THE BEST OF ARIZONA

A Complete, Witty and Rather Opinionated
Guide to the Grand Canyon State

By Don W. Martin & Betty Woo Martin

Pine Cone Press, Walnut Creek, CA 94598

Books by Don & Betty Martin

The Best of San Francisco ● Chronicle Books (1986, revised 1990)
The Best of the Gold Country ● Pine Cone Press (1987)
San Francisco's Ultimate Dining Guide ● Pine Cone Press (1988)
The Best of Arizona ● Pine Cone Press (1990)

This book is dedicated to Martin Litton, riverman and conservationist, whose Grand Canyon dories took us through the world's most magnificent gorge. Martin and his crewmen taught us to love and respect the canyon, and thus the planet.

Copyright (c) 1990 by Don W. Martin and Betty Woo Martin.
All rights reserved. No part of this book may be reproduced in any form without written permission from the publisher. Printed in the United States of America

Library of Congress Cataloguing-in-Publication Data
Martin, Don, 1934; Martin, Betty Woo, 1941
    The Best of Arizona
    Includes index.
    1. Arizona—Description—Guidebooks.
1. Title

ISBN: 0-942053-07-9
Library of Congress Number: 89-92267

Book and cover design ● Charles L. Beucher, Jr.
Cartography ● Jil Weil and Charles L. Beucher Jr.
Photos ● Don W. Martin, unless otherwise credited
Typesetting ● Crosby Associates, Box 248, Sutter Creek, CA 95685

The Cover ● Mission San Xavier near Tucson, affectionately called the "White Dove of the Desert," glistens in a warm Arizona sun. *Photo by Don W. Martin*

Monument Valley—one of Arizona's wonders.

Take time to see the sky
Find shapes in the clouds
Hear the murmur of the wind
And touch the cool water.
Walk softly
We are the intruders
Tolerated briefly
In an infinite universe.

—Jean Henderer,
National Park Service (retired)

CONTENTS

MAPS

THE CALL OF THE CANYON—
AND OTHER PLACES

ARIZONA AND I have been carrying on a flirtation since the 1950s. Back when Phoenix was a manageable size and smog never smudged its skies, I commuted frequently from California. My purpose wasn't tourism; I was wooing a pretty young accordion teacher. That affair never worked out, but it did launch my love affair with the Grand Canyon state. And I hadn't even seen the canyon yet.

A decade or so ago, as associate editor of a San Francisco-based travel magazine, I often sought Arizona assignments. I wrote about Phoenix and Scottsdale, Tucson, dude ranching, Yuma Territorial Prison, Sedona and Oak Creek Canyon and those two cactus national monuments—Organ Pipe and Saguaro. I still hadn't made it to the Grand Canyon.

In the late 1970s, I stopped there briefly while on another Arizona assignment. Later, when Betty and I were in Las Vegas, partying in the name of journalism, we booked a Grand Canyon scenic flight. Although we were disturbed by our aerial intrusion into this wilderness, we were awe-struck by its complex beauty.

Later, we took an 18-day river trip with Grand Canyon Dories, then owned by my friend Martin Litton. We saw the canyon as it should be seen—from the bottom up. After all, this *is* the canyon. The four million people who crowd up to the rims each year only experience the edge.

It occurred to us that we should write a book about the canyon—and the rest of the wonderful state which slopes grandly away to the south. It should be comprehensive, we decided, yet lighthearted. We did not want to produce a boring, encyclopedic tome.

This, then, is your Arizona book. Let it take you by the hand and lead you through one of America's grandest states. Take your time and be selective. Stop to smell the cactus flowers and the pine needles. Explore Arizona as we have, section by section, and savor the best of its wonders.

You might even want to save the Grand Canyon for dessert. It took many million years to get here, and it isn't going anywhere soon.

Don W. Martin
Cape Royal lookout, North Rim
Grand Canyon National Park, Arizona

THE WAY THINGS WORK

THE BEST OF ARIZONA is a remarkably useful and user-friendly guidebook for several good reasons:

● **It's opinionated, straightforward** and even fun to read. Arizona is such a wonderfully diverse state that it's difficult to see all of its attractions. So we've sorted things out. We suggest the best things to see and do in each area, then follow with "the rest," if you have plenty of time on your hands.

● **It's honest.** We accepted no free meals or lodgings, and we paid our way into attractions. We do not charge for listings or accept advertising.

● **It's a complete guide,** listing attractions, activities, restaurants, lodgings, campgrounds and RV parks, shopping areas and popular hikes. It even lists local radio stations to help you find your favorite music as you drive about the state.

● **It features the offbeat as well as the obvious.** Part of the fun of traveling is discovering, so we list little jewels that other guidebooks may have missed. But we won't send you 50 miles over a dirt road to look at a plaque. However, we did find a couple of interesting wagon tracks outside of Kingman.

● **It lets you know before you go.** Easy-to-find chapter headings tell you when to visit, how early to make reservations, who to contact for information and what the weather's like.

● **It maps things out** with directions to attractions and shipping areas.

● **It tells you to take a hike** on some of the state's more popular trails. We won't send you up rock faces with pitons, or into the wilds with seven days' rations. The suggested hikes can be handled by anyone in reasonably good shape. For more serious trekkers, we recommend other guides at the end of the book.

● **It rates restaurants and lodgings.** Many guides merely list them.

How We Rate

We use a simple system, without asking you to memorize a lot of codes, abbreviations and little squiggly figures. We lump attractions into two broad groups: **The Best** and **The Rest.** We start our "Best" rating with our favorite attraction—the must-see for that particular area; the others are alphabetical.

Our restaurant and lodging ratings mean just what you think they mean.

RESTAURANTS

△ **Adequate**—A clean place with basic but edible food.

△△ **Good**— An attractive, well-run cafe with tasty food served in a comfy, pleasant setting.

△△△ **Very Good**—Substantially above average; excellent fare, served with a smile in a fine dining atmosphere.

△△△△ **Excellent**—An exceptionally well-run restaurant with a distinctive setting and tasty, perhaps innovative dishes.

△△△△△ **Awesome**—Gourmet quality by every measure; one of the finest restaurants in the country.

Price ranges are based on the tab for an average dinner, including soup or salad (not including wine or dessert). Obviously, places serving only breakfast and/or lunch are priced accordingly.

$—Average dinner for one is $9 or less

$$—$10 to $14

$$$—$15 to $24

$$$$—$25 to $34

$$$$$—Did you say you were buying?

LODGINGS

Δ **Adequate**—A clean place that meets minimum standards.

ΔΔ **Good**—A well-run establishment with most essentials, such as room phones, color TV and oversized beds.

ΔΔΔ **Very Good**—Substantially above average, generally with a pool, restaurant and other amenities.

ΔΔΔΔ **Excellent**—An exceptional property with elegant rooms; most such places will have extensive resort facilities.

ΔΔΔΔΔ **Awesome**—Outstanding by every measure; one of the best resorts or hotels in the country.

Prices ranges are listed for doubles and singles during high season—the most popular tourist months. Of course, many places reduce their rates during slower months. Conversely, some hike their prices for peak holiday periods or local celebrations.

Price codes below indicate the cost of a standard room for two during the regular season. These prices were furnished to us by the establishments.

$—a double for under $25

$$—$25 to $49

$$$—$50 to $74

$$$$—$75 to $99

$$$$$—$100 or more

It's always wise to made advance reservations. If you don't like the place, you can shop around after the first night and change lodgings (except during some peak seasons, when *all* rooms may be scarce). Without advance reservations, the later you arrive, the more likely you'll be stuck with a higher-priced room, or one hanging over a freeway.

You probably know that most lodging chains have toll-free reservation numbers. If you aren't sure, **dial (800) 555-1212** for toll-free directory assistance.

CLEARING THE AIR

⌀ **No smoking**— This symbol indicates that lodgings have non-smoking rooms and restaurants have smoke-free dining areas.

HOW WE PICK THEM

Our lodging and restaurant selections are somewhat arbitrary, since we can't list all of them. We suggest clean, well-run places that are easy for a stranger to find. We lean toward lodgings near tourist attractions, freeway off-ramps and shopping areas. Further, we seek out motels, hotels and restaurants with a bit of character and charm. We ate anonymously in many cafes, and also relied on suggestions from unbiased residents.

We don't always follow chamber of commerce suggestions, since they tend to favor chamber members. We *do* trust recommendations of the

American Automobile Association, and we often list them. After eighteen years with AAA's northern California affiliate, I know its ratings are un-biased and reliable.

In small towns, we often list places that wouldn't make the cut in larger communities; they may be the only ones available. Don't expect a gourmet delight in Chloride; just expect to be fed for a fair price. Of course, some small towns have great little cafes. If so, rate them that way.

RV PARKS AND CAMPGROUNDS

We look for camping sites in recreation areas, near tourist attractions and freeway off-ramps. We don't list all the national forest campgrounds, but we direct you to forest service offices where you can get lists. Nor do we attempt to list RV parks in areas thick with them, such as the Colorado River strip between Arizona and California. Again, we direct you to sources that will provide lists.

Camping rates are for one vehicle with two people. Bear in mind that many commercial RV parks charge extra for additional bodies, so inquire when you make reservations.

National Forest camping reservations: Several National Forest camping sites in Arizona (and other states) can be reserved via MisTix. For a brochure listing participating campgrounds, write Region, U.S. Forest Service, 517 Gold Ave. S.W., Albuquerque, NM 87102; (505) 842-3292. Or contact: MisTix, P.O. Box 85705, San Diego, CA 92138-5705; (800) 283-CAMP.

BED & BREAKFAST INNS

B&Bs are proliferating rapidly in Arizona. Because of the various types—ranging from restored inns to homestays in someone's spare bedroom—we haven't attempted to rate them. We came across two organizations that provide B&B lists and operate a reservation service. This is not an endorsement; we're merely listing them for your convenience.

Mi Casa-Su Casa, P.O. Box 950, Tempe, AZ 85280-0950; (602) 990-0682; for reservations (800) 456-0682.

Arizona Association of Bed & Breakfast Inns, 3661 N. Campbell Ave. (P.O. Box 237), Tucson, AZ 85719; (602) 622-7167.

MISCELLANY

Credit card abbreviations should be obvious: MC/VISA—MasterCard and VISA; AMEX—American Express; DC—Diner's Club; DISC—The Discover Card. "Major credit cards" indicates the ubiquitous MC/VISA plus American Express and one or more of the other travel cards.

Prices listed in this book are subject to change, invariably upward. Those shown were accurate at the time of publication, as provided by the establishments.

National Park thrift: Arizona has 19 national parks, monuments and other sites, and most have a modest admission charge. You might do well to buy a **Golden Eagle Passport** for $25, which gives your family free admission to all U.S. parks and monuments during a calendar year. **Golden Age** and **Golden Access** passports provide free admission to senior citizens (62 and older) and handicapped persons. Golden Age and Access (but not Eagle) passes also allow fifty percent discounts on camping and other park use fees such as boat launching and cave tours.

National park passports are sold at any park or monument where fees are charged. Golden Age and Golden Access cards are free upon proof of eligibility.

Find it fast: We've cleverly bordered this introductory section in black, so you can flip back to it for quick reference.

CLOSING INTRODUCTORY THOUGHTS

Nobody's perfect, but we try. This book contains thousands of facts and a few are probably wrong. If you catch an error, let us know. Also, drop us a note if you discover that a cafe has become a laundromat or that a passing coyote ate the main attraction at a zoo. Further, if you find a tourist lure, hideaway or awesome little cafe that we overlooked, please share it with us.

All who provide useful information will earn a free copy of the revised edition of **The Best of Arizona** or any other book on our list. (See the back of this book.)

Address your comments to:

Pine Cone Press, 587 Europa Court, Walnut Creek, CA 94598

THANK YOU—

IN A SENSE, guidebooks are written by committee. The thousands of facts must come from many sources and checked by many more. We are greatly indebted to scores of helpful Arizonans, particularly those from chambers of commerce, Indian tribal councils, U.S. Forest Service offices and various national parks and monuments. We requested—and received—additional help from these people and organizations:

Jim Austin, public relations manager, Phoenix & Valley of the Sun Convention & Visitors Bureau; Ross Hilmoe and Randy Swedlund of **Bradshaw Mountain Photo Company** in Prescott for their fine lab work on the photos in this book; **Carol Downey**, resources librarian, Arizona Department of Library, Archives and Public Records; **Brian C. Catts**, Office of Public Service, University of Arizona; **Glen E. Henderson**, superintendent, Montezuma Castle and Tuzigoot National Monuments; **Navajo Tribe** office of tourism; **John C. O'Brien,** chief of visitor services, Grand Canyon National Park; **Barbara Peck,** public relations manager, Metropolitan Tucson Convention & Visitors Bureau; **Fred Shupla,** Office of Research and Planning, the Hopi Tribe; **Karen Whitney,** management assistant, Glen Canyon National Recreation Area; **Maggie Wilson**, media relations manager, Arizona Office of Tourism; **Barry D. Wirth,** regional public affairs officer for the Bureau of Reclamation's Salt Lake City office.

A BIT ABOUT THE AUTHORS

This is the fourth guidebook by the husband and wife team of Don and Betty Martin. Don, who provides most of the adjectives, has been a journalist since he was seventeen. He was a Marine correspondent in the Orient, then he worked for several West Coast newspapers. For eighteen years, he was associate editor of *Motorland*, the travel magazine of the California State Automobile Association. He now devotes his time to writing, photography, travel and—for some strange reason—collecting squirrel and chipmunk artifacts.

Betty, who does much of the research, offers the curious credentials of a doctorate in pharmacy and a California real estate broker's license. She also is a free-lance writer and photographer who has sold material to various newspapers and magazines.

A third and most essential member of the family is ICKYBOD, a green 1979 Volkswagen camper, the Martins' home on the road. Without ICK, they might have been tempted to solicit free lodging and meals, and this guidebook wouldn't be quite so honest.

ARIZONA

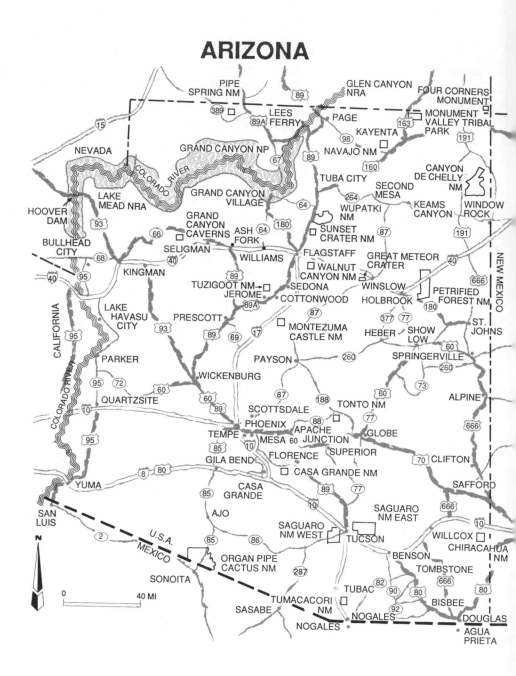

Chapter 1

ARIZONA: GETTING TO KNOW YOU

With beauty before me, I walk;
With beauty behind me, I walk;
with beauty beneath me, I walk;
With beauty above me, I walk;
With beauty all around me, I walk.
        —A Navajo night chant

JUST THE FACTS

Size • 113,909 square miles; sixth largest state; about 340 miles wide by just under 400 miles deep.

Population • About 3,600,000; largest city is Phoenix with just under a million residents. State population density is 27.1 per square mile; ranks 40th among the states.

Elevations • Highest point, Humphreys Peak, 12,633 feet; lowest point, Colorado River as it enters Mexico, 100 feet.

Admitted to the Union • February 14, 1912, as the forty-eighth state; capital—Phoenix.

Time zone • Mountain; one hour later than the West Coast, two hours earlier than the East; only the Navajo Reservation observes summer Daylight Saving Time.

Telephone area code • (602) for the entire state.

Official things • **State motto**—*Didat Deus* (God enriches); **State seal** depicts the five "Cs" of copper, cotton, climate, citrus and cattle; **state bird**—cactus wren (medium-brown with speckled breast, likes to hang around saguaro cactus); **state flower**—saguaro cactus blossom (white with yellow center); **state tree**—paloverde (desert tree identified by green limbs, which is what *palo verde* means in Spanish); **state gem**—

turquoise; **official neck-wear**—bola tie, which (perhaps unfortunately) originated here.

State nicknames ● The Grand Canyon State; the Copper State (appropriate, since it produces more than half of America's copper supply).

Alcohol ● None may be imported from another state (although there are no border checks); sold by the bottle in any licensed store; minimum drinking age 21; legal bar hours 7 a.m. to 1 a.m., Sundays noon to 1 a.m.

Motorists' laws ● Children under four or weighing less than 40 pounds must be secured by child restraints in vehicles. Speed limit is 55 (65 mph on most freeways).

Indian reservations ● They're regarded as sovereign territories, with their own laws—which may differ from those elsewhere in the state. Some, like the Navajo and Hopi nations, require that all vehicle occupants wear safety belts, and they forbid the sale of alcoholic beverages anywhere on the reservation. The Navajo Reservation observes Daylight Saving Time, while the rest of Arizona's Indian lands do not.

Getting there ● Three **interstate highways** cross Arizona from east to west—I-40; I-10 and I-8. Several major **airlines** serve Phoenix and Tucson, and feeder lines fly to Bullhead City, Flagstaff, Kingman, Lake Havasu City, Page, Prescott, Sedona, Winslow and Yuma. **Amtrak** has two routes across Arizona, originating in Los Angeles and connecting to the East; one run stops in Yuma, Phoenix and Tucson; the other hits Kingman, Flagstaff and Winslow.

Road conditions ● Call (602) 279-2000 and punch R-O-A-D to learn about driving conditions.

Hunting and Fishing ● Out-of-state hunting and fishing licenses are available at most sporting goods stores. Anyone over 14 may get one; fees vary. State licenses aren't required on Indian reservations, but each has its own laws and permit fees; check before you go.

To learn more about Arizona, contact

Office of Tourism, 1100 W. Washington St., Phoenix, AZ 85007; (602) 542-3618 Arizona State Parks, 800 W. Washington St., #415, Phoenix, AZ 85007; (602) 542-4174.

Arizona Game & Fish Department, 2222 W. Greenway Rd., Phoenix AZ 85023; (602) 942-3000.

National Park Service, 1115 N. First St., Phoenix, AZ 85004; (602) 261-4956.

Native American Tourism Center, 333 W. Indian School Rd., Phoenix, AZ 85013; (602) 234-2010.

Southwestern Region, U.S. Forest Service, 517 Gold Ave. S.W. Albuquerque, NM 87102; (505) 842-3292.

U.S. Bureau of Land Management, 3707 N. Seventh St., Phoenix AZ 85014; (602) 241-5547.

COMING TO ARIZONA

Every year, about 18 million people vacation in Arizona, leaving behind around $5 billion dollars. A great many of these folks are seeking solace from icy winters back home. Others are drawn by summertime lures.

Presumably, as you thumb through this book—hopefully after purchasing it—you're tempted to add to these numbers. Perhaps you are already there.

But where to go? Arizona is an amazingly diverse state, with pine forests as well as cactus deserts. Although it's famous as a winter retreat, it also attracts many summer tourists. Grand Canyon National Park gets most of its four million annual visitors between June and September. Flagstaff and Sedona, both around a mile high, enjoy four seasons and are primarily summer destinations.

If you seek retreat from winter chill, you have three broad choices: Phoenix and the Valley of the Sun, Tucson and its southern Arizona neighbors, and the Colorado River corridor along the Arizona-California border. Retired? You may want to join the growing ranks of Snowbirds who temporarily swell the state's population by a million or so. The Valley of the Sun gets around 200,000 of them each winter. Yuma's normal population nearly doubles when 40,000 Snowbirds put down temporary roots. In some communities, such as Quartzsite, winter visitors greatly outnumber permanent residents. We devote a special chapter to Snowbird retreats later in this book.

Incidentally, if you don't mind the heat—which is dry and quite tolerable in Arizona—you can get great summer vacation bargains in the Sunbelt areas. Many resorts, motels, golf courses and other facilities drop their rates by as much as 50 percent. Phoenix, which has a "No Sweat" off-season promotion, reports an amazing 78 percent of its summer visitors say they'll return.

We can testify from personal experience that summers in an air-conditioned desert can be great. Just roll your daily clock back a couple of hours. Hit the tennis courts, golf course or bike trail early in the morning, then laze at the pool or prowl air-conditioned shopping malls, museums and other attractions during midday. Desert summer evenings, with their balmy breezes and low humidity, are *wonderful*.

Arizona's peak winter season is November to March. Based on a survey of Phoenix-area long-term visitors, most don't wait for the holidays to make a run for the border. Twenty-five percent come in September and another 32 percent arrive in November. More than half—55 percent—start for home in April.

Obviously, winter to spring is the most crowded period for visitors and locals. Since Arizona's kids are in school, families usually don't take vacations then. They're commuting to work, mingling their cars with the tourists'. Thus, urban areas experience their heaviest traffic in winter.

THE WAY IT IS ● Asking people to describe Arizona is like asking blind men to describe an elephant. It depends on what part they're feeling.

The state fits its desert stereotype. Indeed, two thirds of it is arid. It's the only state in the Union with two national monuments named for varieties of cactus—Organ Pipe and Saguaro.

At the same time, it defies this stereotype. Humphreys Peak north of Flagstaff is one of America's highest, at 12,670 feet. A fourth of the state is covered by forest, and it shelters the largest stand of virgin ponderosa pines in the country. And of course it contains the world's deepest gorge, which is Arizona's grandest stereotype of all.

Chambers of commerce in Oregon and Idaho claim that their Hells Canyon of the Snake River is deeper than Arizona's Grand Canyon. But they measure from the tops of peaks that flank the ravine, and we think that's cheating. Grand Canyon's 5,700-foot depth is measured from the rim of the great Kaibab Plateau.

The shape of Arizona is summed up rather well by Reg Manning, Pulitzer Prize-winning cartoonist for Phoenix's *Arizona Republic*. In his whimsical book, *What Is Arizona Really Like?*, he says the state's topography can be taken in three bites, starting from the Four Corners area in the northeast.

The first bite is a remote, often hauntingly beautiful semi-arid plateau containing the large Navajo and Hopi Indian reservations, Monument Valley and the Painted Desert. The second semi-circle, curving from the north central to the southeastern corner, is a green belt of ponderosa pines, including the forest-rimmed Grand Canyon. The Mogollon Rim, a great fault extending in a 200-mile arc, marks the edge of this high country.

The final bite—consuming nearly two-thirds of the state— is a great sweep of desert, reaching from the northwest to the southeast corner and ranging from sand dunes to flowering cactus gardens. This is the Sunbelt, a term that originated in Arizona and now is used to describe just about anyplace south of a Pennsylvania blizzard.

Although most of Arizona is desert, it isn't necessarily scalding hot. Much of this arid land—particularly in central and northeastern areas—is high desert that's often quite cold in winter. Naturally, the northwestern mountain regions get regular snowfall. Even in the southern Sunbelt, it's best to bring a warm evening wrap for your winter vacation.

Nearly eighty-five percent of Arizona's population is focused in this warm belt. Some say too much of it is focused there. Phoenix, with nearly a million residents, has taken on the sprawl of Los Angeles. More than two million of the state's 3.6 million people live in the Valley of the Sun. Some residents of Tucson—population 700,000—seem determined to catch Phoenix. We think they would be wise to settle for second.

These population centers are not what make Arizona wonderful. Yes, we love to luxuriate at poolside in the resorts of Phoenix and Scottsdale. We have a great affection for sunny, laid-back Tucson. And we like the outdoor patios of Phoenix and Tucson pubs. There, Arizona yuppies sip their Corona Extra in the sunshine, while San Franciscans are huddled indoors, nursing their martinis.

But Arizona's greatest charms lie in its open spaces and scenic wonders; in its small towns with their affable wanna-be-cowboy attitude. We found our Arizona in the high, silent reaches of the San Francisco Peaks and the hidden depths of the Grand Canyon; in the dignity of the Indian nations and the scruffy charm of the Mexican border towns; in the solitude of a wilderness cactus garden reached only by a dusty road.

We'll take our bottle of Corona in El Tovar's cocktail lounge on the rim of the Grand Canyon. We will have earned it by hiking up from Rio Colorado, that great mother river of the Southwest.

THE WAY IT WAS • Arizona is one of the youngest states in the union, admitted as the last of the Lower Forty-eight in 1912. Yet, river-runners and hikers in the Grand Canyon will see two billion year old pre-Cambrian schist, some of the oldest exposed rock on Planet Earth. Native Americans have occupied Arizona's deserts and high plateaus for about 20,000 years.

—Arizona Department of Archives photo

Coronado came looking for gold but found mostly trouble.

Its first residents were nomadic hunters who drifted down from the Great Plains. When droughts drove the mammoths and antelope away, they swapped their spears for plowshares and became—about eleven centuries ago—North America's first farmers. Freed from the constant search for food, they developed complex societies and built large pueblos whose ruins survive today. The state is a treasure house of archaeological sites, ranging from mesa cities to tucked-away cliff dwellings.

Anthropologists call these early people Hohokam, Anasazi, Sinagua and Mogollon. We don't know what they called themselves, for they left no written language. Like most ancient tribes, they probably just referred to their kind as "The People." Through the centuries, they evolved into highly-developed societies, occupying great pueblos of adobe or stone atop mesas or tucked into hidden canyons and precipitous cliffs. They dug irrigation canals and became excellent farmers. Their pottery, weaving and other crafts were among the most advanced of the time.

Around eight hundred years ago, this highly developed society began coming apart at the seams. The great pueblos were abandoned and left to weather away in the hot Arizona sun. Scientists speculate that a persistent drought may have driven them from their corn and bean fields. Or it may have been disease, soil depletion or the arrival of more aggressive tribes.

People identify Navajos and Apaches with Arizona, yet these were latter-day arrivals, coming from the cold north. They were Athabaskans who drifted down from Canada, starting about six hundred years ago. Warlike hunters, they may have driven off many of the native tribes. Ironically, they adopted some of the original residents' farming and weaving techniques.

Scientists have been unable to pinpoint the ultimate fate of the Hohokam, Sinagua or Mogollon. Similarities in culture and crafts suggest that today's Hopi may be descendants of the Anasazi.

Historians have fun feuding over the origin of Arizona's name. There are four Indian versions: *Arizuma,* an Aztec word for "silver bearing"; *Ali shonak* or *Ari-son,* meaning "small spring" or "young spring," which were names of Pima settlements; and a Papago term, *Aleh-zone,* also meaning young spring. Basque settlers insist that Arizona comes from *Aritz ona,* their term for "good oak." This was the name given to a silver strike site in 1736. Some unimaginative scholars suggest that "Arizona" is merely a derivation of "arid zone."

The first appearance of the name in print was in a 1750s document by one Padre Ortega, a Spanish missionary.

Spaniards were the area's first European visitors, and they got here by accident. In 1528, a group led by Alvar Cabeza de Vaca set out to explore Florida's west coast. Part of the group became lost after an Indian attack and spent more than eight years wandering through what is now Texas, New Mexico, Arizona and northern Mexico. Some accounts say they traveled with Indians after De Vaca convinced him that he was a powerful medicine man. When four survivors finally stumbled across some of their countrymen in western Mexico, they reported Indian legends of fabulously wealthy cities which lay to the north.

Antonio de Mendoza, viceroy of New Spain, knew of an eighth century Moorish legend about seven golden cities, hidden somewhere in the unexplored world. Could these be the same? In 1539, with golden greed glittering in his eyes, he dispatched a party of explorers from Mexico City to find these treasure-troves. It was led by Franciscan Father Marcos de Niza.

As the Spaniards approached present-day Arizona, local Indians said the area through which they traveled was called "Cibola". Thus, the legend of the Seven Cities of Cibola was born. Learning that a Zuni pueblo lay ahead, Father de Niza sent an advance party to investigate. Ironically, it was led by a Moorish slave, Estevan, one of the survivors of the De Vaca party. The Zunis weren't very nice hosts; they killed the visitors.

An intimidated Father de Niza kept his distance. But he drew near enough to see that the pueblos glittered in the sun. He returned home and advised the Viceroy of Mexico that he may have found one of the golden cities. A year later, that great and brutal explorer, 30-year-old Francisco Vasquez de Coronado, traveled north to confirm Frey de Niza's reports.

However, the good padre had been fooled by the glitter of mica, embedded in the adobe. Coronado, finding no gold, pillaged a few pueblos and explored as far north as Kansas. After two years, he returned to Mexico City empty-handed. More than a century passed before the curious Spanish again began pestering natives of the Southwest. Then in the late 1600s, Father Eusebio Francisco Kino and other padres came to establish missions. Thousands of Indians were converted to Christianity. They were most likely encouraged by accompanying soldiers who set up military *presidios* to protect the missions.

Most of the Indians did not yield their land or their free spirits easily. Angered by abusive treatment from the Spanish and later Mexican and American intruders, they staged several violent revolts. The Hopi emptied their pueblos of Spaniards in a savage rebellion in 1680.

In the early 1800s, when Mexico won its independence from Spain, most of the soldiers were withdrawn from this northern outpost. Indians—mostly Apaches this time—again went on the warpath, driving frightened settlers to the safety of the walled cities of Tucson and Tubac. In the late 1800s, more than a dozen U.S. Army forts had to be built to protect American settlers.

Not until Geronimo surrendered in 1886 was the area considered safe for settlement.

Today, Indians are a major force in the state, culturally and politically. Vast tracts were set aside as reservations, which have become self-governing entities. The Navajo and Hopi tracts occupy a huge chunk of northeastern Arizona. Combined with other reservations, they comprise a fourth of the state's land area. Arizona has more Indian lands and more Native Americans than any other state. Indians comprise five percent of its population.

Much of what is now Arizona and New Mexico was ceded to the United States in the 1848 Treaty of Guadalupe Hidalgo, at the end of the Mexican War. Sandwiched between California and Texas, they were lumped together as the New Mexico Territory.

California's Forty-niner Gold Rush sent a wave of argonauts across the country. Many preferred a southern route to the precipitous Sierra Nevada range that formed a barrier on California's eastern edge. This path to the gold fields swung down through a slice of Mexico to avoid mountains and hostile Indians. To keep this route secure, the government negotiated the Gadsden Purchase in 1854. Cash-poor Mexico sold 30,000 square miles of its northern desert for $10 million. This later would become a large chunk of southern Arizona.

Four years later, the government awarded the Butterfield Overland Stage Company a contract to forge a mail a route through this area, from St. Louis to San Francisco. It was needed to link fast-growing California with the rest of the U.S., which then ended at the Missouri border.

Settled primarily by Southerners, the New Mexico Territory sided with the South during the Civil War. A Texas militia seized Mesilla, New Mexico, in 1861. The Texans claimed all the land from the Rio Grande to the Pacific as Confederate territory. But a column of Union-sympathizing Californians soon put an end to that. In 1862, the Confederates were routed in the Battle of Picacho Pass, south of Phoenix. Little more than a skirmish with only eight casualties, it was the Civil War's westernmost battle. The following year, perhaps to boost the number of Union supporters, President Lincoln signed a bill creating separate Arizona and New Mexico territories.

For the next two decades, the Arizona Territory epitomized the Wild West. Cattle barons battled over water and grazing rights and knocked down sod-busters' pesky fences. Tombstone and its O.K. Corral shoot-out and Yuma's infamous Territorial Prison became the stuff of which movie legends were made. Then in the 1880s, several minor gold strikes, major copper discoveries and Mormon migrations from Utah brought a more settled kind of citizen to the territory.

The arrival of the railroad completed the taming of this final vestige of the Wild West. Then on St. Valentine's Day in 1912, portly President William Howard Taft signed the proclamation making Arizona the last of the contiguous 48 states.

Hampered by lack of water, the new state grew slowly in the first half of this century. In recent decades, however, it has become one of America's boom areas, aided by air conditioning, the creation of the Snowbird cult, and a court ruling granting it a larger share of Colorado River water.

It grew by a whopping 53.1 percent from the mid-70s to the mid-80s. Among Western states, only California and Washington have larger populations. Phoenix has blossomed into a major city; its suburbs of Mesa, Glen-

—**Arizona Department of Archives** photo
Copper miners pose for the birdie around the turn of the century.

dale and Chandler doubled their populations between 1970 and 1980. The state's growth has tapered now, with about 50,000 a year migrating to the state, compared with more than a hundred thousand annually a few years earlier.

"The slowdown has given us a chance to catch our breath," a Phoenix visitors bureau official told us.

However, with the awarding of additional Colorado River water in the mid-1990s, a new boom is expected.

Phoenix and Tucson are experiencing some of the congestion problems suffered by the rest of the growing Sun Belt. However, compared with the foul air and fouled freeways of Los Angeles and the human compaction of many Eastern cities, Arizona's urban congestion is merely a slight sniffle. And much of the state is still wonderfully uncrowded.

Besides, we're not here to fuss about growing pains. We're here to explore one of America's most fascinating states. Come with us now as we discover the Best of Arizona.

Chapter 2

THE GRAND CANYON

*The wonders of the Grand Canyon cannot be adequately
represented by speech. The glories of form, color and sound
unite in a region never to be duplicated this side of Paradise.*
—John Wesley Powell

WE BEGIN our Arizona exploration with the state's most
famous attraction—that magnificent 227-mile chasm across
the northwest corner.

How does one describe the glorious and complex Grand
Canyon, dropping a mile into the earth's crust from the edge of a great
plateau? It's not just a canyon, but hundreds of canyons, weaving a fantastic
webwork of terraced buttes, pinnacles and ridges.

When we first visited Grand Canyon National Park many years ago, we
were vaguely disappointed. We dutifully drove to Mather Point at the South
Rim, shouldered up to the railing between six tour bus groups and looked
down. There it was, just the way we figured it would be. It was impressive
but we'd already seen it a thousand times—on postcards and posters, in TV
travelogues, and on awful slides at our next-door neighbor's house.

It's difficult to be dazzled by something that has been paraded before
your eyes since childhood.

That evening, at the suggestion of a ranger, we drove to Hopi Point to
watch the sunset. The point, we discovered, was a peninsula projecting into
the chasm. Here, we were no longer merely on the edge. The canyon seemed
to reach over and surround us. Now, we were getting somewhere!

We watched the most incredible light and shadow show we'd ever seen.
As photographers, we were aware of the beauty of early morning and late
afternoon light. It takes on a golden tone and brings out detail by accentuat-
ing shadows.

The receding light turned the Grand Canyon into a castle of colors: red and blue-gray and burnt orange and soft yellow; purples, pinks and tawny browns too subtle for a camera. This stunning scene changed constantly—like time-lapse photography—as the light and shadows shifted. Finally, the canyon was veiled in dark purple and the sky was as pink as Mae West's *boudoir*.

During later visits, we flew above and hiked down into the chasm; we ran the turbulent waters of Rio Colorado. We discovered a complex and

THINGS TO KNOW BEFORE YOU GO

Plan ahead • Make Grand Canyon lodging and camping reservations *as far in advance as possible.* If you plan to stay at Phantom Ranch down in the canyon, reserve space *up to a year* ahead.

Best time to go • Best of all, you'll love the fall, when the park is uncrowded and the weather is crisp and clear. **The South Rim** is open year around. It's 7,000 feet so take a warm wrap, even in summer; it often snows in winter. **The North Rim** is closed in winter, usually from late October to mid-May.

Park entrance fee • $5 per vehicle, good for seven days.

Climate • Warm summers, cold winters with frequent snow.

Useful contacts

Superintendent, Grand Canyon National Park, P.O. Box 129, Grand Canyon, AZ 86023.

Backcountry Reservations Office, P.O. Box 129, Grand Canyon, AZ 86023 (Backcountry hiking and camping reservations only by mail or in person.)

Grand Canyon National Park Lodges (South Rim reservations), P.O. Box 699, Grand Canyon, AZ 86023; (602) 638-2401 or (602) 638-2631.

TW Recreational Services, Inc. (North rim reservations), P.O. Box 400, Cedar City, UT 84720; (801) 586-7686.

Essential phone numbers (602 unless otherwise indicated)

South Rim park information—638-7888/638-7770

North Rim park information—638-7864

South Rim lodging reservations—638-2401

North Rim lodging reservations—638-2611 or (801) 586-768

South Rim (Mather) camping reservations—Ticketron

Park road conditions (recorded)—638-2245

Scheduled activities (recorded)—638-9304

Area radio stations: North Rim

KCCK-FM, 101.1, Kanab, Utah—Country, popular.

KREC-FM, 98.1, St. George, Utah—Light rock, top 40.

KUVR-FM, 90.1, Salt Lake (local booster)—National Public Radio; classical, news, features

KXAZ-FM, 93.5, Page—Easy listening and new wave.

South Rim

KAFF-AM, 930, Flagstaff—Country & Western.

KAFF-FM, 92.9, Flagstaff—Country & Western.

KDBK-FM, 92, Flagstaff—Rock.

KMGN-FM, 93.9, Flagstaff—Talk, news & popular music.

KNAU-FM, 89.7, Flagstaff—National Public Radio.

KVNA-AM, 690, Flagstaff—"Golden oldies."

KVNA-FM, 97.5, Flagstaff—Light rock.

ever-changing wonderland. If you explore the canyon as we do—from within as well as from the edge, at sunup and sundown, in sunshine and in rain—you will never see the same view twice. You will never tire of nature's grandest spectacle.

If we were visiting the Grand Canyon for the first time, we would arrive after dark and go straight to our lodgings. We'd get a good night's sleep, rise before dawn and catch our first view of the chasm at first light. We'd watch the canyon come alive before our eyes.

THE WAY IT WAS • How does one determine the age of the Grand Canyon? Do we begin with the vishnu schist, the two-billion-year-old Precambrian rock at the bottom? Or was the canyon born only a few million years ago when the Colorado River began carving a path through the Kaibab Plateau?

Geologists aren't even quite sure how the Colorado River cut this dramatic chasm. It's known that the gradual uplifting of the Kaibab Plateau allowed the river to cut much more deeply than if the land had been stable. The Kaibab is part of the great Colorado Plateau, whose restless shifting has created magnificent landforms in northern Arizona, Nevada, Utah and New Mexico.

But the plateau isn't flat; it's slightly domed and sloping to the southwest. How did the river get over the hump to ultimately reach the Gulf of California?

One theory holds that two rivers, the ancestral Colorado and the Hualapai, flowed in opposite directions, each originating high on the plateau. The Hualapai reached the Gulf of California while the Colorado emptied into a huge inland sea that geologists call Bidahochi. As the rivers flowed, they eroded further back into the Kaibab until only the crest of the plateau separated them. Then, the Colorado backed up from its inland sea and spilled over the crest, where it was "pirated" by the Hualapai. This occurred about twelve million years ago.

Geologists call this the "Stream Piracy Theory." And it's still just a theory, not accepted by all scientists.

However it was formed, it created not only the world's deepest gorge but two distinct regions, separated by a rushing river and millions of years of evolution. Because of elevation differences and the river barrier, distinctive species developed on each side. For instance, the higher, wetter North Rim is home to the unique Kaibab squirrel, a black-coated critter with a glowing white tail. Found nowhere else on earth, it's an obvious evolutionary cousin to the dark brown Abert squirrel, which scampers about the South Rim.

Since the North Rim is higher and catches more rainfall, it is much more eroded than the lower South Rim. And because the plateau slopes from northeast to southwest, rainfall along the North Rim flows *into* the canyon, while South Rim drizzles flow *away* from it. A cross-section would show a lopsided ravine, with the south side much more precipitous than the north. The river is twice as far from the North Rim as it is from the south.

Any cross-canyon hiker who has strolled down the gently convoluted side canyons of the North Rim, then gasped and struggled up South Rim switchbacks, can verify this fact.

Patient canyon-watchers say the Grand is getting six inches wider every year, with four inches eroding off North Rim cliffs and two inches coming off the southern edge. The canyon, on average, is about ten miles wide.

It is this ten-mile gap that separates northwestern Arizona from the rest of the state. And it separated many early travelers from their appointed destinations. In fact, some explorers didn't think the big ravine was grand at all. Many considered it a pesky wasteland and an obstacle to travel.

A Nineteenth century explorer, Reverend C.B. Spencer, wrote:

"Horror! Tragedy! Silence! Death! Chaos! There is the awful canyon in five words." He'd obviously had trouble getting across. A contemporary of his, C.S. Gleed, agreed, dismissing it as "the grave of the world."

No one knows what prehistoric men and women thought as they descended the canyon's depths. Their petroglyphs depict hunting scenes and the passage of time, but they made no mention of canyon esthetics.

Archaeologists have given the name "Desert Culture People" to the first humans to encounter the canyon, between 6,000 and 2,000 B.C. They were nomadic hunter-gatherers who probably visited the chasm's depths only briefly. They had to rely on the presence of game or edible plants to survive, and such items are scarce a mile into the earth. As evidence of their passing, they left small animal figurines made of split willows. One has been radiocarbon dated around 2145 B.C.

Sometime before the birth of Christ, the Anasazi—probably descendants of the Desert Culture folks—began occupying both rims of the canyon and living in its depths as well. Hundreds of sites have been found here and elsewhere in northern Arizona.

A clever group, the Anasazi practiced simple agriculture, allowing them to subsist deep within the gorge for extended periods. They grew seed grasses on riverside sand bars and on canyon mesas. Cliffside granaries and ruins of their stone houses have been found in several areas. Around the 12th century A.D., most of the Indians abandoned the chasm, probably because of drought or harassment by hostile neighbors.

The first Europeans to see the canyon—and much of the rest of the Southwest—were Spanish conquistadors. Exploration was prompted by rumors of golden cities that lay to the north of Mexico. Obviously, such a quest eventually should bring them to brink the great ravine. Yet decades of searching yielded nothing, not even the Grand Canyon.

In the summer of 1540, Garcia Lopez de Cardenas was dispatched by Francisco Coronado to find an Indian village supposedly situated near a river canyon. Guided by Hopi Indians from a pueblo called Tusayan, Cardenas and his group hiked for 20 days and finally reached the South Rim. Other Spanish explorers had encountered the river lower down, but Cardenas became the first European to see the great chasm itself.

Another 250 years passed before another group of outsiders—also Spanish—concerned themselves with the Grand Canyon. In June, 1776, Father Francisco Tomas Garces visited the canyon while pioneering a new land route between Mission San Xavier del Bac, south of Tucson, and Mission San Gabriel in southern California. Passing near Rio Colorado, he came across a group of Havasupai Indians and accompanied them to their village in the canyon.

He obviously didn't care much for the trip down. He fussed in his diary that he had to follow a dangerous path with "a very lofty cliff" on one side and "a horrible abyss" on the other. Today's trail into that same Havasupai Canyon has been considerably improved.

Grand Canyon panorama from Horseshoe Mesa, off Grandview Trail.

Frey Eusebio Kino, who spent 24 years establishing missions in the Southwest, never visited the canyon. But he is credited with naming the river after crossing it near present-day Yuma in 1701. Rio Colorado—Red River—was inspired by the reddish silt churned up by the swift-moving current.

One James Ohio Pattie may have been the first American to see the canyon. He and a party of French and American trappers bumped into the North Rim in 1826. Like the Spanish, he didn't care much for it. After spending 13 days in a futile search for a crossing, he wrote:

"The river emerges from these horrid mountains, which so cage it up, as to deprive all human beings of the ability to descend to its banks, and make use of its waters."

There are no mountains—horrid or otherwise—flanking the canyon. He may have been referring to the complex buttes and ridges cut into the rugged north rim.

It was daring, one-armed Civil War veteran John Wesley Powell who finally put the Grand Canyon on the map, with his famous down-river trip in 1869. Powell lost his right forearm during the Battle of Shiloh. He went on to fight at Vicksburg and Nashville before being discharged from the Union Army with the rank of major. He kept the title and headed west for an exploration of the Rocky Mountains.

Intrigued by the great Western wilderness, he sought government sponsorship of an expedition down the Colorado River. The Feds showed little interest, but President Ulysses S. Grant did authorize him to draw Army rations for the trip. With Army chow and $500 contributed by a science academy and two Illinois universities, Powell began his trip on the Green River, the Colorado's major tributary.

Ten men left Green River, Wyoming, on May 24, 1869, but only six completed the historic run through the Grand Canyon. One quit after a boat capsized on the Green. Three more, frightened and demoralized by the Grand Canyon's wicked rapids, decided to hike out to a Mormon settlement. Ironically, while Powell and his five remaining companions completed the run without incident, the three hikers were never seen again. They may have been killed by Shivwit Indians, who hated whites because some prospectors had abused their women.

Powell and his men completed their epic voyage on August 30, taking out at the mouth of the Virgin River, about 50 miles southeast of Las Vegas. They had covered 1,048 river miles in 98 days, including 24 days in the Grand Canyon. His crew didn't run all of the Grand's rapids—a feat accomplished routinely by river-runners today. His heavy plank boats, difficult to handle in white water, were portaged around or roped down most of the larger cataracts. But he did accomplish what none had done before: He traveled the length of the Grand Canyon.

The one-armed adventurer made another trip in 1871. Later, he became director of the U.S. Geological Survey and a founder of the Geological Society of America and the National Geographic Society. He died in 1902 at the age of 68.

Grand Canyon tourism began with the arrival of a lively, tale-spinning character named John Hance in the early 1880s. He built a log cabin on the

HOW TO SPEND YOUR GRAND CANYON DAYS

Half day ● If this is all you can invest in Nature's grandest design, perhaps you don't deserve to see it. See the IMAX production, *Grand Canyon: The Hidden Secrets* at Tusayan, then go back to where you came from. Well, maybe you should drive out to Mather Point for a quick look, then follow the East Rim drive 26 miles to the Desert View exit.

First day ● Catch the IMAX show then stop at the visitors center for a park orientation; see the interpretive exhibits and slide shows there. Walk the 1.2-mile South Rim Trail from the visitors center to the Yavapai Museum; take the West Rim drive (via shuttle bus in summer) to Hermits Rest.

Second day ● Experience a sunrise and sunset; take in one or more ranger walks and lectures. Walk the South Rim Trail from the visitors center west to Grand Canyon Village. There, view historic structures such as El Tovar Hotel, Bright Angel Lodge, Hopi House, Kolb Studio and Lookout Studio; walk at least a portion of the West Rim Trail.

Third day ● You're acclimated to the elevation, so take a hike. Either of these will occupy most of a day: Hermit Trail to Lookout Point (eight-mile round-trip) or Grandview Trail to Horseshoe Mesa (six-mile round-trip), with a lunch stop at your turn-around point.

Fourth day ● Resting up from yesterday's hike, take in the *Over the Edge* mixed-media show and visit the Fred Harvey history museum in the Bright Angel Lodge. Drive to Tusayan to prowl the gift shops and arrange a horseback ride or Grand Canyon flight there; do a couple more ranger talks.

Fifth day ● You're in good shape now, so it's time for a *serious* hike! Take the South Kaibab Trail to the Tonto Trail junction, cross the Tonto Plateau to Indian Gardens, then climb the Bright Angel Trail. Total distance 13 miles.

South Rim, near the present Grand Canyon Village, and led tours into the canyon. In 1901, the Santa Fe Railroad completed a spur line to the South Rim from Williams. A fellow named Fred Harvey, who'd gotten his start by opening a restaurant in a Topeka railroad station, built the elegantly rustic El Tovar Hotel and other facilities. Soon, tourism was in full swing.

It hasn't abated since, drawing nearly four million visitors a year. The Fred Harvey Company, now under different corporate ownership, remains the main concessionaire. El Tovar, still open for business, has been designated as a National Historic Landmark.

Despite its popularity, the Grand Canyon didn't become a national park until February 26, 1919. President Theodore Roosevelt, impressed after a visit to the area, created Grand Canyon Game Preserve in 1906. It was given national monument status two years later. Through the years, its size has been doubled to its present 1,982 square miles.

"Do nothing to mar its grandeur," Teddy said. "Keep it for your children and your children's children, and all who come after you, as the one great sight which every American should see."

THE WAY IT IS • Like most older national parks, Grand Canyon provides a plenitude of developed visitor facilities. (Some say it's over-developed. Does a national park really need a dozen gift shops?)

Visitor complexes at the north and south rims offer lodging, camping, restaurants, ranger programs and hikes, mule rides and all those gift shops. In addition, the village of Tusayan, just outside the South Rim entrance, has more lodging, camping and restaurants, a wide-screen movie about the canyon, and wide-screen Monday night football in an awful looking place called Galaxy Four. And, good grief, there's even a McDonald's.

Squadrons of airplanes and helicopters offer scenic flights over the canyon, from Grand Canyon Airport at Tusayan, as well as from Williams, Page, Las Vegas, Flagstaff and even far-away Phoenix. Because of strong objections by environmentalists and a couple of tragic crashes, flights are restricted to certain areas of the canyon, and planes cannot dip below the rim.

Does this place sound busy? It is! Particularly in summer, when swarms of American tourists rub elbows with thousands of foreign tourists, all jockeying for a better view of the Hopi Point sunset. It's difficult to have a wilderness experience while hearing the babble of many tongues and inhaling diesel exhaust from tour buses.

There are better ways—beautiful ways—to experience the Grand Canyon. Try to go during the off-season. Fall is wonderful and spring is nice, too. The South Rim can be both peaceful and stunning in winter, when snow dusts the parapets of the great canyon. Bring your down jacket.

Even in peak summer, you can escape the crowds. Try walking, not driving, the rim trails—particularly the West Rim Trail. Or, simply walk a few hundred feet down one of the trails from the rim, find a peaceful perch and drink in the grandeur. (This doesn't work on the Bright Angel Trail. In summer, it's as busy as San Francisco's Market Street.)

The best way to avoid the crowds is to visit the North Rim, which gets one-tenth as many visitors as the South Rim. It's our favorite side of the canyon. And because we play favorites in this book, that is where our exploration begins.

GRAND CANYON NATIONAL PARK
(North and South rims)

KAIBAB LODGE

NORTH RIM
ENTRANCE

NORTH RIM

THE RIM

MARBLE CANYON

PAINTED DESERT

THE RIM

COLORADO RIVER

UNPAVED ROAD

THE RIM

NORTH RIM
STORE

POINT
SUBLIME

GRAND CANYON
LODGE

CANYON

VISTA
ENCANTADORA

BRIGHT ANGEL
POINT

BRIGHT ANGEL TRAIL

NORTH KAIBAB TRAIL

THE RIM

CAPE
ROYAL

WALHALLA
OVERLOOK

PHANTOM RANCH

BRIGHT ANGEL
TRAIL

PIMA
POINT

HOPI
POINT

SOUTH
KAIBAB TRAIL

HERMITS
REST

VISITOR
CENTER

YAVAPAI POINT

YAKI POINT

COLORADO RIVER

THE RIM

THE WATCHTOWER

DESERT
VIEW STORES

PARK HEADQUARTERS

GRAND
CANYON
VILLAGE

THE RIM

MORAN
POINT

LIPAN
POINT

SOUTH RIM
ENTRANCE

GRANDVIEW
POINT

TUSAYAN
MUSEUM

TUSAYAN
(SHOPS, SERVICES)

GRAND CANYON
AIRPORT

64

SOUTH RIM

TO CAMERON,
FLAGSTAFF
& NORTH RIM

180
to
64

TO FLAGSTAFF,
WILLIAMS & I-40

67

The North Rim
Elevation: 7,450 to 9,000 feet

Your approach will be on State Highway 67. It wanders south from U.S. 89 along the Utah-Arizona border, traveling through the thick pinon-juniper woodlands of Kaibab National Forest.

The first thing you should do, upon paying your $5 per car entrance fee (good for seven days) is pick up a copy of *The Guide.* It's a seasonal newspaper that lists ranger activities, lodging, camping, transportation, food and drink, medical services, lost and found, backcountry hikes, background information and maps. *The Guide* is so complete that you almost don't need this book. But you'd miss the clever writing.

The main difference between the north and south rims, other than crowds and elevation, is that most North Rim vista points are on peninsulas. The South Rim is more of an long, irregular amphitheater. About 350,000 people visit the North Rim each year, compared with the south's 3.5 million. The north side, incidentally, comprises sixty percent of the park area.

The North Rim is much more deeply eroded, cut by long side canyons. Its peninsulas thrust out into the main chasm, where you are nearly surrounded by wedding cake buttes, razorback ridges, pinnacles and other properly awesome formations.

Only eleven miles separate the two rims, as the canyon raven flies. However, it's 215 road miles to the South Rim, via Lees Ferry. Shuttles between the rims are available in summer. (See "Transit" listings in the South Rim section.)

North Rim visitor facilities are clustered around Bright Angel Point. Although they aren't as extensive as those across the gorge, they provide all one's basic needs.

Grand Canyon Lodge is one of those classic national park hotels built of log and stone. A rough stone fireplace dominates the lobby, and the ceiling above is a fascinating webwork of log trusses. The lobby and dining room are perched on the edge of the canyon; tall picture windows offer awesome views. Or one can adjourn to a stone patio and enjoy the vistas from wicker rocking chairs.

A saloon, curio shop, rustic cabins and motel-type units complete the lodge complex. Other facilities include a gasoline station, groceries and national park campground. Ranger programs and hikes are offered during the North Rim's mid-May to mid-October season. The visitor center information desk in the lodge.

ATTRACTIONS

Of course, the canyon is the attraction. You can observe it from several viewpoints reached by auto or on foot. A 21-mile road winds easterly from the visitor area to several vista points.

Bright Angel Viewpoint ● This craggy spur of rock can be reached by a quarter-mile walk along a paved path from Grand Canyon Lodge, or from the visitor area parking lot. Projecting into Bright Angel Canyon, it's a fine place to witness the sunrise or sunset, with lots of formations to capture the moving shadows. From this vantage point you can see—and hear—Roaring Springs far below in Roaring Springs Canyon. The springs provide both water and hydroelectric power for north and south rim visitor facilities.

Roaring Springs empties into Bright Angel Creek, named by Powell because of its crystalline waters. Bright Angel Creek and Garden Creek on the South Rim are part of a fault line that form major side-canyons. Lest you become confused, the North Kaibab Trail follows Bright Angel Canyon down from the North Rim. It connects with the Bright Angel Trail, following Garden Creek up to the South Rim. And yes, the names are confusing.

Point Imperial Viewpoint • Eleven miles from the lodge, Point Imperial is the highest vantage point in the park, at 8,803 feet. It offers a panoramic sweep of the eastern end of Grand Canyon and Marble Canyon to the northeast.

You can see the great Marble Platform—flat as a table top—and the abrupt drop-off of Marble Canyon. Pastel hints of the Painted Desert are farther to the east. To the north are the Vermilion Cliffs, a dramatic red escarpment that extends for 20 miles across the Arizona Strip.

Cape Royal and Angel's Window viewpoints • From Point Imperial, you'll retreat to a "Y" intersection, then follow another winding road to Cape Royal, about 23 miles from the lodge. The end-of-road parking area leads to a pair of lookouts—Cape Royal and Angel's Window. Like Point Imperial, Cape Royal offers a large slice of the eastern Grand Canyon. It projects far out onto the Walhalla Plateau, extending within five miles of the Colorado River.

Angel's Window, reached by the same trail, is a giant peephole through a long, narrow ridge. You can stroll out on the ridge—above the window—for more canyon vistas.

Several turnouts on the way to Point Imperial and Cape Royal are worthy of a stop. At **Vista Encantadora** on the road to Cape Royal, a great razorback ridge rises in the foreground, with buttes and pinnacles beyond. The picture is equally impressive from nearby **Walhalla Viewpoint**; across the road are the ruins of a five-room Anasazi condo.

Toroweap • This overlook is outside the main park area, reached by bumping 65 miles over a dirt road. The route branches south from State Highway 389, nine miles west of Fredonia. Watch for a sign reading *Mt. Trumbull 53 miles*. In good weather, it's navigable by a carefully driven car, but you'd feel more comfortable in a 4-wheel drive.

Your reward for all that bumpity driving is an uncrowded overlook with an impressive canyon view. The gorge falls away 3,000 feet and the river glistens directly below you. You can camp free at a primitive campground near the overlook, but you'll need a permit. It's available from **Backcountry Reservations Office**, P.O. Box 129, Grand Canyon, AZ 86203. Or you can get one at backcountry offices on the north or south rim, or from the Tuweep Ranger Station, about five miles north of the overlook. There is no water, provisions or gasoline along this route, so go prepared. Snow may block the road in winter and summer thunder showers can render it temporarily impassable.

Fall color • The North Rim becomes a spectacular showplace of aspen in the fall, with white bark and yellow leaves glittering against the canyon background. The slender, shimmering trees line the roads to Point Imperial and Cape Royal. Highway 67 leading through Kaibab National Forest also has splashes of color.

Because of the high elevation, fall color comes early—usually in September. Call North Rim park information at 638-7864 to find out when the dazzling yellow leaves hit their peak.

THE BEST HIKING TRAILS

Several trails follow the peninsular contours of the North Rim. The North Kaibab Trail ventures deep into the heart of the canyon, and links with the Bright Angel Trail to offer a rim-to-rim hike, taken by hundreds every year. (See box.)

WARNING: When hiking into the canyon, *always* carry plenty of water and food snacks to maintain your energy level, and wear a shade hat. This is vitally important in summer, since you'll be hiking down into desert climate zones where the temperature routinely tops 100 degrees. Every year, hikers are toppled by thirst and heat-exhaustion; some have died.

THE CANYON FROM RIM TO RIM

For a total canyon experience, hike from one rim to the other. The North Kaibab and Bright Angel trails meet at the Colorado River to offer this popular rim-to-rim trek. And don't worry, there's a bridge across the stream. We'd recommend hiking north to south, since the North Rim is more than a thousand feet higher than the South Rim.

A cross-canyon hike requires advance planning. It's a two or three-day trip, covering more than 23 miles, so you'll need somewhere to spend the night. Phantom Ranch offers rustic accommodations in rooms or dormitories, and meals. Backpackers can camp at Bright Angel Campground or other designated camping sites in the inner canyon. *Reservations for Phantom Ranch or inner canyon campgrounds must be made months in advance.* And of course, you'll have to arrange for a cross-canyon shuttle.

The hike down from the North Rim descends through pine forests to Bright Angel Creek, which leads to Phantom Ranch and the Colorado River. It's 14.2 miles from the North Kaibab trailhead to Phantom, and you'll drop more than a mile in elevation.

You'll want to get an early start the next morning, since it's 9.3 miles from Phantom to the top of Bright Angel Trail. And nearly eight miles of it is uphill. The steepest part comes at the end—a grueling series of switchbacks. Fortunately, there are water and rest stops at Indian Gardens about halfway up, then every mile and a half until you reach the top.

Phantom Ranch reservations (including meals) ● Grand Canyon National Park Lodges, P.O. Box 699, Grand Canyon, AZ 86023; (602) 638-2401. Cabins are $53 for one or two and dormitory beds are $19 each. Meals are $8.50 for breakfast, $6.50 for a sack lunch, $14 for a stew dinner or $23.50 for a steak dinner. Because of heavy booking, give several alternate dates. The best way is to phone and see what dates are available. Meals, which must be arranged in advance, are available for campers as well as for those who stay in the cabins or dorms.

Inner canyon camping reservations ● Backcountry Reservation Office, Box 129, Grand Canyon, AZ 86023 Again, apply early and have alternate dates.

Cross-canyon shuttle ● You can catch the daily van shuttle between the north and south rims for $50 each way, May 7 to October 31 (or until the North Rim closes). It departs the North Rim's Grand Canyon Lodge at 7 a.m., arrives at the South Rim's Bright Angel Lodge at 11:30, starts for the North Rim at 1:30, arriving at 6 p.m. For reservations, call (602) 638-2820.

During the off-season, wear clothes in layers that can be peeled and added, since temperatures can change quickly.

Allow sufficient time for your uphill return. The rule of thumb, if you're in average shape, is to figure twice as much time to climb out as it took to go down. You don't want to be caught stumbling up a narrow trail in darkness. If you plan to be in the park for several days, take a day or so to become acclimated to the higher altitude before attempting strenuous hikes.

Finally, remember that a permit is required from the Backcountry Office for any camping in the canyon.

Cliff Springs Trail ● *Moderately easy hiking; about three miles round trip. Trailhead is a third of a mile from the Cape Royal parking area.* Cliff Springs is our North Rim favorite, and the most unheralded trail in the park. You have to be watchful for the trailhead. Look for a small brown sign on a sweeping turn in the road just before the Cape Royal parking lot. There's limited parking available at a turnout.

The trail begins modestly, passing through a shallow forest ravine. Then it tucks under the dramatic overhang of a redwall cliff for several hundred yards before reaching the dripping springs for which it was named. Many hikers turn around here, but the best part of the trail lies ahead. It follows a redrock ridge into a rough-hewn side canyon, offering great views of sculpted limestone and sandstone formations.

This portion is a bit rough, with some up and down scrambling, but it's easily navigable. The trail ends rather dramatically, dissolving into a great redrock butte.

North Kaibab Trail ● *Steep, some cliff-edge exposure in the upper part; about 14 miles to the river. Trailhead is just over two miles north of the visitor area on the main road.* From the rim, this trail takes you along a dramatic cliff edge to Roaring Springs. It then enters Bright Angel Canyon, following Bright Angel Creek into the Precambrian schists of the inner canyon. After 14.2 miles, you'll reach Phantom Ranch and Bright Angel Campground. It's another mile and a half to the river.

Don't try to make it to the river and back, unless you've made overnight arrangements at Phantom Ranch or an inner canyon campground. However, shorter sections of the trail offer rich variety for day-trippers.

If you're in good shape, you can probably make it from the North Rim to Cottonwood Campground, a 14-mile round trip. It has fresh water, and a manned ranger station in summer. For the rest of us, the 9.4-mile round trip to Roaring Springs will be a good day's work. You'll have to recover an elevation loss of more than 3,000 feet.

Ken Patrick Trail ● *Easy hiking; 10 miles one way. Trailhead is in North Kaibab parking lot.* This rather level path follows the rim to Point Imperial, ducking in an out of forests with frequent canyon views. It offers an ideal day hike if you have a car shuttle. If you want to go only part way on the trail, start your hike at the Point Imperial end. This offers the best canyon vistas.

The trail was named for Ken Patrick, who once served at the Grand Canyon, then was transferred to Point Reyes National Seashore near San Francisco. There, he became the first ranger in the history of the National Park Service to be murdered in the line of duty. He was killed attempting to arrest some poachers.

THE REST

Widforss Trail ● *Moderately easy; some elevation change; ten-mile round trip. Trailhead is 2.7 miles north of the visitor area, then a mile west on a dirt road.* In an area of stunning canyon views, much of this trail is buried in thick forest, which we found to be a bit frustrating. But it emerges occasionally for vivid vistas of Transept Canyon and it passes incredible pinnacles that look like carelessly stacked building blocks, ready to fall.

After a lengthy passage through an aspen-ponderosa forest, it emerges at Widforss Point. Here, you see a pleasant—if not awesome—view of North Rim formations and the pencil-line ridge of the South Rim across the chasm.

If you're short on time, hike to the pinnacle area, then start back just before the trail swings away from the rim to enter the forest. The round trip will take two to three hours.

Uncle Jim Trail ● *Easy hiking; five-mile round trip.* This is a loop trail to a canyon overlook, which spurs off the Ken Patrick Trail about a mile from the North Kaibab trailhead. After passing through a forest, it emerges for nice views of Roaring Springs Canyon and the eastern reaches of the Grand Canyon.

In case you wondered, the trail was named for Jim Owens, a friendly uncle of a man who was the first warden of the Grand Canyon Game Preserve until it became a national park.

ACTIVITIES

Other than the excellent ranger hikes, slide shows and talks, most scheduled activities occur on the South Rim. However, North Rim visitors can book round-trip mule rides down to Roaring Springs. Outside the park at Jacob Lake, 44 miles north, one can arrange for hikes and tours in summer and cross country skiing in winter.

North Kaibab mule rides ● *Contact Grand Canyon Trail Rides, P.O. Box 1638, Cedar City, UT 84720; (602) 638-2292 in summer or (801) 586-7238 the rest of the year.* These are one-day trips that turn around at Roaring Springs; they do not go to the river or Phantom Ranch. Arrangements must be made well in advance.

North Rim hikes and tours ● *Canyoneers, Inc., P.O. Box 2997, Flagstaff, AZ 86003; (602) 526-0924. From May 15 to November 15, call (602) 638-2383 or the Flagstaff number.* The firm offers escorted hikes in Kaibab National Forest near the North Rim and driving-hiking excursions to Grand Canyon overlooks. Prices range from half-day for $25 to overnight trips for $115. The outfit provides equipment rental and overnight stays in yurts for $25 per person. The operation is based at the North Rim Country Store, a provisioning stop between Jacob Lake and the North Rim, just outside the park boundary.

Cross-Country skiing ● *North Rim Nordic Center, c/o Canyoneers, Inc.; same address and phone number as above.* From December 1 to April 1, the country store becomes North Rim Winter Camp for cross-country skiers. Guests are picked up at Jacob Lake in a heated "SnowVan" and taken to the ski camp. From there, they can ski into the park, or follow several miles of a tracked trail system at the camp. Trail fee is $7 for adults and $4.50 for kids under 12. Cross-country ski lessons, equipment rentals, a ski shop and conducted ski tours are available. The firm also offers packaged tours from Jacob Lake to the Ski Camp, yurt rentals and SnowVan tours. Write or call for a detailed brochure.

WHERE TO DINE
Grand Canyon Lodge Dining Room ● ΔΔΔ $$ ∅

P.O. Box 400, Cedar City, UT 84720; (801) 586-7686. American; dinners $7.50 to $16; full bar. Also an informal cafeteria. Breakfast 6:30 to 10 a.m.; lunch 11:30 to 2:30; dinner 5 to 9:30; reservations advised for dining room. All major credit cards. Even if you're on a strict budget, plan at least one meal in the old high-ceiling dining room with its picture-window views of the canyon. For thrift, try the cafeteria.

Jacob Lake Inn Dining Room ● ΔΔ $$

Jacob Lake, AZ 86022; 643-7232. American; dinners $6.50 to $14.50; wine and beer. 6:30 a.m. to 9 p.m.; shorter hours in winter. Major credit cards. This informal, woodsy dining room serves generous portions of home-style cooking.

WHERE TO SLEEP
Grand Canyon Lodge ● Δ to ΔΔΔ $$

P.O. Box 400, Cedar City, UT 84720; (801) 586-7686. Singles or doubles $43 to $57. All major credit cards. Some rooms with canyon view; dining room (listing above). Grand Canyon Lodge offers assorted accommodations, ranging from canyon-view hotel rooms and modern motel wings to small and rather rustic cabins. The lodge essentially serves as the North Rim's visitor center, with a transportation desk, saloon, ranger programs (not in the saloon, of course), park service information desk, dining room (listed above) and cafeteria.

Jacob Lake Inn ● ΔΔ $$

Jacob Lake, AZ 86022; 643-7232. Singles or doubles $40 to $50; two-room units for families $50 to to $58. Major credit cards. Dining room (listing above), tennis court, playground. Located in Kaibab National Forest on Highway 67, 44 miles from the North Rim, Jacob Lake Inn offers motel-style units and some weathered cabins in a pleasant forest setting.

WHERE TO CAMP
Demotte Campground ● *c/o Kaibab National Forest, P.O. Box 248, Fredonia, AZ 86022; 643-7395. RV and tent sites, no hookups, $6. No reservations accepted.* This is a national forest campground on the west side of State Highway 67, 24 miles south of Jacob Lake, about 20 miles from the North Rim. It has pit potties, picnic tables, barbecues. Open May to October.

Jacob Lake Campground ● *c/o Kaibab National Forest, P.O. Box 248, Fredonia, AZ 86022; 643-7395. RV and tent sites, no hookups, $7. Reservations through MisTix; call (800) 283-CAMP.* National forest campground across from Jacob Lake Lodge, at the junction of State Highway 67 and U.S. 89A; 44 miles from the North Rim. Potties, picnic tables, barbecues, groceries. Open May to October.

Jacob Lake RV Park ● *Jacob Lake, AZ 86022; Off-season address: HC 64, Box 25, Fredonia, AZ 86022; (801) 628-8851. RV and tent sites; water and electric $14, no hookups $10, tent sites $7. Reservations accepted; no credit cards.* Pull-throughs, RV dump station; hiking trails nearby. Located in a forested area near Jacob Lake Inn, just south of Jacob Lake Junction.

GRAND CANYON CROSS-SECTION: A SLICE OF THE SOUTH RIM

FORMATION	FEET THICK	LANDFORM	DEPOSITS	DESCRIPTION	GEOLOGIC TIME ERA	GEOLOGIC TIME PERIOD
MOENKOPI FORMATION	400	GENTLE SLOPE, CONCAVE	TIDAL FLAT	Canyon rim: light red to dark brown siltstone, shale and mudstone. Reptile tracks.	Mesozoic	Triassic
KAIBAB LIMESTONE	300	SHEER FACE	MARINE	Light gray limestone; marine fossils	Paleozoic	Permian
TOROWEAP FORMATION	250	SHEER FACE	MARINE	Mix of grayish limestone, siltstone beds, mudstone and sandstone; marine fossils	Paleozoic	Permian
COCONINO SANDSTONE	300	SHEER FACE	DESERT SANDS	Cross-bedded light tan sandstone; fossil tracks.	Paleozoic	Permian
HERMIT SHALE	300	STEEP SLOPE	SAVANNAH	Reddish shale, siltstone and mudstone; fossil plants.	Paleozoic	Permian
SUPAI GROUP	900	LEDGES AND SLOPES	FLOOD PLAIN	Red-colored sandstone, siltstone, shale and limestone; fossil plants and animal tracks.	Paleozoic	Permian and Pennsylvanian
REDWALL LIMESTONE	500	SHEER FACE	MARINE	Limestone stained red by overlying Supai sandstone and Hermit shale; marine fossils and limestone caves.	Paleozoic	Mississippian
TEMPLE BUTTE LIMESTONE	30	SHEER FACE	MARINE	Limestone, soft purple to pinkish gray; fossil rare.	Paleozoic	Devonian
MUAV LIMESTONE	600	CLIFFS, LEDGES, SLOPES	MARINE	Yellow-gray limestone and siltstone; trilobite fossils and wave-action ripples.	Paleozoic	Cambrian
BRIGHT ANGEL SHALE	350-400	LOW SLOPE BENCH	MARINE	Gray-green shale; trilobite and brachiopod fossils; tracks and trails of trilobites and sea worms.	Paleozoic	Cambrian
TAPEATS SANDSTONE	100-300	CLIFF	MARINE	Textured brown sandstone; marine animal track fossils.	Paleozoic	Cambrian
GRAND CANYON SUPER GROUP	UNKNOWN	INNER GORGE	MARINE	Mix of sandstone, limestone, siltstone and shale.	Precambrian	Late
VISHNU SCHIST	UNKNOWN	COLORADO RIVER	MARINE METAMORPHISM, MOLTEN INTRUSIONS	Dark Precambrian schists and gneisses; intrusion from pink and white granite dikes and sills.	Precambrian	Early

The South Rim

Elevation: 5,750 to 7,400 feet

The most direct route to the South Rim is via State Highway 64, north from Williams if you're coming from the west. From the east, take U.S. 180 northwest out of Flagstaff.

We recommend entering the park through the south entrance, then departing via the Desert View gate. This takes you along the East Rim Drive—with its sundry canyon-view turnouts—to the interesting Desert View complex (see "Attractions"). As you leave the eastern end of the park on State Highway 64, you cross a bit of the Navajo Indian reservation. Heading south toward Flagstaff, you can visit Wupatki and Sunset Crater national monuments, just off U.S. 89.

When man sets about to preserve a wilderness, can civilization be far behind?

As you approach the park's south entrance, you'll pass through a commercial area called Tusayan, situated in Kaibab National Forest. It's basically in business to catch the overflow from park facilities. Tusayan offers a campground, several motels, service stations, restaurants, a bowling alley and a restaurant-bar-gift shop complex called Galaxy Four, housed in ugly brown domes. And, yes, there's that McDonald's.

In Tusayan, you can book helicopter and fixed-wing canyon flights, which depart from chopper pads or from the nearby Grand Canyon Airport. Tusayan also is home to an excellent giant-screen movie, *Grand Canyon: The Hidden Secrets*. It offers a fine preview of what you're about to experience in the park.

Passing through the park gate, you might head for Mather Point for your first view of the canyon. It isn't the most impressive canyon vista, but it will certainly whet your appetite. Then head west to the visitor center, or to Yavapai Museum. You can learn about ranger walks, talks and campfire programs, inner canyon hiking, sunset and sunrise times, camping availability and just about anything else you need to know. Pick up a copy of *The Guide* newspaper, which lists whatever the ranger might have overlooked.

During summer, a free shuttle bus runs from Hermits Rest to Grand Canyon Village. Another, operating less frequently, travels to the Kaibab Trailhead at Yaki Point. These are handy for one-way hikers who need to get back to their cars or lodging.

THE BEST ATTRACTIONS

Sunups and sundowns • *Various points along the canyon rim.* It may seem odd to list sunrises and sunsets as attractions, but then, this is an unusual guidebook. And certainly, the canyon is most beautiful during those times. Because you're on a plateau with no mountains or buildings to ruffle the horizon, sunups and sundowns are as crisply defined as they are at sea.

Don't wait until the last minute to catch a sunset. The dramatic canyon lighting starts developing about an hour before. And in the morning, hang around for an hour after you've seen the sun peek over the horizon.

Several turnouts along the east and west rim drives offer fine sunup/sundown vantage points. Hopi Point is particularly popular for sunsets, while Yaki Point offers spectacular sunrises.

GRAND CANYON VILLAGE MAP
(South Rim)

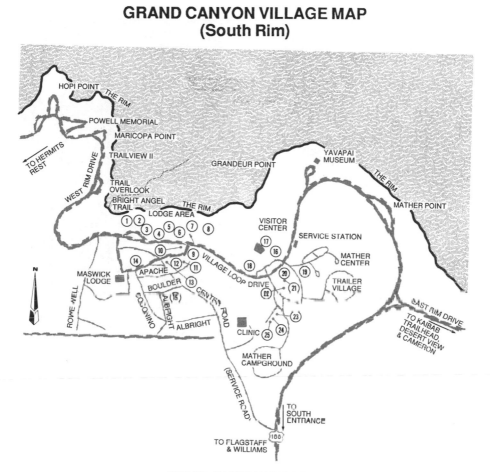

GRAND CANYON VILLAGE

LODGE AREA
1. KOLB STUDIO
2. LOOKOUT STUDIO
3. BRIGHT ANGEL LODGE
4. THUNDERBIRD LODGE
5. KACHINA LODGE
6. EL TOVAR LODGE
7. HOPI HOUSE CURIO SHOP
8. VERKAMP'S CURIO SHOP
9. PUBLIC GARAGE; GENERAL OFFICES
10. RAILROAD STATION
11. YOUTH HOSTEL
12. NATURAL HISTORY ASSN.
13. RANGER OFFICE
14. 'OVER THE EDGE' SHOW
15. EL CRISTO REY PARISH

VISITOR CENTER AREA
16. PARK HEADQUARTERS
17. MATHER AMPHITHEATER
18. SHRINE OF THE AGES

MATHER CENTER
19. YAVAPAI LODGE
20. BANK
21. POST OFFICE
22. BABBIT'S GENERAL STORE

CAMPER SERVICES
23. SHOWERS, LAUNDRY, ICE
24. BACKCOUNTRY RESERVATIONS
25. GRAND CANYON TRAIL GUIDES

—Grand Canyon N. P. photo (#4684)
*Twig figure left by early canyon
inhabitants.*

*Watchtower at Desert View
on the South Rim.*

Our personal preferences are Hopi Overlook (a couple hundred yards beyond Hopi Point) for sunsets and Grandview Point for sunrises. The Hopi Overlook is much less crowded than Hopi Point itself, and it offers a wonderful mix of formations to catch the late light. At Grandview Point, the sun bathes a great proscenium of the canyon with light and shadow. And you see a glittering bit of the Colorado River, like a distant jewel, far below you.

Desert View and the Watchtower ● *About 26 miles east of Grand Canyon Village, off East Rim Drive. Tower open daily 9 to 6; admission is 25 cents.* Desert View is a visitor complex in the eastern corner of the park, offering gift shops, a general store, service station, campground and restaurant. The river is dramatically close here, since this is the upper end of the canyon where it hasn't yet cut so deeply. Appropriate to its name, this overlook also offers a view of the Painted Desert's pastel hues, just to the east.

The area's focal point, other than the canyon view, is the 70-foot stone Watchtower. It was built in 1932 by the Fred Harvey Company as a rather fanciful interpretation of Southwest Indian architecture.

The ground level houses a gift shop, and for a quarter you can climb up the three floors of the tower. It's the best twenty-five cent investment you can make. Walls are decorated with sand paintings and other bright trim, depicting Indian legends. Windows offer fine views of the canyon, particularly from the observatory on top. On the second floor, step out onto the balcony and peek into those odd-looking boxes called Reflectoscopes. Sections of the canyon are reflected into black-glass mirrors, clearly defining their assorted awesome shapes.

East Rim Drive ● *Grand Canyon Village to Desert View.* This 26-mile drive skirts much of the canyon's south rim, with frequent overlooks for a better peek. Among its premier view areas are Yaki Point, which thrusts beyond the rim for an outstanding look at canyon formations; Grandview Point, with its great wide-angle vista; and Lipan Point, where every eroded geological layer of the canyon can be seen.

Before reaching Lipan, watch on your right for a sign indicating the Tusayan Museum and ruin, 22 miles from Grand Canyon Village (see "The Rest" below). The East Rim Drive ends at Desert View. Here, you can see a great serpentine section of Rio Colorado. The park's east entrance station is just beyond here.

Grand Canyon IMAX Theatre ● *In Tusayan, seven miles from the south gate; P.O. Box 1397, Grand Canyon, AZ 86023-1397; (602) 638-2203. Shows hourly on the half hour from 8:30 to 8:30 daily; shorter hours in winter; $6 for adults, $4 for kids under 12.* Beautifully photographed, *Grand Canyon: The Hidden Secrets,* is one of the finest films of this type we've seen. The monster screen draws you right into the ravine, hurls you through the rapids and takes you on dizzying flights between the walls.

Tracing the history of man in the canyon, the movie begins with scenes of rather nubile Indian maidens, then moves on to some outstanding shots of J.W. Powell guiding his long wooden boats through Rio Colorado's violent rapids. Using replicas of the Powell boats, the cast actually ran many of the rapids that the early explorer bypassed.

Closing footage of an ultra-light plane flitting in and out of the canyon shadows like a giant dragonfly is simply smashing.

West Rim Drive ● *Grand Canyon Village to Hermits Rest.* This eight-mile drive offers even more vistas than the more popular East Rim Drive. The route stays closer to the rim for a greater variety of canyon views, and the turnouts generally are less crowded. The best way to savor the changing canyon panorama is to walk—not drive—along the West Rim.

In summer, free shuttles scurry over the drive every few minutes, so you can hop aboard when you've run out of energy. In fact, the drive is closed to other vehicles in summer, so the shuttle is the only way to go—which is great. The drive is open to motorists in the off-season, when the shuttle isn't running.

At Maricopa Point, you'll see ruins of the Orphan Mine with its towering headframe. The Powell Memorial here is an impressive granite column dedicated to the pioneer river-runner. Mohave Point is one of the few viewpoints from which you can see a stretch of the Colorado River. That tiny bit of white foam far below is Hermit Rapids. At the end of the drive is Hermits Rest, a curio shop and refreshment stand in a rough-hewn stone building.

Visitor Center Museum ● *Open daily 7:30 a.m. to 8:30 p.m. in summer; 8:15 to 5 the rest of the year.* This fine museum traces man's intrusion into the canyon, from prehistoric Indians and Spanish explorers to Major Powell, early prospectors and today's tourists. It also exhibits stuffed critters native to the area and an excellent array of Grand Canyon photos.

Slide shows and films help you become better acquainted with the park, and you can buy an assortment of books, maps and videos. As we said earlier, rangers at the information desk here can answer all your Grand Canyon questions.

Yavapai Geological Museum • *Near Yavapai Point. Open 8 to 8 in summer, 9 to 5 in the off-season.* The finest museum in the park, Yavapai offers outstanding exhibits on Grand Canyon geology. Particularly impressive is a time clock that ticks off in three minutes the two billion years that have passed since the first vishnu schist was laid down at the bottom of the canyon. The cutting of the canyon, which took from three to seven million years, and the ascent of man are covered in the final tick!

The museum is perched on the rim's edge; polarized picture windows offer beautifully enhanced canyon views.

THE REST

Fred Harvey History Museum • *Grand Canyon village, in the Bright Angel Lodge. Open daily 9 to 5.* Situated off the Bright Angel lobby, this interesting mini-museum tells the story of the Fred Harvey Company with old photos and memorabilia.

Mr. Harvey, tired of awful meals he was getting on trains, convinced the Santa Fe to let him open a restaurant in the railroad's Topeka, Kansas, station in 1876. From this came a string of "Harvey Houses"—hotel/restaurants along the Santa Fe line. When the railway opened a spur to the Grand Canyon in 1901, Harvey began building many of the dramatically bold log and stone buildings that still house hotels, restaurants and gift shops.

In the museum, you learn that the company's friendly but prim "Harvey Girls" worked for $17.50 a month plus room and board in the 1880s. Women were scarce in the west, and so many girls left their jobs for marriage that Harvey began withholding half of their first year's wages. According to humorist Will Rogers, "Fred Harvey Kept the West in food and wives."

Also of interest here is the Geological Fireplace. It's built of layered stone corresponding to strata in the canyon, from vishnu schist for the hearth to Kaibab limestone atop the ten-foot chimney.

Hopi House • *Grand Canyon Village, near El Tovar. Open daily 9 to 5.* Another of the historic stone structures built by the Harvey Company, Hopi House offers Southwest Indian arts and crafts for sale. It also has several museum-quality artifacts on exhibit. Built in the style of a Hopi pueblo, it's worth a visit even if you aren't in a shopping mood.

Over the Edge Multi-Media Show • *In the Community Building, Grand Canyon Village; 638-2224. Shows every 30 minutes; 9 to 9 in summer, 10 to 3 and 5 to 8 in the off season; $4 for adults and $2 for juniors.* This is a Grand Canyon orientation show, using a dozen slide projectors, strobes and a sound track. It's nice, but not nearly as dramatic as the IMAX show, *The Hidden Secrets.* We'd suggest that the two producers get together and swap titles.

It *does* offer fine examples of photography as reincarnate guide John Hance spins tall tales and takes you on tour "over the edge" of the canyon. The most impressive thing about the show is the technical use of the computer-driven slide projectors.

El Tovar Hotel • *Grand Canyon Village.* Described as "the most expensively constructed and appointed log house in America," El Tovar is perhaps the grandest of the grand hotels built in the early days of the national park system. Completed in 1905 at a cost of $250,000, it is a bold four-story edifice of Kaibab limestone and Douglas fir from Oregon. Dark-stained log columns and beams hold up the lofty ceiling; plush carpets cover the floors. It's an elegant blend of the rustic American west and a luxury Swiss chalet.

Stop by to prowl the lobby, have a drink in the cozy cocktail lounge or really indulge yourself with dinner in the canyon-view dining room.

THE BEST HIKING TRAILS

We begin by repeating our advise from the North Rim section: When hiking into the canyon, *always* carry plenty of water and food snacks, and wear a shade hat. This is vitally important in the summer, since you'll be hiking down into desert climate zones where the temperature tops 100 degrees. Every year, hikers are toppled by thirst and heat-exhaustion. Some have perished.

During the off-season, wear clothes in layers that can be peeled and added, since temperatures can change quickly.

Allow enough time for your uphill return. The rule of thumb, if you're in average shape, is to figure twice as much time to climb out as it took to go down. You don't want to be caught stumbling up a narrow trail in darkness.

If you're going to be in the park for several days, take a day or so to become acclimated to the altitude before attempting strenuous hikes. Finally, remember that a permit is required from the backcountry office for any camping in the canyon.

This hiking advise is particularly important on the south side trails, for the South Rim is much more precipitous and the climb out can pose a serious threat on a hot day. Also, the huge Tonto Plateau crossed by the Tonto Trail is a burning desert in summer. More than one hiker has been felled by the heat there.

South Kaibab Trail ● *Steep incline, a tough climb out; 4.4 miles to Tonto Trail Junction and 6.4 miles to the Colorado River. Trailhead is near Yaki Point.* The Kaibab is our personal preference among the South Rim hikes. Starting in a narrow, shaded side canyon, it descends steeply down Cedar Ridge. It weaves between dramatically eroded formations before leveling out on the Tonto Plateau.

From here, you can cut across on the Tonto Trail to Indian Garden, and then hike up the Bright Angel Trail for a round-trip of around 13 miles. During the cool off-season, a strong hiker can make the 11 mile round trip from the Kaibab trailhead to the river and back in one day. But don't try it in summer! The Kaibab's final climb-out is a torturous switch-back.

Grandview Trail ● *Steep descent; rough climb out; 3 miles to Horseshoe Mesa. Trailhead is at Grandview Point on the East Rim Drive.* The Grandview spirals right down the face of the South Rim, offering impressive panoramas as you hike. Then you pass through narrow side canyons, where you're surrounded by razor ridges, pinnacles and those wedding cake buttes.

The trail emerges onto broad, gently-sloping Horseshoe Mesa, where you'll encounter the ruins of the Last Chance Copper Mine and remnants of prospector Pete Berry's stone cabin. Hike out to the edge of the mesa, and a great amphitheater of canyon opens up around you. If you're doing a day hike, this is a good place to sit with lunch and camera before starting back.

Although it's listed as "unmaintained," most of the Grandview Trail is well-defined and safely terraced. We had no problems with it between the South Rim and Horseshoe Mesa.

From the mesa, the trail merges with the Tonto East and Cottonwood Creek trails. Trails leading down off the plateau are very rough, particularly the descent into Cottonwood Creek Canyon.

Ranger delivers a "rock talk" at Yavapai Point.

Hermit Trail • *Steep descent into the canyon, tough climb out; 8.9 miles to the Colorado River, 4 miles to Lookout Point. Trailhead is just beyond Hermits Rest.* The trail wigs and wags in serpentine twists down through Kaibab limestone to redwall formations. It then follows a dizzying but safe cliff-edge route along a side canyon and emerges onto Lookout Point. This is a nice lunch spot and turn-around for a moderate one-day hike. You don't see a lot of the main canyon unless you go well beyond Lookout Point, but the side canyon scenery is great.

The Hermit climb-out is wearying, so only a seasoned hiker can make the 17-mile round trip to the river. And again, don't try it in summer. Like the Grandview, Hermit also is not maintained, but most of the route is in good shape. You'll encounter a few minor rock slides, but nothing you can't step over.

South Rim Trail • *Easy stroll, four-mile round-trip. Trailhead near Bright Angel Lodge.* This paved trail follows the rim for about two miles through the main visitor area. It takes you past the monumental log and stone buildings of Grand Canyon Village, then along the rim to Grandeur Point and the Yavapai Geologic Museum. A half-mile continuation reaches Mather Point.

As you walk this trail, note the old copper sighting tubes, through which you can spot the canyon's various geological features. About midway to Yavapai Museum, a spur to the south takes you to the amphitheater and visitor center.

West Rim Trail • *Easy—if lengthy—stroll along the canyon rim; about eight miles from Grand Canyon Village to Hermits Rest. Trailhead near Bright Angel Lodge.* This is perhaps the most pleasantly easy trail in the park. It offers wonderful canyon vistas, very little elevation change and it can be taken in manageable sections, depending on your physical shape.

Although it roughly parallels West Rim Drive, the trail hugs the canyon more closely than the road, giving you a wonderful assortment of views. The rim here is much more irregular than on the East Rim Drive, so you find yourself hiking out onto peninsulas, then swinging inland to skirt side canyons.

The trail becomes a bit irregular and rough as it approaches Hermits Rest, and gets mixed in with an old road. Probably the most interesting section is between Bright Angel Lodge and Pima Point. It's paved from Yavapai Museum to Maricopa Point.

THE REST

Bright Angel Trail ● *Steep descent but well maintained, tough climb out; 4.6 miles to Indian Garden, 7.8 miles to the river, 9.7 miles to Phantom Ranch.* No, the Bright Angel Trail didn't make our list of the best. It's too heavily traveled, particularly by mules. We dislike having to stand obediently to one side as the endless mule trains pass, and we particularly dislike having to sidestep what they left behind.

Views from the Bright Angel are certainly impressive, although they don't change much from the rim as you descend. Indian Garden, a spring-fed oasis, is a welcome rest stop. From here, you can hike another mile and a half across the Tonto Plateau to an overlook, where you're just 1,500 feet above the mighty Colorado. A trip from the rim to the overlook and back would make a good day's workout.

Dripping Springs ● *Steep descent, tough climb out; 6-mile round trip; start at Hermit trailhead.* Dripping Springs is a pleasant sylvan glen far back in a side canyon at the head of Hermit Creek. Follow the Hermit Trail 1.5 miles to the Dripping Springs junction, then go another 1.5 miles to the springs.

You're away from the main gorge here, but some of the side canyon formations are quite impressive. Incidentally, the springs barely drip, so take your own water.

Tonto Trail ● *Long, irregular trail, some level, some steep; varying lengths. No rim trailhead.* Tonto is the long trail that parallels the canyon for an amazing 92 miles. It's a real trekker's trail, winding in and out of side canyons, offering everything from river vistas to broad expanses of sloping desert of the great Tonto Plateau.

Two popular places to pick up this route are the South Kaibab trail at the Tonto Junction, and the Bright Angel trail, just below Indian Garden.

ACTIVITIES

Canyon flights ● *Offered by no less than 40 different companies, operating from as far away as Phoenix and Las Vegas, starting at around $50.* The granddaddy of the group is **Grand Canyon Airlines**, which began more than 60 years ago with Ford Tri-motors. Flying out of Grand Canyon airport near Tusayan, the firm now uses more modern equipment. Outside Arizona, call (800) 528-2413 for schedules and prices; locally, call (602) 638-2407.

Other carriers operating from Grand Canyon airport or heli-pads at Tusayan include (area code 602 unless otherwise indicated) **AWR Helicopters**, 638-2833; **AirStar Helicopters**, 638-2622; **Air Grand Canyon**, 638-2686 or toll-free (800) AIR-GRAND; **Windrock Aviation**, 638-9591 or 638-9570; **Kenai Helicopters**, 638-2412; and **Grand Canyon Helicopters**, 638-2419 or toll-free outside Arizona, (800) 528-2418.

Guided tours • *Grand Canyon National Park Lodges, P.O. Box 699, Grand Canyon, AZ 86023. Call 638-2401 for reservations and 638-2631 for information.* Among these "Harveycar" tours are two-hour trips to Hermits Rest for $10; a four-hour Desert View tour for $16; combo six-hour Hermit-Desert View for $18; Sunset Tour to Yaki Point for $6.50; all-day Monument Valley Tour for $65; all-day "Smooth Water" raft excursion through Marble Canyon for $65; and an all-day tour to Wupatki, Sunset Crater and Walnut Canyon national monuments for $60. In all of the above, children's rates are half price.

Historic steam train rides • *Between Williams and Grand Canyon Village; $47 round-trip for adults, $23 for kids 12 and under; major credit cards accepted; Grand Canyon Railway, 518 E. Bill Williams Ave., Williams, AZ 86046; (800) THE-TRAIN or (602) 635-4000.* Using turn-of-the-century steam locomotives and 1920s Pullman cars, Grand Canyon Railway has resumed the historic 64-mile run between Williams and the park. The excursion includes on-board entertainment and complimentary refreshments.

From April through September, two trains leave Williams daily at 8 and 10 a.m., then leave Grand Canyon Village at 2:30 and 4:30 p.m. During March and from October through December, a single train departs Williams daily at 10 and leaves the Grand Canyon at 4:30. There is no service in January and February.

Grand Canyon rail service originally began in 1901, then was discontinued in 1968 because of increased auto use. Ironically, the run has resumed to alleviate traffic congestion at the South Rim, where as many as 4,000 vehicles gather on a summer day.

Horseback riding • *Nags can be booked through Moqui Lodge at Tusayan, P.O. Box 369, Grand Canyon, AZ 86023; (602) 638-2401.* Offerings include a four-hour East Rim ride for $40, wagon ride for $6, one-hour horseback ride for $17.50 and a cowboy breakfast ride for $10.50. Most of these activities occur around Tusayan in Kaibab National Forest, just outside the park.

Mule rides • *They must be reserved months in advance; contact Grand Canyon National Park Lodges, P.O. Box 699, Grand Canyon, AZ 86023; (602) 638-2401.* Rides down the Bright Angel Trail to Phantom Ranch, including one night's accommodations and meals at the ranch, are $206 per person or $359 for two. One-day round-trip mule rides down the Bright Angel Trail to Plateau Point are $64 per person, including lunch. Duffel portage (30 pounds or less) is $34 from rim to river and $25 river to rim. And no, we have no idea why it costs less to pack it out than to take it down.

Riders must weigh under 200 pounds (dressed), be at least four-foot-seven, and not noticeably pregnant. The brochure says they also must be fluent in English. Apparently the mules aren't bi-lingual.

TRANSIT—RAPID & OTHERWISE

Transportation desks at Bright Angel Lodge, Maswik Lodge and Yavapai Lodge on the South Rim and Grand Canyon Lodge on the North Rim can book many of the services listed below. Or contact the firms directly.

Flights to Grand Canyon Airport are offered by **America West** out of Flagstaff and Las Vegas; (800) 247-5692. **Scenic Airlines** flies to the canyon from Las Vegas; call locally 638-2436 or toll-free (800) 634-6801. Also flying from Las Vegas is **Air Nevada**; 638-2441 or (800) 634-6377.

Bus service is provided between the South Rim and Flagstaff or Williams by the **Nava-Hopi Tours**. Operating out of Flagstaff, the company also offers tours in the area. Call (602) 774-5003.

Shuttle service operates between Tusayan, the airport and Grand Canyon Village, hourly from 8:15 a.m. to 7:10 p.m.; more frequent service in the summer. Rates are $4 one way and $7 round trip for adults; $3 and $5 for kids 6 to 12. Call **Tusayan-Grand Canyon Shuttle** at (602) 638-2475 for details. The firm also operates taxi and charter service.

Free shuttles are operated by the park service between Grand Canyon Village and Hermits Rest in the summer. Less frequent shuttles serve the South Kaibab trailhead near Yaki Point.

Rim to rim shuttle service operates daily in summer between Tusayan and the North Rim. It departs Tusayan at 7 a.m., arrives at the North Rim at

---

RAPID TRANSIT ON RIO COLORADO

"You're running the Colorado River in *those* little things?" Occupants of a large pontoon boat stare down at us in disbelief.

For the ultimate Grand Canyon experience, you should run the Colorado River and explore its serpentine side canyons. With dozens of rapids and its enchanting inner-canyon solitude, the Colorado offers America's finest river-running experience.

At last count, 21 companies offered trips of varying lengths. Only one, Grand Canyon Dories, runs Rio Colorado in small, rigid boats. The rest use inflatables of assorted shapes and sizes; they're either oar-powered or motor-driven.

When we ran the river with the dories, folks riding the big rafts were amazed that our oarsmen would tackle the rapids in such fragile-looking craft. As far as we're concerned, it's the *only* way to run the river. Their rigid construction provides a livelier, more exciting ride. Historically, they're more appropriate, since John Wesley Powell used rigid boats on his epic trips.

Of course, the dories are superior to Powell's longboats. Remarkably nimble, they navigate major rapids and deliver their passengers safely—if sometimes soaked. And they're hardly fragile, despite their size; they're made of tough plywood, aluminum or Fiberglas. Measuring about six by 18 feet, the brightly-painted boats are styled after European fishing dories. Each is named for a natural feature that was despoiled by man.

The oar-powered dories move along at a leisurely pace—except when they're splashing through rapids. Full-length trips take nearly as long as Powell, who spent 24 days in the canyon. Like Powell, today's river-runners take time to prowl side canyons, explore Indian ruins, follow crystal creeks to hidden waterfalls and hike the high mesas. They become part of the canyon, not distant observers peering down from the rim.

River-running season extends from April through early November. We prefer spring and fall, since inner-canyon summers can get hot. Most trips put in at Lees Ferry and take out at some point on upper Lake Mead.

Dory trips range from five to 20 days. On shorter runs, guests join or leave the boats at Phantom Ranch or other access points.

For details, contact: **Grand Canyon Dories**, P.O. Box 216, Altaville, CA 95221; (209) 736-0805. For a list of other companies running the Colorado, contact: **River Sub-district**, Grand Canyon National Park, P.O. Box 129, Grand Canyon, AZ 86023; (602) 638-7843.

noon, then leaves for Tusayan at 3, arriving around 7:30. Fare is $50 each way; call 638-2820 or contact any transportation desk.

Car rentals are available from **Budget** (638-9360) and **Dollar Rent-A-Car** (638-2625), operating out of Grand Canyon Airport.

Taxis can be summoned by calling 638-2822 or 638-2475.

OTHER SERVICES

Babbitt's General Store, a bank, post office branch, service station and quickie film processing are located in Mather Center, across from the main visitor center. Laundry, ice machines and coin showers are between Mather Center and Mather Campground. Car repairs are available in Grand Canyon Village and there's a beauty parlor in the Bright Angel Lodge.

Because of the long haul, prices for groceries and other staples are somewhat higher than in towns outside the park.

WHERE TO DINE IN THE PARK

Arizona Steakhouse ● ∆∆∆ $$ ∅

Grand Canyon Village; (602) 638-2401. American; dinners $6 to $16; full bar. Daily 5 p.m. to 10 p.m.; reservations advised. Major credit cards. In the historic Bright Angel Lodge; Western-style interior. Also a coffee shop, open 6:30 a.m. to 10 p.m.

El Tovar Dining Room ● ∆∆∆∆∆ $$$ ∅

Grand Canyon Village; (602) 638-2401. American-Continental; dinners $15 to $25; full bar. Service from 6:30 to 11 a.m., 11:30 to 2 and 5 to 10 p.m.; reservations strongly advised. Major credit cards. Situated on the rim of the Grand Canyon in the elegant El Tovar Hotel, this is one of Arizona's finest restaurants. An award-winning chef, innovative menu and grand setting combine for an outstanding dining experience.

Grand Canyon Village also offers informal dining and cafeterias at the Maswik Lodge, Yavapai Lodge (open 6:30 a.m. to 10 p.m.) and in Babbitt's General Store (serving from 8 a.m. to 7 p.m.). There's cafeteria-style dining at **Desert View**, open 9 to 5.

IN TUSAYAN

Coronado Dining Room ● ∆∆ $$ ∅

Best Western Grand Canyon Squire Inn; (602) 638-2681. American/Southwestern; dinners $8 to $16; full bar. Daily 5 to 10 p.m. Major credit cards. Attractive restaurant with adjoining cocktail lounge. Also, the Squire Coffee Shop, open 6:30 a.m. to 5 p.m.

Moqui Lodge Restaurant ● ∆∆ $$ ∅

Moqui Lodge; (602) 638-2401. Mexican and American; dinners $8 to $16; full bar. Daily 6:30 a.m. to 10 p.m. Rustic-modern dining room with adjacent cocktail lounge. Also an outside dining area, open 5 p.m. to 8 p.m. in summer.

Feather Restaurant ● ∆∆ $$ ∅

Quality Inn Red Feather; (602) 638-2673. American; dinners $5 to $15; full bar. Daily 6 a.m. to 10 p.m., 7 to 9 in the off-season. Serving American steaks, chops, chicken and such.

The Steak House ● ∆∆ $$ ∅

South end of Tusayan; (602) 638-2780. Western American; dinners $6 to $17; full bar service. Lunch 11:30 to 2, dinner 5 to 10. MC/VISA, AMEX. A Western-style place with red-checkered tablecloths, serving barbecue-style steaks and chicken.

WHERE TO SLEEP IN THE PARK

Bright Angel Lodge and Cabins • ∆∆∆ $$ or $$$$

P.O. Box 699, Grand Canyon, AZ 86023; (602) 638-2401. Singles or doubles in lodge or rustic cabins $40 to $51, rim cabins $77 to $92. The Bright Angel is an historic log and stone structure dating back to the turn of the century, located on the rim. Gift shops, cocktail lounge, transportation desk and dining room (listed above).

El Tovar Hotel • ∆∆∆∆ $$$$ to $$$$$

P.O. Box 699, Grand Canyon, AZ 86023; (602) 638-2401. Singles or doubles $90 to $122, suites $142 to $222. Major credit cards. The premier national park lodge; a national historic landmark, with a dining room (listed above), cocktail lounge, patio, gift shops and other amenities. Located on the rim; some rooms with view.

Grand Canyon Youth Hostel • ∆ $

P.O. Box 270, Grand Canyon, AZ 86023; (602) 638-9018. Dormitory sleeping space $10 per night. No credit cards. Located in Grand Canyon Village at 76 Tonto Street, the hostel books up well in advance, so make reservations early.

Kachina and Thunderbird Lodges • ∆∆∆ $$$$

P.O. Box 699, Grand Canyon, AZ 86023; (602) 638-2401. Singles or doubles $81, canyon-side $87. Major credit cards. These twin contemporary lodges just off the rim offer modern accommodations; some with canyon views.

Maswik Lodge • ∆∆ $$

P.O. Box 699, Grand Canyon, AZ 86023; (602) 638-2401. Singles or doubles $40 to $80. Major credit cards. Motel-type units and some rustic cabins in Grand Canyon Village, a short distance from the rim. Cafeteria, cocktail lounge and transportation desk.

Yavapai Lodges • ∆∆ $$$

P.O. Box 699, Grand Canyon, AZ 86023; (602) 638-2401. Singles and doubles $63 to $70. Major credit cards. Yavapai East and West are motel-type units in Mather Center, near the visitor center, a short walk from the rim. Cafeteria, transportation desk and cocktail lounge.

IN TUSAYAN

Best Western Grand Canyon Squire • ∆∆ $$$$ ⊘

P.O. Box 130, Grand Canyon, AZ 86203; (602) 638-2681. Singles and doubles $55 to $85, less in the off-season. Major credit cards. Nine miles from park entrance. Color TV, room phones, heated pool, sauna, tennis courts, dining room (listed above).

Moqui Lodge • ∆∆∆ $$$

P.O. Box 699, Grand Canyon, AZ 86023; (602) 638-2401. Singles and doubles $62; lower off-season rates; closed January-February. Major credit cards. A Fred Harvey lodge in the north end of Tusayan, just outside the park gate. Dining room, cocktail lounge, tennis and horseback rides (see "Activities" above).

Quality Inn Red Feather • ∆∆ $$$ ⊘

P.O. Box 520, Grand Canyon, AZ 86023; (602) 638-2673 or (800) 228-5151. Singles and doubles $68 to $78; lower off-season rates. Major credit cards. TV movies, heated pool, restaurant (listed above).

Seven Mile Lodge and Gift Shop • △△ $$
P.O. Box 56, Grand Canyon, AZ 86023; (602) 638-2291. Doubles $45, singles $38. MC/VISA, AMEX. New motel in Tusayan; color TV, Indian arts and crafts shop.

WHERE TO CAMP IN THE PARK

Mather Campground • *Near Mather Center. Reservations through Tick-etron, Dept. R, 401 Hackensack Ave., Hackensack, NJ 07601; (213) 410-1720, (303) 825-8447 or (602) 340-9033. RV and tent sites, no hookups, $10.* Flush potties, water, RV dump station; coin-operated showers and laundry nearby. Mather is heavily booked in summer, so make reservations as early as possible. It's located in a pleasantly wooded grove with barbecues and picnic tables. Open all year.

Desert View Campground • *Near Desert View Lookout. RV and tent sites, no hookups, $8. Flush potties, water. No advance reservations.* This campground, 26 miles from Grand Canyon Village in the park's eastern end, is open May through October.

Trailer Village • *P.O. Box 699, Grand Canyon, AZ 86023; (602) 638-2401. RV sites, full hookups, $13.50. Reservations accepted; major credit cards.* Flush potties and water; showers nearby. Operated by Fred Harvey Company; located in a woodsy setting in Mather Center beyond Babbitt's General Store. Open all year.

CAMPING OUTSIDE THE PARK

Flintstone Bedrock City • *In Valle, 30 miles south of the park on U.S. 180. Mailing address: Star Route, Williams, AZ 86046; 635-2600. Tent and RV sites, some pull-throughs, full hookups, $10. Reservations accepted; MC/VISA.* Flush potties, showers, restaurant, groceries, Propane and dump station. It has a Flintstone-themed "Prehistoric Playground," along with a movie theater, train ride and gift shop. Open April 1 through October 15.

Grand Canyon Camper Village • *Tusayan, Grand Canyon, AZ 86023; (602) 638-2887. Full hookups $16.80, water and electric $13.65, tent sites $11.55. No credit cards.* Flush potties, coin-operated showers, barbecues and picnic tables. Early reservations are advised, particularly in summer. Groceries, restaurants and other Tusayan facilities are nearby. Open all year.

Ten X Campground • *c/o Kaibab National Forest, Tusayan Ranger District, P.O. Box 3088, Tusayan, AZ 86023; (602) 638-2443. RV and tent sites, no hookups, $7. No reservations.* Water, pit toilets, barbecues and picnic tables. National forest campground located 10.5 miles south of the park entrance on U.S. 180, then half a mile east on Forestry Road 7302C. Open May 1 to October 30.

Chapter 3

GRAND CANYON NEIGHBORS

*Ours...will undoubtedly be the last party to visit this
profitless locality It seems intended by nature that the
Colorado River, along the greater portions of its lonely and
majestic way, shall be forever unvisited and undisturbed.*
                              —Army Lt. Joseph C. Ives in 1858

 GRAND CANYON National Park is certainly the focal point of
northwestern Arizona, but it has some interesting neighbors as
well. To the north is the isolated Arizona Strip, plus great
swatches of ponderosa pines in Kaibab National forest, and the
aquatic playground of Glen Canyon National Recreation Area. To the south,
Hualapai and Havasupai Indians have gotten into the tourist business with
their holdings near the South Rim.

NORTH OF THE NORTH RIM: ARIZONA STRIP

Approaching Arizona from its northwest corner, you'll pass through the
vast and remote Arizona Strip. Isolated from the rest of the state by the
Grand Canyon, this high plateau covering 12,000 square miles is home to
only a handful of people. Many are descendants of early Mormon pioneers
who came down from Utah in the mid-1800s.

If you drive eastward from Las Vegas on Interstate 15, you'll nip a tip of
Arizona, swing north into Utah, then re-enter the Grand Canyon State.
Within this tip, I-15 serpentines through beautiful, rock-ribbed Virgin River
Canyon. It's a mini-Grand Canyon with near vertical walls and terraced but-
tes—a preview of sculpted formations that lay ahead. **Virgin River
Canyon Recreation Area,** operated by the Bureau of Land Management,
offers a rest stop, campground (see listing below), a nature trail, and hiking
trails into the canyon.

Geologically, the Arizona Strip is part of the Colorado Plateau, the great
uplift where time and nature have shaped canyons, buttes and redwall es-

carpments. The Vermilion Cliffs, extending for more than 20 miles to the east near Marble Canyon, is a popular landmark for travelers. They were named for their habit of taking on dazzling red hues at sunset.

Beyond Virgin River Canyon, you encounter prairie country, where cattle roam free and ranch houses sit in the shade of cottonwoods. Settlements are few and tiny and we suspect the ranchers like them that way.

Colorado City

Elevation: Approx. 4,900 feet   **Population: 3,000**

Approaching the strip from Utah on State Highway 59 (Route 389 in Arizona), you pass through the twin border towns of Hilldale, Utah, and Colorado City, Arizona. Both are clean-scrubbed, no-nonsense Mormon settlements. They're rather stern-looking places, brightened somewhat by ruddy-cheeked school girls wearing pretty homemade dresses.

The communities were settled by fundamentalist Mormons who left Utah to escape polygamy prosecution. Gossips say that plural marriage is still practiced here, although federal officers haven't raided Colorado City for several years.

Incidentally, don't expect to find a Bud Light in the busy, well-stocked general store. This is a dry town!

Pipe Spring National Monument • *HC-65, Box 5, Fredonia, AZ 86022 (602) 643-7105. Visitor center/museum open daily from 8 to 4:30; ranch buildings open until 5. Admission $1.* This small national monument, about 17 miles southeast of Colorado City, preserves the great fortified ranch headquarters of an early Mormon cattle spread. Nicknamed Winsor Castle after its English ranch superintendent Anson Perry Winsor, it was created for the Mormon Church's southern Utah "tithing herd." These were cattle tithed to the church; one cow in ten went to the collection plate.

Since Indian raids had killed earlier settlers here, the ranch complex was built as a fort, with two stone buildings linked by thick walls. A spring—from which the monument takes its name—created a virtual oasis of cottonwoods, fruit trees and cattle ponds in this dry country. The fort became a popular way station for travelers from the 1870s until after the turn of the century. Later sold by the church, it was given by its new owners to the National Park Service as a "memorial to Western pioneer life." It became a national monument in 1923.

The sturdy main structure is little changed from its pioneer days. A self-guided tour takes visitors through rooms furnish in early Americana, with oval rugs, rocking chairs and softly ticking grandfather clocks. In the kitchen, chairs are reversed and plates are up-side down, awaiting the supper prayer. Gun ports are cut through the three-foot walls, so this was indeed a fort. It was never attacked, however. Outbuildings contain a blacksmith and harness shops and other ranching essentials.

Authentic farm chickens wander about the yard, along with some the fattest geese we'd ever seen. Ducks occupy a tree-shaded, spring-fed animal pond out front. A short loop trail leads up sandstone cliffs behind the house, providing an impressive view of the lonely, wind-ruffled Arizona Strip.

During summer months, park rangers and docents recapture the spirit of Western pioneers with living history activities such as spinning and weaving, gardening and baking. Adjacent to the visitor center is a gift shop, snack bar and bookstore operated by the Zion Natural History Association.

Beyond Pipe Spring, State Highway 389 passes through the Kaibab Indian Reservation, touches the little settlement of Fredonia, then swings southward into Kaibab National Forest. As the plateau slopes upward toward the Grand Canyon's north rim, prairie grasses give way to the pinon and ponderosa pines. Campgrounds, hiking trails and wilderness areas attract outdoor enthusiasts. A national forest campground, lodge and restaurant are at Jacob Lake; see the "North Rim" section of the previous chapter.

If you pick up U.S. 89A at Jacob Lake and continue eastward across the Strip, you'll drop back into prairie country. Moving across a landscape backdropped by the Vermilion Cliffs, you encounter tiny blips on the map that are essentially motel-restaurant-service station complexes. Basic services are available at House Rock, Cliff Dweller's Lodge and Vermilion Cliffs.

THINGS TO KNOW BEFORE YOU GO

Best time to go ● Summer is peak season for the Arizona Strip and Glen Canyon to the north, and the Indian country to the south. Spring and fall are our favorite times to prowl these areas. Glen Canyon National Recreation Area gets *very* crowded in summer, and it's usually wall-to-wall boaters over the Fourth of July, so make reservations well in advance.

Climate ● Warm, sunny summers and cold winters. July average—high 80 to 90; low 55 to 60. January average—high 45 to 55; low 15 to 35. Snowfall can be heavy at times in the north rim section of Kaibab National Forest. Page and Lake Powell are hotter than other North Rim areas, with July highs ranging from 90 to 105.

Useful contacts—north of the North Rim

> North Kaibab Ranger District, Kaibab National Forest, P.O. Box 248, Fredonia, AZ 86022; (602) 643-7395.

> Visitor Information Center, Kaibab National Forest, Jacob Lake, c/o Fredonia, AZ 86022; (602) 643-7298.

> Page-Lake Powell Visitor & Convention Bureau, Inn at Lake Powell, 716 Rim View Dr. (P.O. Box 727), Page, AZ 86040; (602) 645-2741.

> Glen Canyon National Recreation Area, P.O. Box 1507, Page, AZ 86040; (602) 645-2511.

South of the South Rim

> Tusayan Ranger District, Kaibab National Forest, P.O. Box 3088, Tusayan, AZ 86023; (602) 638-2443.

> Havasupai Tourist Enterprises, Supai, AZ 86435; (602) 448-2121.

> Hualapai Tribal Council, P.O. Box 168, Peach Springs, AZ 85634; (602) 769-2216.

Radio stations—North Rim area

> KCKK-FM, 100.1, Page—Popular variety
> KPGE-AM, 1340, Page—Country & Western.
> KXAZ-FM, 93.5, Page—Variety; new age, light jazz

South Rim area

> See listings for Flagstaff area in Chapter 5.

Marble Canyon

This dramatic, steep-walled chasm is the upstream beginning of the Grand Canyon. It was named by river-runner Powell, who mistook its glossy hard granite walls for marble. You'll get an impressive view of this ravine as you cross the lofty, steel-arch Navajo Bridge. It's the last highway crossing of the Colorado River until Hoover Dam, more than 200 miles southwest.

The community of Marble Canyon offers a lodge, restaurant, landing strip, small store and service station. At Marble Canyon lodge (see below), you can book river trips and Indian country tours.

Lees Ferry

Just north of Marble Canyon, Lees Ferry was the site of the last crossing on the Colorado River before it plunged into its 227-mile ravine. Sitting below redrock cliffs, it's now a thumb of Glen Canyon National Recreation Area and the favored put-in spot for river-runners. A ranger station sits on a hill just above the river, open 8 a.m. to 5 p.m.; it's sometimes closed in the off-season.

The river flows crisp, cold and turquoise-clear, issuing from the innards of Glen Canyon Dam just upstream. A sandy, rock-strewn beach lures fisher-persons and sun-bathers, but few swimmers. Nearby are several large parking areas for river-runners, and the ruins of the original ferry crossing.

Walk across a dirt parking lot just to the left of the launch ramp and you can poke among stone buildings and rusting ranch equipment of Lee's fortress.

Mormon John D. Lee was asked by his church to build a ferry at this strategic point—one of the few areas along the canyon with walls low enough to permit river access. He had another reason for coming here: he was involved in the notorious 1857 Mountain Meadows Massacre. Supposedly, some Mormons joined with Paiute Indians to attack a wagon train of hostile non-Mormons. After the brutal attack, in which all the intruders were slain, Lee was sent to built the ferry to keep him hidden. He completed the job, but federal authorities caught up with him in 1877 and hauled him away to face a firing squad.

Lonely Dell Ranch, named by one of Lees wives, is a short distance north and west of the launch ramp. Look for a sign pointing up a dirt road near the Paria River crossing. The ranch, now designated as an historic district, consists of an old stone, metal-roofed ranch house, a couple of squared log outbuildings and a mixed fruit orchard. Walk past the ranch complex and you'll encounter a pioneer cemetery and an old pump site on the Paria River.

If you're a serious hiker, you can trek the 35-mile **Paria Canyon Wilderness trail**, which starts near Kanab, Utah, and emerges at Lees Ferry. In areas, the gorge towers 2,000 feet over your head. Permits are required. The several-day hike is only allowed downstream (from Kanab) so updated weather information can be imparted, because of the danger of flash floods. For information, contact: **Kanab Area Office, Bureau of Land Management**, 320 N. 100 East (P.O. Box 459), Kanab, UT 84741; (801) 644-2672.

WHERE TO DINE ON THE ARIZONA STRIP

Cliff Dwellers Restaurant ● ΔΔ $$

Highway 89A, eight miles west of Marble Canyon; (602) 355-2228. American; dinners $7 to $14; wine and beer. Open 6 a.m. to 2 p.m. and 5 to 9 p.m. MC/VISA. Generous portions of rural American fare are served in a knotty pine dining room that's decorated with old license plates and other knickknacks. Part of Cliff Dweller's Lodge.

Marble Canyon Lodge Restaurant ● ΔΔ $$

Marble Canyon; (602) 355-2225. American; dinners $7 to $15; full bar. Open 6:30 a.m. to 9 p.m. MC/VISA. Part of the Marble Canyon Lodge, the restaurant serves Western-style American fare and some vegetarian dishes.

Vermilion Cliffs Bar and Grille ● Δ $$

Highway 89A, three miles north of Marble Canyon; (602) 355-2231. American; dinners $7 to $14; full bar. Open 6:30 a.m. to 10 p.m. MC/VISA. This rustic, Western-style dining room is adjacent to Lees Ferry Lodge. Features include home-baked pies, homemade soups; the chef will cook your trout.

WHERE TO SLEEP

Blue Sage Motel & RV Park ● Δ $$

330 S. Main St., Fredonia, AZ 86022; (602) 643-7125. Doubles $32.25, singles $21.50; MC/VISA. In downtown Fredonia; TV in rooms.

Cliff Dweller's Lodge ● Δ $$

Highway 89A, eight miles west of Marble Canyon, AZ 86036; (602) 355-2228. Singles $30, doubles $35; MC/VISA. A contemporary motel has replaced historic Cliff Dwellers Lodge, which was built under the overhang of a huge balanced rock. Its ruins can still be seen, a few hundred feet east of the present lodge.

Lees Ferry Lodge ● Δ $$

HC67-Box 1, Marble Canyon, AZ 86036; (602) 355-2231. Doubles $55, singles $27. MC/VISA. A simple but clean motel located in Vermilion Cliffs, on U.S. 89A, three miles southwest of Marble Canyon. Restaurant (listed above).

Marble Canyon Lodge ● ΔΔ $$

Highway 89A at Navajo Bridge, Marble Canyon, AZ 86036; (602) 355-2225. Doubles $45 to $50, singles $30 to $35, kitchenettes $50, suites $80 to $95. MC/VISA. Nicely restored 1920s resort. Dining room (listed above), trading post and gift shop, landing field nearby.

WHERE TO CAMP

Mad Rabbit Campground ● *State Highway 389, c/o Fredonia, AZ 86022; (602) 643-5545. Tent and RV sites, $10 with hookups, $5 without. No credit cards.* On the Kaibab Indian Reservation, just north of Highway 389. Water, flush potties, showers; convenience market and laundromat nearby. Hiking trails and petroglyphs.

Lees Ferry Campground ● *c/o Glen Canyon National Recreation Area, P.O. Box 1507, Page, AZ 86040; (602) 645-2511. Tent and RV sites, no hookups, $6. No credit cards or reservations.* Located near the Lees Ferry boat launch, the campground has water, flush potties and wind and shade shelters. It's nicely situated among redrock formations.

Virgin River Canyon Recreation Area ● *17 miles west of St. George, Utah. Tent and RV sites, no hookups, $4. No credit cards or reservations.* It comes in two sections—one at riverside and another on a bluff overlooking the river canyon. This Bureau of Land Management campground has flush potties, barbecues and picnic tables. Many sites offer canyon views. Some are pull-throughs.

Page & Lake Powell

Elevation: 4,380 feet   **Population: 6,500**

From Lees Ferry, Highway 89A dips southward, skimming the edge of the Echo Cliffs, then it dissolves into route 89. Turning northward, you climb through a dramatic cleft in those cliffs and head across a desert tableland. Your destination is Glen Canyon Dam and Lake Powell, a pair of statistical rivals to Hoover Dam and Lake Mead.

You can catch an impressive glimpse of the dam and the canyon below it by following a bumpy road down to an overlook, off highway 89 near the Page golf and country club. Park and walk to the vista point, perched dizzily on rippled slickrock, 700 feet above the chasm. Upstream, you see the great concrete plug of Glen Canyon Dam, with the steel-arch Glen Canyon Bridge before it. When the span was completed in 1959, it was the highest bridge in America.

Glen Canyon did not surrender easily to concrete and steel. Conservationists issued predictable cries of protest when the dam was proposed in the 1940s. Once in place, it would drown a beautiful upstream chasm and change forever the flow of the Colorado River through the downstream Grand Canyon.

The concrete arch dam was completed in 1964 to the trumpet call of engineering statistics: 710 feet high, 300 feet thick at the base, containing eight zillion pounds of concrete, enough wiring to link every ghetto-blaster in west Los Angeles, etc., etc. Lake Powell (which finally filled in 1980, then overflowed in 1983 and brought havoc downstream) is America's second largest reservoir, after Lake Mead. With hundreds of finger-like side canyons, it has three times as much shoreline—1,960 miles. And are you now prepared for the ultimate statistic? The lake can hold nine trillion gallons of water.

River-runners, always vocal about these projects, regard the dam with mixed emotions. Water storage has given them a longer, more predictable whitewater season in the Grand Canyon. On the other hand, surge releases dictated by hydroelectric demands are eroding the canyon's beaches. Incidentally, since water is released deep within the face of the dam, it comes out icy cold and clear—too cold for swimming.

The reservoir set the stage for a huge national recreation area, providing easy boating access to the hidden enclaves and serpentine chasms of Glen Canyon. It extends 186 miles upstream like a gnarled, multi-fingered hand. Before exploring it, we'll visit a dam-built town.

Page came into being in 1956 as a construction camp for the dam site. Like many other such towns, it didn't go away after the job was finished. Sitting high on a red dirt shelf above Lake Powell, it thrives on tourist business lured by Glen Canyon National Recreation Area.

Although desert vegetation is rather sparse around here, the town itself is semi-attractive. Planners cleverly bunched the primary and high schools together, then ringed them with the residential area. Downtown is a small collection of stores and shopping centers—more of a business suburb than a city.

Page/Lake Powell Visitor and Convention Bureau is located in the lobby of the Inn at Lake Powell at 716 Rim View Drive; hours are 9 a.m. to 5 p.m. weekdays.

East of Page on Highway 98, the coal-fed **Navajo Generating Plant**— accused of polluting the skies above the Grand Canyon—stands like the superstructure of a monster ship. Consuming 24,000 tons of coal a day brought by rail from nearby mines, it produces enough electricity for a city of three million. Its smokestacks are higher than Glen Canyon Dam, thrusting 775 feet skyward.

PAGE ATTRACTIONS

Powell Memorial Museum ● *P.O. Box 547 (corner of N. Lake Powell Boulevard and Navajo Drive), Page, AZ 86040; (602) 645-9496. Daily 8 a.m. to 7 p.m. May-September and weekdays 9 to 5 October and November, closed December through February.* An oversized but accurate replica of the longboat used by John Wesley Powell on the Colorado River is parked out front of this small museum. It starred in Disney's *Ten Who Dared.*

Within the museum, you can see sketches, photos and other memorabilia of Powell's epic river voyages in 1869 and 1871, along with the usual collection of Indian and pioneer artifacts. Other exhibits focus on the geology of the canyons cut by the Colorado. Films on Lake Powell, dam construction and such are shown on request. The museum also serves as a booking agency for river and lake trips and scenic flights offered by local operators.

Big Lake Trading Post, Museum and Gallery ● *1501 N Highway 98 (two miles east), Page, AZ 86040; (602) 645-2404. Store open daily 6 a.m. to 1 a.m.; donations accepted for museum.* Chris Robinson of ABC-TV's *General Hospital,* a collector of Indian artifacts, opened this combination museum, gas station and general store just east of Page. The museum/Indian crafts shop occupies a balcony above the store. Here, you can view ancient Indian pots and buy modern ones. The museum collection isn't large and there's no attempt at interpretation, but it does contain some rather nice artifacts.

Glen Canyon National Recreation Area

We've sampled a piece of the recreation area at Lees Ferry downstream. However, the heart of it encompasses Glen Canyon Dam, Lake Powell and one million acres of fantastically eroded desert sandstone. Most of the recreation area is in Utah, although the dam and largest marina complex— Wahweap—sit near the border on the Arizona side.

When U.S. Army Lt. Joseph C. Ives explored this sandstone wonderland in 1858, he concluded that it was beyond the reach of development. Major Powell, battling Glen Canyon rapids in his longboats, wondered if such a wild river could ever be useful.

More than a century and one million barrels of concrete later, Glen Canyon Dam is the capstone of the upper Colorado River flood control, water storage and hydroelectric project. Hundreds of thousands of visitors now come to play in this "profitless locality." They water-ski across Lake Powell, pull fat bass from its depths, hike its surrounding deserts and wonder what the canyon must have been like before it was flooded.

A true reflection of Lake Powell's grandeur, in Cascade Canyon.

It must have been beautiful. What's left of it certainly is—a wonderland of buttes, narrow-walled side canyons, terraced cliffs and rippled alluvial fans.

Carl Hayden Visitor Center ● *At Glen Canyon Dam; open daily 8 to 5.* This attractive curved structure at cliff's edge above the reservoir is a good place to begin your exploration. Inside, nicely-done graphics, displays and videos tell you about the dam, the reservoir and their creation. You learn that Glen Canyon Dam is the world's fourth highest, at 710 feet, and that it cost $145 million. A read-out reminds you that it was a good investment as it totes up the value of electricity sold to cities as far away as Nebraska and Wyoming. When we were there, it clicked off $834,295,906.

From the visitor center, you can take a free self-guided tour of the dam. It takes you via elevator deep into its innards, past ranks of humming turbines and along the crest of the dam, where you can stare carefully over the 710-foot drop to the canyon.

Wahweap Marina ● *P.O. Box 1597 (six miles northwest of town), Page, AZ 86040. For concessionaire information and reservations, call (602) 645-2433 or (800) 528-6154.* Wahweap—a Ute Indian word for "bitter water"— is the major activity center for Lake Powell. A concessionaire offers a marina, houseboat and speedboat rentals, boat tours, lodging, gift shop, restaurant, service station and a trailer park (see dining, lodging and camping listings below). The national park service provides a ranger station, campground, boat launch, picnic shelters, rest rooms, a fish-cleaning station and an amphitheater for ranger programs.

Lodging, camping, boat tours, rentals and launchings also are available along the Utah shoreline of Lake Powell at Hall's Crossing, Bullfrog Marina and Hite. Some marinas and campgrounds can be reached only by boat.

Lake Powell is probably America's best recreational boating reservoir, with hundreds of narrow side-canyons to explore and thousands of sandstone shapes to admire. You can skim over the surface on water skis, splash off summer's heat in swimming bays and even don Scuba gear and explore underwater formations and drowned Indian ruins. Houseboating is popular; even on busy summer days, you can find a secret cove to lay in for the night. Fishing is excellent, and you're supposed to get a license for each state. (There's no dotted line to mark the boundary.)

Lake Powell Cruise ● *Departing from Wahweap and other marinas. Call (602) 278-8888 or (800) 528-6154.* If you aren't inclined to rent a boat, you can get a good sampler of the area on this cruise. Half-day and full-day trips leave daily from Wahweap and less frequently from other marinas. During winter, cruises may be canceled unless an adequate number of people show up, so it's best to check in advance.

These water tours take you several miles up the lake, past redrock buttes, pinnacles and other shapes that might have been sculpted in a Disney studio for *Fantasia.* The boatman eases his craft into serpentine canyons, slipping between vertical walls so close that passengers can reach out and touch them. You discover that one of the most awesome things about Lake Powell is the perfect reflections of rock formations cast in the surface, creating geological ink blot tests.

The highlight of the trip is a stop at **Rainbow Bridge National Monument,** the world's largest natural arch. It could be reached only by a 14-mile hike until Glen Canyon Dam backed water within a few hundred feet of it. When the reservoir is full, a finger of the lake actually extends under the structure. Geologists were concerned that the rising water might undermine the base of this great 275-foot arch, but it apparently isn't at risk.

The salmon-pink arch—aptly described by Indians as a "petrified rainbow"—spans Bridge Creek, which trickles into Glen Canyon. During the cruise stop, you can hike up to this natural wonder and even scramble down into the creek bed and pass under it. Appearing fragile from afar, it becomes a massive structure as you approach—42 feet thick and high enough to arch over the nation's capitol.

ACTIVITIES

Speedboat, fishing boat and houseboat rentals and boat tours ● *Lake Powell Resorts and Marinas, P.O. Box 1597, Page, AZ 86040; call (602) 645-2433 or (800) 528-6154.* Boat rentals—particularly houseboats—should be booked early during the summer season.

Scenic flights ● *Lake Powell Air, P.O. Box 1385, Page, AZ 86040; (602) 645-2494.* The firm also offers flights over the Grand Canyon and Monument Valley.

Land tours ● *Lake Powell Overland Adventures, P.O. Box 1144, Page, AZ 86040; (602) 645-5501.* Guided tours with geology and Indian lectures in the Lake Powell area, Grand Canyon, Paria River and Monument Valley.

Para-sailing ● *Lake Powell Para-sailing, c/o Wahweap Marina Store, Page, AZ 86040; (602) 645-2433, ext. 6386.* Trips into the sky also can be booked through the John Wesley Powell Museum and Chamber of Commerce.

ANNUAL EVENTS
Page and Lake Powell
Striper Derby, January-February; **Creative Driftwood Contest,** first Saturday of March; **Lake Powell Hot Air Balloon Regatta,** end of March to first of April; **Page Rodeo,** third weekend of May; **Bass Tournament,** June through August; **Pioneer Days Parade,** second Saturday of July; **Striper Derby,** November-December.

WHERE TO DINE
Bella Napoli ● ΔΔ $$
810 N. Navajo, Page; (602) 645-2706. Italian; dinners $7 to $15; wine and beer. Reservations for six or more. MC/VISA. Cozy little bistro featuring five styles of spaghetti, plus manicotti, seafood cannelloni and pizza; patio dining.

Dynasty Restaurant ● ΔΔΔ $$
704 Rim View Dr. (Inn at Lake Powell), Page; (602) 645-8113. Chinese-American; dinners $5 to $15; full bar service. Daily 6 a.m. to 11 p.m.; reservations accepted. Major credit cards. Large, attractively decorated restaurant with an extensive Chinese menu, plus American steaks, chops and seafood. Nice lake views from the dining room and from an outside patio deck.

Glen Canyon Steakhouse ● ΔΔ $$
201 N. Lake Powell Blvd. (Main Street), Page; (602) 645-3363. American; dinners $7 to $15; full bar service. 5:30 a.m. to 10 p.m.; reservations accepted. MC/VISA. Steaks, seafood and buffets. Adjacent Western-style Cove Lounge features live rock music, big-screen TV, dart tournaments and nibblies.

Rainbow Room of Wahweap Lodge ● ΔΔΔ $$
Wahweap Marina; (602) 645-2433. American; dinners $8 to $16; full bar service. Daily 7 a.m. to 2 p.m. and 6 to 9 p.m.; reservations accepted. Major credit cards. This large, handsome circular dining room offers impressive views of Lake Powell. Menu specialties include steaks, chops and several seafood dishes.

WHERE TO SLEEP
Lake Powell Motel ● ΔΔ $$$
Highway 89 at Lakeshore Drive (P.O. Box 1597), Page, AZ 86040; (602) 645-2433 or (800) 528-6154. Doubles $53, singles $47.75. Major credit cards. TV, room phones; on a bluff overlooking Wahweap Marina; operated by Lake Powell Resorts & Marinas.

Inn at Lake Powell ● ΔΔ $$$ ∅
716 Rim View Dr. (formerly Ramada Inn), Page, AZ 86040; (602) 645-2466 or (800) 826-2718. Doubles $62 to $75, singles $56 to $68, suites $105; lower off-season rates. MC/VISA, AMEX, DC. TV, room phones; pool, spa, lounge, conference room. Some rooms with view of Glen Canyon Dam and Lake Powell. Chamber of Commerce in lobby. Dynasty Restaurant (listed above).

Page-Lake Powell Holiday Inn ● ΔΔ $$$ ∅
287 N. Lake Powell Blvd. (downtown), Page, AZ 86040; (602) 645-8851 or (800) HOLIDAY. Doubles $49 to $89, singles $39 to $79; lower off-season rates. Major credit cards. TV movies, complimentary coffee, balconies; some rooms with lake views; pool, outdoor barbecue, lounge with large-screen TV, gift shop. **Family Tree Restaurant** serves from 6 a.m. to 10 p.m.; American, dinners $7 to $15, non-smoking areas, lake-view dining, full bar service.

Havasu Falls with its baby Niagara travertine pools.

Rainbow Bridge—the world's largest natural arch.

Wahweap Lodge ● △△△ $$$$

Wahweap Marina (P.O. Box 1597), Page, AZ 86040; (602) 645-2433 or (800) 528-6154. Doubles $79.50 to $88, singles $71 to $79.50, suites $150.50; lower off-season rates. Major credit cards. Lakeside resort with gift shop, marina, swimming pool, Rainbow Restaurant (listed above). Rooms have TV, phones, oversized beds, some lake views. Operated by Lake Powell Resorts & Marinas.

WHERE TO CAMP

Wahweap RV Park ● *100 Lakeshore Dr. (at Wahweap Marina), Page, AZ 86040; (602) 645-2313 or (800) 528-6154. RV and tent sites, full hookups $15. Reservations accepted; MC/VISA, AMEX, DISC.* Pull-throughs, flush potties, showers, coin laundry, groceries and supplies, snack bar, dump station; full marina facilities and Wahweap Lodge and restaurant adjacent.

Wahweap Campground ● *Lakeshore Drive (above Wahweap Marina, near national park ranger's office), P.O. Box 1507, Page, AZ 86040; (602) 645-2471. RV and tent sites, no hookups $6. No credit cards or reservations.* Shaded sites above Wahweap Marina; flush potties, tables and barbecues, water.

SOUTH OF THE SOUTH RIM: HUALAPAI AND HAVASUPAI

The broad Coconino Plateau sweeps southwesterly from the Grand Canyon. It's a remote, untamed land of Joshua trees, bunchgrass and pine forests.

Much of the Colorado River's southern shore is bordered by the million-acre Hualapai Indian Reservation. The Havasupai Reservation, with its hidden canyon village of Supai, occupies a 188,077-acre wedge just south of the park boundary. Both tribes have gotten into the tourist business.

State Highway 18, angling northeast from Highway 66 above Seligman, crosses the Hualapai reservation, then enters the Havasupai reserve and terminates at Hualapai Hilltop. This is the trailhead for hikes and mule or horseback rides down into Havasu Canyon.

Before turning onto Highway 18, you might stop and wander through a limestone cave:

Grand Canyon Caverns • *P.O. Box 180, Peach Springs, AZ 86434; (602) 422-3223 or 422-3224. Cave tour $5.75 for adults, $3.75 for kids 4 to 12. Tours 8 to 6 daily in summer and 10 to 5 the rest of the year. Restaurant serves breakfast, lunch and dinner; see listing below. Motel rooms are $18 to $45 for doubles and $16 to $35 for singles. RV parking and camping, with no hookups, is $5 per night.* This limestone cavern is on Route 66, 21 miles west of Seligman. Privately owned, the complex includes a motel, restaurant, gift shop and RV park, in addition to the cave tour.

An elevator takes you the equivalent of 21 stories into the earth, where you're conducted on a one-mile, 45-minute stroll past interesting stalactites, stalagmites and sundry other cave formations.

Caverns Inn Restaurant is open 7 a.m. to 6 p.m. in summer and 9:30 a.m. to 5 p.m. in the off-season. It features American fare, mostly light meals, in a rustic knotty pine dining room. Western outdoor cookouts are held on Thursdays and Fridays in summer.

Hualapai Country

If you like solitude, you'll enjoy exploring the wilds of the Hualapai Indian Reservation. Occupied by fewer than a thousand people, the million-acre reserve offers vast, lonely sweeps of high desert, ponderosa forests and Grand Canyon views.

Rough roads lead to remote corners of the reservation. You'll need a vehicle with good ground clearance for most of them; a four-wheel drive is best. A 21-mile gravel and dirt road will take you to Diamond Creek, one of the rare spots in the canyon where you can drive right to the river's edge. This was the site of the first Grand Canyon tourist facility, a now-departed hotel built in 1884. Other roads, even rougher, lead to other canyon viewpoints.

Peach Springs, the only town on the reservation and home to the Hualapai Tribal Council, is on Highway 66, about 35 miles west of Seligman. The hamlet consists of a few dead service stations, an abandoned motel, a live market, a small museum that's essentially an Indian crafts center, and the tribal office.

Activities • Fees are $3 for day use, $7 for camping (in the boonies; there are no formal campgrounds) and $8 for fishing. One-day and two-day motorized river trips from Diamond Creek to Pearce Ferry are offered by Hualapai River Runners. Prices are $225 to $327, including all meals; the firm accepts VISA and MasterCard. For information, contact: Hualapai River Trips, P.O. Box 246, Peach Springs, AZ 86434; (602) 769-2210, 769-2219; outside Arizona, call (800) 622-4409.

As you enter the reservation, a sign advises: *Anyone caught without a permit will be charged double! No firearms!!!* The Hualapai are long on remote canyon scenery, if a bit short on public relations.

The Havasupai Hike

Beyond the reach of any highway, the remote village of Supai and the beautiful Havasu Canyon have become popular destinations for Arizona visitors.

An easy eight-mile trail reaches the village from Hualapai Hilltop; it offers no services, but plenty of trailhead parking. Instead of hiking, you can rent horses or mules to carry you and your cargo. The trail begins with several switchbacks, then it follows a gentle downslope into Havasu Canyon.

The *AAA Arizona-New Mexico TourBook* calls the trail precipitous, but it's hardly that. The switchbacks are wide enough for a golf cart (although too bumpy), and the rest of the trail is an easy path where you're liable to see a resident chugging along in an all-terrain vehicle.

The route is pleasant, but not awesome as Grand Canyon trails go. The scenery is impressive, although you never see the main gorge. The trail is a busy thoroughfare of horses and mules, as Havasupai tribal members haul tourists and cargo back and forth. So watch where you step. It doesn't always smell so great, either.

On my hike down, I counted fifty passing horses and mules, some with mongrel dogs yapping at their heels. So this is hardly a wilderness experience. One of the dogs abandoned his outbound pack string and dutifully escorted me all the way to the village. Perhaps I smelled a bit better than the mules.

Supai village home with dramatic redrock backdrop.

Lest you get the wrong impression, this is a fascinating and meaningful experience. Arriving at Supai, you discover a neat and tidy village of small pre-fab cottages, a museum, cafe, post office, grocery and a remarkably modern lodge for such a remote spot. With dusty paths for streets, Supai is probably the only community in America with a five-mile-an-hour speed limit.

Supai Lodge is nicely done of wood and stone; each room has two comfortable double beds and complete baths. Havasupai Tribal Cafe serves light meals (see below) and the Havasupai Museum offers exhibits of tribal crafts, including some for sale.

The village is populated by about 500 people and probably an equal number of horses, mules and free-roaming dogs. Nearly every house has a horse or mule in front. The people still live in the saddle, much as their ancestors did after rounding up Spanish strays a couple of centuries ago.

No highway could possibly reach this village, tucked into a dramatic redwall enclave a few miles above the Colorado River. And one gets the impression that the Havasupai like it that way. They've been living here since prehistoric times. Spanish Padre Francisco Tomas Garces visited in 1776 and found the Indians to be quite content with their lot. They still are, since they're among the few Native Americans occupying their ancestral lands.

The reservation's prime tourist attraction is the beautiful Havasu Canyon area below the village. The hike along Havasu Creek is one of the prettiest in the Grand Canyon. Two waterfalls, Havasu and Mooney, take spectacular plunges over lava ledges. Black, gnarled stone fingers reach out from cliff faces, like creatures from the spooky forest scenes in *Snow White*.

Along the cottonwood-shaded creek, water spills over pretty little travertine terraces, like miniature Niagara Falls. The terraces are created when limestone from the mineral-rich water combines with floating leaves and twigs to form curved spill-overs. Some of the larger ones form wonderful swimming holes.

Havasu Campground starts just below Havasu Falls and extends along the creek for nearly a mile to the crest of Mooney Falls. It has picnic tables, barbecues and pit toilets. Wonderfully refreshing, mineral-rich water issues from a spigot in the side of the canyon. This may be the most appealing campsite in the Southwest.

The trail along Havasu Creek is an easy stroll until you reach the top of Mooney Falls. Here, a sign invites only the brave to venture down the rough lava cliff. It can be done, if you're careful and not afraid of heights. Hacked out by early miners, the trail passes through two holes in the cliff face, then ends with a near-vertical, chain-assisted incline at the end.

We made it with only a little heavy breathing. But it was a bit disconcerting to see a trail sign pointing to a hole in the ground.

From here, the trail leads to the Colorado River, eight miles below Mooney Falls. It's alternately easy and rough as it descends into the main gorge.

Supai Village essentials ● *Contact Havasupai Tourist Enterprise, Supai, AZ 86435; call (602) 448-2121 for camping permits, horseback or mule transit and other information. You also can arrange chopper flights in and out of the canyon by contacting Grand Canyon Helicopters, P.O. Box 455, Grand Canyon, AZ 86023; phone (602) 638-2419 in Arizona and (800) 528-2418 outside.*

For lodge reservations, contact Havasupai Lodge, Supai, AZ 86345; (602) 448-2111. All who enter the canyon must pay a $12 entry fee. Lodge rooms are $50 for a double and $45 for a single; the hostel is $10 per person. Camping is $9, horse or mule transit is $70 from Hualapai Hilltop to Supai and $90 from the hilltop to the campground. Upon arriving at the village, you must register at the Havasu Tourist Enterprise office and pay the entry fee. Those with motel reservations can continue to the lodge, since the entry fee is added to the room rate.

Havasupai Tribal Cafe ● *Open 7:30 to 5.* It serves breakfast fare, hamburgers, sandwiches, stew, chili, homemade desserts and a device called an Indian Taco. It's really a cross between a tostada and a pizza—a conglomeration of red beans, chopped lettuce, onions and cheese over tasty, chewy Indian fry bread. (See Indian Taco box in Chapter 13.)

Chapter 4

THE WESTERN EDGE

*Only two commodities have allowed the vast populating of
the arid Southwest—water and hydroelectric power.*
—Dexter K. Oliver, *Desert Lifestyle Magazine*

 THE STORY OF THE WEST is the story of water. Range wars were fought over water rights. Rich placer mines lay idle for lack of water to separate gold from gravel. Farms shriveled and died when cities diverted their irrigation streams.

"Whiskey is for drinking; water is for fighting," Mark Twain once observed.

Nowhere is the role of water more evident than along Arizona's western edge. Here, the mighty Colorado River forms a squiggly border between Arizona, California and the southern tip of Nevada. Walk a hundred feet from the shoreline, and you're in a thirsty desert. Annual rainfall—as little as three inches—supports creosote bush and a few critters with the good sense to keep out of the noonday sun, and not much else.

THE WAY IT WAS • The Colorado River once ran untamed through this desert. After scouring the Grand Canyon ever deeper, it slowed its flow in this shallow basin, dropping much of its load of silt. Thousands of years ago, Native Americans farmed along the river's rich shoreline.

White settlers tried the same thing, as early as the mid-1800s. As settlements grew, small paddlewheel steamboats chugged upstream from the Gulf of California, serving mining camps and bottomland farms along the sun-baked shoreline. They journeyed as much as 300 miles upstream, to the now-defunct Mormon settlement of Callville, near present-day Hoover Dam.

Without the river, there could have been no settlement. But Rio Colorado was unpredictable. Dropping more than 12,000 feet from its Rocky Moun-

64

tain heights and draining 12 percent of America's land area, it often raged across this lowland, flooding farms and beaching boats. In dry years, it would shrink to a trickle by autumn.

For fifty years, riverside farmers gambled with the Colorado's unpredictable flow. Then in 1901, water was diverted into the Imperial Canal near present-day Yuma to irrigate the dry but rich soils of California's Imperial Valley. But the Colorado was reluctant to become domesticated. A flood breached the Imperial Canal in 1905 and the wild river changed course. For 16 months, it flowed unchecked into the Salton Basin, 235 feet below sea level. By the time the breach was finally closed in 1907, the runaway river had created the 40-mile-long Salton Sea, which still exists.

Men were more determined than ever to control the big Red. In 1909, the Laguna Dam was completed just north of Yuma. It provided desert irrigation and put the river steamers out of business. But it was too far south for effective flood control. To subdue the river, the bureau launched one of

THINGS TO KNOW BEFORE YOU GO

Best time to go • The Colorado River corridor is a fall-winter-spring playground. Numerous reservoirs attract legions of Snowbirds; they hit their peak just after Christmas. Some RV parks may fill with seasonal renters, so reservations are advised.

Climate • Warm winters, with some chilly nights; hot summers. July and August really sizzle; communities often set national heat records. July average—high 100 to 105, low 65 to 75; January average—high 70, low 35 to 45; rainfall (Lake Havasu City)—3 to 4 inches; snowfall—none.

Useful contacts

Superintendent, Lake Mead National Recreation Area, 601 Nevada Highway, Boulder City, NV 89005-2426; (702) 293-8907.

Boulder City Chamber of Commerce, 1497 Nevada Highway, Boulder City, NV 89005; (702) 293-2034

Bullhead Area Chamber of Commerce, P.O. Box 66, Bullhead City, AZ 86403; (602) 754-4121.

Kingman Area Chamber of Commerce, P.O. Box 1150, Kingman, AZ 86402; (602) 753-6106.

Lake Havasu City Chamber of Commerce, 1930 Mesquite Ave., Suite #3, Lake Havasu City, AZ 86403; (602) 855-4115.

Parker Area Chamber of Commerce, P.O. Box 627, Parker, AZ 85344; (602) 669-2174.

Quartzsite Chamber of Commerce, P.O. Box 85, Quartzsite, AZ 85346; (602) 927-5600.

Area radio stations

KAAA-AM, 1230, Kingman—Country & Western.

KDKB-FM, 92.1, Kingman—Rock.

KJUL-FM, 104.3, Las Vegas (Hoover Dam area)—Light rock and pop.

KNPR-FM, 89.5, Las Vegas—National public radio; classic, news

KORK-AM, 920, Las Vegas—Nostalgia, big band and pops.

KSLX-FM, 98.3, Kingman—Rock.

KUNB-FM, 91.5, Las Vegas—Jazz.

KWAZ-FM, 97.9, Needles, Calif.—Top 40, tilted toward light rock.

KZUL-FM, 105.1, Lake Havasu City—Light rock.

KZZZ-FM, 94.7, Kingman—Light rock, pop.

the largest public works programs in history—the construction of a 762-foot high concrete dam in the narrow, steep-walled Black Canyon. Hoover Dam's completion in 1935 marked the end of the free-flowing Colorado and the beginning of major development along its shorelines.

THE WAY IT IS • The river is now completely domesticated—thrust into harness to provide water, power and flood control in the arid Southwest. So many dams now straddle the stream that they've formed a chain of lakes for hundreds of miles, from Colorado to Mexico's Gulf of California.

No other river in the world—except perhaps Egypt's Nile—is so essential to the survival of so many million people. Without Rio Colorado, the Los Angeles, Las Vegas and Phoenix of today wouldn't exist. There would be no Imperial Valley farmlands; no inexpensive iceberg lettuce in February.

Men no longer fight water wars with guns, but political feuds still rage over who should get how much of the Colorado's water and hydroelectric output. While politician poke holes in the air with their fingers, Snowbirds flock to the river like geese on a hot day. Its shoreline offers the greatest concentration of reservoirs and rec vehicle parks in the world.

The advent of air conditioning has spawned a string of skinny little towns that hug reservoir shorelines, stretching from Hoover Dam south to Parker. At night, these slender cities sparkle across the desert like a milky way. It's an impressive sight as you fly over the area or approach the river by highway.

Most of the riverside towns are unplanned and not very pretty. The subtle beauty of the desert suffers under the weight of asphalt and the glare of neon. They are lively places, however, where glossy speedboats skim over placid reservoirs and senior citizens live out their American dream of a winter place in the sun.

Hoover Dam and Lake Mead

Elevation: 1,232   **Population: 2,500 (Boulder City)**

Hoover Dam was the happy result of unfortunate timing. Early in this century, the Bureau of Reclamation wanted to build a major upstream dam on the Colorado River. The site selected was a narrow gorge variously called Boulder Canyon and Black Canyon.

However, several years passed before the Southwestern states could agree on how the water and hydroelectric power should be divided. By the time final plans were drawn, America was deep in the Depression. But instead of hampering the dam project, it provided a ready flow of men, willing to work in the hot sun for fifty cents an hour. Since the area was then a remote wasteland, a complete town—Boulder City—was built on the Nevada side of the river.

More than 5,000 men, working in shifts around the clock, finished the massive concrete dam two years ahead of schedule. When it was completed in 1935, it was the world's highest dam, holding back the world's largest man-made reservoir. It has been declared one of America's seven civil engineering marvels. Originally called Boulder Dam, it was re-named Hoover Dam in 1947 to honor Herbert Hoover, the man largely responsible for its creation—first as secretary of commerce and later as President.

This incredible wedge, still the Western Hemisphere's highest concrete dam, provides a dramatic entry into Arizona from Nevada. U.S. Highway 93 twists down through craggy riverside peaks into narrow Black Canyon, then crosses this spade-shaped chunk of concrete. If you park and look dizzily down the curving sweep of the dam, you'll sense the immensity of this project.

Take the tour and you'll be assaulted by friendly tour-guide superlatives. The dam is 660 feet thick at the base, tapering to 45 feet at the top and it contains 4.4 million cubic yards of concrete. Behind it, Lake Mead can hold 28.5 million acre feet of water. It reaches 110 miles north and east toward the Grand Canyon and has a surface area twice the size of Rhode Island.

"At peak capacity, 118,000 six-packs per second go through penstocks that feed 17 generators," our guide burbled happily.

She said the dam was built beyond specifications, designed to last 2,000 years. She didn't add that Lake Mead likely would be silted up by then, and Hoover Dam would be holding back nothing but a giant alluvial fan.

The dam is a handsome structure, finished with striking Art Deco trim. Copper doors, ornate grill work, fluted intake columns in the forebay and sleek winged statues seem designed for a world's fair instead of a flood control project.

Further, it was built with tourism in mind. Visitors are taken deep into the concrete wedge on oversized elevators and escorted through the dam's innards along terrazzo-tiled hallways. From balconies, they stare down into the giant generator rooms, where millions of kilowatts are sent humming to Los Angeles and Las Vegas.

A RIVER BE DAMMED

The Colorado is the most harnessed river in America. Dams of the lower Colorado River Reclamation Project provide water for 11 million people in Arizona, California and Nevada and generate 5.7 billion kilowatt-hours of electricity each year. Reading from north to south, these are the dams of the lower Colorado and their functions:

Hoover Dam ● Completed in 1935, is the keystone to the project, providing flood control, water storage and hydroelectric power. It's a concrete arch dam, holding back Lake Mead, capable of storing 30 million acre-feet of water.

Davis Dam ● This earth and rock-fill dam was completed in 1953 and is used primarily to store water for delivery—via lower dams—to Mexico under the Mexican Water Treaty. It also generates electricity. Its reservoir, Lake Mohave, can store 1.8 million acre-feet of water.

Parker Dam ● An earth and rock-fill near-twin to Davis, it was completed in 1938 to provide water storage and hydroelectric power. Water from its 1.5 million acre-foot Lake Havasu goes primarily to Southern California.

Palo Verde Diversion Dam ● This earth and rock-fill structure was completed in 1957 to divert water to California's Palo Verde Valley.

Senator Wash Dam ● It's an earthfill embankment dam designed to store excess water in a small reservoir for later use. After release from a 12,250 acre-foot reservoir, water passes through hydroelectric turbines.

Imperial Dam ● Two miles below Senator Wash, this concrete dam was completed in 1938. It provides water for southwestern Arizona through the Yuma Project and to southern California through the All-American Canal.

Laguna Dam ● The granddaddy of the project, Laguna was completed in 1909 and now augments water deliveries of Imperial Dam, five miles upstream.

"More than 26 million pairs of feet have walked over this terrazzo since 1936, and it's holding up pretty well," our guide beamed at the end of the tour. Then she concluded, unfortunately: "Now, wasn't that the best dam tour you've ever taken?"

Lake Mead National Recreation Area's desert aquatic playland encompasses Lake Mead to the north and Lake Mohave below the dam. Mohave, occupying a rugged and often steep-walled canyon, is formed by Davis Dam, about 65 miles below Hoover Dam, near Bullhead City.

The cliche "boater's paradise" is appropriate here. Between the two reservoirs, boaters can explore hundreds of miles of shoreline. Nine developed sites have lengthy lists of recreational facilities. Swimming beaches and picnic areas are scattered along the shorelines as well.

Trailer villages at the marinas are popular with Snowbirds and a few year-around residents. They've learned that summer desert survival is easy if you have plenty of Coors in the refrigerator and keep the air conditioner cranked up.

Fishing is excellent on the two reservoirs, according to the people who like that sort of thing. Most marinas have serious tackle shops. Fisherpersons often catch their limits of striped and largemouth bass and rainbow trout. Willow Beach Fish Hatchery on the Arizona side is in business to keep the fake lakes stocked.

LAKE MEAD AREA ATTRACTIONS

Hoover Dam • *Guided tours $1 for adults; kids under 15 free. Daily 8 a.m. to 6:45 p.m. Memorial Weekend through Labor Day; 9 a.m. to 4:15 the rest of the year; closed Christmas Day. Small visitor center on the Nevada side is open 8 a.m. to 7:30 p.m. Memorial Weekend through Labor Day; 8:30 to 5 the rest of the year. (All times are Pacific.) Phone (702) 293-8367*

Ticket offices for dam tours are on the dam itself. Visitors follow guides deep within the concrete giant for a look at inspection corridors and huge penstocks that feed 17 generators, which can crank out nearly two million kilowatts at peak capacity. Upgrading of the generators is increasing this by 60 percent by 1992.

Parking is available on both the Arizona and Nevada sides, with free shuttle service to the dam during busy periods. At a Nevada-side visitor center, a sound and light show playing over a relief map tells the story of the harnessing of the Colorado River. In a nearby pressure-dome tent, TV star Michael Landon relates a mixed-media slide show, *How Water Won the West.*

A "Snacketeria" built over the dam's forebay offers hotdogs, hamburgers and other snacks. A gift shop is adjacent. For a mere $3.95, you can take home a souvenir coffee mug that tells your friends: "I ate a dam dog at the Hoover Dam Snacketeria."

A program to expand an improve parking and to build a new visitors center is under way. Completion—depending on the whims of government funding—is anticipated around 1995.

Alan Bible Visitor Center, Lake Mead NRA • *Junction of U.S. Highway 93 and State Highway 166, on the Nevada side, three miles from the dam; (702) 293-4041. Open daily 8:30 to 5.* It's best to have a boat to explore the 110-mile-long Lake Mead and 67-mile Lake Mohave. But if you're landbound, a stop at the visitor center will acquaint you to this large twin reservoir complex.

Hoover Dam's forebay with Art Deco intake towers.

It has films on Lake Mead and Hoover Dam construction, wildlife exhibits, a botanical garden, a gift shop and bookstore. A fifty-cent *Lake Mead Auto Tourguide,* available at the center, details driving trips on the Arizona and Nevada sides of Lake Mead and Lake Mohave.

Brochures available at the visitor center list nine marinas—six on Lake Mead and three on Lake Mohave. If you're frustrated at being land-bound, you can rent boats at most of them, or book boat tours. For a complete list of marinas and their facilities, contact: Lake Mead National Recreation Area, 601 Nevada Highway, Boulder City, NV 89005-2426; (702) 293-8907

These are the four Arizona-side marinas and their offerings:

Willow Beach • *On Lake Mohave, 15 miles southeast of Hoover Dam on U.S. 93, then four miles west.* It has a ranger station, motel, trailer village, marina, restaurant, grocery store, gasoline, picnic area, laundry and houseboat rentals. Nearby is Willow Beach National Fish Hatchery. (See listing below.)

Temple Bar • *On Lake Mead, 19 miles southeast of Hoover Dam on U.S. 93, then 28 miles northeast.* Facilities include a ranger station, motel, trailer village and campground, marina, restaurant, grocery store, gasoline, picnic area and laundry. Note the impressive "Mormon Temple," a great butte rising from Lake Mead. It was named by Daniel Bonelli, an 1875 pioneer who established a ferry crossing upstream.

South Cove/Pearce Ferry • *On Lake Mead, 41 miles southeast of Hoover Dam on U.S. 93, then 48 miles northeast.* Both are in remote and scenic areas on Lake Mead's Arizona shoreline, with boat launches but no developed facilities. There's a ranger station in the community of Meadview on the national recreation area border and primitive no-fee camping at Pearce Ferry.

Even though facilities are limited, we recommend the drive northeast from Highway 93 toward South Cove. After passing the scattered and scruffy community of Donlan Springs, you'll enter a virtual forest of Joshua trees. These hairy-armed desert plants resemble trees and many are certainly tall enough, but they're members of the lily family. Just short of Lake Mead, you enter Meadview, a low-budget resort and retirement community. It's comprised mostly of double-wide trailers on desert lots. Groceries and gasoline are available.

From here, you begin catching striking views of Lake Mead, rimmed on both sides by barren, craggy peaks. A paved road winds down through a shallow canyon toward South Cove. The desert flora, following some biological dictate, shifts from Joshua trees to cactus, yucca and mesquite. South Cove itself has only a boat launch and bisexual pit pottie. But the setting of the blue reservoir against wrinkled brown butcher-paper mountains is impressive.

Even more eye-catching is the backdrop for Pearce Ferry, reached by a four-mile dirt road. The route down—easily handled by an ordinary sedan— takes you into serious canyon country with its red and tawny stratified walls and wedding cake buttes. You're near the uppermost reach of Lake Mead here and the Grand Canyon is just around the next rocky bend. The park's western boundary, in fact, is about a mile away.

If you're driving an RV or have a tent in the trunk of your car, consider spending a night here. Facilities are primitive, with only a pit toilet, but the setting is grand and peaceful. The only sound you're likely to hear is the campground host's generator, but he turns that off at night.

Willow Beach National Fish Hatchery • *Lake Mohave; P.O. Box 757, Boulder City, NV 89005; (602) 767-3456. Open daily 7 a.m. to sunset; free.* Despite the address, the fish hatchery is on the Arizona side. Visitors can take self-guided strolls past the hatching room and raceways. Here, hundreds of thousands of rainbow and brook trout are being reared for Lake Mohave and Lake Mead anglers. You'll learn a bit about the history of the Colorado River in an exhibit room, and you'll see enough fish to drive Garfield or Sylvester out of their feline minds. About 1.2 million trout are freed each year, mostly in the two reservoirs.

Boulder City deserves mention here, even though this is an Arizona guidebook. Sitting on a knoll seven miles from the dam, it's a pretty little community fronted by a park that adds a rich splash of green to this tawny desert.

Like the dam, the company town was built with esthetics in mind. The old arcaded business district along Arizona Street is a well-preserved Art Deco Main Street USA. Downtown's centerpiece is the gleaming white Dutch colonial Hoover Dam Hotel, with a handsome turn of the century lobby.

Old Boulder City has earned a spot on the National Register of Historic Places. Its suburbs are more modern, typical of any middle class community. Interestingly, the citizens of this Nevada town of 2,500 have voted to ban gambling. It's the only community in the state with nary a slot machine or spinning roulette wheel.

If you need the feel of dice in your hands, you can stop at Gold Strike Inn. It's a typically garish Nevada casino occupying a swatch of asphalt on Highway 93, midway between the town and the dam. The glitter gulch of Las Vegas is but 23 miles away.

BOULDER CITY ATTRACTIONS

Boulder City/Hoover Dam Museum • *444 Hotel Plaza (P.O. Box 516), Boulder City, NV 89005-0516; (702) 294-1988. Daily 9 to 5; admission $1 for adults; 50 cents for seniors and children under 12.* This small museum in the Boulder City historic district exhibits photos, documents and artifacts concerning Hoover Dam's construction. A gift shop sells souvenirs and a film relates the story of the dam project. Nearby, along Arizona Street and Hotel Plaza, you can stroll beneath the sidewalk overhangs of the Art Deco shops and stores of old Boulder City.

Boulder Dam Hotel • *1305 Arizona St., Boulder City, NV 89005; (702) 293-1808.* Restored to its 1930s Art Deco elegance, this fine old hotel is worth a peek even if you don't need a room. Step into the fashionable lobby with its oak paneling, period furnishings and brick fireplace, and have a drink beneath the heavy wood beams of the Spillway Lounge, decorated with pictures of the dam and early Boulder City.

WHERE TO DINE

Captain's Table • ∆∆ $$
Temple Bar Resort; 767-3211. American; dinners $7 to $13; full bar. Daily 8 a.m. to 7 p.m. MC/VISA. The menu tilts toward seafood with catfish a specialty. Lake view from the dining room.

Carlos' Restaurant • ∆∆ $
1300 Arizona St. (Hotel Plaza), Boulder City; (702) 295-5828. Mexican; dinners $5 to $10; full bar. Tuesday-Sunday 4 to 10 p.m. MC/VISA. It's an attractive little Mexican cafe with bentwood chairs, white nappery and silk flowers on the tables.

Oasis Restaurant • ∆∆ $$
Highway 93, 37 miles southeast of Hoover Dam; (602) 767-3222. American; dinners $4 to $11; full bar service. Daily 7 a.m. to 10 p.m. MC/VISA. Boasting that it's not in the middle of nowhere, but in the middle of everywhere, the Oasis is a rustic cafe and RV park between the Temple Bar and South Cove turnoffs. Menu offerings are steak, chicken, chops and seafood.

Willow Beach Resort Restaurant • ∆∆ $$
Willow Beach Road, Willow Beach Marina; (602) 767-3311 or 767-3331. American; dinners $5 to $13; full bar. Daily 8 a.m. to 6 p.m. MC/VISA. The dining room features views of Lake Mohave; menu is the usual mix of steak, fish and chicken, with the emphasis on beef.

WHERE TO SLEEP

Boulder Dam Hotel • ∆∆∆ $$
1305 Arizona St., Boulder City, NV 89005; (702) 293-1808. Doubles $35 to $40 ($10 higher on weekends). Major credit cards. Many guest rooms in this 1933 hotel feature period decor such wrought iron beds, lace curtains and print wall coverings. **Restaurant** and cocktail lounge.

Gold Strike Inn • ∆∆∆ $$
Highway 93, Boulder City, NV 89005; (702) 293-5000 or (800) 245-6380. Singles and doubles $30 to $46 ($10 higher on weekends). Major credit cards. Part of the Gold Strike Casino; rooms have TV, phones and oversized beds. **Restaurant**, cocktail lounges, gaming, gift shop, live entertainment.

Temple Bar Resort • ∆∆ $$
Temple Bar, AZ 86443-0545; (602) 767-3211 or (800) 752-9669. Singles

and doubles $55 to $65; housekeeping units $35 to $85. MC/VISA. Color TV in some units; marina, boat and water ski rentals, restaurant (listed above).

Willow Beach Resort ● ▵▵ $$$

Willow Beach Road, Willow Beach, AZ 86445; (602) 767-3311 or 767-3331. Singles and doubles $48. MC/VISA. Color TV; marina, boat rentals, restaurant (listed above).

WHERE TO CAMP

Hemenway Harbor ● *Lake Mead National Recreation Area; (702) 293-8907. RV and tent sites; no hookups, $6. No reservations or credit cards.* Pleasant oleander-shaded campground is on the Nevada side of Lake Mead, a mile north of the Alan Bible Visitor Center on State Highway 166. Flush potties, water, picnic tables and barbecues; boat launch and swimming areas nearby.

Oasis RV Park ● *Highway 93, Oasis (c/o P.O. Box 980, HC 37, Kingman, AZ 86401); 27 miles southeast of Hoover Dam; (602) 767-3222. RV sites, full hookups, $12.50. MC/VISA.* Flush potties, showers, coin laundry, groceries, Propane, snack bar, dump station, pool, hot tub and clubhouse. Located behind the Oasis Restaurant (listed above).

Pierce Ferry ● *Lake Mead National Recreation Area; (702) 293-8907. Primitive camping with no hookups or water; free.* On the Arizona shore of Lake Mead at Pearce Ferry boat launch. Pit potties; no designated campsites but campers must stay at least 100 feet from the water's edge.

Temple Bar Trailer Park ● *Temple Bar, AZ 86443; (602) 767-3211. Full hookups, $15. Reservations, MC/VISA.* There's also a Lake Mead NRA campground here, no hookups, $6. No reservations or credit cards. Temple Bar Resort and the NRA campground are on the Arizona shore of Lake Mead. Marina, restaurant, laundry, groceries and fuel are nearby. Barbecues and picnic tables at the NRA campground, along with flush potties and water.

Willow Beach Resort ● *Willow Beach, AZ 86445; (602) 767-3311 or 767-3331. Full hookups, $8.50. Reservations, MC/VISA.* On the Arizona shore of Lake Mohave. RVs only; no camping. Marina facilities nearby, including restaurant, laundry, groceries and fuel.

SOUTH TO CHLORIDE AND KINGMAN

If you follow the Colorado River corridor south, you'll first skirt inland on U.S. 93 through the Detrital Valley. It's a remote desert area populated mostly by creosote bush. As you continue south, the Cerbat Mountains form a rocky, rough-hewn backdrop. The lure of silver brought prospectors into these mean mountains in the 1860s. They stayed around to establish one of Arizona's longest surviving mining camps.

Chloride

Our first impression was that scruffy old Chloride was about as pretty as its name. The town, named for silver-chloride deposits in the nearby hills, is a gathering of dog-eared buildings, a couple of stray dogs and a few junk cars.

However, it does a rather good job of playing funky tourist spot, and the folks are very friendly. Many of Chloride's hundred or so residents are retired, attracted by the small-town atmosphere and cheap lodging. The

Rock paintings above Chloride by artist Roy Purcell.

citizens stage mock gunfights on Saturdays and operate a weekend flea market. Visitors can prowl through a few galleries and antique stores or peek into a restored miner's shack at Shep's store, a block and a half south of the post office.

Melodramas hit the boards at the Silver Belle Playhouse on Saturdays at 10:30 a.m. and 2:30 p.m., from March through May and September through November. There's no admission charge; the players pass the hat after the show. These are delightfully amateurish skits that are rife with silly puns. The performers are brightly costumed and seem to be having as much fun as the audience. And no, they'll never make it on Broadway. Or even off.

Rock paintings, not Indian but quite contemporary, are the town's main attraction. Follow a bumpy route out Tennessee Avenue to view artist Roy Purcell's large murals, painted on the stone faces of a dry wash canyon. "Journey: Images from an inward search for self" is what Purcell calls his strange offerings, painted in 1966 and 1975. They're a surrealistic-impressionistic mix—sort of a blend of Picasso, Mexican art and petroglyphs.

A couple of restaurants in town provide simple fare. **Old Tennessee Saloon** in the 1928 Chloride General Store is a basic formica place with an American menu and a full bar. It's open daily from 7 a.m. to 9 p.m. **Cajun West** serves light meals—a mix of Cajun, American and Mexican. It also has a bar, and is open weekdays from 11 a.m. to 8 p.m. and weekends from 7 a.m. to 8 p.m.

Continuing southeast toward Kingman, you'll encounter **Santa Claus,** a sort of low-budget Christmas village in a red, white and green bungalow. It's been here since 1937. The small restaurant serves breakfast and lunch, including hamburgers with predictable names like Elf's Delight. Hours are 8 to 5 Sunday through Thursday and 8 to 7 Friday and Saturday. Christmas trimmings and folk craft items are sold in the gift shop. Santa Claus takes VISA and MasterCard.

Kingman

Elevation: 3,336 feet   **Population: 12,345**

This community of 11,000 occupies an attractive valley of eroded cliffs and buttes at the junction of Interstate 40 and U.S. 93. Dating from 1882, it was named for surveyor Lewis Kingman, who was plotting a rail route between Needles, California, and Albuquerque, New Mexico. But it was the discovery of silver and copper in the surrounding hills that kept the town on the map.

Local history buffs say Kingman became the seat of Mohave County in a rather curious manner. It seems that residents of nearby Mineral Park refused to surrender county records, even though they'd lost the seat to Kingman in an election. So the good folks of Kingman slipped over to the rival community and snatched the records under cover of darkness.

Mining declined during the 1930s and was virtually shut down by World War II. The surrounding countryside is dotted with ghost towns and semi-ghost towns worthy of exploring. They include the aforementioned Chloride, Cerbat, Mineral Park, Goldroad, Old Trails and Oatman.

While those towns withered, Kingman survived as a provisioning center for travelers on the Santa Fe railway and historic Route 66. The first path through here dates back to 1859, when Army Lt. Edward Beale's construction crew carved a wagon road that eventually led from Arkansas to Los Angeles. It was the first federally-funded road in the Southwest; old U.S. 66 roughly follows its course.

Two years earlier, the lieutenant passed here with a rather curious procession—a herd of camels. He'd convinced the Army that the beasts would be useful for southwestern transport, and he made this crossing to demonstrate his point. The cranky critters proved their worth but the government, preoccupied with the coming Civil War, abandoned the project.

Kingman is still an important crossroad and a popular pausing place for motorists hurrying along I-40. Chamber of commerce officials claim there's nearly 1,500 rooms in the motels lining the main streets.

Incidentally, the town's favorite son isn't Surveyor Kingman or a former mining baron. It's a rotund character actor with a gravelly voice named Andy Devine, who was born in nearby Flagstaff and grew up here. The main street is named for the late actor, and he's featured in a special exhibit at the local museum (see below).

The turn-of-the-century downtown looks a bit sleepy these days, since most of the business has shifted to suburban shopping centers. Take time to drive these old streets and admire architectural gems such as the Spanish colonial Santa Fe depot at Andy Devine Avenue and Fourth Street, the mission revival 1915 IOOF building at Fifth and Beale and the classic Greek-style tufa-stone, glass-domed Mohave County Courthouse at Spring and Fourth.

Folks at the **Chamber of Commerce visitor center** (333 W. Andy Devine Ave., near the town museum) will tell you everything you think you need to know about this community and the surrounding countryside.

THE BEST ATTRACTIONS

Mohave Museum of History and Arts ● *400 W. Beale St. (Grandview), Kingman, AZ 86401; (602) 753-3195. Free; donations requested. Monday-Friday 10 to 5 and weekends 1 to 5; closed major holidays.* A cut above the

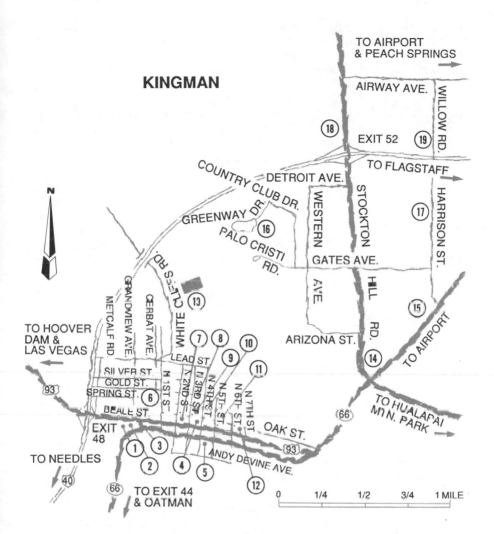

KINGMAN

DIRECTORY

1. MOHAVE MUSEUM
2. CHAMBER OF COMMERCE
3. LOCOMOTIVE PARK
4. OLD BEALE HOTEL
5. SANTA FE RAILWAY STATION
6. DOWNTOWN HISTORIC DISTRICT
7. BUS STATION
8. COUNTY COURTHOUSE
9. LIBRARY, P.O. BRANCH
10. BONELLI HOUSE
11. HISTORIC IOOF BUILDING
12. KAYSER HOUSE
13. WHITE CLIFFS WAGON TRACKS
14. MAIN POST OFFICE
15. KINGMAN CITY PARK
16. KINGMAN GOLF COURSE
17. MOHAVE COUNTY FAIRGROUNDS
18. KINGMAN MEDICAL CENTER
19. CENTENNIAL PARK

typical small-town museum, it tells the story of this valley's settlement, from Native Americans through the silver and copper rush to the present. It also features a complete set of painter Lawrence Williams' portraits of U.S. Presidents and their ladies, and a rather extensive book shop.

The sizable Andy Devine exhibit is titled "The good guys wore white hats." Filled with photos and other memorabilia, it traces the portly performer's life from his boyhood through his movie career to his passing in 1977. His larynx was damaged when he fell on a stick as a child. This left him with a gravelly voice that became famous in dozens of Western movies. He was the captain in TV's *Flipper* series and was the voice of Friar Tuck in Disney's *Robinhood.*

Bonelli House ● *430 E. Spring St. (N. Fifth), Kingman, AZ 86401. Free; donations requested. Thursday-Monday 1 to 5 p.m.; closed major holidays.* The Bonellis were Swiss Mormons who made a modest fortune as jewelers and merchants in Kingman and nearby Chloride. Their impressive tufa-stone, balconied mansion, built in 1915, has become a museum of turn-of-the-century elegance. Rooms contain period furnishings such as music boxes, antique wall clocks, brass beds and an unusual water-jacketed stove.

Docents conduct tours of the sturdy, square-shouldered, two-story structure, which architects call the "Anglo-territorial style."

Hualapai Mountain Park ● *13 miles from Kingman on Hualapai Mountain Road; (602) 757-3859.* This Mohave County park spreads over the forested slopes of the Hualapai Mountains, offering a refreshing alpine retreat from Kingman's high desert. A visitor center features exhibits of the geology, plants and critters of the area. With altitudes ranging from 5,000 to 8,500 feet, the park has hiking trails, picnicking, camping and a play field. Overlooks provide striking views of the desert below. Rustic cabins and campsites (see camping section below) can be reserved through the Mohave County Parks Department, P.O. Box 390, Kingman, AZ 86402.

THE REST

Kingman historic district ● *Downtown area; maps available at the chamber of commerce and museum.* Several dozen 18th century and early 19th century buildings dot Kingman's neighborhoods. By following a map, you can see everything from Victorian to tufa to simple adobe homes.

Railroad Park ● *Between Andy Devine Avenue and Beale Street, just east of the museum.* A 1927 Baldwin steam engine with a bright red caboose is the centerpiece in this attractive downtown park. It once paused here to take on water during its Santa Fe run between Los Angeles and Chicago.

White Cliffs Wagon Road ● *Off White Cliff Road about half a mile from downtown.* Deep ruts cut into tufa bedrock are all that remain of an 1863 wagon road used to haul ore from the Stockton Hill Mines north of Flagstaff. To find the old road—in the White Cliffs historic area—drive northeast on Lead Street, which swings north and becomes White Cliffs Road. It turns to dirt and winds up through a rugged canyon. Watch on your right for a battered footbridge and a rock shelter. Walk across the bridge (carefully) and you'll encounter the tracks. Alongside the ruts you'll note curious—and historically unexplained—depressions, as if people were trying to pole the ore wagons along.

The Kayser House ● *616 E. Beale St. (between Sixth and Seventh); open daily 10 to 5.* This cute little turn-of-the-century bungalow is now a country

Mohave County Courthouse and war memorial in Kingman.

store and gift shop. It features hand-made quilts, along with folk art such as baskets, potpourri and dried flower arrangements.

ANNUAL EVENTS

Kingman Spring Carnival, first weekend of March; **Downtown Antique Fair,** first Saturday of June; **Mohave County Fair,** second week of September; **Andy Devine Days,** last weekend of September; **Winter Carnival,** first weekend of November.

WHERE TO SHOP

Most of Kingman's commercial business is scattered along Andy Devine Avenue and Beale Street, one-way parallel streets through the downtown area. The two merge at the eastern end, where you'll find a couple of regional shopping centers.

WHERE TO DINE

Calico's Restaurant • ∆∆ $$ ∅

418 Beale St. (Beale exit from I-40), Kingman; (602) 753-5005. American and Mexican; dinners $3 to $15; full bar. Daily 5:30 to 10 p.m. MC/VISA. This handsomely-decorated restaurant features a mix of Mexican and regional American foods.

House of Chan • ∆∆ $$ ∅

960 W. Beale St. (near I-40 exit 48), Kingman; (602) 753-3232. Chinese and American; dinners $6 to $20; full bar. Monday-Saturday 11 a.m. to 10 p.m. MC/VISA, AMEX. It specializes in Cantonese dishes and American fare, including prime rib.

The Kingman Deli • ∆ $

419 Beale St. (between Fourth and Fifth), Kingman; (602) 753-4151.

American; meals from $3 to $6; no alcohol. Monday Friday 10 to 3:30, Saturday 10 to 2:30. No credit cards. More of a small cafe than a deli, it offers 36 varieties of sandwiches, salads, soups, chili and other light meals.

Route 66 Distillery • ∆∆∆ $$ ∅
1400 E. Andy Devine Ave. (in the Quality Inn), Kingman; (602) 753-5531. American; dinners $5 to $12; full bar. Daily 5:30 a.m. to 10 p.m. Major credit cards. The Distillery is a virtual museum of historic Route 66, with memorabilia from the 50s and 60s.

WHERE TO SLEEP

Best Western Kings Inn • ∆∆ $$ ∅
2930 E. Andy Devine (I-40 exit 53 then right), Kingman, AZ 86401; (602) 753-6101 or (800) 528-1234. Doubles $48 to $52, singles $33; lower off-season rates. Major credit cards. TV movies, whirlpool and sauna.

Quality Inn • ∆∆∆ $$ ∅
1400 E. Andy Devine, Kingman, AZ 86401; (602) 753-5531 or (800) 221-2222. Doubles $43 to $48, singles $38 to $43, kitchenettes $48 to $53; lower prices are off-season rates. Major credit cards. In-room coffee, refrigerators, whirlpool and sauna, gift shop, beauty salon, VCR rentals, fitness room. Route 66 Distillery restaurant (listed above).

Rodeway Inn • ∆∆ $$$ ∅
411 W. Beale St. (across from Mohave Museum), Kingman, AZ 86401; (602) 228-2000. Doubles $44 to $55, singles $38 to $45; lower off-season rates. Major credit cards. Swimming pool, room phones, TV movies. **Coffee shop** open 6 a.m. to 9 p.m., American-Mexican, dinners $4 to $9, beer and wine.

Royal 8 Inn • ∆∆ $$$ ∅
424 Beale St. (I-40 exit 48, then half mile south), Kingman, AZ 86401; (602) 753-9222. Doubles $48 to $55, singles $40. MC/VISA, AMEX. TV movies, room phones, pool, whirlpool. **Restaurant** open Monday-Saturday 5:30 a.m. to 10 p.m., Sunday 5:30 to 9, American menu, dinners $9 to $12, full bar.

Sunny 8 Motel • ∆∆ $$ ∅
3275 E. Andy Devine (I-40 exit 53, then one block east), Kingman, AZ 86401; (602) 757-1188. Doubles $30 to $34, singles $27. MC/VISA, AMEX. TV movies, room phones, pool.

WHERE TO CAMP

Hualapai Mountain Park • *County Park 13 miles from Kingman on Hualapai Mountain Road; (602) 757-3859. Tent and RV sites; no hookups; $5 to $10. Reservations through Mohave County Parks, P.O. Box 390, Kingman, AZ 86402; no credit cards.* Flush potties, barbecues, picnic tables, play field, nature trails.

Kingman KOA • *3820 N. Roosevelt Ave. (I-40 exit 53 then a mile west on Airway Avenue), Kingman, AZ 86401; (602) 757-4397. RV and tent sites, full hookups $12.75; Reservations accepted; MC/VISA.* Some pull-throughs; disposal station, flush potties and showers, coin laundry, pool, groceries and Propane, miniature golf.

King's Rest RV Park • *3131 McDonald (a block off Andy Devine), Kingman, AZ 86401; (602) 753-2277. RV sites, full hookups $17. Reservations accepted; MC/VISA.* Coin laundry, flush potties, showers.

SOUTH TO BULLHEAD AND LAKE HAVASU

As you swing back toward Rio Colorado, head southwest briefly on I-40, then take a old Route 66 to the gold rush town of Oatman. It's tucked into the rough ramparts of the Black Mountains—dramatic spires and ridges that look like dark, storm-tossed waves on a petrified ocean.

Oatman

Like Chloride, Oatman is a scruffily charming shadow of its former self. As in Chloride, its citizens work hard at attracting visitors. They even encourage wild burros to wander the streets, providing a little local color—and a definite down home aroma. Most merchants sell burro food for a quarter.

In addition to this informal petting zoo, Oatman has the usual assortment of antique and gift shops. A large flea market occurs on most weekends, and local good old boys stage shoot-outs for visitors.

The rickety **Oatman Hotel** has a museum scattered through its upstairs rooms, with early 20th century memorabilia, including old movie posters, theatre costumes and rusty mining equipment. Room 15 has a curious claim to fame: Clark Gable and Carol Lombard spent their wedding night here after getting hitched in Kingman on March 18, 1939. One of her dresses is displayed on the nuptial bed.

For grub, try the basic American fare at the appropriately scruffy **Gold City Saloon and Cafe** (part of the Oatman Hotel) or the equally rustic **Silvercreek Saloon and Steakhouse**.

Gold was discovered around Elephant's Tooth pinnacle above town, just after the turn of the century. The Tom Reed Mine and other diggin's produced $30 million until 1942, when the last shaft was closed.

Oatman basks at the base of the craggy Black Mountains.

Bullhead City

Elevation: 540 feet   **Population: 13,600**

Our route next takes us to this fast-growing winter haven sitting just north of the triangle where Arizona, Nevada and California merge. Named for a rock promontory now submerged into Lake Mohave, it's a low-rise scatter of housing tracts, modular homes and mobile home parks. This sun-warmed jumble of hasty settlement is the first of a skinny string of towns stretching along Rio Colorado's desert shoreline.

South along State Highway 95, unincorporated communities of Riviera, Fort Mohave and Golden Shores stretch Bullhead's outskirts to Interstate 40. Much of this area is encompassed in Fort Mohave Indian Reservation.

Bullhead City wasn't incorporated until 1984, but its roots go back to the 1945, when it was the construction camp for Davis Dam, immediately north. A mere 504 feet above sea level, it often earns the dubious honor of being the nation's summer hot spot. Tourist officials wish people wouldn't talk about that. Then in winter, thousands of folks fleeing the nation's—and Canada's—coldest spots triple Bullhead's population. About 20 RV and mobile home parks line the river's shores.

Aquatically-inclined visitors can rent speedboats, water-ski gear and houseboats. The area also lures fishermen to Bullhead's Colorado River reservoir, the world's largest inland fishing grounds for striped bass.

Laughlin, Nevada, across the reservoir, is another reason for Bullhead's popularity. A few years ago, entrepreneur Don Laughlin guessed that winter vacationers might like to pass the time pulling a few slot machine handles. He built a casino, more followed, and a sudden city blossomed in the desert. Laughlin immodestly named it for himself.

Nearly a dozen casinos now line the Nevada side, beguiling Bullhead residents and visitors with the seductive glitter of neon. To make things easier, large parking lots have been paved at Bullhead City's north end and launches provide free casino shuttles.

As a commentary on the town's priorities, the new casinos are large and substantial, obviously built to stay, while Laughlin's justice court is in a portable classroom.

To learn more about Bullhead, stop in at the **Chamber of Commerce** at 625 Highway 95 near the community park. Hours are 8 to 5 weekdays and 9 to 3 Saturdays.

Davis Dam • *Just north of Bullhead City, it offers free self-guiding tours daily from 7:30 a.m. to 3:30 p.m.* Sixty-five miles downstream from Hoover Dam, Davis forms craggy, steep-walled Lake Mohave. It provides flood control and sends hydroelectric power into the Southwest. Tours take you into the concrete and earthfill structure, where you can look down the line of huge humming turbines. Stepping onto the dam's lower deck, you can watch the water boiling up from their penstocks. From here, it flows briefly downstream before bumping into another reservoir formed by its near twin, Parker Dam.

ANNUAL EVENTS

Lake Mohave Boat Show, first weekend of April; **Chili Cook-off,** last weekend of April; **Laughlin River Days,** second weekend of May; **Western Craft Fair,** second weekend of October; **Bullhead-Laughlin**

Rodeo, fourth weekend of November; **Boat Parade of Lights,** mid-December.

WHERE TO SHOP
Bullhead City's main street is Highway 95 and most of its stores and small shopping centers are scattered along it. Laughlin, Nevada, is thus far too preoccupied with casino construction to offer much in the way of shopping essentials, but stores were under construction when we passed through.

WHERE TO DINE
The best dining bargains are on the Nevada side, where Laughlin casinos lower prices to lure visitors to their gaming tables. These restaurants in Bullhead are worthy of note:

Captain's Table ● ∆∆ $$
Seventh and Long streets (in the River Queen Resort); (602) 754-3214. American; dinners $6 to $30; full bar. Sunday-Thursday 7 to 10 p.m., to 11 Friday-Saturday. Major credit cards. Seafood and steak are specialties.

Lake Mohave Resort Restaurant ● ∆∆ $$
Katherine Landing (just above Davis Dam), in Lake Mead National Recreation Area; (602) 754-3245. American; dinners $9 to $15; full bar. Sunday-Thursday 8 a.m. to 8 p.m., Friday-Saturday 7 a.m. to 8 p.m. MC/VISA. The menu tilts toward seafood in this resort restaurant on the shores of Lake Mohave.

Rick's Restaurant ● ∆∆ $$
1081 Highway 95 (in Arizona Clearwater Resort, 1.5 miles south of Davis Dam bridge); (602) 754-2201. American; dinners $7 to $14; full bar. Daily 6 a.m. to 11 p.m. MC/VISA, AMEX. Ribs and steaks are featured in this river-view restaurant.

Silver Creek Inn ● ∆∆∆ $$$
1120 Highway 95 (1.5 miles south of town), (602) 763-8400. American; dinners $6 to $13; full bar. Sunday-Thursday 7 a.m. to 2 p.m. and 5 to 10 p.m., Friday-Saturday to 11 p.m. MC/VISA, AMEX. Family-style dining, steaks-chops-seafood menu.

WHERE TO SLEEP
Arizona Clearwater Resort Hotel ● ∆∆ $$ ∅
1081 Highway 95 (1.5 miles south of Davis Dam bridge), Bullhead City, AZ 86430; (602) 754-2201 or (800) 654-7126 within Arizona and (800) 443-2201 outside. Singles and doubles $45 to $55, suites $60 to $75; lower in the off-season. MC/VISA, AMEX. Room refrigerators, continental breakfast, TV movies, pool, spa, launch ramp and boat dock, Rick's Restaurant (listed above).

Best Western Grand Vista ● ∆∆∆ $$$ ∅
1817 Arcadia Plaza (on Highway 95), Bullhead City, AZ 86430; (602) 763-3300 or (800) 528-1234. Singles and doubles $39 to $75. Major credit cards. TV movies, room phones, pool, spa, free dinners at nearby casinos. (**Restaurant** under construction at press time.)

Desert Rancho Motel ● ∆∆ $$$
1041 Highway 95 (a mile south of the bridge), Bullhead City, AZ 86430; (602) 754-2578. Doubles $47 to $65, singles $40 to $60, family units $65 to $110; lower rates Sunday-Thursday. MC/VISA. TV, room phones, room refrigerators, pool.

River Queen Resort • ▵▵▵ $$
Seventh and Long, off Highway 95 (P.O. Box 218), Bullhead City, AZ 86430; (602) 754-3214. Singles and doubles $43 to $53, kitchenettes $48 to $58, suites $60 to $100. Major credit cards. TV, phones, pool, some suites and family units on the river, Captain's Table restaurant (listed above).
Silver Creek Inn • ▵▵▵ $$$
1120 Highway 95 (1.5 miles south of town), Bullhead City, AZ 86442; (602) 763-8400. Singles and doubles $54 to $59; lower Sunday-Thursday. MC/VISA, AMEX. Room refrigerators, TV, phones, pool; large units; restaurant (listed above).

WHERE TO CAMP

About 20 RV parks are crowded around Bullhead City; most are set up for long-term stays. For a complete list, contact the Bullhead City Chamber of Commerce. These are among the places that accept overnighters:

Bullhead RV Park • *1000 Highway 95 (a mile south of town), Bullhead City, AZ 86430; (602) 763-8353. RV sites, full hookups, $12.50. Reservations accepted; MC/VISA.* Flush potties, showers, coin laundry, groceries, pool, disposal station.

Katherine Landing • *(five miles north on Lake Mohave), Lake Mead National Recreation Area, (702) 293-8907. Tent and RV sites, no hookups, $6 per night. No reservations or credit cards.* Flush potties, showers, ranger station; adjacent Lake Mohave Resort (below) has additional facilities.

Lake Mohave Resort • *c/o Katherine Landing, Bullhead City, AZ 86430-4016; (602) 754-3245 or (800) 752-9669. RVs only (tents at Katherine Landing above), full hookups, $15. Reservations accepted.* Flush potties, showers, ranger station, boat ramp, marina, palm-shaded landscaping, restaurant, groceries.

Mohave County Park • *North end of town, below Davis Dam; (602) 754-4606. RV and tent sites, $7 to $12; no credit cards or reservations.* Flush potties, visitor center, boat ramp, water sports.

River City RV Park • *2225 Merrill Ave. (a mile south, then a block east of Highway 95) Bullhead City, AZ 86442; (602) 754-2121. RV sites, full hookups, $14. Reservations accepted; MC/VISA.* Coin laundry, heated pool, flush potties, showers.

Riverview RV Resort • *2000 E. Ramar Rd. (Three miles south on Highway 95, then a mile east on Ramar Road), Bullhead City, AZ 86442; (602) 763-5800. RVs only, full hookups, $14.25. Reservations accepted.* Pools, spa, tennis, par-three golf, recreation and exercise rooms, coin laundry, groceries.

Lake Havasu City

Elevation: 482 feet   **Population 17,300**

You've likely heard the story by now. The London Bridge, while not falling down, was too old and narrow to handle modern traffic, so city officials put it up for sale. They didn't really expect any buyers, but entrepreneur Robert P. McCulloch offered $2,460,000 in 1968. He said he wanted to move it to the Arizona desert, where he'd purchased a piece of Lake Havasu shoreline.

The Arizona desert? The London Bridge?

About $9 million later, McCulloch had accomplished the ridiculous. The bridge was dismantled stone by stone and reconstructed over an Arizona

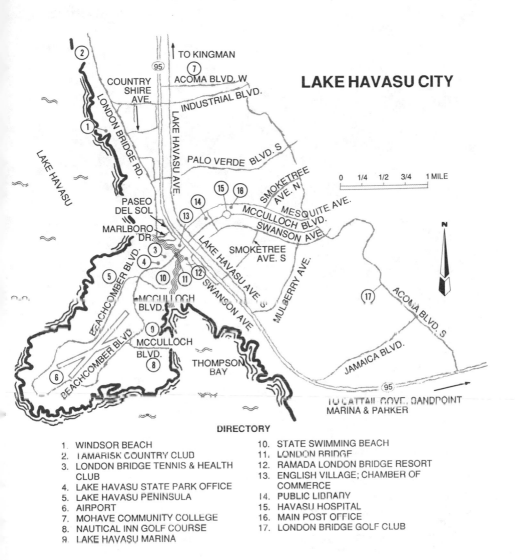

LAKE HAVASU CITY

TO KINGMAN

95 · 7 · ACOMA BLVD. W

COUNTRY SHIRE AVE.

INDUSTRIAL BLVD.

LONDON BRIDGE RD.

LAKE HAVASU

LAKE HAVASU AVE.

PALO VERDE BLVD. S

PASEO DEL SOL

MARLBORO DR.

SMOKETREE AVE. N

MCCULLOCH BLVD.

MESQUITE AVE.

SWANSON AVE.

SMOKETREE AVE. S

BEACHCOMBER BLVD.

LAKE HAVASU AVE. S

SWANSON AVE.

MCCULLOCH BLVD.

MCCULLOCH BLVD.

THOMPSON BAY

MULBERRY AVE.

ACOMA BLVD. S

JAMAICA BLVD.

95

TO CATTAIL COVE, SANDPOINT MARINA & PARKER

0   1/4   1/2   3/4   1 MILE

N

DIRECTORY

1. WINDSOR BEACH
2. TAMARISK COUNTRY CLUB
3. LONDON BRIDGE TENNIS & HEALTH CLUB
4. LAKE HAVASU STATE PARK OFFICE
5. LAKE HAVASU PENINSULA
6. AIRPORT
7. MOHAVE COMMUNITY COLLEGE
8. NAUTICAL INN GOLF COURSE
9. LAKE HAVASU MARINA
10. STATE SWIMMING BEACH
11. LONDON BRIDGE
12. RAMADA LONDON BRIDGE RESORT
13. ENGLISH VILLAGE; CHAMBER OF COMMERCE
14. PUBLIC LIBRARY
15. HAVASU HOSPITAL
16. MAIN POST OFFICE
17. LONDON BRIDGE GOLF CLUB

sandpile. Then the sand was scooped out and the venerable bridge spanned a narrow channel, linking the mainland to a peninsula-turned-island in Lake Havasu.

Voila! McCulloch had the centerpiece for his planned city in the desert. Incidentally, there were some pieces left over, and you can buy them at local souvenir shops.

Lake Havasu City is the largest of the new resort communities along Rio Colorado, pushing 20,000 residents. Local officials say The Bridge is Arizona's second most-visited attraction. The McCulloch folks decided to provide a bit of British atmosphere for the bridge's desert locale, so they built an "authentic" English village at its base. It features a London cab, double-decker bus and a proper pub—the City of London Arms.

London Bridge and ersatz English Village on Lake Havasu.

The problem was—and still is—that they didn't know when to stop. Ye olde English Village has become schlock city with fast-food stands, a ratty-looking carousel and curio shops selling souvenirs of dubious taste and usefulness. The only thing curious about the Old Curiosity Shoppe is why anyone would pay $4 for a London bridge souvenir ashtray labeled "Grandpaw's Butts." Another English Village curiosity is a cowboy-themed gift shop thinly disguised as a wild West museum.

Out on the pond, watercycles and paddleboats paddle about and *Miss Havasu II* takes visitors on an historical tour of Lake Havasu for $6.

Historical? Lake Havasu?

A visit to Lake Havasu City can be rewarding, however. The bridge *is* impressive and even beautiful when it's bathed in night lighting. A faithful replica of Britain's gold coronation coach sits in a recess in the lobby of the Ramada Inn London Bridge Resort. And at least one English Village store— the London Gift Shop—offers good quality English imports, including an extensive Beatrix Potter ceramic and book collection.

At the **Chamber of Commerce** office in English Village, you can learn more about the bridge and pick up recreation, dining, lodging and camping information. It's open daily from 9 to 5; phone 855-5655. The city's main chamber office is at 1930 Mesquite Ave. (855-4115); also open weekdays from 9 to 5.

ANNUAL EVENTS

Dixieland Jazz Festival, third weekend of January; **Snowbird Jamboree,** fourth weekend of February; **Blue Water Invitational Regatta,** second weekend of March; **Square Dance Jubilee,** first weekend of April; **Lake Havasu Pro-Am golf tourney,** third week of April; **Lake Havasu Striper Derby,** third weekend of May; **London Bridge Days,** second week of October; **Havasu Classic Outboard World Championships,** fourth weekend of November; **Annual Striper Derby,** December through March.

WHERE TO SHOP

Lake Havasu City's downtown is uptown—on a bluff overlooking London Bridge. Most of its shops are along McCulloch Boulevard, Mesquite Avenue and Swanson Avenue, three parallel streets that are perpendicular to Highway 95. Drive northeast from London Bridge on McCulloch Boulevard. Of course, English Village has its souvenir shops, but don't expect to find a loaf of bread or bag of ice there.

WHERE TO DINE

London Arms Pub and Restaurant • △△△ $$

In Ramada London Bridge Resort at 1477 Queens Bay; (602) 855-0888. American; dinners $7 to $25; full bar. Daily 11 a.m. to 10 p.m. (Adjoining Kings Retreat Cafe serves 6 a.m. to 10 p.m.) Major credit cards. This tudor-style restaurant blends English specialties with its American menu.

London Bridge Chinese Restaurant • △△△ $$

1971 McCulloch Blvd. (Riviera); (602) 453-5002. Chinese; dinners $8.25 to $15; full bar. Daily 11 a.m. to 10 p.m. MC/VISA. Despite the name, this modern, roomy restaurant does not serve English-style Chinese food. The menu tilts toward spicy Szechuan and Hunan fare.

Max and Ma's Restaurant • △△△ $

90 Swanson Ave. (near the Ramada London Bridge Resort); (602) 855-2524. American; dinners $5 to $11; full bar. Breakfast, lunch and dinner daily. MC/VISA, AMEX. The busy menu in this handsome early American-style restaurant ranges from daily fresh fish to chicken, spaghetti and steak. A salad bar features more than 60 items.

Shugru's Restaurant • △△△ $$ ∅

1425 McCulloch Blvd. (near Island Fashion Mall across London Bridge); (602) 453-1400. American/Continental; dinners $8 to $20; full bar. Daily 11 a.m. to 1 a.m. MC/VISA. Fresh seafood, steak and wok specialties are featured menu items. This attractive restaurant has a view of London Bridge.

WHERE TO SLEEP

Blue Danube Inn • △△ $$$ ∅

2176 Birch Square (Mulberry Avenue), Lake Havasu City, AZ 86403; (602) 855-5566. Singles and doubles $45 to $75, kitchenettes $60 to $90, suites $110 to $140. MC/VISA. TV, room phones, room refrigerators, pool, spa.

Holiday Inn • △△△ $$$ ∅

245 London Bridge Road (Highway 95 and Mesquite), Lake Havasu City, AZ 86403; (602) 855-4071 or (800) HOLIDAY. Doubles $51 to $72, singles $43 to $68, suites $95 to $130. Major credit cards. Some room refrigerators, TV movies, room phones, pool, spa, laundry. **Bridgeroom Restaurant** serves from 6 a.m. to 2 p.m. and 5 to 10 p.m., American, dinners $5 to $15, cocktail lounge with nightly entertainment.

Ramada London Bridge Resort • △△△△ $$$ ∅

1477 Queens Bay (just above the bridge and English Village), Lake Havasu City, AZ 86403; (602) 855-0888 or (800) 225-2879 in Arizona and (800) 624-7939 outside. Singles and doubles $65 to $125, suites $125 to $225. Major credit cards. A large resort with two pools, spa, tennis courts. Kings Retreat Cafe and London Arms Pub and Restaurant (see London Arms listing above).

Sands Vacation Resort • △△ $$$

2040 Mesquite Ave., Lake Havasu City, AZ 86403; (602) 855-1388 or

(800) 521-0360. An all-suite hotel; singles and doubles $69 to $89. MC/VISA, AMEX. TV movies, room phones, pool, room refrigerators, continental breakfast and complimentary happy hour.

Shakespeare Inn • △△△ $$
2190 McCulloch Blvd. (Acoma), Lake Havasu City, AZ 86403; (602) 855-4157 or (800) 942-8278. Singles and doubles $24 to $49, kitchenettes and suites $49 to $99. MC/VISA, AMEX. TV, rental movies, room phones, pool; **Shakespeare Restaurant**, American, dinners from $5 to $20, full bar; open 24 hours.

Super 8 Motel • △△ $$ ∅
305 London Bridge Rd. (two blocks from bridge), Lake Havasu City, AZ 86403; (602) 855-8844 or (800) 843-1991. Singles and doubles $28.88 to $46.88. Major credit cards. TV movies, room phones, pool, spa, free coffee.

WHERE TO CAMP

Crazy Horse Campground • *1534 Beachcomber Blvd. (in Lake Havasu State Park, across London Bridge), Lake Havasu City, AZ 86403; (602) 855-4033. RV sites, full hookups $15 to $17, no hookups $9. Reservations accepted; MC/VISA.* Western-theme store, flush potties, showers, some lakeside sites, disposal station, coin laundry, groceries, Propane, spa, swimming beach, boat dock and launch, recreation room.

Islander RV Resort • *751 Beachcomber Blvd. (on the peninsula, across London Bridge), Lake Havasu City, AZ 86403; (602) 855-5005. RV sites, full hookups, $20. Reservations accepted.* A new resort with a clubhouse, rest rooms and showers, laundromat, library, billiard and cardroom, TV lounge. Also shuffleboard and horseshoe pits, pools, spas, barbecue area, boat ramp, swimming beaches and nature trails.

Sandpoint Marina and RV Park • *P.O. Box 1469 (10 miles south off Highway 95, near Cattail Cove), Lake Havasu City, AZ 86403; (602) 855-0540 or (602) 855-0549. RV sites, full hookups, $14; also trailer rentals $40 to $60. Reservations accepted.* Flush potties, showers, store, service station, cafe, marina with boat launch, boat and houseboat rentals.

Lake Havasu State Park • *Two state beaches, Cat-Tail Cove and Windsor Beach, have sites for $3 to $8, with flush potties, boat ramps and swimming areas. No reservations or credit cards.* Cat-Tail Cove (17 miles south on Highway 95) has RV sites only, with a disposal station, flush potties, coin laundry, Propane and rental boats. Windsor Beach (1350 McCulloch Blvd.) has tent and RV sites, with a swimming beach and boat ramp.

SOUTH TO PARKER & QUARTZSITE

Continuing south beside the Colorado River's chain of lakes on Highway 95, you'll encounter Parker, a pleasantly nondescript town on the Colorado River Indian Reservation.

Lake Moovalya is another of Rio Colorado's reservoirs; it's cradled between Headgate Rock Dam below and Parker Dam above. People have trouble pronouncing *Moovalya*, so the 11-mile stretch of water recreation area is simply called the Parker Strip.

Parker

Elevation: 450 feet   **Population: 3,035**

A community of about 3,000, Parker is practically wall-to-wall RV parks.

There are five in town, 23 on the Arizona side of Parker Strip and 20 on the California side.

Parker Chamber of Commerce, 1217 California Ave., (602) 669-2174), invites visitors to "catch river fever." It's open from 9 to 5 weekdays; closed weekends.

Parker Dam • *North of town and outside the reservation, is a near twin to Davis Dam upstream. Free self-guided tours are available daily 7:30 to 4 on the California side (Pacific time).* Parker offers a feature unique to Colorado River dam tours—you can step inside a huge turbine pit and watch the shaft spinning. It has the look, smell and feel of a ship's engine room. And you can inspect one of the 40,000 horsepower, 60,000 pound turbines, on display in the massive generator room.

Colorado River Indian Tribes Museum • *Agency and Mohave roads, Parker; (602) 669-9211. Open weekdays 8 to 5 and Saturday 10 to 4 (closed during the lunch hour); free admission.* Exhibits feature tribal lore of the Mohave, Chemehuevi, Navajo and Hopi Indians and their prehistoric predecessors. Indian crafts and publications are sold at a small gift shop.

ANNUAL EVENTS

Parker Enduro Classic Boat Races, last weekend of March, **Parker Rodeo,** second weekend of October; **Mini-Boat Enduro races,** third weekend of November; **Christmas Lighted Boat Parade,** second Saturday in December.

WHERE TO SHOP

California Avenue (Highway 72) is downtown Parker, running from southeast to northwest; most of its stores are in a ten-block section here. Other shopping areas, including Moovalya Plaza center, are on Riverside Drive Highway 95 headed northeast.

WHERE TO DINE

Coffee Ern's • △ $
1720 California (adjacent to Kofa Inn); (602) 669-8145. American; meals $5 to $8; no alcohol. Open 24 hours; MC/VISA. This small coffee shop features around-the-clock breakfast and other basic American fare.

El Palacio Mexican Restaurant • △△ $$
1884 Highway 95; (602) 763-2494. Mexican; dinners $3.50 to $15; full bar. Daily 11 a.m. to 11 p.m.; MC/VISA. Homemade Mexican fare, including pork tamales, menudo, fajitas and *frutitas* for dessert. Live Mexican music; Sunday brunch buffet.

Paradise Cafe • △△ $
Highway 95 at Casa del Rio (Parker Dam turnoff), Parker; (602) 667-2404. American barbecue; dinners $6 to $12. Weekdays 4:30 to 9, weekends 4:30 to 10; MC/VISA. Calling itself "a fun place with a serious kitchen," this homey little cafe specializes in barbecue ribs and chicken and homemade pies and desserts.

WHERE TO SLEEP

El Rancho Motel • △△ $$ ∅
709 California Ave. (north end of town, near the river), Parker, AZ 85344; (602) 669-2231. Doubles and kitchenettes $30 to $40, singles $27 to $35. Major credit cards. TV movies, room refrigerators, room phones, pool, in-room coffee.

Holiday Kasbah Motel ● ∆∆ $$ ∅
604 California Ave. (Riverside Drive), Parker, AZ 85344; (602) 669-2133.
Doubles $40 to $50, singles $30 to $37, suites $53 to $71. Major credit cards.
TV movies, room phones, refrigerators, continental breakfast.

Kofa Inn ● ∆∆ $$
1700 California Ave. (Highway 95), Parker, AZ 85344; (602) 669-2101.
Doubles $35.87, singles $31.65. Major credit cards. TV, room phones, pool.
Coffee Ern's cafe adjacent (listed above).

Stardust Motel ● ∆∆ $$
700 California Ave. (Seventh Street), Parker, AZ 85344; (602) 669-2278.
Doubles $35 to $75, singles $30 to $50, suites $45 to $100. MC/VISA, AMEX.
TV movies, room phones, pool; most rooms have refrigerators and
microwave ovens.

WHERE TO CAMP

For a list of the many commercial RV parks in the area, contact the
chamber of commerce. Here are three state or county operated ones that ac-
cept overnighters:

Buckskin Mountain River Island Unit ● *P.O. Box BA (12 miles north on*
the river), Parker, AZ 85344; (602) 667-3386. RV and camp sites, no hookups,
$6, day use $3. No credit cards or reservations. Boat launch ramp, flush pot-
ties, lawn areas, barbecues and picnic tables.

Buckskin Mountain State Park ● *P.O. Box BA (11 miles north on the*
river), Parker, AZ 85344; (602) 667-3231. Tent and RV sites; shade cabanas
with hookups, $11; regular hookups, $8; no hookups $6, day use $3. No credit
cards or reservations. Boat launch ramp, flush potties, grassy lawn area, bar-
becues and picnic tables.

La Paz County Park ● *Route 2, Box 706 (eight miles north on the river),*
Parker, AZ 85344; (602) 667-2069. RV and tent sites, $6 to $9. No credit
cards or reservations. Flush potties, disposal station, boat ramp, swimming
beach, tennis, nature trails, playground, bike paths; golf course across the
road.

Quartzsite

Elevation: 875 feet   **Population: 900**

It might be the strangest town in Arizona, and possibly on the planet. Ac-
tually, it isn't exactly a town, but more of a scraped-away piece of desert
covered with RV parks.

Quartzsite dates back to 1856 when one Charles Tyson built a civilian
fort and stage stop. Today, it resembles a huge traveling show that's about
to pull up stakes. As a matter of fact, most of its residents do just that, since
they're Snowbirds who flee north to beat the summer heat. This annual
spring exodus shrinks the population from 200,000 to a handful. A few of
the town's structures are anchored to the desert dirt, but most business is
conducted out of tents and shade ramadas.

This dusty desert village has no town government, no sewer or water sys-
tem, no schools, police department or zoning regulations. What it has is a
mobile population who's median age is somewhere between Social Security
and infinity. They're having the time of their lives at barbecues, potluck din-
ners and dances. Some merely unfold camp chairs on a swatch of Astroturf
beside their RVs and breathe the clean desert air. At Stardusty Ballroom,

which has only a floor—no walls or ceiling—oldsters fox-trot to music of the swinging years. "Dance at your own risk," a sign warns.

Restaurants cater to their clientele with fare that is bland and easy to chew. "Ninety-five percent of my customers wear false teeth," one restaurateur explained.

Cheap rent is one of the town's main attraction. With dozens of RV parks competing for customers, space rent is the lowest in Arizona. Further, the Bureau of Land Management will let you park at La Posa Recreation Area for just $25 for six months. Located south of I-10, La Posa offers no utilities, not even water, but you can't beat the rates.

The town's transient 200,000 swells to more than 500,000 during the Quartzsite Gemboree, a monster gem and mineral show, flea market and RV rendezvous held each winter. During the show, folks say you can walk from one end of town to the other over the roof tops of RVs.

ATTRACTIONS

Quartzsite Gemboree ● *Late January through early February in three overlapping shows: The Main Event, Quartzsite PowWow and Tyson Wells Sell-A-Rama.* Some people say Howard Armstrong's Main Event is the main reason for Quartzsite's existence. It's the largest of the gem show/flea market/desert festivals.

Started in 1964 by a few rock-swappers tail-gating out of their pickups, Quartzsite's annual Bedouin bazaar has become the world's largest gem show. And the three overlapping festivals are considerably more than that. About 6,000 booths peddle everything from 7,000-pound quartz boulders and petrified dinosaur poop to snow cones and hotdogs. During the two-week run, the festivals feature antiques and collectibles exhibits, flea markets, an auto show, a professional rodeo, country and Western music jamboree, camel and ostrich races, live entertainment and—good grief!—even a history of Quartzsite pageant.

During the rest of the year, **The Main Event** is a large restaurant, service station, shopping and RV complex (restaurant listing below). To learn about the next Quartzsite Gemboree, contact: Howard Armstrong, P.O. Box 2801, Quartzsite, AZ 85346; (602) 927-5213.

Quartzsite Museum ● *In an adobe brick building downtown, (north side of the freeway); open Wednesday through Saturday 10 to 3. It's free; donations are appreciated.* Occupying the former Tyson Wells stage stop, the museum exhibits old bottles, mineral specimens, pioneer artifacts and a mock-up school room and assay office.

Hi Jolly grave site ● *In the local cemetery, surrounded by RV parks.* When Lieutenant Edward Beale marched his camel corps through the Southwest in 1857 (see Kingman listing), he was accompanied by a Syrian camel herder named Haiji Ali. That's as difficult to pronounced as Moovalya, so he became "Hi Jolly." After the camels were disbanded, Hi Jolly remained in Quartzsite until his death in 1902. He grave is marked with a pyramid and a camel silhouette that looks like it was copied from a cigarette pack.

WHERE TO DINE

Saguaro Inn ● △△ $
At Main Event on business loop 10; (602) 927-5974. American; dinners $3 to $15; full bar. Daily 7 a.m. to 9 p.m. MC/VISA. Specials include a grits and gravy buffet for $1.49 and a $2.99 breakfast. Check out the fanciful carv-

ings, including a wooden giraffe with his neck in one room and his southern end in another.

WHERE TO CAMP

Good grief, practically anywhere! There are too many RV parks in Quartzsite to even think about listing them. Some are rather nice places with landscaping, palms and pools. Others are merely dirt patches, where the fragile desert has been rudely scraped away.

You can "dry camp" with no hookups for as little as $3, or you can merely go outside of town and park beside a creosote bush. For a list of RV parks, contact the **Quartzsite Chamber of Commerce,** P.O. Box 85, Quartzsite, AZ 85346; (602) 927-5600.

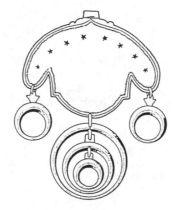

Chapter 5

THE NORTHERN MIDDLE

Flagstaff has, free for the taking, the healthiest and most invigorating of climates, its surrounding scenic beauties will fill to overflowing the enjoyment of any vacationist who will but come to commune with nature.
—*Coconino County, the Wonderland of Nature* guidebook, 1916

 ALTHOUGH THIS IS ARIZONA, you may think you've taken a wrong turn and wound up in the Pacific Northwest. Great stands of ponderosa pines carpet Coconino National Forest, and the serrated San Francisco Peaks thrust more than 12,000 feet into the sky.

North central Arizona occupies the southern reaches of the Colorado Plateau. This tableland—4,000 to 8,000 feet high—extends down from the Grand Canyon and drops off abruptly at the 200-mile-long Mogollon Rim. It's a wonderfully mixed land of alpine lakes, volcanic peaks and red rock canyons, offering Arizona's greatest variety of lures.

At the center of all this is Flagstaff, seat of government for huge Coconino County. It's Arizona's second largest, covering 18,629 square miles. Within a day's drive are seven national parks and monuments, including several intriguing Indian ruins. Flagstaff and Williams each claim to be the southern gateway to the Grand Canyon. Williams is closer; Flagstaff offers more accommodations.

Flagstaff

Elevation: 6,905 feet   **Population: 37,200**

THE WAY IT WAS ● First, there were the true natives, drawn to these high, cool pine forests around 15 to 20 thousand years ago. They shared the land with antelope, bison and camels, migrating with the seasons to hunt and forage. About four thousand years ago, they began rudimentary agriculture, getting their balanced protein from a blend of corn, squash and beans.

From these early tribes evolved the Sinagua *(si-NAU-wa)*, who settled around present-day Flagstaff and south through Oak Creek Canyon around 1000 A.D. Although they occupied much of the green Colorado Plateau, their name in Spanish means "without water." It was a reference to the porous, leaky volcanic soil in the eastern region of the plateau, where their abandoned pueblos were first noted by Spanish explorers. An advanced society, the Sinagua farmed, built irrigation canals and constructed elaborate adobe pueblos above ground and in the niches of protective cliffs.

Then curiously, by the time those Spanish travelers passed through here in the 16th century, the Sinagua had gone. Were they driven out by drought, disease or the arrival of warlike Athabaskans from the north? Archaeologists can only speculate. Thousands of ruins have been found to prove they were here; nothing has been found to confirm why they left. It's possible that the Hopi of northeastern Arizona are their descendants, although they're more commonly linked to another prehistoric group, the Anasazi.

White settlement of the region didn't begin until the 1870s, after the Apaches had been cornered—but still not defeated—in southeastern Arizona. Judge Samuel Cozzens spent three years exploring the area, then went back East and returned with a group of colonizers in 1876. They started a settlement called Agassiz near San Francisco Peaks. But they, too, left, deciding the area wasn't good for farming or mining.

Finally, sheepherder Thomas Forsythe McMillan arrived, concluded that it was good sheep country and stayed. By 1880, the area's population had

---

THINGS TO KNOW BEFORE YOU GO

Best time to go • The Colorado Plateau and San Francisco Peaks offer an all-year playground. This is forest country, not cactus country. Summers are pleasantly warm and occasional winter snows dust Flagstaff, the area's commercial center. Fairfield Snowbowl is a popular winter sports resort.

Climate • Warm summers; cool to cold winters. July average—high 82, low 51; January average—high 42, low 15; rainfall (Flagstaff)—20 inches; snowfall—80 inches.

Useful contacts

Coconino National Forest, 2323 Greenlaw Way, Flagstaff, AZ 86001; (602) 527-7400.

Flagstaff Chamber of Commerce, 101 W. Santa Fe, Flagstaff, AZ 86001; (800) 842-7293 or (602) 774-9541.

Kaibab National Forest, 800 S. Sixth St., Williams, AZ 86046; (602) 635-2681.

Williams-Grand Canyon Chamber of Commerce, 820 Bill Williams Ave. (P.O. Box 235), Williams, AZ 86046; (602) 635-2041.

Winslow Chamber of Commerce, 300 W. North Road (P.O. Box 460), Winslow, AZ 86047; (602) 289-2434.

Area radio stations

KAFF-AM, 930, Flagstaff—Country & Western.

KAFF-FM, 92.9, Flagstaff—Country & Western.

KDBK-FM, 92, Flagstaff—Rock.

KMGN-FM, 93.9, Flagstaff—Talk, news & popular music.

KNAU-FM, 89.7, Flagstaff—National Public Radio.

KVNA-AM, 690, Flagstaff—"Golden oldies."

KVNA-FM, 97.5, Flagstaff—Light rock.

swelled to 67. The railroad came through two years later and Flagstaff's future was assured.

The town's curious name came from a flagpole that may or may not have existed. Some historians say that limbs were stripped from a tall ponderosa and a flag was hoisted on July 4, 1876, to honor the centennial of America's independence. Others insist that the pole was a marker to guide travelers headed west.

Some attribute the pole to that ubiquitous camel-herder, Army Lt. Edward Beale. Later, the tree was chopped down and used as firewood at Sandy Donahue's Saloon. So much for historic preservation.

The name Flagstaff was selected by a group of citizens in 1881, meeting in P.J. Brennen's tent store. Twice in three years, the new settlement was burned and rebuilt. Fortunately, there was plenty of lumber in the area. The city was incorporated in 1894.

Lumbering is still an important industry and the county is home to more than half of Arizona's domestic sheep. However, tourism is Flagstaff's major enterprise. Interestingly, Northern Arizona University is its largest employer, with a staff of 1,600.

THE WAY IT IS ● Flagstaff is the most versatile small city in Arizona, both for visitors and residents. The university provides cultural opportunities, while excellent museums and historic buildings preserve the area's past. The nearby San Francisco Peaks offer alpine lures. Climb a steep street from downtown Flagstaff and you're at Lowell Observatory, where the existence of the planet Pluto was confirmed in 1930.

A short drive east takes you to Indian cliff dwellings at Walnut Canyon. Swing north and you're in the scenic volcanic wilds of Sunset Crater National Monument and the scattered Sinagua pueblos of Wupatki National Monument. Head south and you descend the red-walled depths of Oak Creek Canyon.

Coconino County offers an abundance of open space. More than 92 percent of its land area is within a national forest, park, monument or other federal preserve. By contrast, Flagstaff is a mini-metropolitan center; half the county's 80,000 residents live there. It's a four-season vacation land with balmy summers and pockets of stunning fall color in cottonwood and sycamore groves. Nearly 7,000 feet in elevation, Flagstaff receives about 80 inches of snow each winter but it stays on the ground only on the higher peaks.

Naturally, such a tourist-oriented area offers plenty of places to stay. Motels line the main drag—Santa Fe Avenue—and others are clustered around freeway off ramps. Several RV parks are within minutes of downtown.

As in most most older Arizona communities, Flagstaff's downtown is a mix of turn-of-the-century and modern buildings. Catch a glimpse of the Gothic-style lava stone Church of the Nativity at 16 W. Cherry Avenue and the multi-gabled Santa Fe railway station at Santa Fe and Humphreys.

Most of Flagstaff's shopping has moved to the suburbs. The downtown area is compact and quite active and attractive. There is none of the scruffiness seen in some towns that suffer from suburban scatter.

Flagstaff Chamber of Commerce Visitors Center at 101 Santa Fe Avenue (Beaver Street) is open Monday-Saturday 8 to 6 and Sunday 8 to 5. Phone 774-4505. For current events, call 779-3733.

THE BEST ATTRACTIONS

Museum of Northern Arizona ● *Fort Valley Road (U.S. 180, three miles north); mailing address is Route 4, Box 720, Flagstaff, AZ 86001; (602) 774-5211. Adults $3, ages 5 to 21 $1.50. Daily 9 to 5.* Housed in a handsome fieldstone and timber building complex in a shady ponderosa grove, the museum is "dedicated to the anthropology, biology, geology and fine arts of the Colorado Plateau."

This may sound like a lofty order, but the museum handles it with professional skill. Although the museum is old—dating back to 1935—its exhibits are innovative and modern.

An interesting Orientation Wall describes the shelter, settlement patterns, social organizations, crafts and food sources of northern Arizona's various Indian tribes. A complete skeletal reconstruction of a ground sloth is the centerpiece of the prehistoric exhibit. A display of early and modern

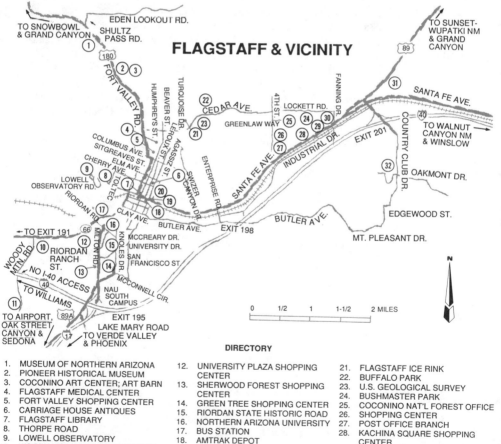

DIRECTORY

1. MUSEUM OF NORTHERN ARIZONA
2. PIONEER HISTORICAL MUSEUM
3. COCONINO ART CENTER; ART BARN
4. FLAGSTAFF MEDICAL CENTER
5. FORT VALLEY SHOPPING CENTER
6. CARRIAGE HOUSE ANTIQUES
7. FLAGSTAFF LIBRARY
8. THORPE ROAD
9. LOWELL OBSERVATORY
10. WOODY MOUNTAIN CAMPGROUND
11. ARBORETUM AT FLAGSTAFF
12. UNIVERSITY PLAZA SHOPPING CENTER
13. SHERWOOD FOREST SHOPPING CENTER
14. GREEN TREE SHOPPING CENTER
15. RIORDAN STATE HISTORIC ROAD
16. NORTHERN ARIZONA UNIVERSITY
17. BUS STATION
18. AMTRAK DEPOT
19. CHAMBER OF COMMERCE
20. MAIN POST OFFICE
21. FLAGSTAFF ICE RINK
22. BUFFALO PARK
23. U.S. GEOLOGICAL SURVEY
24. BUSHMASTER PARK
25. COCONINO NAT'L FOREST OFFICE
26. SHOPPING CENTER
27. POST OFFICE BRANCH
28. KACHINA SQUARE SHOPPING CENTER
29. MUSEUM CLUB
30. PARK SANTA FE SHOPPING CENTER

Navajo silver work is highlighted by a silver-mounted saddle that would be the envy of Roy and Dale—and even Trigger. In a special loft room, kids can fondle bit of rock, fur, cactus wood and such. The museum also has a gift shop and book store with a good selection of Arizona lore.

This world-class museum has tens of thousands of biological, fossil rock and mineral specimens and more than 2,000 paintings and sculptures in its collections. It earns international recognition for its annual Hopi, Navajo and Zuni shows.

Lowell Observatory ● *1400 West Mars Hill Road (follow Santa Fe Avenue west and uphill), Flagstaff, AZ 86001; (602) 774-2096. Adults $1, $3 per family. Tuesday-Saturday 9:30-4:30 June through August, with tours at 10 and 1:30; shorter hours the rest of the year. Public telescope viewing Friday and Saturday evenings from 8 to 10 in summer, less frequently the rest of the year.*

Privately-endowed Lowell Observatory sits atop a pine-covered mesa, less than a mile from downtown. Its primary focus is the study of the solar system. Boston businessman and author Percival Lowell founded the institution in 1894 and it's still one of America's leading astronomical centers.

It was this wealthy amateur astronomer who first determined—in 1902—that a ninth plant existed beyond Uranus and Neptune. Nearly three decades later, the observatory's Clyde Tombaugh pinpointed and named Pluto. Studies at Lowell also led to the theory of the expanding universe.

Although a skilled observer, Lowell sometimes let his imagination work overtime. He titillated other astronomers—and science fiction writers—by discovering "canals" on Mars. This led to his conclusion that Martians were scampering about up there. Subsequent Mars landings, of course, have found no canals and no little green men. Lowell died in 1916 and left his fortune to the continuing operation of the observatory.

Visitors can view stellar exhibits and join hour-and-a-half lecture tours. Evening visits are particularly intriguing, when you can peer through one of the observatory's telescopes.

Even if the visitor center is closed, you can pick up a leaflet from a door rack and take a self-guiding tour about the grounds. Our favorite exhibit is an outdoor "Pluto Walk," where you can stroll through a sidewalk solar system. The sun and planets are sized proportionately, although the walk has been condensed 20 times to save space and shoe-leather. If the block-long path were on a normal scale, a sign advises, you'd have to hike to Boise, Idaho, to reach *Proxima Centauri*, our nearest star.

Northern Arizona University ● *P.O. Box 1842 (southwest of downtown) Flagstaff, AZ 86011; (602) 523-9011. Visitor parking pass and campus maps available at the Parking Office outside Lumberjack Stadium. For a complete run-down of activities both on and off campus, get a copy of the free newsletter, "Un-tv, the Northern Arizona Arts and Entertainment Guide."* The presence of the university elevates Flagstaff from a pleasant mid-sized town to a pleasing cultural center.

Arts and crafts exhibits, live entertainment, Flagstaff Symphony concerts and activities ranging from *tai chi* to tennis tournaments abound on campus and off. On-campus lures include the NAU Observatory, open for public viewing on clear Thursday evenings from 7:30 to 10, the NAU Art Gallery (523-3471), the Skydome and Lumberjack Stadium for sports events and an indoor swimming pool.

A free shuttle bus, running at 15-minute intervals, takes visitors around campus during the school year on weekdays from about 7:30 a.m. to 10 p.m.

Pioneer Museum ● *Fort Lowell Road (U.S. 180, two miles north); (602) 774-6272. Free admission; donations appreciated. Monday-Saturday 9 to 5, Sunday 1:30 to 5.* Operated by the Arizona Historical Society, the museum offers an extensive collection of Flagstaff area lore. Exhibits include memorabilia from astronomer Percival Lowell and Grand Canyon photographer Emery Kolb, plus the usual array of high-button shoes, branding irons and yesterday photos.

The building itself is a museum piece. Built in 1907-08 of volcanic tufa, it originally served as the Coconino County Hospital for the Indigent. A transportation annex out back garages horseless carriages, surreys and the like.

Riordan State Historic Park ● *Riordan Ranch Road (off Milton and Riordan roads in the downtown area); P.O. Box 217, Flagstaff, AZ 86002; (602). Adults $2, kids 18 and under free. Daily 8 to 5 in summer, 12:30 to 5 the rest of the year.* Flagstaff has swelled outward and surrounded this large ranch-style estate, once the home of a pioneer lumbering and merchant family. State park rangers conduct tours of the bold fieldstone, shingle-sided structure. It's actually two homes, once occupied by the Riordan brothers and their families. It's joined in the middle by a communal meeting and recreation room.

Furnishings are appropriate to the turn-of-the-century period when Michael and Timothy Riordan built this Carpenter-style, 13,000 square foot house. A visitor center, occupying the carriage house, offers historical exhibits and a touch table, where you can pick up and peer through a stereo-

Riordan brothers' home at state historic park in Flagstaff.

optigan. The extensive pine-shaded grounds, framed by split-rail fences and now hemmed in by the city, has a picnic area.

THE REST

The Arboretum at Flagstaff • *Woody Mountain Road (west on old Highway 66, then south 3.8 miles on Woody Mountain Road), P.O. Box 670, Flagstaff, AZ 86001; (602) 774-1441. Free; donations appreciated. Monday-Friday 10 to 3; guided tours at 11 a.m. and 1 p.m.* Plants of northern Arizona's high desert, forest and alpine climate zones flourish at this rather new botanical garden, which occupies a 200-acre meadow surrounded by ponderosa forest. Visit a humid, solar-heated "production house" and stroll the winding paths to communicate with local flora. If you're a real plant enthusiast, you can attend exciting events such as a bulb-forcing class.

The Carriage House Antique and Craft Mall • *413 N. San Francisco Street (Dale), Flagstaff, AZ 86001; (602) 774-1337. Monday-Saturday 10 to 5, Sunday 11 to 4.* Antique and crafts zealots can explore 19 different shops, all tucked under the roof of an early 20th century two-story brick mansion.

Coconino Center for the Arts and the Art Barn • *Fort Lowell Road (U.S. 180, two miles north).* Occupying a modern building beneath the pines, the Coconino Center for the Arts (779-6921) is a focal point for local artists and other things cultural, with galleries, a bookstore, art shop and an auditorium for special events. The next-door Art Barn (Tuesday-Saturday 10 to 5; 774-0822) is in fact housed an old barn. It exhibits the works of local artists. Both share a woodsy complex with the Pioneer Museum (listed above). A yearly Native American exhibit, running from late June through August, features Southwestern Indian arts, crafts, music, dance and cultural workshops.

Museum Club of Flagstaff • *3404 E. Santa Fe Ave. (east end, near Fanning Drive; (602) 526-9434.* No, it's not a museum, but a wonderfully funky cowboy bar, built from huge timbers in 1918. You can tell this is a high-class joint because the parking area out front is full of pickups. Passing through an inverted tree-fork entrance, you enter a barn-like interior held up by polished tree trunks. If you don't step onto the dance floor and try the cowboy two-step, you just aren't with it, dude.

U.S. Geological Survey • *McMillan Mesa (off Cedar Avenue, a mile and a half northeast), Flagstaff, AZ 86001; (602) 527-7000. Weekdays 8 to 4:30; free.* This isn't a museum either, but a geological survey field office specializing in astrogeology. Scientists study and interpret space photos and "Landsat" (land-satellite) images of the earth, taken from space.

There are no tours or exhibit rooms, but visitors can stroll the hallways to admire the giant color wall maps and photos of the moon and planets, including impressive photos of Planet Earth. Many of these photos, with computer-enhanced color and detail, are spectacular. Most are in Building 1, along with a science library.

THE OUTDOOR THING

Coconino National Forest headquarters at 2323 E. Greenlaw Way (east end of town, off Fourth Street behind Knoles Village Shopping Center) has assorted hiking maps, campground lists and such. Most of the material is free; $2 will get you a detailed national forest map, essential for the explorations we describe below. Phone (602) 527-7400.

National forest lands spill down from the San Francisco Peaks, skirt Flagstaff and continue south through Oak Creek Canyon and Sedona—which we'll discuss in he next chapter. Obviously, this wilderness largess provides sightseeing, hiking, backpacking, camping, fishing and hunting, all within minutes of Flagstaff.

Fairfield Snowbowl • *P.O. Box 2430 (Eight miles north on U.S. 180, then six miles northeast to the ski area); Flagstaff, AZ 86002; (602) 779-1951. Sky rides, 10 a.m. to 4 p.m., June to Labor Day; weekends only during May, September and October.* Although primarily a winter ski area (winter sports listing below), the Snowbowl is certainly worth a snowless visit. The 14-mile drive from downtown Flagstaff will take you into a handsome alpine country in Coconino National Forest.

Hop on a sky ride for a journey from the 9,500-foot base to the dizzying heights of the San Francisco Peaks at 11,500. Or hike from base camp into the Kachina Wilderness Area (see "Hiking" below). Fall color can be awesome along the twisting, aspen-lined road from U.S. 180 to the ski area. Call the chamber at (602) 774-4505 or the forest service at (602) 527-7400 to find out when the leaves are turning.

Hiking • Miles of trails traverse Coconino National Forest, particularly in the Kachina Wilderness and San Francisco Volcanic Field just north of Flagstaff. Maps are available at national forest offices. Summer is hiking season for the high country, since snow closes trails most of the rest of the year. Be wary of lightning storms during July and August.

One of the most challenging trails leads to the top of **Humphreys Peak,** the highest point in Arizona at 12,633 feet. Although this isn't a technical hike that requires rock-scaling and cliff-hanging, it is a difficult all-day outing. You'll need considerable endurance. Elevation gain is more than 3,000 feet; plan on eight or nine hours for the nine-mile trudge to the summit and back. The trailhead is at the Fairfield Snow Bowl. Check with the forest service to determine when the trail is clear of snow.

Other interesting hikes are up 9,299-foot **Mount Elden,** with trailheads off U.S. 89 north of Flagstaff and off Schulz Pass Road; the **Weatherford** and **Inner Basin** trails that wind through Kachina Peaks Wilderness and the **Kendrick Peak** trails northwest of Flagstaff, which offer awesome views of the area.

Crater Climbing • Want to scramble down into the jaws of a crater? Several cinder cones in the San Francisco Volcanic Field are climbable. Two easily reached by dirt roads are **SP** and **Colton** craters. Drive 27 miles north of Flagstaff on U.S. 89, then turn west just below Hanks Trading Post at milepost 446. You'll see SP Crater directly ahead. Get a national forest map for specific directions.

"SP" is a tactful abbreviation for "S—-Pot," a tactless description of the crater's spattered rim by early ranchers. Actually, it's more attractive than that, with a nearly symmetrical cone. An 800-foot scramble will get you to the top. Colton Crater, south of SP, offers an easier climb—around 300 feet.

Red Mountain • This is a large, low-rise cindercone with a huge, fantastically-eroded crater that invites exploration. Drive 33 miles north on U.S. 180, then turn west onto a dirt road for a mile and a half. You can drive right to the base and enter the crater through an eroded cleft in the rim.

Schulz Pass scenic drive • Many roads extending into the national forest offer pleasant alpine vistas. Particularly pretty is Schulz Pass Road, a graded thoroughfare that branches to the east from U.S. 180 just above the Museum of Northern Arizona. It tucks in through the foothills of the San Francisco Peaks and joins U.S. 89 just south of the Sunset Crater National Monument turnoff.

WINTER SPORTS

DOWNHILL—Fairfield Snowbowl ● *P.O. Box 2430 (8 miles north on U.S. 180, then 6 miles northeast to the ski area); (800) 352-5777 in Arizona and (800) 526-1004 outside; locally (602) 779-1951 or 774-1863; snow reports (602) 779-4577.* Fairfield Snowbowl attracts skiers to its four chair lifts and 32 trails ranging from novice to advanced. Operating in conjunction with Fairfield Flagstaff Resort near downtown, it offers an assortment of lodging-skiing packages.

The ski area follows the downslope of the San Francisco Peaks, with a vertical drop of 2,300 feet. Facilities include group lessons, "Ski-wee" learning program for kids, equipment sales, rental and repair and baby-sitting. All-day lift tickets are $25; ski-boot-pole equipment package are $13, snowboards $15.

To ease parking, skiers can catch a $3 round trip shuttle from Fort Valley Lodge at the Highway 180 junction. The lodge serves as a base camp with light meals and sundry supplies. Cafes, bars and warming huts also function at the base of the ski area.

Ski Lift Lodge at U.S. 180 and Snowbowl Road (602) 774-0729, is the nearest lodging to the slopes. (See listing under "Where to Stay".)

Other snowbowl packages are offered by **Fairfield Flagstaff Resort**, (602) 526-3232 or (800) 352-5777 in Arizona and (800) 526-1004 outside; **Twilite Motel**, (602) 774-3364; **Evergreen Inn**, (602) 774-7356; **Days Inn**, (602) 774-5221; **Little America of Flagstaff**, (779-2741) or (800) 352-4386; and **Ramada Inn**, (602) 526-1150 or (800) 228-2828.

CROSS-COUNTRY—Flagstaff Nordic Center ● *Route 4, Box 958 (15 miles north on U.S. 180), Flagstaff, AZ 86001; (602) 774-6216. Adult all-day pass $6 on weekdays, $8 on weekends and holidays; kids 5-12 $3 on weekdays and $4 weekends and holidays; runs open 8 to 4:30.* Twenty-five miles of groomed trails lure beginner, intermediate and advanced Nordic skiers to Bob Alexander's cross-country center.

The facility, in Coconino National Forest, has a rental package for $12, pro shop, group and private lessons, moonlight tours, amateur ski races and other special events. A grill offers barbecued chicken, hamburgers, hotdogs and drinks from 11:30 to 2:30 weekends; dispensing machines keep skiers going the rest of the time.

Little America of Flagstaff, (602) 779-2741 or (800) 352-4386, offers a cross-country ski package.

WHERE TO SHOP

Business I-40 takes you through the heart of Flagstaff's shopping areas. Coming from the west, you'll be on Milton Road, then swing right onto Santa Fe Avenue; both are lined with shops and shopping centers. Downtown Flagstaff, the best place for curio and Indian crafts shops, is opposite the Amtrak station, around Santa Fe and Humphreys.

Fourth Street, north of Santa Fe Avenue in eastern Flagstaff, leads to a neighborhood shopping area. Flagstaff Mall, the town's large enclosed shopping center, is at the east end, off Santa Fe.

WHERE TO DINE

Alpine Spaghetti Station ● ∆∆ $

2400 E. Santa Fe (Fourth Street); (602) 779-4138. Italian; dinners $5 to $8; full bar. Daily 11 a.m. to 10 p.m. in summer; 4 to 10 the rest of the year. MC/VISA, AMEX. A cozy cottage-style cafe, it offers an abundance of Italian atmosphere with its pizzas, lasagna, manicotti and fettucini.

Black Bart's Steakhouse ● ∆∆∆ $$

2760 E. Butler (I-40 exit 198; across from Little America); (602) 779-3142. American; dinners $9 to $23; full bar. Sunday-Thursday 5 to 9 p.m., Friday-Saturday 5 to 10. Reservations advised; MC/VISA, AMEX. This busy Western-themed complex includes a restaurant, dinner theater, saloon with bat-wing doors, RV park (listed below) and adjacent antique shop. Singing waiters entertain diners in the rustic barnwood interior; dinner-theater variety shows are scheduled in summer.

Charly's Restaurant and Pub ● ∆∆ $$ ∅

23 North Leroux (downtown, a block north of the train station); (602) 779-1919. American/Southwestern; dinners $6 to $19; full bar. Lunch 11 to 2 daily, breakfast 8 to 12 weekends; dinner Monday-Saturday 6 to 10 in summer and Thursday-Saturday 6 to 10 the rest of the year. Reservations advised; MC/VISA, AMEX. Located in the 1897 Weatherford Hotel, Charly's offers Old World decor and a menu featuring steak, seafood, chicken, Navajo tacos and other Southwestern specialties.

Cottage Place ● ∆∆∆ $$$

126 W. Cottage Ave. (downtown, near Beaver Street); (602) 774-8431. Continental; dinners $14 to $22; wine and beer. Tuesday-Saturday 5 p.m. to 10 p.m. Reservations advised; MC/VISA, AMEX. Housed in a refurbished old cottage, this charming restaurant features such continental fare as scampi, veal Regina, Turkish style braised lamb and chateaubriand.

Crazy Bill's Steakhouse ● ∆∆∆ $

3130 E. Santa Fe Ave. (near Pony Soldier Motel, east end); (602) 526-4752. Western; dinners $6 to $11; full bar. Daily 10 a.m. to 1 a.m. Reservations advised on weekends; MC/VISA. This funky, lively Western-style cafe features steak, seafood and barbecued ribs and chicken. It's one of Flagstaff's better restaurant bargains and it offers an excellent, spicy beef jerky. The adjoining saloon is a popular sports bar.

El Chilito Restaurant ● ∆∆ $ ∅

1551 Milton Road (half mile north of I-17/I-40 interchange); (602) 774-4666. Mexican; dinners $5 to $8; full bar. Daily 11:30 a.m. to 11 p.m. Reservations suggested; MC/VISA, AMEX. A Mexican restaurant with a modern look, El Chilito also features Southwest fare.

The Clark House ● ∆∆∆ $$$ ∅

503 N. Humphreys (W. Elm Street, near downtown); (602) 774-1343. French-Italian; dinners $9 to $16; full bar. Lunch daily 11:30 to 3, dinner Sunday-Thursday 5 to 9 and Friday-Saturday 5 to 10. Reservations essential; MC/VISA, AMEX. Housed in a 1911 tufa-stone home, the Clark House combines an elegant setting with a Continental menu. Furnished with period antiques, this Craftsman bungalow is listed on the National Register of Historic Places.

Fiddlers Restaurant & Lounge ● ∆∆∆ $$ ∅

702 S. Milton (at Highway 66 downtown); (602) 774-6689. American; dinners $6 to $25; full bar. Lunch Monday-Friday 11:30 to 2:30, dinner daily

5 to 10. *Reservations advised; MC/VISA, AMEX.* Modern, upscale Fiddlers features prime rib, charbroiled steak, seafood, chops and pasta. There's live music on weekends in the adjoining cocktail lounge.

Horsemen Lodge ● △△△ $$

North Highway 89 (three miles north of Flagstaff Mall); (602) 526-2655. American; dinners $10 to $18; full bar. Monday-Saturday 5 to 10 p.m. Reservations advised; MC/VISA. This ranch-style log and stone restaurant trimmed with knotty pine, Navajo blankets and hunting trophies, is a popular local favorite. The American country menu focuses on fresh trout, steak and oak pit barbecued chicken and ribs. A huge fieldstone fireplace is a nice spot for before-dinner drinks.

Kelly's Christmas Tree Restaurant ● △△△ $$ ∅

1903 Second Street (Second Avenue, near downtown); (602) 779-5888. American; dinners $7 to $18; full bar. Lunch Tuesday-Friday 11:30 to 2, dinner Tuesday-Sunday from 5:30 (closed Monday). Reservations advised; MC/VISA, AMEX. This comely restaurant with an early American look and a light touch of Christmas trim features an "Americana" menu. Offerings include chicken and dumplings, chicken curry, barbecued pork ribs, prime rib and such. Live entertainment is featured in the new cocktail lounge.

Mandarin Gardens Restaurant ● △△ $$

3518 E. Santa Fe (east end, in the Park Santa Fe Shopping Center); (602) 526-5033. Northern Chinese; dinners $8 to $15; wine and beer. Monday-Saturday 11 a.m. to 9 p.m., Sunday 4 to 9 p.m. MC/VISA. This simply-decorated restaurant serves tasty examples of the spicy fare of Hunan, Szechuan, Mongolia and other Mandarin foods.

Mason Jar Restaurant ● △△ $$ ∅

2610 E. Santa Fe Avenue (Five Flags Inn, listed below); (602) 526-1399. American; dinners $6.25 to $11.75; full bar. Daily 6 a.m. to 10 p.m. Major credit cards. Early American decor provides a homey atmosphere: print wallpaper, tulip chandeliers and—a cute touch—mason jars filled with colored beans as table decorations. The menu matches the theme, offering "home-style" regional American dishes.

WHERE TO SLEEP

Best Western Kings House ● △△ $$$ ∅

1560 E. Santa Fe Ave (I-40 exit 198, east of downtown), Flagstaff, AZ 86001; (602) 774-7186 or (800) 528-1234. Doubles $60 to $70, singles $55 to $65; lower off-season rates. Major credit cards. TV movies, room phones, pool, free continental breakfast.

Best Western Pony Soldier ● △△△ $$$ ∅

3030 E. Santa Fe (near Kachina Square Shopping Center), Flagstaff, AZ 86004; (602) 526-2388 or (800) 528-1234. Doubles $68, singles $55, suites $85 to $95; lower in the off-season. Major credit cards. TV movies, room phones, pool, fireside lounge. **Afton House Restaurant** serves American and Chinese fare 6 a.m. to 10 p.m., dinners $4 to $15, full bar.

Comfort Inn ● △△ $$$ ∅

914 S. Milton Road (I-40 exit 195B, then a mile north), Flagstaff, AZ 86001; (602) 774-7326 or (800) 221-2222. Singles and doubles $54 to $59; lower in the off-season. Major credit cards. TV movies, room phones, pool; free use of adjacent fitness center.

Evergreen Inn • ∆∆ $$ ∅
1008 E. Santa Fe Ave. (downtown) Flagstaff, AZ 86004; (602) 774-7356. Doubles $39 to $55, singles $29 to $49, kitchenettes and suites $55 to $75; lower in the off-season. Major credit cards. TV, room phones, pool.

Five Flags Inn • ∆∆∆ $$$ ∅
2610 E. Santa Fe Ave. (Country Club Drive off-ramp from I-40); Flagstaff, AZ 86004; (602) 526-1399. Doubles $42 to $65, singles $38 to $61, kitchenettes $85 to $115; lower in the off-season. MC/VISA. TV movies, room phones, pool; winter ski packages. Mason Jar Restaurant (listed above).

Ramada Flagstaff/Grand Canyon • ∆∆∆ $$$ ∅
2320 E. Lucky Lane (Butler exit from I-40), Flagstaff, AZ 86004; (602) 526-1150. Doubles $68 to $78, singles $62 to $72, suites $130 to $160; lower October 15 to April 15. Major credit cards. TV movies, room phones, pool, spa, airport service, ski packages, golf and tennis available. **Humphreys Restaurant**, 6 a.m. to 10 p.m., serving American fare, $6 to $12 for dinner; non-smoking areas.

Ski Lift Lodge • ∆ $$
Highway 180 and Snow Bowl Road. (Route 4, Box 957) Flagstaff, AZ 86001; (602) 774-0729. Doubles $48 to $56; singles $44 to $52; lower rates October 1 to March 1. MC/VISA, AMEX. Special ski packages with lodging and all-day lift tickets. This small complex includes a restaurant, lounge, ski rental shop and liquor store. **Restaurant** hours are 6 a.m. to 9 p.m.; it serves home-style American fare, dinners $5 to $12.

TraveLodge I-40 • ∆∆∆ $$$ ∅
2520 E. Lucky Lane (Butler Avenue exit from I-40), Flagstaff, AZ 86004; (602) 779-5121 or (800) 255-3050. Doubles $54 to $59, singles $45 to $49, kitchenettes $57 to $62; lower off-season rates. Major credit cards. TV movies, room phones, pool, refrigerators and microwaves in some rooms, spa.

University Inn • ∆∆ $$ ∅
602 Mikes Pike (off Milton Road, across from university campus), Flagstaff, AZ 86001; (602) 774-4581 or (800) 654-4667. Doubles $35 to $40, singles $25 to $30, kitchenettes and suites $65 to $85. MC/VISA, AMEX. TV movies, room phones, spa, lounge. **Coffee shop** serving American fare, 6:30 a.m. to 9 p.m.; dinners $4 to $10; no-smoking areas.

BED & BREAKFAST INNS

Dirker House Bed & Breakfast • *423 W. Cherry (Park), Flagstaff, AZ 86001; (602) 774-3249. From $40 per couple and $26 per person; full breakfast. No smoking indoors.* European-style comforts in a restored early 20th century home; furnished with antiques.

Birch Tree Inn • *824 W. Birch (Toltec, off Santa Fe), Flagstaff, AZ 86001; (602) 774-1042. From $60 to $75 per couple; full breakfast. No smoking indoors.* Period furnishings in a restored 1917 home with a colonnaded porch; billiard room; off-street parking; afternoon wine or tea.

Red's Bed & Breakfast • *2217 N. Talkington Dr. (off Fort Valley Road near Museum of Northern Arizona), Flagstaff, AZ 86001; (602) 774-7851. $30 to $45 per couple; full breakfast. No smoking indoors.* All private baths, outside deck (breakfast served there in summer), afternoon wine.

WHERE TO CAMP

Black Bart's RV Park • *2760 E. Butler (Butler exit off I-40), Flagstaff, AZ 86004; (602) 774-1912 or (800) 774-1912. RV and a few tent sites, full* *hookups $16, tents $10. reservations accepted; MC/VISA.* Flush potties, coin laundry, groceries; restaurant (listed above) and antique shop nearby.

Flagstaff KOA ● *5803 N. Highway 89 (exit 201 off I-40, then three stoplights north on U.S. 89), Flagstaff, AZ 86004; (602) 526-9926. RV and tent sites, full hookups $18, water and electric or no hookups $17. Reservations accepted; MC/VISA and DISC.* Coin laundry, showers $4, groceries, Propane, dump station; planned summer recreational activities, playground, cookouts, hiking trails.

Fort Tuthill County Park ● *U.S. 89A (take Fort Tuthill exit from I-17 south of Flagstaff); (602) 774-5139. RV and tent sites, no hookups $6. No reservations or credit cards.* Open from May 15 to September 15 only; barbecues and picnic tables, play area, nature trails, racquetball courts.

J and H RV Park ● *7901 N. Highway 89 (three miles north), Flagstaff, AZ 86004; (602) 526-1829. RV sites, full hookups $10, no hookups $8. Reservations accepted; MC/VISA.* Flush potties, showers, barbecue grills and picnic tables, horseshoe pits, small store.

Munds Park RV Campground ● *P.O. Box J (Munds Park exit, 18 miles south on I-17, Munds Park, AZ 86017; (602) 286-1309. RV and tent sites, full hookups $16, tents $13. Reservations accepted; MC/VISA.* Flush potties and showers, coin laundry, groceries, pool, spa, recreation room, playground.

NORTH TOWARD THE GRAND CANYON

Heading north of Flagstaff on U.S. 89 or northwest on U.S. 180, you climb quickly into the foothills of the San Francisco Peaks. Both routes skirt the edge of the range and travel across semi-arid expanses of the Colorado Plateau.

But the peaks seem to stay with you, lurking in your rearview mirror. Wherever you travel in north central Arizona, you see this mighty mountain cluster, like a mystery ship floating on the horizon. The main peaks—Humphreys, Fremont, Doyle and Agassiz—are craggy remnants of a million-year-old volcano that may have jutted 15,000 feet skyward. Scattered about their flanks are more recent cinder cones and lava flows.

Wupatki & Sunset Crater National Monuments

A few miles north of Flagstaff, you'll encounter two national monuments on this semi-arid downslope. Although each has its own identity and visitor center, they're jointly administered by the National Park Service, with an office at 2717 N. Steves Blvd., Suite 3, Flagstaff, AZ 86004.

Sunset Crater National Monument ● *Twelve miles north on U.S. 89, then east; (602) 527-7042. Visitor center open daily 8 to 5; $3 per car (includes admission to Wupatki). Bonito Campground near the visitor center is operated by the U.S. Forest service; water, no hookups, $7; open late spring through early fall.* You have to look for it, but in the right light, the bold brown cindercone of Sunset Crater has an orange-red cast to it, and thus the name. Tinged by iron oxide, it's the centerpiece of a starkly beautiful volcanic area.

Although Sunset Crater last erupted more than 700 years ago, the klinkery, jagged lava fields look as if they were deposited just last week. Scrub ponderosas share the lava landscape with assorted desert fauna. A few aspens contribute brilliant fall yellow to the stark moon-like landscape.

Wukoki ruin at Wupatki National Monument.

Sinagua, Anasazi and Cohonina Indians once occupied this arid lands, building hilltop pueblos and pit houses and tilling the rough soil. Sunset Crater's eruption obviously sent them scurrying for shelter. Hundreds of ruins have been found in the area, mostly in present-day Wupatki National Monument to the north.

The visitor center features exhibits on vulcanism in general and Sunset Crater's formation about eight centuries ago. Films of Hawaii's Kilauea eruption convey the drama that the startled Indians must have experienced. Ranger programs and hikes are conducted in and about the visitor center, mostly in summer.

Beyond the visitor center, a one-mile loop trail near the base of Sunset Crater offers a first-hand study of vulcanism at work. You can't climb the crater itself, but hiking is permitted on Lenox Crater, a smaller cinder cone about a mile east of the visitor center.

Outside the park, you can drive almost to the top of **O'Leary Peak**, then hike the rest of the way. A lava dome nearly 9,000 feet high, it offers impressive views of the surrounding landscape. If the climb intimidates your vehicle, you can park and hike the last mile. Views of the peaks and lava fields are worth the effort.

As you motor northeast through the monument, heading for Wupatki, pause at the Painted Desert Overlook for a view of the color-banded peaks, mesas and badlands on the distant horizon. Picnic tables may entice you to take a lunch break.

Wupatki National Monument ● *Fourteen miles north of Sunset Crater; (602) 527-7040. Visitor center open daily 8 to 5; $3 per car (includes admission to Sunset Crater).* Wupatki is home to one of the Southwest's largest and most intriguing Indian ruins. Wupatki Pueblo, a short walk from the visitor center, is a four-story, 100-room village created from Moencopi sandstone building blocks.

Nearby is an oval "ball court" and an amphitheater whose functions still puzzle scientists. The ball court resembles those of Mexico's Mayan and Toltec cultures, but did they play road games this far north?

In a rare show of congeniality, the Sinagua, Anasazi and Cohonina shared farming and construction methods and even intermarried. Through this mosaic of cultures, they developed one of the most advanced societies of their day. They abandoned the area in the 13th century.

Although Wupatki is the monument's largest ruin, hundreds more are scattered about this lava plain. This is one of the intrigues of the area. If you first register at the visitor center, you can get off by yourself and explore several unexplored ruins, perhaps pretending you're an archaeologist who's just tripped over a rare find. Of course, you are expected to mind your archaeological manners and disturb nothing you see.

Wupatki Pueblo's rooms can't be entered because of its heavy visitor traffic, but you may probe into several less popular sites. You can poke around the roof-less rooms of **Wukoki** Pueblo, just beyond the visitor center. **The Citadel** is a toppled-over ruin occupying a low butte. Vertical rows of slate-thin sandstone indicate where walls have collapsed. **Lomaki** is our favorite discovery in the monument. Remarkably well-preserved, it's tucked into the protective walls of a small canyon. Some of the homes were built on the canyon rim, complete with view balconies.

Leaving Wupatki and continuing north on U.S. 89, you enter the Navajo Reservation that occupies a husky chunk of northeastern Arizona. The communities of **Gray Mountain** and **Cameron** offer gasoline, modest-priced motels, restaurants and gift shops featuring souvenirs and local Indian crafts.

Cameron is particularly interesting, dating back to 1916 as a Navajo trading post. Sitting near the junction of U.S. 89 and State Highway 64, it's a popular stopover for Grand Canyon visitors; the park's Desert View area is 57 miles away. A large curio shop occupies the stone and brick main building, with pole ceilings and whitewashed walls.

Cameron Trading Post ● *P.O. Box 339, Cameron, AZ 86020; (602) 679-2231. Motel rates are $40 double and $30 single. Overnight at the RV park, with hookups, is $12.60; MC/VISA.* A woodsy-looking restaurant beyond the curio shop is set off by a large fireplace and an unusual pressed tin ceiling. The area also has a post office, art gallery and an RV park.

Little Colorado River Gorge Navajo Tribal Park ● *12 miles east of Cameron on Highway 64.* Whether you're canyon-bound or not, you might drive a few miles up Highway 64 to catch splendid vistas of the Little Colorado River's sheer-walled gorges. Signs mark two canyon-view turnouts. One viewpoint features a large outdoor market of Navajo jewelry, blankets and other crafts. Smaller versions of these markets are scattered along U.S. 89 and State Highway 64 within the reservation.

WEST TO SELIGMAN

Interstate 40 hurries through roadside stands of ponderosas as it heads west toward Williams, Ash Fork and Seligman. All were early stops along the Santa Fe Railway and old Highway 66. (See box.) Historic 66 parallels I-

40 for a few miles out of Flagstaff, then it disappears under the new freeway and re-appears at Ash Fork.

The first town of any consequence on this route is a community which, in setting and temperament, is sort of a mini-Flagstaff.

Williams

Elevation: 6,752 feet   **Population: 2,500**

Like Flagstaff, Williams is rimmed by a national forest—Kaibab, in this instance. It's nearly as high as Flagstaff—6,762 feet, but it's much smaller, with a population of 2,500 or so.

At 58 miles, Williams is the closest town to the Grand Canyon's South Rim, and the chamber likes to boast about that. In fact, it calls itself the **Williams-Grand Canyon Chamber of Commerce**. The office is near the west end of town at 820 Bill Williams Avenue. It's open daily from 8 a.m. to 5 p.m.

Because of this canyon proximity, the town is top-heavy with motels. There were about 25 at last count, lining the parallel one-way thorough-fares—Bill Williams Avenue and Railroad Avenue. The small business district is caught in a pleasant 1930s time-warp. Other than the new motels, it has changed little from the days when it was an important pause on the Santa Fe Railway and old Route 66.

Like most communities along this route, Williams was put on the map by the early railway. Cattle ranching began in the late 1870s, then the coming

---

GETTING YOUR HISTORICAL KICKS

There was a time, in the 1960s, when we were humming Bobby Troupe's *Get your kicks on Route 66*. We watched the weekly adventures of two young men who traveled that historic highway in their Corvette. (I never did figure out where they put their luggage.)

Like the Santa Fe Railway before it, U.S. Highway 66 tied Chicago to Los Angeles. It provided a pathway for generations of tourists and migrants who flocked to the sunny Southwest. Now, most of the old highway has disappeared under the multi-lane asphalt of I-40; towns along its route have been bypassed.

The last section was decommissioned as a federal highway when the freeway link between Kingman and Flagstaff was completed in the 1980s. A weepy little ceremony was held in Williams in October of 1894, with Troupe in attendance.

Some of the bypassed towns, like Topock, Oatman, Hackberry, Truxton and Peach Springs, went to sleep. Those near I-40 interchanges, such as Kingman, Seligman, Ash Fork, Williams and Flagstaff, survive in varying degrees of prosperity.

The longest remaining stretch of the old route is between Ash Fork and Kingman. **Historic Route 66 Association of Arizona** was formed to call attention to the highway and encourage preservation of its towns. For a route map and brochure, contact the group at P.O. Box 66, Kingman, AZ 86402; (602) 753-5001.

If you grow weary of high-speed eighteen-wheelers on busy I-40, you may find it pleasant to take this parallel road. Pause along the way to explore the sleeping hamlets that once got their kicks along Route 6-6.

of the rails in the 1880s spurred the local timber industry and the town began growing.

The settlement takes its name from a randy old mountain man and guide, Bill Williams, who prowled these parts for a quarter of a century until Ute Indians got to him in 1849. To honor his spirit, townfolk dress up as Bill Williams Mountain Men and Shady Ladies. They stage frontier-style celebrations over Memorial Day and Labor Day weekends.

Kaibab National Forest office is downtown office at 501 W. Bill Williams Avenue, Williams, AZ 86046; (602) 635-2676. Another office is on the western edge town; follow signs on the I-40 frontage road. Both are open weekdays only, from 7:30 to 4. You can learn about the area's forest service campgrounds, hiking trails and such at these offices. Maps of the southern section and northern section (essentially the Grand Canyon North Rim area) of the forest are on sale for $2 each.

Worthy of exploration is **Sycamore Canyon**, virtually unknown compared to Sedona's Oak Creek Canyon, but nearly as attractive. To get there, drive south from town on Fourth Street; after eight miles, turn left onto Forestry Road 110 and follow it 15 miles to its end. From Sycamore Canyon Point, you'll get an awesome view of the canyon and the alpine countryside. The 11-mile Sycamore Trail provides a more intimate exploration of this area.

ATTRACTIONS, ACTIVITIES & SUCH

Grand Canyon Railway • *Historic steam train rides between Williams and Grand Canyon Village. 518 E. Bill Williams Ave., Williams, AZ 86046; (800) THE-TRAIN or (602) 635-4000. Adult round-trip $47; kids 12 and under $23; plus $2 park admission. Major credit cards.* Using vintage steam equipment, Grand Canyon Railway has resumed the historic run from Williams to the park that began in 1901. From April through September, two trains depart daily from Williams 8 and 10 a.m., then leave Grand Canyon Village at 2:30 and 4:30 p.m. From March 1 to 31 and from October through December, a single train departs Williams daily at 10 and leaves the Grand Canyon at 4:30. There is no service in January and February. (See "Activities" under Grand Canyon South Rim in Chapter 2 for more details.)

Broken Spoke Stage Line • *635-4061* offers horse-drawn tours of Williams in the summer for $3 per person for $5 per couple. The firm also does hay rides, so bring your Seldane.

Fray Marcos Hotel and Williams Depot • *518 E. Bill Williams Ave., downtown.* The firm that re-activated historic steam train rides between Williams and the Grand Canyon (see above) renovated the venerable Fray Marcos Hotel in 1989-90 as its depot and Grand Canyon Railway Museum. One of the original Harvey Houses, the Fray Marcos was completed in 1908 as the first poured concrete building in Arizona. Naturally, it's been elevated to the National Register of Historic Places. The museum, which is free, displays artifacts and photos of early railroading, mining, ranching, logging, plus a display on the Fred Harvey Company.

Grand Canyon Deer Farm • *100 Deer Farm Road (eight miles east, just off I-40), Williams, AZ 86046; (602) 635-4073. Daily from 9 a.m. to dusk in spring and fall, 8 a.m. to dusk in summer, 10 to 5 in winter (subject to weather conditions). Adults $3.95, kids 3 to 12 $2; MC/VISA.* Who can resist all those doe-eyed deer strolling about their pine-shaded enclosure? You can pet and feed a regiment of spotted fallow deer and axis deer, along with assorted antelope, sheep and goats (stay downwind of the latter). A few volunteer Abert squirrels, an emu from Australia and a bored-looking buffalo complete the menagerie. It's a clean, well run operation, fronted by a large souvenir shop and snack bar in a big red barn. Naturally, you can buy critter food.

ANNUAL EVENTS

May Rendevous Days, Memorial Day Weekend; **Arizona High School Rodeo,** first weekend in June; **Cowboy Shooting Competition and Encampment,** mid-July; **Cowpunchers Reunion Rodeo**, first weekend in August.

WHERE TO SHOP

Downtown Williams is rather compact, focused along Bill Williams Avenue, which parallels I-40. Most commercial growth—what little there is—will be found in the eastern end.

WHERE TO DINE

Parker House Restaurant ΔΔ $ ∅
525 W. Bill Williams Ave. (west end I-40 interchange); (602) 635-4590. American; dinners $5 to $9; no alcohol. Daily 6 a.m. to 9:30 p.m. MC/VISA, AMEX. A few Mexican dishes are mixed in the the American menu. Try some of the inexpensive lunch specials.

Old Smoky's Restaurant ΔΔΔ $ ∅
624 W. Bill Williams (near west end interchange); (602) 635-2091. American; breakfast and lunch only, Monday-Saturday 6 a.m. to 2 p.m. and Sunday 6 to 1. From $4 to $9. MC/VISA. It's Williams' most funkily charming restaurant. The interior is frontier West and the waitstaff scampers about in coonskin caps. Breakfasts have a spicy Mexican accent; there's also a large assortment of waffles. Lunches include assorted hamburgers and other sandwiches. Try the homemade bakery goods, such as cinnamon raisin, banana nut, zucchini and pumpkin raisin breads.

Rod's Steakhouse ΔΔ $$
301 E. Bill Williams Ave. (Slagle); (602) 635-2671. American; dinners from $8 to $16; full bar. Daily 11 a.m. to 10 p.m. MC/VISA, DISC. Featuring a cozy, warm-wood dining room with flagstone tile, this attractive restaurant focuses on mesquite-broiled steak and prime rib, with a couple of chicken and chop items.

WHERE TO SLEEP

Days Inn of Williams ΔΔΔ $$$$ ∅
2488 W. Bill Williams Ave. (at west interchange), Williams, AZ 86046; (602) 635-4051 or (800) 325-2525. Doubles $86 to $96, singles $66 to $76, suites $95 to $135; lower in the off-season. Major credit cards. New motel with TV movies, free in-room coffee, room phones, indoor pool and spa. **Denny's Restaurant** is adjacent, serving dinners from $4 to $10, open 24 hours, full bar.

Mountain Side Inn ΔΔΔ $$$
642 E. Bill Williams Ave. (east interchange, just north of freeway); Williams, AZ 86046; (602) 635-4431. Singles and doubles $63 to $75; lower in the off-season. Major credit cards. In a pleasant foothills setting; TV, room

phones, pool. The **Dining Car Restaurant** opened in mid-1990; American, dinners from $7 to $19; 6 a.m. to 10 p.m. full bar.

Norris Motel ΔΔ $$ ∅

1001 W. Bill Williams Ave. (P.O. Box 388), Williams, AZ 86046; (602) 635-2202. Doubles $38 to $46, singles $38; lower in the off-season. MC/VISA, AMEX. TV, room phones, some refrigerators, indoor spa.

WHERE TO CAMP

Circle Pines KOA • *1000 Circle Pines Rd. (near I-10 exit 167); Williams, AZ 86046; (602) 635-4545. Tent and RV sites, full hookups $13.95; also "Kamping Kabins" $20 per couple. Reservations accepted; MC/VISA.* Pull-through sites, flush potties, showers, disposal station, coin laundry, groceries and Propane; indoor pool and spa, recreation room, playground. Pancake breakfasts and nightly outdoor stake fry from June through August.

Grand Canyon KOA • *North Highway 64, Williams, AZ 86046; 635-2307. Tent and RV sites, full hookups, $13.50; also "Kamping Kabins" $20 per couple. Reservations accepted; VISA/MC.* Flush potties, coin laundry, groceries, Propane. Situated on State Highway 64, seven miles northeast of Williams and 52 miles south of Grand Canyon National Park. It offers amenities such as free movies, hay rides and "cowboy steak dinners" in summer; an indoor pool and spa, grocery and gift shop.

Ash Fork

Elevation: 5,140 feet   **Population: 650**

From Williams, I-40 drops from pine forests to a high prairie and skirts the hamlet of Ash Fork. A large flagstone tile company is this burg's primary industry. It also catches a few tourists for meals, gas and overnight stops. Several motels line the main street; some are rather scruffy. Here's a couple that aren't.

WHERE TO SLEEP

Stage Coach Motel • Δ $$ ∅

823 Park Avenue (west end), Ash Fork, AZ 86320; (602) 637-2278. Doubles from $30 to $45, singles from $22 to $30; lower off-season rates. MC/VISA, AMEX. TV movies.

Ash Fork Inn • ΔΔ $$

Ash Fork, AZ 86320 (west end); (602) 637-2511. Singles and doubles $31.60. Major credit cards. TV movies, room phones, 24-hour restaurant.

For dining, you might try **Ted's Bullpen Restaurant** at the east end of town. It's a big trucker's hangout with hearty American fare, open 24 hours. There's also a service station (with diesel, obviously) and general store. **Little Fat Lady Restaurant** next to the Ash Fork Inn, serves inexpensive American and Mexican food, with beer and wine; MC/VISA.

WHERE TO CAMP

Ash Fork Grand Canyon KOA • *P.O. Box 357 (Ninth and Pine, at freeway exits 144 or 146), Ash Fork, AZ 86320; (602) 637-2521. Tent and RV sites, full hookups $15.50, water and electric $14, tents $10, Kamper Kabins $20. Reservations accepted, MC/VISA.* Flush potties, showers, coin laundry, groceries, snackbar, Propane, dump station. Shaded sites with playground, VCR movie rental, free coffee.

Seligman

Elevation: 5,250 feet   **Population: 600**

Continuing west (either on I-40 or old Highway 66), you'll breeze into the little pretend Western town of Seligman, which has been around since 1886. A mock-up of false front stores stands beside a good old boy bar called the **OK Saloon**. The saloon is real; the fake storefronts cleverly disguise a corral. Beside it is an old jail that supposedly contained Three-Fingered Jack, Jim Younger and—good grief!—even Seligman Slim.

Who?

WHERE TO SLEEP

Navajo Motel ● △ $$

500 W. Chino, Seligman, AZ 86337; (602) 422-3204. Doubles $32 to $37, singles $24 to $32. MC/VISA, AMEX. TV movies, room phones.

Romney Motel ● △ $$

155 W. Chino, Seligman, AZ 86337; (602) 422-3394. Doubles $25 to $40, singles $21 to $25; MC/VISA. TV, room phones.

Catch a meal at the **Copper Cart** on the east end of town, open 6 a.m. to 10 p.m., serving the usual steaks, chicken and chops for $5 to $12; Beer and wine; MC/VISA. Near the west end is **Mr. J's Coffee Shop**, similar hours, similar menu but a bit cheaper than the Cart; no alcohol; MC/VISA.

You can camp at the **Northern Arizona Campground** near the OK Saloon and Corral. It's scruffy but clean, offering showers, coin laundry and a store with groceries, a fast-food counter and Indian curios. It's $11.55 with full hookups, $8 for dry-camping.

EAST TOWARD A BIG HOLE IN THE GROUND

Two important lures draw tourists west of Flagstaff on I-40. Not far from town is one of our favorite Arizona Indian ruins, Walnut Canyon National Monument. About 40 miles beyond is Meteor Crater, where a stony visitor slammed into the earth 49,500 years ago. Another ten miles gets us to that "takin' it easy" town of pop music fame—Winslow, Arizona.

Heading east, you'll soon put Coconino's forests behind, and you won't see another serious stand of timber along I-40.

Walnut Canyon National Monument ● *Walnut Canyon Road (Seven miles east on I-40, then three miles south), Flagstaff, AZ 86004; (602) 526-3367. Daily from 8 to 5, the Island Trail closes at 4; $1 per person or $3 per family.* About 800 years ago, a band of Sinagua Indians found an idyllic home, deep in the sheltering recesses of Walnut Canyon. They mysteriously departed around 1250, leaving behind a fine set of cliff condos.

Recessed in overhangs between the rim and floor of the canyon, the dwellings can be reached by a 251-step trail from the visitor center. Keep that number in mind as you start back up. The path past two dozen ruins is called the Island trail, since many of the relics are on a free-standing ridge in the middle of the canyon.

We like to visit the ravine late in the day, when most of the others have gone and slanting light bathes the ruddy adobe niches. We can retreat to the shade of one of the dwellings and ponder how the Sinagua passed their days half a millennium ago.

The interpretive center, perched dramatically on the rim, offers a picture-window view of the rock-ribbed, forested canyon. It also provides a quick

Sinagua dwellings tucked into Walnut Canyon.

study of the Sinagua and the geology of the area. There's a good selection of natural history books available as well. Rangers conduct walks and talks daily in the summer and on weekends at 11 and 2 in the off-season. A half-mile rim trail provides impressive views of the narrow chasm.

Meteor Crater ● *Forty miles east of Flagstaff to Meteor Crater exit, then six miles south c/o; Meteor Crater Enterprises, 603 N. Beaver, Suite C, Flagstaff, AZ 86001; (602) 774-8350. Daily from 6 a.m. to 6 p.m. in summer, 7 to 5 from mid-September to mid-November, 8 to 5 mid-November to mid-March and 7 to 5 mid-March to mid-May. (You get all that?) Adults $6; seniors $5; kids 12 to 17, $2; 5 to 11, $1.*

Imagine this: A monster chunk of nickel and iron weighing millions of tons streaks earthward at 43,000 miles an hour. It slams into the earth with a force that buries fragments hundreds of feet deep. Most of the mass explodes into a gaseous cloud that flattens trees and kills every living thing for miles around. When the dust settles, an impact crater 560 feet deep and nearly a mile across steams silently on the broad plain.

Operators of the privately-owned Meteor Crater have done an outstanding job preserving and interpreting this awesome hole in the ground. A large visitor center perched on the rim houses a fine astrogeology museum, where graphic illustrations portray the meteor's lethal impact. Studying the exhibits brings to mind the dust cloud theory of dinosaur extinction. The museum also provides a quick study of space exploration, exhibiting a space capsule, space suits, photos, badges and other regalia of every American space flight. Videos teach visitors about the mysteries of the world beyond. One particularly moving film is dedicated to the lost crew of the Challenger space shuttle.

In order to protect the site, visitors aren't allowed to hike down into the depression. But you can take the mile and a half walk around the rim. Get to the visitor center at least an hour before closing time if you want to do the loop, and allow another hour to study exhibits in the museum.

The best-preserved impact crater in the world, this site has been used by astronauts to get a feel of outer-world terrain. When the great depression was first discovered in 1871, folks thought it was of volcanic origin. Philadelphia mining engineer Daniel Moreau Barringer spent the last 25 years of his life in an obsessive quest to prove that the crater had been caused by a meteor impact. It was finally accepted by the scientific community when he died in 1929.

Meteor Crater RV Park ● *Meteor Crater turnoff from I-40 (c/o 603 N. Beaver St., Suite C, Flagstaff, AZ 86001); (602) 282-4002. RV and tent sites, full hookups $24, water and electric $12, no hookups $10.* Coin laundry, free showers, individual bathrooms, play area, mini-golf, horse shoes, service station.

Winslow

Elevation: 4,856 feet   **Population: 8,500**

From a 49,500-year-old hole in the ground, we move to lures of somewhat more recent vintage. Winslow is an old-fashioned town of 8,000 residents, with a sturdy brick business district. Nearby are considerably older villages—the Homol'ovi ruins of the ancient Anasazi.

The railroad gave birth to the town in 1882 and it thrived as a cattle and freight center. Today, it touts its position in the center of things touristy. Chamber officials point out that Winslow is central to Northern Arizona's tourist lures, from the Meteor Crater to the Navajo and Hopi lands to the north east.

The **Chamber of Commerce Visitor Center,** is at 300 W. North Road (at the central I-40 interchange), Winslow, AZ 86407; (602) 289-2434; open Monday-Saturday, 8 a.m. to 5 p.m. In addition to tourist information, it features a small museum with a diorama depicting area Indians, early white settlers and Arizona points of interest. Look for a totem and railway caboose outside.

We like this little Western town, and it offers a good selection of motels for those who want to pause.

ATTRACTIONS

Homol'ovi Ruins State Park ● *North one-half mile on State Highway 87 from I-40, then west on a dirt road.* If you enjoy exploring untouched archaeological sites, far from tourist crowds, you'll like Homol'ovi Ruins State Park. Anasazi clans did their thing here from the 13th to 16th centuries. The ruins are along a dirt but easily navigable road just north and west of Winslow.

No highway sign marks the route, but if you take the first dirt road left from Highway 87 after leaving the freeway interchange, you'll find the ruins. After a mile, a sign will assure you that you're on the right track.

The first ruin is on the left, about two miles in. It's little more than a low mesa with tell-tale ridges of collapsed flagstone walls. Hundreds of potsherds are scattered about. It's intriguing to pick up what seems to be a

Little Painted Desert above Winslow.

sandstone fragment, then see a wavy dark line painted by a steady hand 600 years ago. Now, put it back where you found it!

Homol'ovi II is 3.5 miles beyond the first ruin. Park in a small box canyon and hike through a draw to this hilltop pueblo. A sign tells you that this collapsed city once held 800 rooms. It likely was an important regional center for trading food, stone tools, pottery and turquoise. One small area has been restored but the rest has been left as the archaeologists first found it. Sadly, the ruin is riddled with pits dug by vandalizing pot-hunters.

Little Painted Desert County Park ● *Just off State Highway 87, 13 miles north of Winslow; gates open from 8 a.m. to 9 p.m. Flush potties and picnic ramada.* This is a surprising jewel of a park—a mini-badlands of softly contoured, pastel-hued sandstone. From a parking area, you can drive or walk along rim roads in either direction for varied vistas of this fluted amphitheater of erosion.

A trail from the north rim road takes you into this sensuously rounded landscape; railroad ties help you keep your footing as you descend from a shallow cliff edge. Plan your Little Painted Desert visit in the early morning or late afternoon. The light and shadow effects on the russet, tawny green and gray ridges and ravines are awesome.

Old Trails Museum ● *212 Kinsley Ave. (between Second and Third), Winslow, AZ 86047; (602) 289-5861. Tuesday-Sunday 3 to 7 p.m. June through October; closed the rest of the year. Free admission, donations accepted.* This small storefront museum in downtown Winslow has pictures and artifacts of the area's Native Americans, railroading, mining, ranching and other things historical.

ANNUAL EVENTS

Bluegrass Festival, last weekend of June; **"West's Best" Rodeo,** last weekend of September.

WHERE TO SHOP

Most of Winslow's regional shopping is on North Park, clustered around the central freeway exit, near the Chamber of Commerce. Second and Third street are parallel commercial streets downtown, running from east to west.

WHERE TO DINE

El Papagayo Restaurant • △△ $

1942 W. Third St., Winslow; (602) 289-3379. Mexican-American; dinners $5.25 to $12; full bar. Daily 10 a.m. to 11 p.m. MC/VISA. Mexican specialties including fajitas and *pollo asado,* American steaks, chops, seafood.

The Falcon • △△ $

1113 E. Third St. (east end), Winslow; (602) 289-2342. American, dinners from $6 to $11; full bar. Daily from 5:30 a.m. to 9:30 p.m. MC/VISA. A popular local restaurant since 1955, the Falcon features homestyle steaks, seafood, chops and such. Soups and pies are created on the premises.

WHERE TO SLEEP

Best Western Adobe Inn • △△△ $$$ ⌀

1701 N. Park Dr. (I-40 exit 253), Winslow, AZ 86047; (602) 289-4638. Doubles $48 to $54, singles $38 to $48; lower off-season rates. Major credit cards. TV movies, phones; indoor pool and spa. **Restaurant** serves from 6 a.m. to 2 p.m. and 4 to 10 p.m., American, dinners $6 to $12, full bar.

Best Western Town House Lodge • △△ $$

1914 W. Third St. (I-40 exit 252, then half mile east), Winslow, AZ 86407; (602) 289-4611. Doubles $44 to $54, singles $38 to $48, lower off-season rates. Major credit cards. TV movies, phones; pool, coin laundry, playground. **Restaurant** serves 6 a.m. to 9:30 p.m., American, dinners $6 to $13, full bar service.

EconoLodge • △ $$

I-40 at Northpark Dr. (exit 2530), Winslow, AZ 86407; (602) 289-4687. Doubles $33 to $44, singles $29 to $44; lower off-season rates. Major credit cards. TV, phones; pool.

Super 8 Motel • △△ $$ ⌀

1916 W. Third St. (I-40 exit 252, then half mile east); Winslow, AZ 86407; (602) 289-4606. Doubles $41 to $45, singles $37 to $41. TV movies, phones.

Chapter 6

THE RED ROCK MIDDLE

There are only two places in the world I want to live—
Paris and Sedona.
      —German painter Max Ernst's comment in the 1940s

 THE LAND BELOW FLAGSTAFF is a mosaic of natural beauty, from the stunning rose-colored monoliths of Oak Creek Canyon to the thick forests embracing Prescott. The area is rich in history as well. Visitors can explore ancient pueblos of the Sinagua, the old mining district of Jerome and Prescott's territorial capital.

Other than Sedona, which sits in a corner of Coconino, this diverse landscape is packaged in Yavapai County. Sloping from ponderosa pines to tawny desert, it contains a fourth of the state's working and worked-out mining claims.

Oak Creek Canyon & Sedona

Sedona elevation: 4,400 feet   **Population: 10,255**

This may be the world's most beautiful community setting. When Frank Lloyd Wright first saw Oak Creek Canyon, he said simply: "Nothing should ever be built here."

Picture a narrow chasm, walls cloaked with pines, a sun-sparkled stream wandering about its floor, set off by fairy castle shapes of redrock cliffs. Then place an art colony in the lower end. Finally, give it a nice feminine name, Sedona.

Most chasms are admired from the rim. Oak Creek, however, is a lived-in canyon. You can explore its depths from winding roads and admire its ramparts from picture-window restaurants and motel decks. Sedona and Oak Creek Canyon are Arizona's most popular in-house retreats. Natives come by the thousands, seeking solace from the summer sun of Phoenix. They return in the fall to admire the saffron leaves of sycamore, aspen and cottonwood along Oak Creek and the Verde River.

More than 10,000 people have the good sense to live here year-around.

Sunlight and shadows play off the red sandstone buttes, spires and fluted cliffs that surround Sedona. Every daylight hour and every season brings new form and color to this crimson backdrop. We find it hard to believe that all 10,000 residents don't drop whatever they're doing each evening to admire the sunset.

Although most Arizonans approach Sedona from the south, the most dramatic access is from the north, through the upper reaches of Oak Creek Canyon. Highway 89A from Flagstaff crosses a forested plateau, then spirals into the narrow chasm. The route brushes by creekside resorts and national forest campgrounds. Sedona occupies the southern end, where the canyon widens into an amphitheater of redrock formations.

Before you drop into the canyon, stop at Oak Creek Vista for an overlook of the area you're about to experience. You can do a bit of shopping here as

THINGS TO KNOW BEFORE YOU GO

Best time to go • This is spring-summer-fall country. Sedona, Prescott and the Verde Valley are havens for Arizona desert-dwellers fleeing the heat, so make lodging reservations early. Sedona attracts nearly three million visitors a year; it's *very* crowded on summer weekends. Oak Creek Canyon and the Verde River offer striking fall color, generally from late October to mid-November.

Climate • Warm summers; cool winters. **Sedona**: July average—high 95, low 65; January average—high 55, low 30; rainfall—17 inches; snowfall—9 inches. **Prescott**: July average—high 89, low 56; January average—high 50, low 20 to 25; rainfall—18 inches; snowfall—24 inches.

Useful contacts

Camp Verde Chamber of Commerce, Main & Turner (P.O. Box 1665) Camp Verde, AZ 86322; (602) 567-3341.

Coconino National Forest, 225 Brewer Road (P.O. Box 300), Sedona, AZ 86336; (602) 282-4119.

Jerome Chamber of Commerce, 426 Hull Ave. (P.O. Box 788), Jerome, AZ 86331; (602) 634-9425 or 634-5716.

Prescott Chamber of Commerce, 117 W. Goodwin St. (P.O. Box 1147), Prescott, AZ 86302; (602) 445-2000.

Prescott National Forest, 344 S. Cortez St., Prescott, AZ 86303; (602) 445-1762.

Sedona-Oak Creek Canyon Chamber of Commerce, 89A & Forest Rd. (P.O. Box 487), Sedona, AZ 86336; (602) 282-7722.

Area radio stations

KAHM-FM, 102.1, Prescott—Easy listening.

KAZM-AM, 780, Sedona—Old and new popular music, talk, news.

KLKY-AM, 1130, Prescott—Popular music and news.

KNOT-AM, 1450, Prescott—Country and Western.

KNOT-FM, 98.3, Prescott—Country and Western.

KQST-FM, 100.1 Sedona; 104.9 Cottonwood-Verde-Prescott—Adult contemporary, jazz, "New Age."

KYCA-AM, 1490, Prescott—News and talk.

well. From April through October, Navajo and Hopi craftsmen gather at the canyon overlook to display and sell their turquoise, silver and other jewelry. These are licensed vendors, so you can be confident that their stuff is authentic.

THE WAY IT WAS ● As always, the first dwellers were native Americans. Hohokam and Sinagua Indians sowed and weeded their crops along Oak Creek eight to ten thousand years ago.

Despite its tempting beauty, the area didn't attract permanent white settlement until 1876 when one James Thompson began farming here. More families followed, and by 1902, the colony was large enough to be put on the map. Brothers Ellsworth and Carl Schnebly, the town's founders, petitioned for a post office. Carl and his wife Sedona offered to operate it from their boarding house. Carl suggested a couple of names, but the post office department said they wouldn't fit on a cancellation stamp.

"Keep it simple," Ellsworth said. "Let's just name it after your wife."

Ellsworth's suggestion was fortunate, since one of Carl's proposals was "Schnebly Crossing."

Schnebly Hill Road bears the family name, however. Carl built it to haul produce to Flagstaff, in exchange for lumber. It's now a popular scenic drive.

Early in this century, Hollywood movie makers were attracted by the area's handsome rock formations; the first film was a silent version of Zane Gray's *Call of the Canyon*. Artists began settling in, drawn by the isolation and beauty. Then resort-builders arrived. They put a end to the isolation but more or less protected the setting.

THE WAY IT IS ● Sedona has grown considerably in recent years, more than doubling its population since 1976. Surprisingly, it wasn't incorporated until 1987. While not a model of urban planning, the town still retains much of its early-day charm. There are no high-rises to block those orange-hued rocks and no neon to compete with the canyon's light-and-shadow shows.

Sedona is divided into three sections by a mid-town "Y" at the junction of U.S. 89A and State Highway 179. It's also split between Coconino and Yavapai counties. The original site in Coconino county (which locals call "Uptown Sedona") hasn't changed much in the 20 years since we first visited here.

Most of the growth is concentrated south on 179 (still in Coconino) and along 89A on the Yavapai County side. Although these new areas are a bit sprawled, developers have taken a cue from Uptown and resisted neon and high-rises. Route 89A through "new" Sedona is lined with spur streets leading to planned residential areas with predictable names like Shadows Estates, Settlers Rest, the Palisades, Western Hills, Rolling Hills and Harmony Hills.

The town is unabashedly tourist-oriented and it is upscale tourism, for the most part. More than two dozen galleries display fine examples of Western and other contemporary art. About 300 artists live here. In a 1988 reader survey by *Southwest Art* magazine, Sedona was rated as the sixth best place in America to buy art; it even finished ahead of New York. Performing arts thrive as well. Musicales and plays are presented at the Sedona Arts

SEDONA

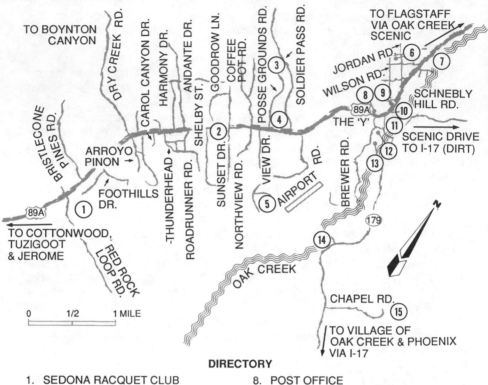

DIRECTORY

1. SEDONA RACQUET CLUB
2. BASHAS' SHOPPING CENTER
3. COMMUNITY CENTER
4. BAYLESS SHOPPING CENTER; FLICKER SHACK
5. SEDONA AIRPORT
6. SEDONA LIBRARY
7. SEDONA ARTS CENTER
8. POST OFFICE
9. CHAMBER OF COMMERCE
10. L'AUBERGE DE SEDONA
11. ARTESANIA PLAZA
12. TLAQUEPAQUE
13. COCONINO NAT'L FOREST OFFICE
14. POCO DIABLO RESORT
15. CHAPEL OF THE HOLY CROSS

Center. Each summer, the community sponsors the Jazz on the Rocks festival and the Sedona Chamber Music Festival.

Some of Arizona's finest resorts are tucked against the canyon's redrock cliffs and the town has a deserved reputation as a dining center. It also offers the usual curio shops with their real and imagined turquoise and other native crafts. Most stop short of being tacky.

Naturally, the town is rife with cutesy boutique names, like Chocolate Suicide, The Bear Facts, eScentuals and—for those seeking truth in advertising—The Tourist Trap.

A jolly little trolley dingalings through the downtown area, taking visitors between there and Tlaquepaque, a handsome arts and crafts village on the edge of town.

The primary tourist pastime is staring at all those rock formations, from every conceivable angle. You can take jeep tours through them or hot air balloon flights above them. Several scenic drives are on the chamber of commerce must-see list. National forest trails offer some of the prettiest hiking you'll find anywhere.

As you explore the area, you'll learn to recognize such promontories as the Coffee Pot, Sugar Loaf, Capital Butte, Courthouse Rock, Chimney Rock and the majestic Cathedral Rock, which seems to be in nearly every photo of Sedona. Look to the west of Highway 179 and you might recognize a more contemporary shape: Snoopy Rock.

Sedona Chamber of Commerce is right downtown—sorry, Uptown—at the corner of Forest Road and Highway 89A. It's on the right as you arrive from Oak Creek Canyon, just above the "Y". Hours are weekdays from 8 to 5 and weekends from 9 to 5; (602) 282-7722.

THE BEST SCENIC DRIVES

Scenic drives lead our list, as well as the chamber's. Here are some of the better ones:

Dry Creek Road ● Although not touted by the chamber, this is one of the more attractive drives in the area. Follow 89A about three miles through new Sedona, then turn right onto Dry Creek. It forks after five miles, with one branch going to Long Canyon and the other to Boynton Canyon. Take both. The left branch takes you to Boynton Canyon trailhead and to the elegant resort setting of John Gardiner's Enchantment (both discussed below). The other route leads you past beautiful rock formations before it dead-ends into one of them.

Red Rock Loop ● This popular scenic drive loops through about 15 miles of redrock country; it's partly paved and partly not. Drive south through new Sedona on U.S. 89A about four miles, then turn left onto Red Rock Loop Road. After a couple of miles, turn left onto Chavez Road and follow it to Red Rock Crossing. This is the most popular photo spot in Sedona, with Cathedral Rock reflected in the shallow waters of Oak Creek.

Despite its name, this is no longer a crossing, so double back and continue your Red Rock loop. You'll eventually return to 89A.

Schnebly Hill Road ● It isn't in much better shape than it was when Carl Schnebly hacked it out as a wagon road, but the vistas are worth the bumps. To find it, turn south at the "Y" onto 179, cross Oak Creek, then turn left (uphill) at the sign. You'll leave pavement after a few blocks.

The road gets increasingly bumpier and more scenic as you climb out of the canyon. At several inviting turnouts, you can park and hike among the redrock formations. Schnebly Hill Vista is a particularly impressive viewpoint. After 12 miles, the road connects with I-17 at Munds Park. Don't try it in winter without a road check (282-4119); the route is often closed by snow or bogged by mud.

Verde Valley School Road ● It offers another approach to Red Rock Crossing. To find it, follow Highway 179 south 15 miles to the Village of Oak Creek, a satellite art colony to Sedona. Turn west onto Verde Valley School Road and follow it past the base of Cathedral Rock to the crossing.

THE BEST NON-DRIVING ATTRACTIONS

Chapel of the Holy Cross ● *Chapel Road off Highway 179 (two miles south); (602) 282-4069. Daily 8 a.m. to 6 p.m. April through October, 9 to 5*

Chapel of the Holy Cross, cradled by redrock formations.

the rest of the year. Some call it the most striking religious structure in America. Rising from the red rocks with a bold cross for a facade, the chapel rivals the rocks themselves as Sedona's best-known landmark. Within this grand setting, soft music and soft lights mellow you out for a spiritual experience.

Unfortunately, this experience is being disturbed somewhat by encroaching suburbia. Expensive houses are creeping up the surrounding hills.

Rising between two redstone pinnacles, the chapel looks to be a creation of the late Frank Lloyd Wright. Actually it was built by one of his disciples, Marguerite Brunswig Staude. Although part of the local Catholic dioceses, this is not a church with regular services but a chapel for quiet retreat.

Sedona Arts Center ● *Art Barn road, north end of town; (602) 282-3809. Tuesday-Saturday 10:30 to 4:30, Sunday 1:30 to 4:30, closed December 24 to January 5; free admission.* This is a center for both creative arts and performing arts. The art barn hosts plays, music recitals and readings, as well as exhibiting the works of local artists. Paintings, batiks, sculptures, ceramics and other things artistic are on sale in the gallery shop.

Tlaquepaque ● *Just south of uptown on Highway 179; most shops open daily 10 to 6 (shorter hours in the off-season).* This Spanish colonial style shopping complex was named for an arts and crafts colony in the suburbs of Guadalajara, Mexico. However, Sedona's Tlaquepaque is much more elegant than the rather scruffy original. It's built around handsome, tiled courtyards, shaded by giant sycamores. Dozens of shops, galleries and cafes are tucked into arcaded buildings. Looking more like a formal garden than a shopping center, it's worth a visit even if you aren't artistically inclined.

THE REST

Art galleries ● They're concentrated in Uptown Sedona along 89A and along Highway 179 to the south. Most galleries have copies of the *Sedona Art Galleries Guide* with a map that will direct you to many of the others.

Co-op Gallery ● *Uptown Sedona at Apple Avenue and Jordan Road; 282-2215; Monday-Saturday 10 to 5, Sunday 11 to 3.* Of the more than 20 galleries, we single this one out because it's a non-profit consortium of local artists. You can find rather good buys here in paintings, ceramics and sculptures. The Co-op also conducts classes in silk screening, drawing, block print, painting and illustration.

Garden of Gethsemane sculpture ● *In Oak Creek Canyon about two miles from Sedona, east side of Highway 89A.* This unusual sand and water casting of Jesus in his final meeting with the Disciples was created 20 years ago by southern California artist Ed Conibar. Regrettably, it is periodically vandalized. Ed, now in his 80s, is regarded as the only sand cast artist in the country. He returns now and then to repair his work.

ACTIVITIES

As we mentioned earlier, an assortment of companies market trips over, above, around and through the red and orange ramparts of Oak Creek Canyon. Here's a sampling:

Balloon Flights ● They're offered by Northern Light Balloon Expeditions, P.O. Box 1695, Sedona, AZ 86336; (602) 282-2274; and Inflated Ego, 3230 Valley Vista Drive, Sedona, AZ 86336; (602) 284-9483.

Helicopter Flights ● Arizona Helicopter Adventures operates out of Sedona Airport, P.O. Box 299, Sedona, AZ 86336; (602) 282-0904. The firm also flies folks to Monument Valley and Lake Powell, and it'll deliver a romantic couple and dinner to some secluded panorama, and pick them up after dessert.

Jeep Tours ● This is the most popular way to get next to the redrock landscape, although we're bothered by the black tire tracks left in the wake of these off-road outings.

Those garish vehicles of **Sedona Pink Jeep Tours** have been at it the longest, operating out of an office across from the Chamber of Commerce; the address is P.O. Box 1447, Sedona, AZ 86336; (800) 8-SEDONA or (602) 282-5000. Other firms are **Sedona Adventures** in the Uptown Mall, (P.O. Box 1476), Sedona, AZ 86336, (602) 282-4114; **Sedona Red Rock Jeep Tours** with locations at 260 N. Highway 89A and 251 Highway 179 (P.O. Box 10305), Sedona, AZ 86336, (800) 848-7728 or (602) 282-6826 and (602) 282-2026; and **Time Expeditions,** 309 N. Highway 89A, Sedona, AZ 86336; (602) 282-2137.

Feel any strange vibes? Some say there are mystical forces loose in this area, with focal points for magnetic feminine and electric masculine vortex fields. Masculine vortex vibes are best at Bell Rock, while feminine energies are focused at Cathedral rock. Need some of both? Boynton Canyon offers an "electromagnetic masculine-feminine combination."

Taking all this somewhat semi-seriously is the **Eye of the Vortex Bookcenter** at 1405 W. Highway 89A (P.O. Box 1044), Sedona, AZ 86336. The folks there will point your Nikes or rental horse in the right direction. The jeep companies offer Sedona Vortex tours to "put you in touch with the dynamic energies of your inner self."

Fasten your seat belts.

OAK CREEK CANYON RECREATION AREA

TO FLAGSTAFF

89A

OAK CREEK VISTA

WEST FORK OF OAK CREEK

PINE FLAT CAMPGROUND

CAVE SPRING CAMPGROUND

SURVEYOR CANYON

OAK CREEK

BOOTLEGGER CAMPGROUND

BANJO BILL CAMPGROUND

HALFWAY PICNIC AREA

SLIDE ROCK STATE PARK

MANZANITA CAMPGROUND

ENCINOSO PICNIC AREA

WILSON MOUNTAIN

MUNDS CANYON

OAK CREEK

SOLDIER WASH

WILSON CANYON

CASNER CANYON

GRASSHOPPER SWIMMING AREA

SEDONA

89A

SCHNEBLY HILL RD.

TO I-17 (DIRT)

TO COTTONWOOD & JEROME

179

0 1/2 1 1-1/2 2 MILES

TO I-17

THE OUTDOOR THING

Coconino National Forest office is at 225 Brewer Road. Go right at the "Y" on 89A, then turn left opposite the post office. It's open weekdays 7:30 to 4:30; the phone number is 282-4119. The national forest virtually surrounds Sedona. The office can provide maps and lists of campgrounds.

Focal point of the forest is Oak Creek Canyon, a busy recreation area with five campgrounds (see listings below), two picnic areas, natural swimming holes and hiking trails. An occasional trout is pulled from Oak Creek in the summer.

Slide Rock State Park ● *In Oak Creek Canyon, 6.5 miles north. Daily 8 a.m. to 6 p.m.; $3 per vehicle, $1 for pedestrians.* The park offers picnic and barbecue facilities and a snack bar, plus an old farm and apple orchard established by early homesteaders.

Adjacent, within Coconino National Forest is Oak Creek Canyon's "ole swimmin' hole"—a slickrock chute that offers a natural water slide. But don't wear your teeny-weenie bikini or Australian beach briefs; you're likely to lose them on the rough rocks. It gets jammed on summer weekends and parking is at a premium. Do your water-sliding during the week if possible. You can use the Slide Rock swimming area without paying the park fee, although the park offers convenient parking.

Hiking into Coconino National Forest will bring you into close contact with the area's redrock formations. Here are some of our favorite trails:

West Fork of Oak Creek ● *Easy hike, mostly level; varying lengths.* This is probably Oak Creek Canyon's worst-kept secret. Thousands of tourists come and go without knowing this pretty hiking trail through Oak Creek's west fork exists, for there is no marked trailhead. However, thousands of others obviously know where it is, because it's so heavily impacted that forest service officials are pondering the possibility of limiting access to this fragile stream-side environment.

Meanwhile, folks at the forest service office will tell you how to find it—and whether or not access is limited.

The trail starts just north of Don Hoel's Cabins and leads into the higher reaches of the canyon. Most people content themselves with a scenic mile or three, then return to the highway. Incidentally, this is not a hike into solitude. During the summer, and on fall color weekends, you'll have more than enough company on the trail.

Sterling Pass Trail ● *Moderate to difficult; 2.4 miles.* Less crowded than the over-used West Fork trail, this route starts at Manzanita Campground in Oak Creek and climbs switchbacks through a pretty, heavily-wooded unnamed canyon to Sterling Pass. From there, it drops down into Sterling Canyon and meets Vultee Arch Trail (described below).

Vultee Arch Trail ● *Easy to moderate; 3.5 miles round-trip.* This is a relatively easy hike up Sterling Canyon, reached from a trailhead off Dry Creek Road (in south Sedona, not in Oak Creek Canyon). To reach the trailhead, turn right onto Dry Creek Road, go two miles to Forest Road 152, then go right five miles. This gently inclined trail leads to a natural arch, named for Gerard and Sylvia Vultee. The noted aircraft designer and his wife died when their plane crashed nearby in 1938.

The trail isn't difficult, but there's a hitch. The last time we visited, the road to the trailhead—Route 152—was badly eroded and could be traversed

Redrock ramparts of Boynton Canyon shelters Enchantment resort.

only by a four-wheel drive. Even our high-clearance VW van, Ickybod, was turned back after a few hundred feet. However, the trail was being upgraded at this writing. Check with the Sedona office of Coconino National Forest about its condition. If you don't want to drive it, you can walk five miles along the approach road; it's a nice all-day outing through redrock country. Total round-trip is 13.5 miles.

Boynton Canyon ● *Five miles, easy to moderate.* Like the West Fork of Oak Creek, this also is heavily used, so you might want to avoid it on weekends. Take our earlier-described scenic drive up Dry Creek Road to Boynton Canyon. You'll find the trailhead on the right, just short of the John Gardiner resort. The trail skirts the edge of the resort, then winds up into a narrow redrock canyon.

After about an hour of moderate elevation gains, the trail enters a dramatic box canyon, with redrock formations rising all about you. Sit down, catch your breath and have lunch. This is one of the most dramatically beautiful spots you'll ever find.

Devil's Bridge Trail ● *Moderately steep, two-mile round-trip.* This is a shorter version of the above trail, leading to another natural arch. Take Dry Creek Road to the same bumpy Forest Road 152. Then walk—or drive if you can—1.2 miles to the Devil's Bridge trailhead. If you walk all the way from the Dry Creek road turnoff, the round trip is about 4.5 miles.

ANNUAL EVENTS

Sedona Heritage Days, first weekend of May; **Sedona Chamber Music Festival** at various locations, second half of June; **Symphony in the Park,** second weekend of September; **Sedona Jazz on the Rocks,** third weekend of September; **Apple Fair,** second weekend of October; **Fes-**

tival of Lights, luminarias at Tlaquepaque, starts second weekend of December.

WHERE TO SHOP

For shoppers, Sedona comes in three pieces. Most of the crafts and curio shops, motels and some galleries are Uptown. The fine Tlaquepaque complex and several other galleries are along State Highway 179 south of Uptown. For practical supplies and such, regional shopping centers line Highway 89A in West Sedona, on the Yavapai County side.

WHERE TO DINE

Eat Your Heart Out ● ∆∆ $$
350 Jordan Rd. (Uptown, north end); (602) 282-1471. American; dinners $9 to $14; beer and wine. Daily 11 a.m. to 2 p.m. and 5 to 9 p.m. (to 9:30 Friday-Saturday); MC/VISA. A small, changing menu in this intimate restaurant features items such as Cajun spiced chicken, baked salmon and other American regional specialties. Excellent dessert cart.

El Rincon ● ∆∆ $
In Tlaquepaque on Highway 179; (602) 282-4648. Mexican; dinners $6 to $10; full bar service. Sunday noon to 5, Tuesday-Saturday 11 a.m. to 9 p.m., closed Monday; no credit cards. Navajo accents such as Indian fry bread influences the Mexican fare at this pretty garden restaurant. You can dine indoors or on a patio beside Oak Creek.

Hitching Post Restaurant ● ∆ $
269 W. Highway 89A (across from Canyon Portal Motel); (602) 282-7761. American; dinners $5 to $8; no alcohol. Daily from 7 a.m. to 8 p.m.; no credit cards. This cozy little restaurant features basic, inexpensive American fare, including luncheon specials starting at $3.95.

Humphreys ● ∆∆∆ $$ ∅
1405 W. Highway 89A (across from the Flicker Shack); (602) 282-7748. American; dinners $10 to $20; full bar. Daily 3.30 to 9 p.m. Reservations suggested; MC/VISA. This nautical theme place specializes in fresh seafood, prime rib and mesquite grilled steaks. Live entertainment in the lounge several nights a week.

L'Auberge de Sedona Restaurant ● ∆∆∆∆ $$$$ ∅
301 Little Lane (Uptown, in L'Auberge resort); (602) 282-7131. French; dinners $40; full bar. Daily 7 to 10 a.m., noon to 3 and 5:30 to 10. Reservations essential; Major credit cards. This small, opulent restaurant with picture-window views of Oak Creek offers a six-course *prix-fixe* dinner for $40 with a selection of several appetizers, soup and salad, a choice of seven or eight entrees and dessert. The food and service are worth the price.

Oak Creek Owl Restaurant ● ∆∆∆∆ $$$ ∅
329 Highway 179 (just beyond the "Y"); (602) 282-3532. Continental; dinners $15 to $25; full bar. Open daily, lunch 11:30 to 3, dinner 5 to 11. Reservations suggested; MC/VISA, DC. Elegant and cozy with owl art decor, it's one of central Arizona's leading restaurants and a winner of several awards. Skillfully prepared Continental cuisine is complimented by an extensive wine list.

Rene at Tlaquepaque ● ∆∆∆ $$
In Tlaquepaque on Highway 179; (602) 282-9225. American and Continental; dinners $10 to $16; full bar. Thursday-Monday 11:30 to 2:30 and 5:30 to 10 (to 8 p.m. Sunday). Reservations suggested; Major credit cards. The

decor is Spanish provincial; the menu is a mix of American and Continental, tilted toward French. Patio dining in summer.

Shugru's Restaurant, Bakery & Bar ● △△ $$$ ∅
2250 W. Highway 89A (opposite First Interstate Bank); (602) 282-2943. Continental & Mexican; dinners $12 to $24; full bar. Sunday & Tuesday-Thursday 8 a.m. to 9 p.m., Friday-Saturday 8 to 10, Monday 11 to 9. Reservations suggested; MC/VISA, AMEX. The eclectic menu at this stylish place includes steaks, seafoods, wok dishes and Mexican specialties, backed up by baked beans and cinnamon rolls. Omelets are a breakfast specialty.

WHERE TO SLEEP

Bell Rock Inn ● △△△ $$$
6246 Highway 179 (near Oak Creek Village), Sedona, AZ 86336; (602) 282-4161. Doubles $47 to $80, singles $37 to $62, suites $61.50 to $94; lower off-season rates. MC/VISA, AMEX. TV, room phones, pool, spa, tennis, golf packages. **Restaurant** open 7 a.m. to 9:30 p.m., Continental, dinners $7 to $18, Southwest decor, full bar.

Black Forest House ● △△ $$$ ∅
50 Willow Way (just off 89A in west Sedona), Sedona, AZ 86336; (602) 282-2835 or 282-9416. Doubles $50 to $60, singles $45 to $57; lower off-season rates. MC/VISA. New motor hotel with TV, refrigerators and microwave ovens. **Gourmet Club of Sedona** restaurant, serving German and French meals around a campfire garden, daily 5 to 9 p.m., $8.25 to $14.50, no alcohol.

Cedars Resort ● △△ $$ ∅
Highway 89A and 179 (P.O. Box 292), Sedona, AZ 86336; (602) 282-7010. Doubles and singles $40 to $68; lower off-season rates. MC/VISA, AMEX. TV movies, phones, refrigerators, pool, spa.

Cimarron Inn ● △△ $$ ∅
2991 W. Highway 89A, Sedona, AZ 86336; (602) 282-7010. Doubles and singles $48 to $58. MC/VISA, AMEX. New motel, opened spring of 1990; TV movies, phones, refrigerators, pool, spa.

Enchantment Resort ● △△△△△ $$$$ ∅
525 Boynton Canyon Road (Dry Creek road off 89A in west Sedona), Sedona, AZ 86336; (800) 843-1691 in Arizona and (800) 826-4180 outside; local (602) 282-2900. Doubles $180 to $640, singles $180 to $270, kitchenettes $450 to $640, suites $230 to $640; lower off-season rates. Major credit cards. Set in a secluded canyon against red rock cliffs, John Gardiner's Enchantment is perhaps the most elegant and beautifully situated resort in Arizona. All the usual room amenities; tennis, croquet, pools, full health spa, six-hole golf course. **Enchantment Dining Room**; breakfast 7:30 to 10, lunch noon to 2, dinner 7 to 9; non-smoking areas, American cuisine with Southwestern accent; dinners from $35, full bar.

Junipine Resort Condo Hotel ● △△△△ $$$$ ∅
8351 N. Highway 89A (8 miles north in Oak Creek Canyon); Sedona, AZ 86336; (602) 282-3375 or (800) 842-2121 in Arizona and (800) 542-8484 outside. All condo units with full kitchens; doubles $176 to $236, singles $115 to $158; lower off-season rates. Major credit cards. Handsome "creekhouse" suites in a hideaway Oak Creek setting; TV movies, room phones, some fireplaces; spa, grocery store. **Junipine Cafe** serves daily 8 a.m. to 9 p.m., American, dinners $13 to $21, non-smoking area, beer and wine.

L'Auberge de Sedona Resort ● ∆∆∆∆ $$$$$ ∅

301 Little Lane (P.O. Box B); Sedona, AZ 86336; (800) 272-6777 or (602) 282-1661. Doubles $140, singles $120, cottages $250 to $350; lower off-season rates. Major credit cards. Posh resort in a secluded creekside setting in the heart of Uptown Sedona; TV movies and radios, room phones; pool, spa, tennis, exercise room, health club and massage. L'Auberge Restaurant (listed above).

Oak Creek Terrace ● ∆∆∆ $$$

4548 N. Highway 89A (in Oak Creek Canyon, four miles north), Sedona, AZ 86336; (602) 282-3562 or (800) 224-2229 in Arizona and (800) 658-5866 outside. Doubles or singles $60 to $75, kitchenettes $89 to $115, suites $150. MC/VISA. TV movies, fireplaces, Jacuzzi tubs; some units have private decks over Oak Creek.

Poco Diablo Resort ● ∆∆∆∆ $$$$$ ∅

Highway 179 two miles south (P.O. Box 1709) Sedona, AZ 86336; (602) 282-7333. Singles and doubles $95 to $150; lower off-season rates. Major credit cards. Luxury resort on 25 acres at the foot of redrock cliffs near Oak Creek; some suites; room fireplaces, phones, TV movies, refrigerators, whirlpool tubs; par-three golf, tennis, pools, spas, racquetball. **Restaurant** open daily 6 a.m. to 10 p.m., American-Continental, dinners $8 to $18, no smoking areas, full bar.

Star Motel ● ∆ $$

295 Jordan Road (Uptown, just off 89A), Sedona, AZ 86336; (602) 282-3641. Doubles $31 to $44, singles $26 to $40, kitchenettes $35 to $45. MC/VISA. Modest, inexpensive; TV in rooms.

Sugar Loaf Lodge ● ∆∆ $$ ∅

1870 W. Highway 89A (West Sedona a mile from "Y"), Sedona, AZ 86336; (602) 282-9451. Doubles $36 to $60, singles $28 to $45, lower prices listed are off-season rates. Major credit cards. TV movies, phones, room refrigerators.

BED & BREAKFAST INNS

Cathedral Rock Lodge Bed & Breakfast ● *Off Highway 89A, downstream from Red Rock Crossing (Star Route 2, Box 8560), Sedona, AZ 86336; (602) 282-7608. From $65 to $90 per couple; private baths; full breakfasts; MC/VISA.* Rambling country home with gardens and spacious wooded grounds; barbecue and picnic areas; redrock views. Fireplace lounge; videotape collection of movies filmed in the area. Rooms furnished with antiques; smoking outside only.

Graham's Bed & Breakfast Inn ● *150 Canyon Circle Drive, two blocks from intersection of Highway 179 and Bell Rock Boulevard), P.O. Box 912, Sedona, AZ 86336; (602) 284-1425. From $90 to $125 per couple; $10 less for singles. Private baths; full breakfasts; MC/VISA.* A Southwest-style B&B inn with a mix of antique, Art Deco and Southwest furnishings. Late afternoon refreshments, pool and spa (closed during winter); patio; fireplace in the dining room. Redrock view; all rooms have balconies. Smoking on balcony and outside only.

WHERE TO CAMP

Oak Creek Canyon ● *Five Coconino National Forest campgrounds; (602) 282-4119. RV and tent sites, no hookups, $8. No reservations or credit cards.* Pine Flat Campground, 12 miles north of Sedona on 89A is open all year.

The others—Manzanita, Banjo Bill, Bootlegger and Cave Creek—are closed in the off-season. All are on Highway 89A and all have pit toilets, picnic tables and barbecues; most offer nature trails and swimming and fishing in Oak Creek. All but Bootlegger (which costs $5) have drinking water.

Hawkeye/Red Rock RV Park ● *40 Art Barn Road (off 89A, near Uptown) Sedona, AZ 86336; (602) 282-2222 or (800) 229-2822. RV and tent sites; full hookups $17, water-electric $14, no hookups $10. Reservations accepted; Major credit cards.* Flush potties, showers, coin laundry, groceries, snack bar, Propane, dump station. Swimming and fishing in nearby Oak Creek. Within walking distance of town.

Rancho Sedona RV Park ● *135 Bear Wallow Road, just off Schnebly Hill Road near Uptown (P.O. Box 450), Sedona, AZ 86336; (602) 282-7255. RV and tent sites; full hookups $18.25, water-electric or tent $16.50. Reservations accepted; no credit cards.* Flush potties, showers, coin laundry, dump station. Along Oak Creek; short walk to Tlaquepaque and Uptown Sedona.

SOUTH OF SEDONA

Oak Creek Canyon fans out into the semi-arid Verde Valley to the south, where the ancient Sinagua once tilled their beans, squash and corn. The Verde River is appropriately named for the green swath it leaves in this high desert below the Mogollon Rim. It's fed by several creeks draining the Colorado Plateau, including Oak, Sycamore, West Clear and a couple called Wet and Dry Beaver creeks.

Two Indians ruins in the area are preserved in national monuments—Tuzigoot to the southwest and Montezuma Castle, the well-known cliff dwelling directly south. Men and women of a more recent vintage came looking for gold, silver and copper. They left in their wake a cliff dwelling of quite another sort—the scruffy copper mining town of Jerome, steeply terraced into the face of Mingus Mountain.

Yet another attraction in the area preserves a troubling link between Native Americans and the new Americans. At Fort Verde State Historic Park, we learn about the troops brought to protect white settlers from the Yavapai and Tonto Apaches. It's no wonder they needed protection; they were stealing the the Indians' land.

Camp Verde

Elevation: 3,160 feet   **Population: 6,000**

The Verde Valley offers blazing bits of fall color in late October through mid-November, particularly along the course of Verde River. Otherwise, it's a rather ordinary-looking agricultural basin offering four interesting tourist lures.

Settlement here dates from 1863 when a minor gold rush drew prospectors to the Hassayampa River and Lynx Creek. They didn't find much gold, but farmers and ranchers later settled in and began unsettling the Indians. The Army arrived in 1865, after several skirmishes between the newcomers and the original residents.

THE ATTRACTIONS

Montezuma Castle National Monument ● *P.O. Box 219, Camp Verde, AZ 86322; (602) 567-3322. Daily 8 a.m. to 7 p.m. in summer, 8 to 5 the rest of the year. Adults $1, families $3, kids 17 and under free.* Montezuma Castle is small as ruins go. However, the drama of its perch high in a cliff face and its legend have caught the attention of visitors. Early settlers fancied this to be the refuge of the last Aztec ruler, who supposedly fled here to escape Cortez in the 16th century.

We know now that it's a Sinagua cliff dwelling in an extraordinary setting, framed by giant sycamores. The only Aztecs to have come this far north are green-carders and tourists. The structure is a five-story apartment containing 20 rooms, probably built in the 12th century. Nearby Castle "A" was even larger—six stories with perhaps 45 rooms, but it's badly deteriorated.

Visitors can't climb up to the fragile castle, but the view from a self-guiding nature path is impressive. A diorama nearby features a cutaway of Montezuma Castle, with a recording about a day in the life of those who occupied it. The visitor center does its usual excellent job of interpreting the geology of the area and the sociology of the Sinagua and Hohokam Indians who once occupied the Verde Valley.

Montezuma Well ● *An extension of Montezuma Castle National Monument, 11 miles northeast. Same hours; no fee.* Well, golly students, if Montezuma II was holed up in that castle, he needed a sacrificial well in which to toss an occasional virgin, right?

Wrong, of course.

Montezuma Well is a limestone sinkhole rimmed by several pueblo ruins. We prefer the well to the castle, which is less visited. A trail down to the sink, 55 feet from the rim, offers a close-up of several ruins near the water's edge. If the water weren't so green and scummy and if a sign didn't warn of leeches, this might be a tempting swimming hole.

Another trail leads to a vent outside the rim, where warm, clean water flows into nearby Wet Beaver Creek. Both Hohokam and later-arriving Sinagua used the well for irrigation, and traces of their limestone-lined ditches can still be seen.

This is a wonderful little spot, shaded by a giant leaning sycamore. It was here that we found the inscription which begins this book, penned by retired National Park Service employee Jean Henderer. It is worth repeating:

> *Take time to see the sky*
> *Find shapes in the clouds*
> *Hear the murmur of the wind*
> *And touch the cool water.*
> *Walk softly—*
> *We are the intruders*
> *Tolerated briefly*
> *In an infinite universe.*

Fort Verde State Historic Park ● *P.O. Box 397 (off Lane Street downtown), Camp Verde, AZ 86322; (602) 567-3275. Daily 8 to 5; adults $1, kids 17 and under free.* As its original name implies, "Camp" Verde was not a walled fort, but an encampment from which U.S. Army troops sallied forth to quell angry Indians.

Camp Verde was built in the early 1870s, then re-named Fort Verde in 1879 to imply a permanent Army presence. Yet three years later, the Apaches were defeated and the fort was abandoned. Local settlers helped themselves to most of the lumber. By the time citizens began preserving the relic in 1956, only a few buildings remained.

Visitors today can take a self-guiding tour through the furnished commanding officer's quarters, hospital and bachelor officers' quarters. The administration building is now a museum with relics of the period.

The commanding officer's structure—with its Victorian furniture, fireplace and organ—suggests that life wasn't terribly rough in frontier Arizona if you were the boss.

Yavapai-Apache Visitor Activity Center • *Montezuma Castle exit 289 from I-17, Camp Verde; (602) 567-5276. Daily 8 to 5; free.* Designed by Hopi architect Dennis Numkena, the structure suggests a surrealistic pueblo with cut-stone walls and a ladder-like superstructure soaring five stories skyward.

The facility is operated jointly by the National Park Service and Verde Valley Yavapai-Apache tribe. It features a museum of Indian culture and crafts, photo murals of Verde Valley attractions and a gift shop. Films, videos and slide shows tout tourist lures of the valley and the rest of Arizona. With luck, you may stop by when an Indian craftsperson is demonstrating jewelry-making or basket-weaving.

ACTIVITIES

Montezuma Outback Tours • *P.O. Box 2074, Camp Verde, AZ 86322; (602) 567-9519. Cave tours $20 per person, high country tours $35.* This firm takes visitors in air-conditioned jeeps to caves once occupied by man in the remote desert and to the high country of the Mogollon Rim. Other offerings include hikes to Indian petroglyphs and dwellings, paddle-wheel boat rides on the Verde River and Camp Verde area historical tours.

The Verde Float • *c/o Worldwide Explorations, P.O. Box 686, Flagstaff, AZ 86022-0686; (602) 774-6462 or (800) 2-PADDLE. Half-day float trips $30, kids 13 to 17, $24, kids 12 and under in adult's boat, $15.* These float trips take visitors through the riparian environment of the Verde River in inflatable kayaks, departing from Cliff Castle Lodge in Camp Verde.

ANNUAL EVENTS

Annual Catfish Contest, Memorial Day Weekend; **Fort Verde Days Celebration,** second weekend in October.

WHERE TO DINE

Olde Adobe Grille • ∆∆ $$ ∅
Main Street (in Sutler's Stores); (602) 567-5229. American, Southwestern; dinners $8 to $17; full bar service. Daily 11:30 to 10 p.m.; reservations suggested. MC/VISA. Southwestern fare, ribs, seafood and chops; Santa Fe decor in an 1871 adobe building. Jazz and guitar music in adjoining cocktail lounge.

Valley View Copper Room Restaurant • ∆∆ $$
Arnold and Main streets (P.O. Box 767), Camp Verde; (602) 567-3592. American; dinners $6 to $17; full bar. Daily 8 a.m. to 9 p.m. MC/VISA. An attractive restaurant and lounge; steaks, chops and seafood menu with ethnic specials; piano bar in the lounge Friday and Saturday evenings.

Cottonwood

Elevation: 3,100 feet   **Population: 11,000**

Traveling 20 miles southwest of Sedona on U.S. 89A, you'll encounter the town of Cottonwood. Once a small farming community, it's now the commercial center for the Verde Valley. In an important secondary role, it offers more affordable housing for the employees of Sedona's smart shops and restaurants.

Its collection of motels provides a good base for exploring the Verde Valley. Predictably, the lodgings are less expensive than those in Sedona.

Beyond the shopping centers, motels and service stations of the newer community is Old Cottonwood, with a handful of false front stores housing Indian crafts shops, antique stores and a couple of souvenir places.

Verde Valley Chamber of Commerce at the junction of 89A and State Highway 279, is open daily from 9 to 5; phone (602) 634-7593.

Tuzigoot National Monument ● *(between Cottonwood and Clarkdale on Tuzigoot Road) P.O. Box 68, Clarkdale, AZ 86324; (602) 634-5564. Adults $1; $3 per family. Daily 8 a.m. to 5 p.m. (to 7 p.m. in summer).* These extensive ruins, once housing about 250 Sinaguas, crown a low ridge north of town. Signs in Cottonwood will direct you there. "Tuzigoot" is an Apache word meaning "Crooked Water," referring to the Verde River that meanders nearby.

Built in the latter stages of the Sinagua society, Tuzigoot may have hosted families driven from other areas by a drought in the 13th century. Ultimately, it, too, was abandoned perhaps due to the same persistent famine. Archaeologists excavating the ruin in the 1930s found 450 burial sites. From this they drew some interesting conclusions about a typical Sinagua's life on earth. Life expectancy was in the mid-forties and two-thirds of Tuzigoot's residents never saw their 21st birthday. A strapping male was about five feet, six inches tall.

The complex was restored as a Depression-era WPA project. Almost as interesting as the ruin is the visitor center, also a WPA undertaking. It was fashioned of river stone with a pole and twig ceiling similar to the pueblo. Exhibits provide a quick study of the Sinagua lifestyle—tool-making, pottery-shaping, weaving and such.

Our next stop, the copper mining town of Jerome, is visible from here, on the slopes of Mingus Mountain. The scruffy mining camp left an odd legacy for Tuzigoot—a shallow tailing dump pumped as slurry from the mines. They look like dead rice paddies, fanning out from the base of the Tuzigoot mesa.

ANNUAL EVENTS

Verde Valley Fair, last weekend in April; **Annual Historic Symposium,** in Clarkdale, third Saturday in August; **Verde River Days,** last Saturday in September.

WHERE TO DINE & SHOP

La Cafe Market Place ● △△ $ ∅

747 S. Main Street (Highway 89-A); (602) 634-8472. Daily 8:30 a.m. to 5 p.m. MC/VISA. The Market Place is a cute little cafe and shopping complex in a Southwest-style turquoise and white structure. Small, individual shops offer gourmet foods and coffee, bakery items, antiques, crafts, pottery, stained glass and such. The cafe serves light breakfasts and lunches, including soups, salads and deli-style sandwiches. Incidentally, we like a sign that says "You're welcome to smoke outside."

Parlor Company ● △△ $

202 N. Main Street; (602) 634-7835. Lunch weekdays 11 to 3, gift shop 11 to 3. This attractive country-style cafe and gift shop is housed in a schoolhouse built in 1913. Fare includes deli sandwiches, salads and home-style soups, breads and desserts.

WHERE TO SLEEP

Best Western Cottonwood Inn ● ∆∆ $$ ∅

993 S. Main St., Cottonwood, AZ 86326; (602) 634-5575 or (800) 528-1234. Doubles $44 to $53, singles $36 to $49, suites $64 to $79; lower off-season rates. Major credit cards. TV, room phones, spa. **Paragon Restaurant** open 6:30 to 2:30 and 5 to 9 p.m. daily, Continental cuisine, dinners $7 to $14, non-smoking areas, full bar service.

Sundial Motel & Apartments ● ∆∆ $$ ∅

1034 N. Main St. (in Old Cottonwood), Cottonwood, AZ 86326; (602) 634-8031. Doubles $34.50 to $38.50, singles $28 to $30.10, kitchenettes $95 to $115 per week, suites from $48.50 per day; lower off-season rates. MC/VISA. TV, room phones, free coffee; barbecue facilities; Sunday brunch. Spanish-Indian style structure built around a courtyard, near the Verde River.

Willow Tree Inn ● ∆ $$ ∅

1089 Highway 279 (across from Walmart shopping center), Cottonwood, AZ 86326; (602) 634-3678. Doubles $38 to $58, singles $32 to $42, kitchenettes $38 to $58. Major credit cards. TV, VCR and movie rental, room phones.

WHERE TO CAMP

Camelot RV Center ● *858 E. Main St. (2 miles south of Highway 89A-279 junction), Cottonwood, AZ 86326; (602) 634-3011. RV sites; full hookups $13. MC/VISA.* An adult RV park with flush potties, showers and coin laundry.

Dead Horse Ranch State Park ● *P.O. Box 144, Cottonwood, AZ 86326; (602) 634-5283. RV and tent sites; hookups $8, no hookups $6, day use $3.* On the site of a former working ranch, the state park offers swimming in the Verde River, fishing in a stocked lagoon, picnic tables and barbecues. To reach it, turn north off Main Street onto Fifth, drive less than a mile and cross a river ford.

Rio Verde RV Park ● *3420 Highway 89A, Cottonwood, AZ 86326; (602) 634-5990. Full hookups $13. Reservations accepted.* Flush potties, showers, coin laundry, disposal station.

A few miles beyond Cottonwood and Tuzigoot is **Clarkdale**, a trim 1930s style town with brickfront stores and a city park boasting an old fashioned gazebo. It began life in 1912 as a smelter site for William A. Clark's Jerome copper mine. It seems there wasn't enough level land in Jerome itself for a decent-sized smelter.

From Clarkdale, we follow Highway 89A toward that once-bustling hillside hamlet.

Jerome

Elevation: 5,435 feet   **Population: 500**

Scruffy can be beautiful if you're a member of the Jerome Historical Society, trying to convince tourists to follow a twisting highway up the side of a dry, brushy peak.

Historians say Jerome never was pretty. Cantilevered into the slopes of Cleopatra Hill, halfway up Mingus Mountain, it was one of Arizona's largest and raunchiest mining camps. In 1903, a visiting *New York Sun* reporter called it "the wickedest town in America."

Its terraced streets were lined with saloons and bawdy houses. Sloping yards sprouted tailing dumps and mining gear instead of rose bushes. Homes were so steeply terraced, claim old-timers, that you could look down your neighbor's chimney. Slides were common and the town jail skidded several dozen feet downhill, where it remains to this day.

Smelters belched pollution. Nearly a mile underground, men stood in boot-deep water, groveling for copper ore in humid 100-degree heat. Dozens died from falls, blasts and other miscalculations.

The bawdy houses and smelters are gone, along with most of the littered mining machinery. An occasional rose bush grows among the weathered houses. Jerome has become a mecca for visitors fascinated by the town's wicked past. It has attracted a rather youthful population of artists and shopkeepers, as well. Instead of old miners dozing in the sun, one is more likely to see pretty young entrepreneurs who would look more at home in a bikini on Malibu Beach.

The business district, appropriately scruffy, is terraced on three levels as the highway switchbacks through town. Galleries, curio shops and antique shops occupy many of its old buildings. Red and green scars are still evident in the hillsides, where miners dug for gold, silver and copper.

The first claim was filed on Mingus Mountain in 1876. Prospectors found a little gold and silver and a lot of copper. In 1883 the United Verde Copper Company built a smelter and the boom began. At its peak, Jerome bustled with 15,000 citizens. In less than 80 years, a billion dollars worth of copper, gold, silver, lead and zinc was rooted from the ground. Alternately leveled by fire and rebuilt, the town thrived until 1953, when the last copper mine was shut down.

The year that mine closed, some folks decided they were history, so they formed the Jerome Historical Society. They hoped visitors and new residents might be attracted by the town's intriguing past. Population dwindled to 100, then slowly climbed back to its present count of 500 or so.

ATTRACTIONS

Jerome State Historic Park ● *P.O. Box D, Jerome AZ 86331; (602) 634-5381. Open daily 8 to 5; $1 for adults, kids free.* The park embraces the estate of James S. Douglas, owner of the Little Daisy mine. It became an historic park in 1967, after it was donated to the state by the sons of "Rawhide Jimmy."

Occupying a ridge with sweeping views of Jerome above and the Verde Valley below, the large, square-shouldered mansion is now a museum to the town's yesterdays. Some of the oversized rooms contain period furniture; others display mining memorabilia and mineral displays. One of the more interesting exhibits is a three-dimensional model of Jerome with its complex webwork of mine shafts. A cleverly-done video recounts the history of the rowdy mining camp through the eyes of a "ghost." He recalls that an 1880 fire burned 24 saloons and 14 Chinese restaurants.

A couple of picnic tables invite lingering on the landscaped grounds.

Gold King Mine Museum ● *P.O. Box 125, Jerome, AZ 86331. Adults $2, kids 6 to 17, $1. Daily 9 to 5:30.* Located on the site of the Hayes mining camp a mile east of Jerome, the Gold King is a cluttered scatter of early-day memories. "Where the pavement ends, the Old West begins," reads a sign at the entrance. Is that an invitation or warning?

This place walks a fine line between museum and junkyard. But the owners make it interesting. They'll fire up a 1914 sawmill powered by a burping, coughing kerosene engine; a jowely blacksmith hammers out souvenirs; peacocks and goats wander about a petting zoo.

Outdoor exhibits range from stamp mills and farm machinery to cast-off toilet seats. Inside the gift shop, you can buy souvenirs and rural scenes painted on saws and hinges.

Jerome Historical Society Mine Museum and Gift Shop ● *200 Main Street, Jerome, AZ 86331; (602) 634-5477. Daily 9 to 5 (museum closes at 4:30); fifty cents.* A small collection of mining and household implements— from mining stock certificates to old photos—recalls Jerome's early days. The up-front gift shop, as large as the back-room museum, offers a good selection of crafts and curios.

ANNUAL EVENTS

Paseo de Casas (Tour of Homes), the third full weekend of May; **Jerome Music Festival** with everything from mariachi to bluegrass the third Saturday of September.

WHERE TO DINE

House of Joy ● ∆∆∆ $$
Hull Avenue (just off the lower tier of Main Street); (602) 643-5339. American-Continental; dinners $10 to $15; wine and beer. Saturday and Sunday only, 3 to 9 p.m.; reservations required, sometimes weeks in advance. No credit cards. Housed in an old bordello, it's one of central Arizona's in-vogue restaurants. The menu and old fashioned dining room are both small; fare is not awesome but the setting is worth it.

Betty's Ore House ● ∆∆ $
315 Main Street (second tier); (602) 634-5094. American; dinners under $10; full bar. Weekdays 8 to 8, weekends 8 to 10. MC/VISA. Sharing an early-day building with the Miners' Roost Hotel, the Ore House features light American-style dinners such as steak, seafood, and liver and onions, plus breakfasts and lunch-time sandwiches and salads.

WHERE TO CAMP

Mingus Mountain and Potato Patch ● *These are two Prescott National Forest campgrounds, six miles southwest of Jerome on Highway 89A; (602) 567-4121. No hookups; no fee. No credit cards or reservations.* Pit toilets, water; hiking trails, picnic tables and barbecues. Groceries at Potato Patch.

Gold King Mine ● *P.O. Box 125, Jerome, AZ 86331. No hookups, $5. No credit cards or reservations.* Rudimentary camping on an old mine tailing dump next to the museum; showers, flush potties.

Prescott

Elevation: 5,346 feet   **Population: 21,500**

Prescott appears to be a community quite pleased with itself. Safe from the rumble of freeways, it's one of the best-balanced and most self-contained towns in the state.

Friendly natives may gently correct you when you say "Pres-kott." It's "PRESS-kit," with the last syllable bitten off quickly. Even local radio announcers, alleged guardians of proper pronunciation, say it that way.

Once you've learned the language, townsfolk will boast of PRESS-kit's idyllic location, between the dry high desert and the cool pines of PRESS-kit National Forest. It's cooler in summer than Sedona, they'll tell you, and not nearly so crowded.

PRESS-kit has its art galleries, they point out, and an active performing arts center. Two colleges and an aeronautical university provide an academic base. The town has a few museums and the whole of the Bradshaw Mountains for a playground. History? Why, PRESS-kit was where Arizona began! Territorial capital, it was. Hadn't you heard?

THE WAY IT WAS • When Arizona was sliced free from New Mexico to become its own territory in 1863, the new governor—John N. Goodwin—

PRESCOTT & VICINITY

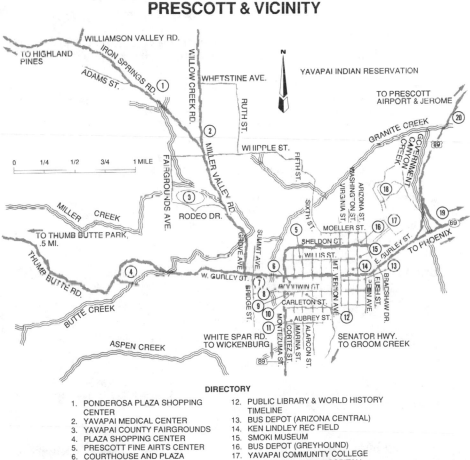

DIRECTORY

1. PONDEROSA PLAZA SHOPPING CENTER
2. YAVAPAI MEDICAL CENTER
3. YAVAPAI COUNTY FAIRGROUNDS
4. PLAZA SHOPPING CENTER
5. PRESCOTT FINE AIRTS CENTER
6. COURTHOUSE AND PLAZA
7. SHARLOT HALL MUSEUM
8. WHISKEY ROW; BEAD MUSEUM
9. CHAMBER OF COMMERCE
10. POST OFFICE
11. PRESCOTT NAT'L FOREST OFFICE
12. PUBLIC LIBRARY & WORLD HISTORY TIMELINE
13. BUS DEPOT (ARIZONA CENTRAL)
14. KEN LINDLEY REC FIELD
15. SMOKI MUSEUM
16. BUS DEPOT (GREYHOUND)
17. YAVAPAI COMMUNITY COLLEGE
18. FORT WHIPPLE (VA HOSPITAL)
19. PRESCOTT NAT'L FOREST (BRADSHAW DISTRICT)
20. PHIPPEN WESTERN ART MUSEUM

began casting about for a capital site. The mineral-rich central highland seemed most logical, so a temporary capital was set up at Fort Whipple near Del Rio Springs, in the nearby Chino Valley.

Later, a permanent site was selected about 22 miles south on Granite Creek. Well, it was *supposed* to be permanent.

A town was laid out in a neat grid and a sturdy log and whipsaw-board governor's mansion was constructed. The fort was moved here to protect the new capital. But in 1867, before something fancier than an oversized log cabin could be built, the government was shifted to Tucson.

Prescott citizens lured the capital back briefly in 1877 before it settled for good in Phoenix. No matter, the people said. Who wanted all that political ruckus and traffic, anyhow?

They were left with an attractive community in a pretty location at the foot of the Bradshaws. After fighting off Indians late in the 19th century, the town grew up as a mining, lumbering and farming center. A 1900 fire destroyed most of it, but the citizens put it back together again.

THE WAY IT IS ● Prescott looks more like a vintage New England village than a Southwestern community. The bold, doric-columned Yavapai County Courthouse occupies a large town square. Early American homes and occasional Victorians line streets shaded by mature trees. Many business buildings are of sturdy red brick. The downtown area seems prosperous despite a commercial exodus to suburban shopping centers.

Don't be fooled by Prescott's Eastern look. The town is decidedly Western, with several cowboy shops and galleries. Locals claim that their annual Frontier Days is America's oldest rodeo, dating back to 1888.

An abundance of motels, restaurants and a few curio shops serve the thousands of tourist drawn to this contented, tree-shaded community.

Prescott Chamber of Commerce, 117 W. Goodwin St., just off courthouse plaza, is open daily 9 to 5. On weekends, it is staffed by members of an adjacent real estate office who can find a brochure for you, even if chamber employees aren't there.

THE BEST ATTRACTIONS

Sharlot Hall Museum ● *415 W. Gurley St., Prescott, AZ 86302; (602) 445-3122. Tuesday-Saturday 10 to 5 (closes at 4 p.m., November through March), Sunday 1 to 5. Free; donations appreciated.* Covering more than a city block, the Sharlot Hall complex contains a dozen historic buildings, either original or re-constructed. Plan a couple of hours to stroll about the landscaped grounds and poke into these memories of Prescott's past.

The Governor's Mansion has been faithfully reconstructed from old photos. Inside, you'll see period furnishings ranging from elegant to rudimentary—from a Victorian settee to packing crates. The cut log structure seems rather inelegant for a governor's mansion. However, since most of the townspeople were living in ragtag tents at the time, Mr. Goodwin's digs were classy indeed.

A second hand-hewn building on the museum grounds was occupied by another territorial governor—the much-traveled John C. Fremont. The Victorian-era Bashford House contains a stylish little gift shop, and a transportation building displays a stagecoach, prairie schooner and Model-A Ford. The modern Museum Center offers permanent and changing art and historic

—Arizona Department of Archives photo
Governor's "Mansion" in Prescott—a humble beginning for the new Arizona Territory.

exhibits while the Sharlot Hall building features a retrospective of the founder's busy life.

Ms. Hall was a remarkable woman who came to Arizona in 1882. Fascinated with the frontier, she began collecting artifacts and writing history as it happened. She served as Arizona's historian for several years, then opened a museum in the old Governor's Mansion in 1928.

"I couldn't be a tame house cat woman," the energetic lady once said.

Prescott's Phippen Museum of Western Art ● *4701 Highway 89 North (seven miles from town), Prescott, AZ 86302; (602) 778-1385. Adults $2, kids $1. May 16 to December 31—Sunday 1 to 4, Monday and Wednesday-Saturday 10 to 4, closed Tuesday; January 1-May 15—daily except Tuesday, 1 to 4.* The museum sits all by itself in the countryside outside Prescott. To find it, go north on U.S. 89, just past its junction with 89A.

Paintings, bronzes, sculptures and ceramics of past and contemporary Western artists are displayed in this attractive structure, which looks like an upscale ranch house. Some of these works can be purchased in the gift shop. The privately-endowed museum was opened in 1984 to honor the late George Phippen, a local artist who was co-founder and first president of the Cowboy Artists of America.

Smoki Museum ● *100 N. Arizona St. (P.O. Box 123), Prescott, AZ 86302; (602) 445-1230. Adults $1, kids under 12 free. Tuesday-Saturday 10 to 4 and Sunday 1 to 4, June 1 through August 31, by appointment only the rest of the year. (Contact the chamber.)* Never assume a pronunciation in PRESS-kit. The "Smoke-Eye" Museum has a significant collection of artifacts of Southwest Indian tribes, including stone tools, baskets and pottery excavated from local sites. With barred grills on the windows, this rough-hewn, cut-stone structure has more the look of a fortress than a museum.

The Smoki are members of a non-Indian group organized in the 1920s to stage mock tribal dances for tourists. Through the years, this rather secretive society has become serious about collecting and displaying artifacts. Members still stage their elaborate ceremonials, which many *real* native Americans—particularly the Hopi—find objectionable.

The Bead Museum ● *140 S. Montezuma (Gurley), Prescott, AZ 86303; (602) 445-2431. Monday-Saturday 9:30 to 4:30, Sunday by appointment. Free.* This curious little museum features beadwork and trade beads from all over the world. It's more interesting than the name may imply. We spent more than an hour there, peering curiously at ancient Indian tribal beads, huge beads from West Africa, a beaded alligator, beaded tapestry that looks as fine as embroidery and beaded sashes. The place also sells every conceivable kind and shape of bead—strung and unstrung, along with Indian crafts and sundry other giftwares.

Yavapai County Courthouse and Plaza ● *Gurley and Montezuma.* After admiring the classic Greco-Roman lines of the courthouse, spend a few moments exploring the Plaza surrounding it. On the north side is a bronze statue of a mounted Bucky O'Neill, former sheriff, mayor and newspaperman. He died in Teddy Roosevelt's Rough Rider charge up Cuba's San Juan Hill. The sculptor was Solon Borglum, the lesser-known but perhaps equally talented brother of Gutzon Borglum, flamboyant creator of the Mount Rushmore Memorial.

Extending out from the memorial is an intriguing Yavapai "time-line," with the county's history carved and painted chronologically in concrete. It's a bit like the Mann's Chinese Theater forecourt in Hollywood, without the stars. Nearby is a gazebo and a bronze sculpture entitled Medivac, which is a memorial to Yavapai County residents who died in America's conflicts, from World War I to Vietnam.

THE REST

Antique shops ● They abound in Prescott, both downtown and on the edges. Step into any antique shop and ask for a pink flyer that will direct

Mannequin soldiers in bachelor quarters of Governor's Mansion.

you to a score more of them. Six are concentrated along Cortez Street, between Gurley and Sheldon. Another half dozen are along Montezuma between Gurley and Leroux.

Prescott Animal Park ● *Heritage Drive at Willow Creek Road, Prescott, AZ 86302; (602) 778-4242. Daily 10 to 5 (closed Mondays November through April); adults $2, kids 14 and under $1.* This is a small animal compound devoted to protection of endangered species and conservation education.

Prescott Fine Arts Center ● *Marina and E. Willis (P.O. Box 1267), Prescott, AZ 86302; (602) 445-3286. Gallery-gift shop open Wednesday-Sunday 11 to 5; MC/VISA.* When a local congregation outgrew the town's 19th century Sacred Heart Church, a citizen bought it—lock, stock and bible racks—and donated it to the Prescott Fine Arts Association.

The church, listed on the National Register of Historic Places, has become the group's 200-seat theater, where it offers a season of dramas, concerts and children's plays. The rectory on Marina Street is now a gallery, where one can buy the works of local artists. During our last visit, offerings ranged attractive hand-woven tapestries and beaded purses to innovative costume jewelry and a giant wooden centipede.

Whiskey Row ● *Montezuma Street between Gurley and Goodwin.* Once the bawdy district, it burned with most of the rest of downtown Prescott in 1900. This solid rank of storefronts was quickly rebuilt. Of course, the bawdy ladies have faded into the night, but several saloons survive to recall those bad old days. Have a Corona Extra w/lime wedge at Matt's Saloon, the Palace Bar, Billy's Western Bar or the Birdcage Saloon. Most retain their Old West ambiance.

World history time-line ● *In front of the city library on Goodwin Street between Alarcon and Marina.* It's similar to the Plaza timeline, but on a global scale. Sidewalk etchings and paintings trace the history of our weary old world from 3300 B.C. Optimistically, it continues to 2050.

THE OUTDOOR THING

Prescott National Forest offices are at 344 S. Cortez St. (Aubrey Street), downtown; (602) 445-1762 and 2230 E. Highway 69 (east of town); (602) 445-7253. Prescott sits in the middle of this 1.25 million acre national forest, offering 11 campgrounds, fishing lakes and reservoirs, picnic sites, hiking trails and the like. A $2 map detailing these lures is available at the supervisor's office in Prescott, and at any of the district offices.

These are some of the more appealing outdoor recreation areas and hikes in and about Prescott:

Granite Dells ● *At Watson Lake Park, four miles north on U.S. 89.* Day-hikers, rock-climbers and picnickers are attracted to this strange land of huge boulders jutting up from a brushy hillside. (Outside the national forest.)

Granite Mountain Wilderness ● *About three miles northwest of Prescott on State Highway 255, then north on Forest Road 375.* Several trails branch into the wilderness from Granite Basin Lake Campground. They range in difficulty from moderate to wearying; check with a ranger for suggested routes.

Thumb Butte Park ● *On Thumb Butte Road (an extension of Gurley Street). Hiking trails, picnic areas; free.* This basaltic monolith four miles south of town is the area's most prominent landmark. Should you get turned around in Prescott, it will help you get oriented. Several trails from the picnic area wind in and about this rock-ribbed butte. Only skilled rock-climbers should attempt to reach the top, however.

ANNUAL EVENTS

Spring Arts Festival, second weekend of March; **Prescott Valley Days** parade and fiddlers' contest, first Saturday in June; **Territorial Days,** second weekend in June; **Yavapai Inter-Tribal Pow Wow,** fourth weekend in June; **Frontier Days Rodeo,** five days over Fourth of July; **Blue Grass Festival,** third weekend of July; **Smoki Ceremonials,** second Saturday in August; Arts and Crafts **Faire on the Square,** Labor Day Weekend; **Yavapai County Fair,** fourth weekend of September; **Governor's Cup Antique Car Display and Rally,** first weekend of October.

WHERE TO SHOP

Western shops and galleries, Indian crafts and curio shops are centered downtown, along east-to-west Gurley Street, then south along Montezuma Street. Continuing west on Gurley, you'll encounter the Plaza West regional shopping area.

If you turn north off Gurley onto Grove Avenue (which becomes Miller Valley Road), then fork left onto Iron Springs Road, you'll hit another regional shopping district. Two of our recommended restaurants, Dry Gulch Steakhouse and K-Bob's, are out this way.

WHERE TO DINE

Berry's Pine Pantry & Restaurant • △△ $ ∅

111 Grove Ave. (Gurley Street); (602) 778-3038. American; dinners $6 to $10; no alcohol. Daily 10 a.m. to 9 p.m. No credit cards. This cute cafe in a 1895 Victorian house features 16 varieties of pies, in addition to a light menu of soups, chili and sandwiches.

Dry Gulch Steakhouse • △ $$

1630 Adams St. (off Iron Springs Road northwest of town); (602) 778-9693. American; dinners $9 to $21; full bar service. Tuesday-Friday 11:30 a.m. to 9:30 p.m., Saturday-Sunday 4 to 9. Major credit cards. A local hangout, this Western-style restaurant specializes in beef, with a few chicken-chop-fish items.

El Charro Restaurant • △△ $ ∅

120 N. Montezuma (Gurley); (602) 445-7130. Mexican; dinners $3 to $8; margaritas, beer and wine. Monday-Thursday 11 a.m. to 8 p.m., Friday-Saturday 11 to 8:30, Sunday noon to 7. MC/VISA. It's one of several good, inexpensive Mexican cafes; the menu features the typical smashed beans and rice items.

Golden Gate Restaurant • △△ $ ∅

620 E. Gurley (Washington, near Ken Lindley Field); (602) 778-0042. Chinese; dinners $6.50 to $9.50; full bar service. Monday-Saturday 11 to 2 and 5 to 9. Reservations accepted; MC/VISA. This attractive establishment runs the Chinese gamut from Cantonese to spicy Hunan and Szechuan.

K-Bob's Steakhouse • △△ $$ ∅

1355 Iron Springs Road (northwest of town, opposite Ponderosa Mall); (602) 778-0866. American; dinners $5 to $12; full bar service. Sunday-Thursday 11 a.m. to 9 p.m., Friday-Saturday 11 to 10. MC/VISA. A large salad bar in a mock-up wagon bed is a focal point in this attractive, locally popular spot. Steak, chicken and seafood are specialties.

Mario's ● ∆∆ $ ∅
1505 E. Gurley (opposite Sheraton Resort); (602) 445-1122. Italian-American; dinners $5 to $10; full bar. Sunday noon to 10 p.m., Monday-Saturday 11 a.m. to 11 p.m. Major credit cards. This lively place offers all-you-can eat specials, pizza and some American dishes. A jumping cocktail lounge features dancing, wide screen TV and a fireplace.

Murphy's ● ∆∆∆∆ $$ ∅
201 N. Cortez St. (Willis), (602) 445-4044. American; dinners $8 to $18; full bar. Sunday-Thursday 11 to 3 and 4:30 to 10, Friday-Saturday 11 to 3 and 4:30 to 11. Reservations advised; MC/VISA, AMEX. Housed in a beautifully-restored 1890 mercantile building, Murphy's offers one of the best dining buys in Arizona. Prime rib, mesquite broiled seafood and steaks and home-style bread are served in an elegant setting of antiques and greenery.

Peacock Room ● ∆∆∆ $$ ∅
112 E. Gurley (in Hassayampa Inn at Marina); (602) 778-9434. American; dinners $10 to $20; full bar. Daily 7 a.m. to 2:30 and 4 to 10. Reservations advised; Major credit cards. Centerpiece of the recently-restored Hassayampa Inn, the restaurant features steak, fish and chop specialties, served amidst 1920s ambiance.

Penelope Parkenfarker's Bar & Grill ● ∆∆∆ $
128 N. Cortez (Gurley), (602) 445-6848. American; dinners $6 to $10; full bar. Sunday-Thursday 11 to 11, Friday-Saturday 11 to midnight. MC/VISA. It's a lively sports bar with good camaraderie and half a dozen TV sets picking up the games; sandwiches and other light meals.

Ranch House ● ∆ $ ∅
401 S. Montezuma (Aubrey), (602) 445-3139. American; dinners $4 to $7; beer and wine. Sunday-Thursday 6 a.m. to 3 p.m., Friday-Saturday 6 a.m. to 8 p.m. MC/VISA. This family-style restaurant features remarkably inexpensive lunch and dinner all-you-can eat specials.

WHERE TO SLEEP

Airport Centre Motel ● ∆∆ $$ ∅
6000 Willow Creek Rd. (Highway 89 North near airport turnoff), Prescott, AZ 86301; (602) 778-6000. Doubles $43, singles $33, kings and suites $48 to $65; lower off-season rates. MC/VISA, AMEX. TV, room phones, free coffee, coin laundry, convenience store, free airport shuttle; 10 townhouse apartments with full kitchens, by the night or longer.

Best Western Prescottonian ● ∆∆∆ $$$ ∅
1317 E. Gurley (Highway 69 and 89 junction), Prescott, AZ 86301; (602) 445-3096 or (800) 528-1234. Doubles $60 to $75, singles $45 to $60, suites $115 to $150; lower off-season rates. Major credit cards. TV, rental movies, spa, pool; refrigerators and coffee makers in some rooms. **Restaurant** open 5 a.m. to 10 p.m., American, dinners $5 to $12, non-smoking area, full bar service.

Cascade Motel ● ∆ $$
805 White Spar Rd. (Highway 89 south), Prescott, AZ 86301; (602) 445-1232. Doubles and singles $20 to $39, kitchenettes $24 to $49; lower off-season rates. MC/VISA. TV.

Hassayampa Inn ● ∆∆∆∆ $$$ ∅
122 E. Gurley St. (Marina), Prescott, AZ 86301; (602) 778-9434 or (800) 626-4886. Doubles $75 to $96, singles $65 to $91, suites $90 to $141; lower

off-season rates. Major credit cards. Attractive luxury lodging in downtown Prescott; TV movies, room phones; free coffee and snacks in the lobby. Peacock Restaurant and lounge (listed above).

Hi Acre Resort • ΔΔ $$

1001 White Spar Rd. (Highway 89 south), Prescott, AZ 86301; (602) 445-0588. Doubles and singles $22 to $49, kitchenettes $26 to $90, suites $35 to $105; lower off-season rates. MC/VISA. TV, room phones, room refrigerators; attractive wooded grounds on a creek; picnic tables.

Hotel Vendome • ΔΔΔΔ $$

230 S. Cortez St. (Carleton), Prescott, AZ 86301; (602) 776-0900. Doubles and singles $35 to $70; lower price is the off-season rate. Major credit cards. A beautifully-restored 1917 lodging house in downtown Prescott. Period furnishings in the lobby and cozy lobby bar; contemporary-early American mix in the rooms. Phones, TV, brass ceiling fans.

Mile High Motel • Δ $$ ∅

409 S. Montezuma (Aubrey), Prescott, AZ 86301; (602) 445-2050. All kitchenettes; doubles $28 to $45, singles $22 to $35; lower off-season rates. MC/VISA. TV; Ranch House restaurant next door (listed above).

Pine View Motel • ΔΔ $$ ∅

500 Copper Basin Rd. (U.S. 89, a mile south of the courthouse), Prescott, AZ 86301; (602) 445-4660 or 445-4030. Doubles $30 to $40, singles $25 to $35, kitchenettes $30 to $40, suites $40 to $50. MC/VISA, AMEX. Remote TV/stereo, room phones, room refrigerators and microwaves.

Senator Inn • ΔΔΔ $$$

1117 E. Gurley St. (Sheldon), Prescott, AZ 86301; (602) 445-1440. Doubles $45 to $65, singles $40 to $60, suites $85 to $125; lower off-season and commercial rates. Major credit cards. TV movies, pool, spa; refrigerators in some rooms; gas grill on patio; coffee, tea, and hot chocolate in front office. Some "romantic getaway" suites $85 to $125.

Sheraton Resort & Convention Center • ΔΔΔ $$$ ∅

1500 Highway 69 (east side, near Highway 89 junction), Prescott, AZ 86301; (602) 776-1666 or (800) 325-3535. Doubles $75 to $85, singles $55 to $65; lower off-season rates. Major credit cards. Crowning a hill in east Prescott, this new facility offers a pool, spa, sauna, tennis and racquetball courts and massage. Room phones, TV/stereo, movies. **Restaurant;** dinners $7 to $22, no-smoking area. Cocktail lounge, entertainment.

Sierra Inn • ΔΔ $$

809 White Spar Road (1.5 miles south on Highway 89), Prescott, AZ 86301; (602) 445-1250. Doubles $40 to $45, singles $30 to $40, kitchenettes and suites $50 to $79; lower off-season rates. Major credit cards. TV movies, room phones, some fireplaces; guest laundry, pool, spa; free coffee, tea and snacks.

BED & BREAKFAST INNS

Prescott Country Inn Bed & Breakfast • *503 S. Montezuma (downtown, three blocks from plaza), Prescott, AZ 86301; (602) 445-7991. From $49 to $109 per couple; lower off-season rates. MC/VISA.* Private cottages with baths, kitchens, TV, coffee makers; full breakfast served in units. Furnished with antiques, live plants and artworks. Landscaped grounds with outdoor barbecues; parlor with fireplace, books and games.

Prescott Pines Bed & Breakfast • *901 White Spar Rd. (Highway 89 south), Prescott, AZ 86301; (602) 445-7270 or (800) 541-5374. From $44 to*

Arcosanti—a curious growth in the desert.

$69 per couple, kitchenettes from $48 to $69, chalet $145 for up to 8 people; lower off-season rates. MC/VISA. Landscaped grounds around a refurbished 1902 country-style home. Victorian furnishings; some fireplaces and kitchens; TV and phones in all rooms.

WHERE TO CAMP

Point of Rocks Campground ● *Route 5, Box 636 (4 miles south on U.S. 89), Prescott, AZ 86301; (602) 445-9018. RV sites, full hookups $12. Reservations accepted; MC/VISA.* Phone and TV hookups, flush potties, showers, coin laundry, groceries and Propane.

White Spar Campground ● *S. 89 (2.5 miles south) c/o Prescott National Forest; (602) 445-7253. No hookups, $6. Reservations through MisTix, P.O. Box 85705, San Diego, CA 92138-5705; (800) 283-CAMP.* Water, pit toilets, no showers. Nature trails.

Driving southeast from Prescott on State Highway 69, you'll drop quickly from pines to cactus. At the interchange with I-17 at Cordes Junction, you can follow signs to a most curious development.

Arcosanti ● *c/o Mayer, AZ 86333; (602) 632-7135. Daily 9 to 5; tours on the hour 10 a.m. to 4 p.m.; four people minimum, $4 per person. Arcosanti bakery serves whole-grain pastries and light meals from 10 to 4; brunch at 10:30.* Arcosanti is the curious creation of Italian architect and visionary Paolo Soleri. Seeking to solve most of the world's problems in one architectural swoop, he has conceived an idyllic, energy-efficient, space-saving community. Here, energized yet mellowed out people would live blissfully together in a smoke-free, drug-free, stress-free environment.

In reality, Arcosanti looks like a scruffy space station that crash-landed in the desert. Or perhaps a low-budget EPCOT Center. Its geometric pre-cast concrete shapes have begun to weather in the 20 years since Soleri's disciples started construction. The creator himself doesn't live here; he's in Scottsdale, where he operates an arts center and bell-making shop that finances the project.

The famous free-form Soleri bells—both bronze and clay—are made here, too. They can be purchased in the gift shop. The bell works is part of a tour, conducted by Soleri's workers. As you walk, you learn that the oddly geometrical community is but a small beginning of Soleri's dream city.

"We have only 40 to 50 residents now," says our young guide. "We have to reach critical mass—about 500 permanent residents—before this is a cohesive city." He doesn't sound very convincing as he speaks.

Students pay a few hundred dollars to absorb Soleri's philosophy, along with his peculiar architectural techniques or bell-casting skills. Then if a job is available, they work a 40-hour week at minimum wage. Life at Soleri is not costly; housing in the small living cells is only $50 a month. Some work a few months, save their modest wages, then travel. Many return for a later tenure in the idyllic city.

This is not a sect or cult, our guide points out. Soleri waves no political or religious banner. His message is simple: Mankind must learn to live and work in close harmony, taking up less space and consuming less. He calls his discipline "arcology"—a blend of architecture and ecology. When he really starts dreaming, he envisions a megalopolis triple the height of the Empire State Building, a mile and a half wide, with living and working space for a million people.

You will find no vertical Los Angeles at Arcosanti, but a rather squat collection of odd shapes. You can get a better feel for the place from afar. Up close, it looks weathered and disjointed—in a cohesive sort of way. After the tour, follow a bumpy road to the base of a shallow cliff, across a ravine from the complex, for an overview. You can get a map at the reception center.

Soleri was a Frank Lloyd Wright disciple who supposedly became disenchanted with the master. Yet his Arcosanti seems to clash with the desert, instead of enhancing it, as Wright's structures do. If Wright were alive to see this curious creation, we wonder if the teacher would be as disenchanted as the pupil.

Chapter 7

THE COSMOPOLITAN MIDDLE

Phoenix is a curious mixture of modern convenience and the crudities of a frontier town. Indians and cowboys pass our doors every hour. On the other hand, I have rarely been in a community where the churches were better attended, or where there was less public disorder.

—1896 letter by Whitelaw Read, ambassador to Great Britain

MORE THAN SIXTY PERCENT of Arizona's population lives in a mountain-rimmed desert basin called the Valley of the Sun. Phoenix and its neighboring cities form a megalopolis that rivals Los Angeles in size. For purposes of geography, we'll discuss Phoenix and its next-door neighbors of Scottsdale, Tempe and Mesa in this chapter, then catch the more outlying towns in the next.

The Valley of the Sun is a delightfully curious mix of Old West and New Wave. You can pull on your Levi's and eat cowboy steaks or wrap yourself in society's most sophisticated trappings. Some Scottsdale shops rival those of Rodeo Drive in Beverly Hills. Resorts like the Arizona Biltmore, Marriott's Camelback Inn and the new Phoenician have no equals. Without question, this area is the resorting, dining and shopping mecca of Arizona.

Incidentally, that "Valley of the Sun" label is the creation of tourism promoters, not map-makers. Officially, it's the Salt River Valley, but that sounds a bit astringent for a vacation paradise. And with more than 300 days of sunshine a year, promoters have the right to brag.

Phoenix

Elevation: 1,083 feet   **Population: 1,036,000**

Valley of the Sun population: 2,103,800

It's wonderful that the Phoenix bird rose to build a new city over prehistoric Hohokam canals. But did the old bird have to get this big?

It has become a major metropolitan center with attendant congestion and even an occasional tinge of smog. In less than 50 years, it has made the transition from cow ponies to helicopter traffic spotters. Of course, it offers some of Arizona's finest tourist facilities, attracting nine million visitors each year. So, let's stop fussing and let the superlatives flow:

THINGS TO KNOW BEFORE YOU GO

Best time to go ● Fall through spring are the Valley of the Sun's idyllic days. Tourism reaches its peak between January and March, so make reservations early if you're going then.

Climate ● It's no secret that the summer sun sizzles, although it's not as hot as the Colorado River corridor. If you seek a winter suntan, Phoenix is a bit warmer than rival Tucson. July average—high 104, low 78; January average—high 65; low 35; rainfall—7 inches; snowfall—are you kidding?

Useful contacts

Phoenix & Valley of the Sun Convention and Visitors Bureau, 505 N. Second St., Suite 300, Phoenix, AZ 85004-3998; (602) 254-6500.

Visitor Information Hotline (recording): 252-5588.

Visitor Centers are located on the northwest corner of Adams and Second streets in the Hyatt Regency hotel block downtown, and in Terminals 2 and 3 at Sky Harbor International Airport.

Toll-free reservations number: (800) 528-0483; in Arizona, call collect (602) 257-4111. These numbers can be used to reserve hotels, motels, apartments, condos, car rental, ground and air tours.

Phoenix Transit System: (602) 253-5000.

Local art events (recording): 257-1222.

Fountain Hills Chamber of Commerce, P.O. Box 17598, Fountain Hills, AZ 85269; (602) 837-1654.

Greater Paradise Valley Chamber of Commerce, 16042 N. 32nd St., C-2, Phoenix, AZ 85032; (602) 482-3344.

Mesa Convention and Visitors Bureau, 120 N. Center St., Mesa, AZ 85201; (602) 969-1307.

Scottsdale Chamber of Commerce, 7333 Scottsdale Mall, Scottsdale, AZ 85251-4498; (602) 945-8481.

Tempe Chamber of Commerce, 60 E. Fifth St., Tempe, AZ 85281; (602) 894-8158.

Tonto National Forest, 2324 E. McDowell Rd., Phoenix, AZ 85010; (602) 225-5200.

Area radio stations

KDKB-FM, 93.3—Rock.
KESZ-FM, 99.9—Adult contemporary (popular).
KFNN-AM, 1510—Business and financial news.
KFYI-AM, 910—News and talk.
KGRX-FM, 100.3—New wave, soft jazz, light rock.
KJZZ-FM, 91.5—Jazz and news.
KKFR-FM, 92.3—Contemporary top forty.
KMEO,FM, 96.9—Easy listening pops, light rock, oldies.
KNIX-FM, 102.5—Country and Western.
KONC-FM, 106.3—Classical.
KOOL-FM, 94.5—"Golden Oldies."
KSLX-FM, 100.7—Classic rock.
KUPD-FM, 97.9—Rock.

Phoenix was rated second in the nation for visitor services, accommodations and dining by the New York-based Zagat Guide survey in 1988. It has more *Mobil Travel Guide* five-star resorts than any other city in the country. The American Automobile Association also gives Phoenix-Scottsdale high marks, awarding its prestigious five-diamond rating to four resorts.

Even with all these amenities, Phoenix is one of the least expensive major cities in America. A recent survey showed that a business traveler could do nicely on $78 a day for lodging and meals, the third lowest in the country. This compares with $164 in Los Angeles and $245 in New York. Boise, Idaho, was cheaper than Phoenix, with $76. But have you ever tried a winter in Boise?

THE WAY IT WAS ● In a state rich with Spanish, Mexican and cowboy lore, Phoenix had a rather conventional beginning. Hohokam Indians farmed the area for several centuries, diverting water from the Salt River. Judging from archaeological sites, their population may have reached 100,000. Then they mysteriously vanished around 1400 A.D., abandoning their irrigation canals.

Later Pima Indians noted the ditches and called their builders "Hohokam," which means "gone away" or "used up."

This Sonoran Desert basin dozed in the sun until a fellow with the memorable name of John Smith started a hay camp in 1864. Ex-Confederate soldier Jack Swilling arrived three years later and formed a company of unemployed miners to dig out the abandoned Hohokam canals. The group soon had a fine wheat and barley crop. One of the settlers, a sophisticated Englishman named Darrel Duppa, predicted that a great city would rise from the site of the former Indian camp, as the Phoenix bird rises from its own ashes every 500 years.

This Phoenix didn't take 500 years.

A town was surveyed in 1870 and a few adobe houses went up. The railroad arrived in 1887, bringing new settlers anxious to get a look at the Wild West. Many stayed, replacing those mud huts with Victorian houses and brick bungalows that gave the place a prosperous New England-in-the-desert look. Just 19 years after its founding, Phoenix snatched the state capitol from Prescott.

In 1911, the Roosevelt Dam was completed on the Salt River, encouraging major agricultural expansion. Then Arizona got a share of Colorado River water and the Phoenix bird took off—like the roadrunner with Wile E. Coyote on its tail. It has never looked back.

World War II brought the military, looking for year-around weather for flight and combat training. At the war's end, that tempting sunshine brought a lot of the GI's back.

THE WAY IT IS ● By every measure, Phoenix is the economic, agricultural, manufacturing and certainly political capital of the state. Its growth has been staggering.

From 1980 to 1987, it ranked first in population gain among major U.S. cities, swelling by 30 percent. It's now the tenth largest city in the United States.

Phoenix is the core of a fused-together glop of 20 communities in the Valley of the Sun. These peripheral towns have grown even faster than their

THE VALLEY OF THE SUN

DIRECTORY

1. STATE CAPITOL
2. CIVIC PLAZA
3. HEARD MUSEUM
4. SKY HARBOR INT'L AIRPORT
5. PAPAGO PARK (ZOO & BOTANICAL GARDEN)
6. OLD TOWN SCOTTSDALE
7. ARIZONA STATE UNIVERSITY
8. TALIESIN WEST
9. OUT OF AFRICA
10. CHAMPLIN FIGHTER MUSEUM
11. ARIZONA MORMON TEMPLE
12. BUCKHORN MINERAL WELLS

leader. In ten years, places like Mesa, Glendale, Tempe and Scottsdale have doubled or tripled their population. Chandler, on the valley's eastern rim, was America's fastest growing city *of any size* in 1986.

Growth slowed a bit toward the end of the decade, but it didn't stop.

"The slowdown just allowed us to catch our breath," said Jim Austin of the Convention and Visitors Bureau.

While it's doing that, Phoenix has plunged into the largest municipal improvement project in America's history. In 1988, citizens voted a $1.1 billion bond issue for a total revamping of the downtown area. By the time the dust has settled in the mid-1990s, the town will have a new art museum, history museum, science and technology museum, theater for the performing arts, aquatic center and several new public parks.

Meanwhile, out at Sky Harbor—a great name for an airport—a new 48-gate terminal is being added. And yes, Sky Harbor International is the fastest growing airport in the country.

And you ain't seen nothin' yet, according to planners of this growth-hungry metropolis. In 1993, after a decades-long dispute with California, Arizona gets its full share of Colorado River water. Much of that will flow into thirsty Phoenix. The Valley of the Sun, already busy with more than two million residents, is expected to reach 2.8 million by the turn of the century.

FINDING YOUR WAY ● Phoenix is an easy city to learn. Although its sheer sprawl can be intimidating, most of it is laid out in a precise grid. I-10 approaches from the west and merges with north-south I-17 just northeast of the downtown core. It does an abrupt 90-degree turn, heads east toward Tempe, then swings south. The Superstition Freeway, State Highway 360, branches off I-10 in Tempe and goes through Mesa before it becomes a surface street.

Some areas aren't served by freeways, including the Scottsdale and Paradise Valley regions popular with tourists. But cross-town freeways are under construction and may be completed by the time you get there. If not, fairly direct surface streets will get you where you're going.

Many Phoenix motels are clustered along Van Buren, including some of the less expensive ones. Others hover around I-10 and I-17 off-ramps. Most of the luxury resorts are northeast of downtown, in and about Scottsdale and Paradise Valley.

The area's attractions are divided between Phoenix and Scottsdale. Most of the museums are in Phoenix while the Scottsdale area is tilted more toward Western lures. Both have extensive shopping facilities and a good restaurant selection. We shall begin in Phoenix, then shift to Scottsdale. Downtown Phoenix has two high-rise clusters—the main core just east of the state capitol and a secondary "mid-town" area to the north along Central Avenue. Redevelopment is focused in the main core, around the attractively landscaped Phoenix Civic Plaza.

Most streets here are one-way, with east-west ones named for U.S. Presidents; Washington is the axis street. Central Avenue is the dividing north-south thoroughfare. Numbered avenues parallel it to the west and numbered streets are to the east. Addresses co-incide with numbered streets and avenues for the most part. (For instance, the 300 block of west Van Buren starts at Van Buren and Third Avenue.)

What you will see, as you tour downtown Phoenix, is a remarkably clean and spacious city, despite its cluster of high-rises. You will see buildings in

Phoenix Skyline and the Mercado—a mix of Spanish and modern.

various levels of erection and parks in various stages of planting.

And incredibly, in the heart of the tenth largest city in America, you will be able to find a place to park.

THE BEST ATTRACTIONS

The Heard Museum ● *22 E. Monte Vista (Central Avenue), Phoenix, AZ 85004; (602) 252-8840 or 252-8848 (taped information). Monday-Saturday 10 to 5, Sunday 1 to 5; guided tours Tuesday at 1:30, Saturday at 11, 1:30 and 3 and Sunday at 1:30 and 3. Adults $3, seniors $2.50, students $1.*

Quite simply, the Heard is the finest museum in Arizona and probably the world's greatest monument to Native Americans. Although it dates back to 1929, this treasury of American Indian cultures is a state of the art facility. With more than 30,000 objects to draw from, its staff exercises artistic discipline in keeping displays both simple and topical. Every exhibit is designed to interpret and inform.

This is a living museum as well as a repository of the past. Entering the Southwest-style courtyard, you're likely to see a Hopi working on a modern sculpture or a Navajo weaving on an ancient loom. A herd of happy school children might be bent over grinding stones, pulverizing corn.

The major exhibit offers a simple and enlightening study of Arizona's ancient and modern Indian cultures with artifacts, graphics and mock-ups. Displays teach you about the people who have occupied—and still occupy—Arizona's three basic landforms: the Sonoran Desert, the Uplands and the Colorado Plateau. You first encounter an audio-visual show with slides of Arizona's Indian country and its residents. They discuss their heritage and their efforts to embrace a society thrust upon them. Entering a mock-up mud-roofed Navajo hogan, you see a blending of past and present with traditional utensils and blankets—and a Propane tank.

Other displays include modern Native American art, jewelry, costuming and a large brightly-colored *kachina* doll collection. Special exhibits focus on native peoples in other parts of the world who have been impacted by conquest, colonization and tourism.

An excellent museum shop offers a fine assortment of Indian arts and artifacts and one of the state's largest selections of books on Arizona and Native American lore.

Arizona Historical Society Museum • *1242 N. Central Ave. (Culver Street), Phoenix, AZ 85004; (602) 255-4470. Tuesday-Saturday 10 to 4; free.* A new Historical Society museum is to open in Papago Park by the spring of 1992. The original repository, in a three-story brown brick Victorian near the Central Avenue overpass, is being renovated. It opens in the spring of 1991 as a typically-furnished late 1800s home; tours will be available.

In the meantime, you can see exhibits in the temporary "Museum on Wheels" at 1120 N Third Avenue. They include artifacts, photos and dioramas of Arizona's yesterdays, from the coming of the Spanish, the Mexican era, cowboys and bad guys to the 20th century irrigation projects that blossomed the desert.

Arizona Mineral Museum • *McDowell Road and 19th Avenue (state fairgrounds), Phoenix, AZ 85009; (602) 255-3791. Weekdays 8 to 5, Saturday 1-5; free.* This museum on the southwest corner of the fairgrounds focuses on the mining end of minerals, with core samples, tools and mine models. Mineral specimens include radiant examples of copper ore, gemstones and things that glow under different ultraviolet wave-lengths.

It's probably the state's most comprehensive museum of this type, with lapidary exhibits, rock specimens from around the state and around the world and a gift shop selling everything from minerals to mining books to gold pans. Knowledgeable staffers can tell you where the next gem show is scheduled and suggest local rock shops for more browsing and shopping.

Arizona Museum of Science and Technology • *80 N. Second Street (Adams), Phoenix, AZ 85004; (602) 256-9388. Monday-Saturday 9 to 5, Sunday noon to 5. Adults $3.50, kids 4 to 12 and seniors $2.50.* By the time you scan this, the science and technology museum may be a state-of-the-art facility in brand new quarters. It's part of the $1.1 billion downtown renovation. Otherwise, you'll find a small but well-done facility with hands-on exhibits.

The original museum is directed primarily toward grade-school youngsters; the newer one will have a broader appeal. The museum is both active and contemporary. Docents give rock talks and conduct lab experiments. Exhibits depict attempts to feed the world's hungry with fast-growing *leucaena* trees, solar stoves and hand-powered irrigation pumps.

Arizona State Capitol Museum • *1700 W. Washington (17th Avenue), Phoenix, AZ 85007; (602) 255-4675. Weekdays 8 to 5; tours at 10 a.m. and 2 p.m.; free.* Arizona outgrew its copper-domed, tufa and granite state capitol in 1972 and moved to a modern structure. Sitting in the shadow of its replacement, the old Grecian-style relic has become a museum of the state's early government. It was built in 1900 as the territorial capital, 12 years before statehood.

—Arizona
Department of
Archives photo

*State capitol in a fanciful
early-day etching.*

Senate and house chambers and several other offices have been returned to their 1912 look, with wooden desks, tulip chandeliers and spittoons. Other rooms serve as museums to the state's political past. Special exhibits honor Arizona's Supreme Court justice, Sandra Day O'Connor, and the Battleship Arizona, sunk at Pearl Harbor. In the governor's office, a waxen George W.P. Hunt, Arizona's first head of state, sits behind his cluttered desk.

The old and new capitol are an unlovely combination, with the squared high-rise towering over the distinguished copper dome. Frank Lloyd Wright had a better idea. In 1957, he submitted plans and a model for a sweeping, open-air, honeycombed structure called "Oasis." It was a grand design with a skeletal canopy and open breezeways to take advantage of the sunny climate. It's a pity the state didn't take him up on his offer.

Champlin Fighter Museum ● *See Mesa listing below.*

Desert Botanical Garden ● *1201 N. Galvin Parkway (in Papago Park), Phoenix, AZ 85008; (602) 941-1225. September-May 9 a.m. to sunset, June-August 8 a.m. to sunset; gift shop open 9 to 5. Adults $3.50, seniors $3, and kids 5 to 12, $1.* In Arizona's finest botanical garden, you'll see desert plants from around the globe, including more than half of the world's cactus varieties. You'll even learn the difference between a *stenocereus griseus* and a *stenocereus thurberi.* March to May is the desert garden's peak blooming season.

A special exhibit shows how the Hohokam and other Indians used plants to survive and thrive in this dry environment. Winding paths take you past a Tohono O'odham saguaro-harvesting ramada, an Apache wickiup, a Pima house with its outdoor kitchen and other desert structures.

Docents station themselves about this beautifully-maintained garden to discuss things botanical. Guided tours are conducted periodically. You can buy botanical books, souvenirs and your own personal "dish garden" in the gift shop. Serious cactus shoppers can get all sorts of prickly plants in the large sales greenhouse.

Hall of Flame Firefighting Museum • *6101 E. Van Buren St. (in Papago Park), Phoenix, AZ 85008; (602) 275-3473. Monday-Saturday 9 to 5. Adults $3, seniors $2 and kids 6-17, $1.* Every kid of every age whose pulse is quickened by the shriek of a siren and the red flash of a fire engine will love this place. It's the world's largest museum of firefighting equipment, exhibiting glittering ranks of hand-drawn pumpers, early hook-and-ladder rigs and other smoke-chasing classics.

More than 100 restored fire engines are on display, from a 1725 English hand pumper to 1920s ladder and chemical trucks. Most interesting are the pre-20th century pumpers; some are works of art with scrollwork, rosettes and dainty brass lanterns with cut glass.

The extensive collection also includes badges, helmets and uniforms, plus lithographs, drawings and photos of firemen in action. Exhibits trace the history of "America's most dangerous profession" from Benjamin Franklin's Philadelphia volunteers to modern fire control techniques.

Heritage Square • *Sixth Street and Monroe (downtown, a block east of Civic Plaza); 262-5071.* This is a scene from Phoenix yesterday—eight structures dating from the late 19th and early 20th centuries. They're gathered around an attractive patio garden, shaded by a curved-wood lath house. These are the buildings and their present functions:

Rosson House, handsomely restored to its 1895 brick Victorian finery, is open for tours from 10 to 3:30 Wednesday through Saturday and noon to 3:30 Sunday. Tour price is $2 for ages 13 and up and 50 cents for kids 3 to 12. Admire the pressed tin ceiling, carved staircase and attractve period furnishings.

Brass lamps with etched glass adorning 1889 hand-drawn pumper at Hall of Flame Museum.

DOWNTOWN PHOENIX

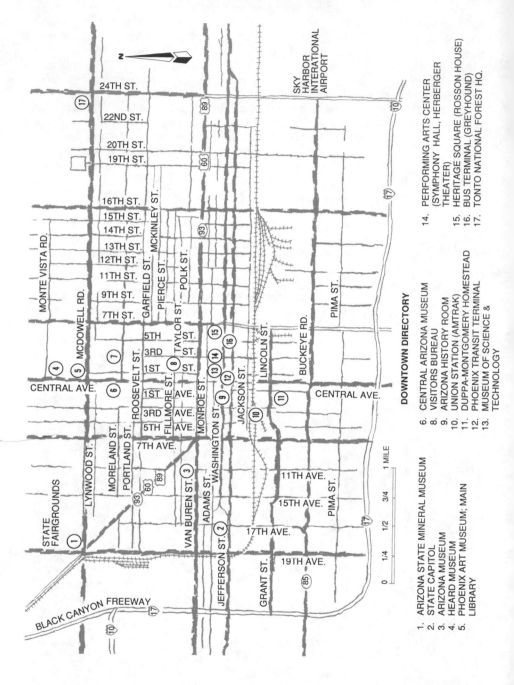

DOWNTOWN DIRECTORY

1. ARIZONA STATE MINERAL MUSEUM
2. STATE CAPITOL
3. ARIZONA MUSEUM
4. HEARD MUSEUM
5. PHOENIX ART MUSEUM; MAIN LIBRARY
6. CENTRAL ARIZONA MUSEUM
8. VISITORS BUREAU
9. ARIZONA HISTORY ROOM
10. UNION STATION (AMTRAK)
11. DUPPA-MONTGOMERY HOMESTEAD
12. PHOENIX TRANSIT TERMINAL
13. MUSEUM OF SCIENCE & TECHNOLOGY
14. PERFORMING ARTS CENTER (SYMPHONY HALL, HERBERGER THEATER)
15. HERITAGE SQUARE (ROSSON HOUSE)
16. BUS TERMINAL (GREYHOUND)
17. TONTO NATIONAL FOREST HQ.

The Bovier-Teeter House, an 1899 Midwestern-style bungalow, contains the Heritage Cafe, serving American and Continental fare. It's furnished with antiques and artifacts from the Arizona Historical Society's collection. Hours are Monday-Saturday from 10 to 4 and Sunday from noon to 4.

The Carriage House, built at the turn of the century, is a snack shop annex to the Heritage Cafe, serving frozen yogurt and other goodies that can be enjoyed on the adjacent patio. Hours are Monday-Friday 9 to 4, Saturday 10 to 4 and Sunday noon to 4.

The Silva House is a classic "revival bungalow" built in 1900. The Salt River Project maintains a turn-of-the-century lifestyle museum, focusing on the development of the domestic use of water and electricity. Hours are Tuesday-Saturday from 10 to 4 and Sunday noon to 4.

The Stevens-Haustgen House is a 1911 brick bungalow occupied by the Craftsmen's Cooperative Gallery. It sells garments, ceramics, sculptures and costume jewelry crafted by local artists. Hours are Monday-Saturday from 10 to 4 and Sunday from noon to 4.

The Stevens House, a 1901 bungalow, is home to the Arizona Doll and Toy Museum, open Tuesday through Saturday from 10 to 4 and Sunday noon to 4. Exhibits include American, English and Japanese dolls, advertising symbols such as the Campbell Soup kids and Crackerjack sailor, 25 years of G.I. Joe and a cute little school room scene with dolls at miniature old-fashioned desks.

A 1923 **"Duplex"** brick bungalow shelters offices of the Heritage Square foundation.

Phoenix Art Museum ● *1625 N. Central Ave. (McDowell Road), Phoenix, AZ 85004; (602) 257-1222. Tuesday-Saturday 10 to 5 (Wednesday to 9), Sunday 1 to 5; guided tours Sunday at 1:30, Wednesday at 7:30 and Friday at 1:15. Adults $3, seniors $2.50 and students $1.50.* The American West and the Old World are featured in Phoenix' eclectic municipal museum. Permanent collections include a gallery of Western Art, galleries of early European and American art, an Asian gallery, costume displays and decorative arts.

We were intrigued by the "Art-Attack Gallery" in which art examples are employed to show how artists use line, texture, shape and color to get their message across. In the Thorne Gallery, you see exquisite detail in early American and European rooms done in miniature.

In a special exhibit on Napoleon—with paintings, coins and other artifacts of his era—you'll note that the French emperor bore a startling resemblance to Marlon Brando.

The museum sponsors study programs, concerts, lectures and tours. Its changing exhibits range from Frank Lloyd Wright drawings to Rodin sculptures to Ansel Adams photos.

Phoenix Zoo ● *5180 E. Van Buren (in Papago Park), Phoenix, AZ 85072; (602) 273-1341. Daily 9 to 5. Adults $6, kids 4 to 12, $3; safari train trips $1.* This would be a pleasant place to stroll even if it weren't stocked with 1,200 animals. Occupying 125 acres of Papago Park between Phoenix and Scottsdale, the zoo encloses a handsome slice of desert terrain. It's landscaped with giant eucalyptus trees, pools, trickling streams and shady patios. Rather young for a zoological garden, it was opened in 1963. It reflects the current zoo trend of providing open-air enclosures and focusing on procreation of endangered species.

Taking advantage of the climate, the zoo specializes in the display and preservation of scarce desert critters such as bighorn sheep and the African oryx. They have their own personal mountain as a habitat. Special features include a children's petting zoo with a big red barn theme, an Arizona exhibit where the roadrunner and coyote are kept a respectable distance apart, and a nocturnal display where you can squint into the dimness at a screech owl, kit fox and—ugh!—vampire bat.

The extensive grounds requires a lot of walking, so you might want to spend a dollar for a tram; it's a handy way to get oriented.

Pioneer Arizona Living History Museum • *c/o Black Canyon Stage (Pioneer Road exit 225 from I-17, 30 miles north), Phoenix, AZ 85027; (602) 993-0212. Wednesday-Friday 9 to 3, weekends 9 to 4, shorter hours during the summer. Adults $4.50; seniors and students 16 and older, $4; kids 4 to 12, $3.* Since 1956, a non-profit group has been assembling an historic Arizona town on a chunk of desert 30 miles north of Phoenix. A couple of dozen buildings—either accurate reconstructions or originals—now occupy the site. More are due in future years. It's a sampler town of Arizona from its earliest Spanish days to statehood.

Although the site seems a bit disconnected and some of the graphics need a good preparator's touch, the exhibits are well worth the drive north.

HOW TO SPEND YOUR VALLEY OF THE SUN DAYS

First day • Head for the Heard, the finest Indian Museum in America. You can spend at least a full morning there. If you have more than one day in town, take time for the nearby Phoenix Art Museum. Otherwise, have lunch and drive a mile south for a look at the State Capitol Museum, Heritage Square with its turn-of-the-century homes, and the downtown area with its new Mercado and Arizona Center shopping malls.

Second day • Light out for Scottsdale's old West downtown area, then continue on to Paradise Valley's Luxury resorts. Visit Taliesin West, Frank Lloyd Wright's studio and architectural school. Stop by Rawhide, then continue north to the Westerny communities of Carefree and Cave Creek. Toward sunset, drive up to Pinnacle Peak and watch the city twinkle in the dusk. Have a Western-style dinner at one of the Pinnacle Peak or Cave Creek restaurants (see listings below).

Third day • Visit the attractions in Papago Park between Phoenix and Scottsdale: the Phoenix Zoo, Desert Botanical Gardens and Hall of Flame Firefighting Museum. Then tour the Arizona State University campus in Tempe and the Mesa Southwest Museum and Champlin Fighter Museum in Mesa.

Fourth day • Tour the rest of Phoenix' cultural offerings: Arizona Museum of Science and Technology, Arizona Hall of Fame and the State Capitol Museum if you didn't catch it the first day. Museumed out? Visit one of the shopping malls listed below.

Fifth day • Get to know the desert-mountain wilderness surrounding the city. Picnic and hike in North Mountain and South Mountain parks. Take a desert jeep tour; several operators are listed under "Activities and Entertainment" below.

Some—such as a turn-of-the century brick bank and a wood frame Victorian—are handsomely furnished. The adobe sheriff's office and jail looks right out of *Rio Bravo*. You expect John Wayne to step outside and confront the bad guys.

Other worthy structures are a log and mud-chink "northern cabin," an opera house where live melodramas are performed, and the Whiskey-Road-to-Ruin Saloon. Its handsome wooden bar and back bar came around the Horn to San Francisco and somehow found its way to Gila Bend and finally to the pioneer village.

History indeed lives at this museum. A lady in a gingham dress prepares supper on an old wood stove in the Victorian farmhouse; a printer prints things on 19th century presses; a blacksmith does a fine job, employing traditional tools to bend hot iron into every shape imaginable; a lady in the northern cabin spins, weaves, tats and embroiders. The village also is the scene of frequent special living-history events involving the miners, cowboys, soldiers and other pioneers of Arizona's lively past.

The Stagecoach Restaurant, adjacent to the Whiskey-Road-to-Ruin Saloon, serves homestyle meals for $4 to $12. You can accompany your grub with a sip of sarsaparilla or beer from the bar. The saloon and restaurant can be patronized without paying admission to the park.

Pueblo Grande Museum • *4619 E. Washington St. (44th Street), Phoenix, AZ 85034; (602) 275-1897. Monday-Saturday 9 to 4:45, Sunday 1 to 4:45. Admission 50 cents.* Now surrounded by the expanding city, this site preserves a large Hohokam pueblo. There's little left of the village, which can be viewed from an overlook. Ridges and depressions suggest the shapes of an ancient ball court and canal banks.

The museum does an excellent job of presenting slices of life from the early days. Exhibits include a scale-model Hohokam home and artifacts taken from the site. Excavations, which have been continuing since 1887, indicate that this was a major village served by at least 17 canals. It was occupied from about 700 to 1450 A.D. One of the first prehistoric ruins to be excavated in Arizona, Pueblo Grande is a part of the Phoenix Park, Recreation and Library Department.

THE REST

Arizona Hall of Fame Museum • *1101 W. Washington St. (in the old Carnegie Public Library at 11th Street), Phoenix, AZ 85007; (602) 255-4675. Weekdays 8 to 5; free.* Rehabilitated in 1984, the old Carnegie Public Library now houses offices of the Arizona Department of Library, Archives and Public Records. A museum features photos and memorabilia of Arizona's "famous, not yet famous and perhaps infamous," including Arizona women and the state's Medal of Honor winners.

A special exhibit honors the Navajo Code-Talkers, who used their native language as the basis for a communications code in the Pacific during World War II. Since Navajo is little known outside Arizona, the code was never broken and it was used again by Navajo Marines and soldiers during the Korean and Vietnam conflicts.

Arizona History Room • *100 W. Washington (First Avenue, in First Interstate Plaza downtown), Phoenix, AZ 85003; (602) 271-6879. Weekdays 10 to 3; free.* Exhibits focus on Western Americana and Arizona history in this small museum on the main floor of the First Interstate Bank building. Displays are changed periodically.

Arizona Military Museum ● *5636 E. McDowell Rd. (in the Arizona National Guard complex seven miles east, near 52nd Street) Phoenix, AZ 85008; (602) 267-2676. Weekends only, 1 to 4; free.* A World War II concentration camp, this place made headlines just after Christmas in 1944 when 19 German prisoners of war tunneled free. They were all recaptured. The former prison camp headquarters is now a museum of Arizona's military past. Regalia includes uniforms, weapons and old photos of men in uniform from the Spanish to the present.

Arizona Museum ● *1002 W. Van Buren (in University Park, at 10th Avenue), Phoenix, AZ 85007; (602) 253-2734. Wednesday-Sunday 11-4. Free; donations appreciated.* This facility attempts to stuff 2000 years of Arizona history into two small rooms. Exhibits include Hohokam artifacts, battleship Arizona mementos, an egg from a former Phoenix ostrich farm, a rifle collection, modern Kachina dolls, ancient Indian baskets, the first Phoenix newspaper press, early Arizona paintings, old maps and minerals. Two steam locomotives from early Arizona mines wouldn't fit, so they're parked outside, along with a decaying wagon.

Constructed in 1927 of adobe brick, this is Arizona's oldest museum building.

Duppa-Montgomery Homestead ● *116 W. Sherman (First Street), Phoenix, AZ 85003; (602) 253-5557 or 255-4470. Sundays 2 to 5, November through May; free.* This weathered adobe may be the oldest home in Phoenix, situated on land homesteaded by city-namer Darrel Duppa. He didn't occupy the structure itself, however; it was built later by the pioneering Montgomery family. It's now surrounded by growing neighborhoods and an industrial area. Inside—when it's open to the public—you'll find period furnishings and artifacts.

Mystery Castle ● *800 E. Mineral Rd. (at the end of Seventh Street, near South Mountain Park), Phoenix, AZ 85040; (602) 268-1581. Open October 1 to July 4—Tuesday-Sunday 11-5. Adults $2.50, kids 4 to 14, 50 cents.* Mary Lou Gulley, daughter of eccentric builder Boyce Luther Gulley, conducts short tours through this curious conglomeration. It's more of a complicated multi-gabled house than a castle. Her father built it in erratic stages from 1927 until his death in 1945. The structure is an assemblage of native stone and odd bits and pieces that Gulley scavenged through the years.

To reach it, drive south on Seventh Street, jogging slightly to the right on Baseline Road, then continuing on Seventh up toward South Mountain.

Plotkin Judaica Museum ● *3310 N. Tenth Ave. (at Osborn Road in Temple Beth Israel), Phoenix, AZ 85013; (602) 264-4428. September through May—Tuesday-Thursday 9 to 2 and Sunday 9 to 12; free.* Artifacts and documents teach about the history of Judism and Jewish holidays. Permanent exhibits, plus occasional touring shows.

Salt River Project History Center ● *1521 Project Dr. (at the "Y" between Washington and Van Buren), Tempe, AZ 85281; (602) 236-2208. Weekdays 9 to 4; free.* Located in the Salt River administration building, this small museum centers on the reclamation project that provides much of the Valley of the Sun's water. Exhibits, artifacts and videos trace the history of the project from the Hohokam canals through the construction of Roosevelt Dam to modern water delivery methods.

World Wildlife Zoo ● *Northern Avenue (18 miles west of I-17, three miles west of Lichfield Road), Lichfield Park, AZ 85340; (602) 935-WILD. Mid-Sep-*

tember to mid-June—daily 9 to 5; summers—Monday-Friday 8 to noon, weekends 8 to 6. Adults $4, kids 1 to 12, $2.50. Several endangered species are members of this small zoo, including the African oryx, Saharan addax and a monkey that can whip along at more than 30 miles an hour. Its large collection of birds—many of them in a walk-in aviary—includes sundry ostriches, rare New Guinea pigeons and Philippine Palawan pheasants. The zoo started as an endangered species breeding farm.

THE OUTDOOR THING: REGIONAL PARKS

Although Phoenix is a major city, the wilds are never far away. The metropolis is surrounded by desert and mountain parks and some are tucked within the city itself. Most are administered by the city or Maricopa County. The 2.9 million acre Tonto National Forest lies just to the northeast. Here, you can hike the trails, camp the campgrounds and swim and boat in the Verde River and Salt River reservoirs.

Tonto National Forest maintains an office in Phoenix at 2324 E. McDowell Road; phone 225-5200. There's another between Cave Creek and Carefree. Hours are 8 to 5 weekdays. Two dollars will get you the detailed forest recreation map. The office also has free hiking, camping and fishing information.

Black Canyon Shooting Range • *Just off I-17 (exit 223), 25 miles north; (602) 582-5296.* Target shooting, trap, skeet and archery ranges are available at this recreation area. There's also picnicking and camping areas (no hookups, but showers are available).

Echo Canyon Recreation Area • *East MacDonald Drive at Tatum Boulevard; (602) 256-3220. Open 6 a.m. to sunset.* This is a hikers' and climbers' park on Camelback Mountain. Sheer 200-foot cliffs challenge climbers, and hikers can follow a variety of trails, including a trek to the top of Camelback. At 2,704 feet above sea level, it's the highest point in the Phoenix Mountains.

Encanto Park • *North 15th Avenue and West Encanto Boulevard. Open daily 5:30 a.m. to 12:30 a.m.* Lagoons, lakes, a swimming pool, two golf courses, tennis courts and picnic areas dot this 222-acre park two miles north of downtown. Water play and other sports equipment can be checked out from the recreation building.

Estrella Mountain Regional Park • *Twenty miles west of Phoenix on State Highway 85, then three miles south of Avondale on Bullard Avenue; (602) 932-3811.* A golf course adds a bit of civilized green to this 18,600-acre park, but most of it is rugged desert terrain that lures hikers and equestrians. Undeveloped campsites are available. Other facilities include an archery range, golf pro shop and snack bar.

Lake Pleasant Regional Park • *Thirty miles north; take I-17 to State Highway 74 (exit 223), then go west; (602) 566-0405. Admission $4 per car, $2 per motorcycle.* This is a 14,400-acre desert garden with two lakes and stands of saguaro cactus. Dirty Shirt Campgrounds offers undeveloped sites. The lakes are centers for sailing, bass fishing, wind-surfing and swimming. Rowboats, wind-sails and small sailboats can be rented.

North Mountain Recreation Area • *Off Seventh Street and Peoria Avenue; (602) 276-2221. Open from 5:30 a.m. to 12:30 a.m.* North Mountain park is a true urban wilderness, with few developed facilities other than picnic areas. Hiking trails take you to some spectacular city viewpoints.

Papago Park • *Between Phoenix and Scottsdale; (602) 256-3220; open from 6:30 a.m. to midnight.* Perhaps the city's most visited park, Papago's hilly desert terrain is host to the Phoenix Zoo, Botanical Garden and Hall of Flame; Phoenix Municipal Stadium is on the edge. Other facilities include picnic areas, an 18-hole golf course, quiet lagoons, game fields and hiking and biking trails.

South Mountain Park • *Eight miles south on Central Avenue; (602) 276-2221. Daily 5:30 a.m. to midnight; free.* Billed as the world's largest city park, this 16,000-acre wilderness contains jagged canyons, pinnacle peaks, extensive cactus gardens and awesome city vistas. You can hike or follow a paved road to the top for impressive Valley of the Sun views from 2,330-foot Dobbins Lookout. Facilities include a children's playground, picnic areas, 40 miles of hiking trails and riding stables (just outside the entrance).

Squaw Peak Park • *West of Paradise Valley, nine miles from downtown Phoenix; take 24th Street to Lincoln Drive, go left, then turn right onto Squaw Peak Drive; (602) 276-2221. Daily from 5:30 a.m. to 12:30 a.m.* Jutting skyward between the populated suburbs of north Phoenix and Paradise Valley, this park has been left in its natural state, with few developed facilities. A steep trail winds through terraced desert gardens to the 2,068-foot Squaw Peak, one of the area's most noted landmarks. The view from this rocky aerie is spectacular.

Saguaro Lake • *East on Freeway 360, then north on Power Road, which becomes Bush Highway; follow signs to the reservoir; (602) 986-0969.* The Salt River Project has turned the stream into a chain of lakes; Saguaro is

Squaw Peak and the lush grounds of the Arizona Biltmore in Phoenix.

closest to Phoenix—about 25 miles east. It's a popular spot that fills up quickly on summer weekends, so arrive early to claim your picnic or camping site. Call ahead for boat rentals at 986-0969.

The 10-mile-long reservoir offers a marina and boat ramp, with boat rentals (fish or ski), a snack bar and boating supplies. You can book a lake excursion aboard the *Desert Belle* by calling (602) 671-0000. Or write to: Arizona Steamboat Cruises, P.O. Box 977, Apache Junction, AZ 85217-0977. Boat tours up the lake are conducted from October through April. Bagley Flat Campgrounds offers primitive sites for no fee; boat camping along the reservoir is permitted.

ACTIVITIES & ENTERTAINMENT
Including Scottsdale, Tempe and Mesa

Aquatic parks • *Two parks prove that it's fun to get all wet.* **Big Surf** is at 1500 N. Hayden Rd. (McClintock Dr.), Tempe, AZ 85281; (602) (946-SURF). This Polynesian-theme water park brings the ocean to Arizona with a large wave-making machines. It offers swimming, surfing and boogie-boarding. **Waterworld U.S.A.** is at 4243 W. Pinnacle Peak Rd., Phoenix, AZ 85027; (602) 266-5299. This 20-acre water-play park features slides, swimming pools and a wave machine.

Desert jeep excursions • *Several companies offer tours into the surrounding Sonoran desert, Superstition Mountains, along the Apache Trail and to nearby ghost towns and gold-panning areas.* Among the operators are **Arizona Awareness Jeep Tours**, 2422 N. 72nd Place, Scottsdale, AZ 85257, (602) 947-7852; **Arizona Bound Tours**, 8061 E. Krail St., Scottsdale, AZ 85250; (602) 994-0580; **Arizona Desert Jeep Adventures**, 10410 E. Cholla St., Scottsdale, AZ 85259; (602) 391-1542; **Arizona Scenic Desert Tours**, 3520 E. Everette, Phoenix, AZ 85032, (602) 971-3601; **Arizona's Old West Trails Tours**, 841 E. Paradise Ln., Phoenix, AZ 85022, (602) 942-3361; **Buck's Scottsdale Superstition Jeep Tours** (narrated by Barry Goldwater), 5320 E. Evans Dr., Scottsdale, AZ 85254; (602) 953-1970; **Trail Blazer Tours**, 6922 Fifth Ave., Scottsdale, AZ 85251, (602) 481-0223; and **Trailmaster Adventures/Cimarron River Co.** (jeep and float trips), P.O. Box 10483, Scottsdale, AZ 85271, (602) 947-4565.

Hiking and backpacking: Expeditions on Foot • *2925 E. Villa Maria Dr., Phoenix, AZ 85032; (602) 482-3992.* The firm conducts guided hikes of one or more days, from gentle to difficult. Treks go into the Phoenix mountains, Sedona's redrock canyons and the pine forests and volcanic mountains around Flagstaff.

Hot Air Ballooning • *These firms market balloon flights over the Valley of the Sun:* **A Aeronautical Adventure**, 10001 N. 28th Place, Phoenix, AZ 85028, (602) 992-2627; **A Balloon Experience**, P.O. Box C4200-363, Scottsdale, AZ 85252; (602) 820-3866; **Arizona Balloonport**, 4901 E. Bloomfield, Scottsdale, AZ 85254; (602) 953-3924; **Pegasus Balloon Company**, P.O. Box 50893, Phoenix, AZ 85044; (602) 224-6111; **Sky Climber Balloon Adventure**, 5822 E. Larkspur Dr., Scottsdale, AZ 85254; (602) 483-8208; and **Unicorn Balloon Company**, 15001 N. 74th St., Ste. F, Scottsdale, AZ 85260; 991-3666.

Performing Arts • *Several theatrical groups keep the area occupied with cultural offerings.* Professional theatrics hit the boards in the **Herberger**

Theater Center, 222 E. Monroe, Phoenix, (252-TIXS), with more than 600 yearly performances in two Broadway-style theaters. **Phoenix Little Theatre** offers popular productions in its facility at 25 E. Coronado Rd. (near Central; 254-2151). At Arizona State University Campus in Tempe, **Gammage Center for the Performing Arts** (965-3434) offers concerts, theater and variety shows. **Sundome Center,** 19403 Johnson Blvd., Sun City West (584-3188), has a busy performing arts program for the west Phoenix area.

CACTUS LEAGUE: SUN COUNTRY BASEBALL

Every March, shouts of "play ball!" echo among the Southwest's sunny deserts as eight members of the Majors launch their Cactus League spring training. The Valley of the Sun is the focal point, hosting five clubs—the Chicago Cubs, Milwaukee Brewers, Oakland A's, San Francisco Giants and Seattle Mariners. The Cleveland Indians work out in Tucson, the San Diego Padres set up shop in Yuma and the California Angels practice in Palm Springs, California.

The Cactus League is a major economic asset to the area—a fact driven home painfully when owners locked out the players for most of the 1990 preseason. A recent survey indicated that spring baseball brings nearly $150 million to host communities. It generates thousands of additional tourists in the guise of adoring fans. Three-fourths of these hot dog clutchers come from out of state and two-thirds come specifically to witness spring baseball action.

Fans like the informality and the vigor of spring training, and the intimacy of the small stadiums. It's baseball played with enthusiasm, gusto—and mistakes; the way they played as kids on the America's sandlots. They like the ticket prices, too: $5 to $7 for the best seats in the stands.

If you're one of those baseball junkies, here's where you can catch the action—presuming the owners let their players play. Unless otherwise indicated, teams practice on their home fields. Tickets for all Cactus League games are available through Dillard's box offices, or call (602) 829-5555 in Arizona (293-1008 in the Tucson area) and (800) 366-3269 out of state. All games start at 1 p.m.

Chicago Cubs play at HoHoKam Park, 1238 Center St. (near Brown Road) in Mesa; (602) 964-4467.

Cleveland Indians play at Hi Corbett Field in Reid Park, 22nd Street and Randolph Way in Tucson; (602) 293-1008.

Milwaukee Brewers play at Compadre Stadium, 1425 W. Ocotillo Rd. (off Arizona Avenue), in Chandler; (602) 821-2200.

Oakland A's play at Phoenix Municipal Stadium, 5999 E. Van Buren (near Galvin Parkway in Papago Park), Phoenix. They practice at Scottsdale Community College, 9000 E. Chaparral Road in Scottsdale.

San Diego Padres play at Desert Sun Stadium, 1440 Desert Hills Dr. (off Avenue A), in Yuma; (602) 782-2567.

San Francisco Giants play at Scottsdale Stadium, 7408 E. Osborn Rd., Scottsdale; (602) 994-5123. They work out at Indian Bend Park, 4289 N. Hayden Road in Scottsdale, and in Scottsdale Stadium.

Seattle Mariners play at Diablo Stadium, 2200 W. Alameda (near Diablo Way), in Tempe; (602) 731-8381.

California Angels work out at Gene Autry Park, 4125 E. McKellips in Mesa, from mid-February to mid-March before adjourning to Angel Stadium in Palm Springs.

Phoenix Symphony Orchestra • *3707 N. Seventh St., Phoenix, AZ 85014; (602) 264-4754.* Concerts ranging from pops to classics, including world-noted guest stars, are held in the Center for the Performing Arts.

Professional sports • *Ticket information at these outlets.* **Phoenix Cardinals,** 51 W. Third St., Tempe; (602) 967-1010. **Phoenix Suns,** ticket offices at 2910 N. Central Ave., Phoenix, and Veterans Memorial Coliseum, 1826 McDowell Rd., Phoenix; phone 263-SUNS. **Cactus Baseball League:** Several major league baseball teams compete in the Valley of the Sun during March-April spring training; see box.

River rafting • *Two firms specialize in white-water rafting on the upper Salt and the Verde rivers. One outfit provides tubes and shuttle service for floating the lower Salt.*

Salt River Canyon Raft Trips • *2242 W. Main, Mesa, AZ 85201 (968-1552), offers whitewater trips down Salt River Canyon.* **Desert Voyagers,** P.O. Box 9053, Scottsdale, AZ 85252 (998-RAFT) has one to four-day whitewater trips on the Verde and Salt rivers and half-day floats on the Salt.

Salt River Recreation, P.O. Box 6568, Mesa, AZ 85216 (984-3305), offers rental tubes and shuttle service on the Lower Salt River. There are several shuttle stops, so you can float for a couple of hours or all day. The lower Salt River turns into a giant pool party on summer weekends, so you might want to schedule a weekday float.

Western-style entertainment and dining • *Several operators bring the Old West back to life with cookouts, cowboy outings and country saloons. Most are in or about Scottsdale, northeast of Phoenix. Here's a sampler.*

Cowboy Adventures, 15862 Trevino Dr., Fountain Hills, AZ 85268 (837-8585), wrangler-style outings with riding and roping lessons, cowboy cookouts, sing alongs and dancing; **Cowtown AZ,** 10402 W. Carefree Hwy., Phoenix, AZ 85029 (866-7698), a Western movie location and entertainment center with gunfights, a museum, shops and shooting gallery; **Frontier Town,** 6245 E. Cave Creek Rd., Cave Creek, AZ 85331 (488-9129), Old West town with shops, gold-panning lessons, Western entertainment, jeep tours and Crazy Ed's Satisfied Frog Restaurant (reviewed below); **Pinnacle Peak Patio,** 10426 E. Jomax Rd., Scottsdale (967-8082), steakhouse, country music, false-front stores, dramatic valley view; **Rawhide,** 23023 Scottsdale Road, Scottsdale, an 1880s reconstructed Western town (reviewed below).

Rockin' R Ranch, 6136 E. Baseline Rd., Mesa, AZ 85206 (832-1539), Wild West town, chuck wagon suppers, gunfights, wagon rides, Indian dancers and gunfighters; **Rustler's Rooste,** The Pointe at South Mountain, 7777 Pointe Parkway, Phoenix, AZ 85044 (231-9111), a Western-style steakhouse with a nightly Western hoedown; **Toolies Country Saloon and Dance Hall,** 4231 W. Thomas Rd., Phoenix, AZ 85019 (272-3100), a 12,000-square foot saloon, dance hall and "general store" with Western souvenirs; **Wagons Ho,** P.O. Box 60098, Phoenix, AZ 85082 (230-1801), wagon train rides, cookouts and campfire circles, to the tune of Western music.

ANNUAL EVENTS

Includes nearby communities

Arizona National Livestock Show, New Year's weekend; **Fiesta Bowl Football Classic,** Sun Devil Stadium, ASU, January 1; **Phoenix**

Open, last week of January; *Parada del Sol* Rodeo, first week of February; **Wild, Wild West** rodeo in Mesa, second weekend of February; **Arizona Renaissance Festival,** in Apache Junction, weekends from mid-February to mid-March; **Heard Museum Guild Indian Fair,** first weekend of March; **Phoenix Grand Prix,** second weekend of March; **Scottsdale Arts Festival,** second weekend of March; **Maricopa County Fair,** third weekend of March; **Phoenix Festival,** featuring Southwestern arts, crafts, cuisine and entertainment, third weekend of March; **Tempe Spring Festival of the Arts,** late March to early April.

Phoenix Jazz Festival, first weekend of April; **Scottsdale All-Indian Days,** second weekend of April; **Legends Classic** golf tournament, third weekend of April; **Cinco de Mayo** celebrations in most communities, May 5; **Indian Pow Wow,** arts and crafts, Mesa, second weekend of October; **Arizona State Fair** mid-October; **Thunderbird Hot Air Balloon Classic,** first weekend of November; **Fine Folk Festival,** arts, crafts and entertainment, Mesa, first weekend of November.

WHERE TO SHOP
Also see Scottsdale, below

As in most Western cities, the major Phoenix shopping malls are in the 'burbs. However, downtown does host several large department stores, including **Goldwater's, Saks Fifth Avenue, Dillard's** and **The Broadway Southwest**.

Among the city's more impressive malls are the Spanish-Moorish **Mercado** at Seventh Street and Van Buren (just east of downtown); the **Metrocenter** at 9617 Metro Parkway (northwest of downtown; take Peoria Avenue west off I-17); **Paradise Valley Mall** at 4568 E. Cactus Rd. (northeast of downtown, near Paradise Village Parkway, west off Tatum); **Park Central Mall** at Central Avenue and Earll Drive (just north of downtown) and **Westridge Mall** at 7611 W. Thomas Rd. (west of downtown, near 75th Avenue).

Three malls are northeast, on Camelback Road between 19th and 25th streets: **The Colonnade** at 1919 E. Camelback, **Town and Country Mall** at 2101 E. Camelback and **Biltmore Fashion Mall** at 2470 E. Camelback.

For Indian crafts, try the **Heard Museum** gift shop at 22 E. Monte Vista Rd. (just north of downtown, between Central and Third Street); and **Gilbert Ortega's,** with stores at 122 N. Second St. (downtown, near Phoenix Civic Plaza) and 1803 E. Camelback Rd. (18th Street). Ortega's has four other locations in Scottsdale.

WHERE TO DINE
American
Another Pointe in Tyme ● △△△△ $$$ ∅

7777 S. Pointe Parkway (The Pointe on South Mountain Resort); (602) 438-9000, ext. 4350. American; dinners $11 to $23; full bar. Daily 6:30 to 10 (Friday-Saturday to 11). Reservations advised; major credit cards. Swordfish and prime rib are specialties in this handsome restaurant with warm wood decor. Cocktail lounge entertainment on Friday and Saturday nights.

Ed Debevic's ● △△ $

2102 E. Highland Ave. (Town and Country Shopping Center at Highland); (602) 956-2760. American diner; dinners $4 to $7; full bar service. Sunday-

Thursday 11 to 10, Friday-Saturday 11 to midnight. MC/VISA. A 1950s diner
with nostalgic decor and old fashioned "juiceboxes."

The Golden Eagle ● △△△△ $$$ ∅
*201 N. Central Ave. (at Van Buren, atop Valley Bank Center); (602) 257-
7700. American nouvelle and Southwestern; dinners $15 to $22; full bar.
Monday-Friday 11:30 to 2, Monday-Saturday 5:30 to 9:30. Reservations ad-
vised; major credit cards.* Travel-Holiday Award-winning restaurant on the
37th floor of Valley Bank Center; impressive valley view. Piano bar Friday
and Saturday nights. Varied American, Southwestern and Continental menu.

Orangerie at the Arizona Biltmore ● △△△△△ $$$$ ∅
*Missouri and 24th Street; (602) 954-2507. American; dinners $24 to $32;
full bar service. Lunch Monday-Friday 11:30 to 2:30, dinner Monday-Saturday
6 to 10. Reservations required; major credit cards.* Elegant award-winning
dining room in the Arizona Biltmore. "New American" menu features bam-
boo-steamed Maine Lobster, skillet-seared medallions of antelope, Cajun
beef and other regional dishes. Nightly dinner music by harpist.

Oscar Taylor ● △△△ $$
*2420 E. Camelback Rd. (in Biltmore Fashion Park); (602) 956-5705.
American steakhouse; dinners $15 to $26; full bar service. Sunday-Thursday
11 a.m. to 10 p.m., Friday-Saturday 11 to 11. Reservations advised; MC/VISA,
AMEX, DC.* A Roaring 20s Chicago-style bistro with ceiling fans, globe chandeliers and brick walls. It serves dry-aged prime steak, ribs and homemade
desserts and breads; some fresh fish.

Tom's Tavern ● △△ $ ∅
*#2 N. Central (Washington); (602) 257-1688. American; dinners $8 to
$9; full bar. Weekdays 7 a.m. to 7 p.m. MC/VISA, AMEX.* Lively old-fashioned
pool hall atmosphere; chili, hamburgers and fresh seafood.

Continental

Caf' Casino ● △△ $ ∅
*4842 N. 24th St. (Camelback); (602) 955-3430. French; dinners $6 to
$11; wine and beer. Sunday-Thursday 7 a.m. to 9 p.m., Friday-Saturday 7 to
10. MC/VISA.* Cute French bistro and sidewalk cafe with inexpensive
entrees, salads and pastries.

Goldie's 1895 House Restaurant ● △△△ $$$ ∅
*362 N. Second Ave. (Van Buren, downtown); (602) 254-0338. Varied
menu; dinners $14 to $20; full bar service. Monday 10 to 3, Tuesday-Thursday
10 to 9, Friday 10 to 11, Saturday 5 to 11, Sunday 4:30 to 8. Reservations ad-
vised; major credit cards.* Handsomely appointed restaurant in Phoenix'
oldest Victorian. Steaks, seafood and Continental fare. Classic and folk
guitarist in adjoining cocktail lounge.

Ristorante Pronto ● △△ $$ ∅
*3950 E. Campbell Ave. (40th Street); (602) 956-4049. Italian-Swiss; din-
ners $8 to $15; full bar service. Weekdays 11:30 a.m. to 11 p.m., weekends 5
to 11; reservations accepted. Major credit cards.* Cozy little Ticino-style restaurant featuring northern Italian and Swiss fare.

Mexican

La Parilla Suiza ● △△ $$
*3508 W. Peoria; (602) 978-8334. Dinners $9 to $16; full bar service. Sun-
day 1 to 10 p.m., Monday-Thursday 11 to 10, Friday-Saturday 11 to 11; reser-
vations accepted. Major credit cards.* This Mexico-based restaurant serves

excellent charcoal-broiled specialties, including unusual dishes such as a chicken melt and beef-onion-bellpepper taco.

Macayo ● ΔΔ $$ ∅

7829 W. Thomas Road (near Westridge Mall); (602) 873-0313. Dinners $7 to $15; full bar service. Open daily 11 a.m. to 10 p.m., to midnight Friday-Saturday. MC/VISA, AMEX. Cheerful restaurant serving Sonoran and other Mexican fare.

Marilyn's First Mexican Restaurant ● ΔΔ $$

12631 Tatum Blvd. (Paradise Valley Mall); (602) 953-2121. Dinners $6 to $12; full bar service. Open daily 11 a.m. to 10 p.m. Major credit cards. A charming and cheerful little place noted for its fajitas, chimichangas and beef chili rellenos; generous portions.

Oriental

Autumn Court ● ΔΔ $ ∅

4302 N. Central Ave.; (602) 234-0512. Chinese; dinners $8 to $12; full bar service. Daily 11:30 a.m. to 10 p.m.; reservations accepted. Major credit cards. Brightly decorated restaurant with white nappery, specializing in both spicier Mandarin and more subtle Cantonese dishes.

Ayako of Tokyo ● ΔΔ $$ ∅

2564 E. Camelback Rd. (Biltmore Fashion Park); 955-0777. Japanese; dinners $10 to $15; full bar service. Daily 11:30 to 10; reservations accepted. Major credit cards. Chefs chop and cook at tableside in this upscale Americanized Japanese restaurant; also a sushi bar and cocktail lounge.

Golden Phoenix ● ΔΔ $ ∅

6048 N. 16th St. (263-8049) and 1534 W. Camelback Rd. (279-4447). Chinese; dinners $8 to $12. Daily 11:30 a.m. to 10 p.m.; reservations accepted. Major credit cards. Extensive menu features Szechuan, Hunan and other spicy northern China dishes; large portions at modest prices.

WHERE TO SLEEP

Ambassador Inn ● ΔΔ $$$ ∅

4727 E. Thomas Rd. (44th Street), Phoenix, AZ 85018; (602) 840-7500. All kitchenette units with refrigerators and stoves; doubles $45 to $60; lower off-season rates. Major credit cards. TV, room phones; pool. **Cafe Ambassador** serves 7 a.m. to 10 p.m., American and Mexican, dinners $5 to $11, non-smoking areas, full bar service.

American Lodge Motel ● ΔΔ $$ ∅

965 E. Van Buren (Civic Plaza near Convention Center), Phoenix, AZ 85006; (602) 252-6823. Doubles $32 to $38, singles $24 to $28; lower off-season rates. MC/VISA, AMEX. TV movies, room phones; pool.

Best Western Bell Motel ● ΔΔ $$ ∅

17211 N. Black Canyon Hwy. (Bell Road East exit off I-17), Phoenix, AZ 85023; (602) 993-8300; (800) 528-1234. Doubles $35 to $65, singles $30 to $65. Major credit cards. TV movies, room phones, pool, spa, in-room coffee. Adjacent **Carrows** and **Waffle House** restaurants open 24 hours; American, dinners $3 to $15 (not connected to motel).

Comfort Inn Airport ● ΔΔ $$ ∅

4120 E. Van Buren, Phoenix, AZ 85008; (602) 275-5746 or (800) 221-2222. Doubles $41 to $49, singles $33 to $43, kitchenettes $43; lower off-season rates. Major credit cards. TV, room phones, pool.

Courtyard by Marriott • ∆∆∆ $$$ ∅
9631 N. Black Canyon (Metrocenter, near I-17), Phoenix, AZ 85021; (602) 944-7373 or (800) 321-2211. Doubles $54 to $89, singles $44 to $79; lower off-season rates. Major credit cards. TV movies, room phones; pool, spa, exercise room, coin laundry. **Restaurant** serves from 6:30 a.m. to 10 p.m., American, dinners $6 to $13, full bar.

Days Inn San Carlos • ∆∆ $$$
202 N. Central Ave. (Monroe), Phoenix, AZ 85004; (602) 253-4121 or (800) 325-2525. Doubles $45 to $60, singles $35 to $40, suites $95 to $125; lower off-season rates. Major credit cards. TV, room phones, complimentary breakfast; pool. Small hotel in historic building. **Philly's Finest** and **Purple Cow** serve breakfast and lunch from 7 a.m. to 3 p.m., meals from $2 to $6, no alcohol.

Doubletree Suites at Phoenix Gateway • ∆∆∆∆ $$$$ ∅
320 N. 44th St. (Van Buren), Phoenix, AZ 85008; (602) 225-0500 or (800) 528-0444. All suites; doubles $75 to $135, singles $65 to $125; lower off-season rates. Major credit cards. TV movies, room phones, free cooked-to-order breakfast, coffee, refrigerator and wet bar in rooms; pool. **Toppers and T-Salters Restaurant** serves 6:30 a.m. to 10 p.m., American and Continental, dinners $12 to $20, non-smoking areas, full bar service.

EconoLodge Airport Central • ∆∆ $$ ∅
2247 E. Van Buren (between airport and downtown), Phoenix, AZ 85006; (602) 244-9341 or (800) 492-2904. Doubles $25 to $38, singles $22 to $28; lower off-season rates. MC/VISA, AMEX and DC. TV, room phones, pool; gift shop, coin laundry. **Vintage Restaurant** serves from 6 a.m. to 10 p.m., American, dinners $5.50 to $11, non-smoking areas, full bar service.

Embassy Suites Thomas Road • ∆∆∆ $$$$ ∅
2333 E. Thomas Rd. (1/4 mile from Squaw Peak Parkway), Phoenix, AZ 85016; (602) 957-1910 or (800) EMBASSY. All suites; from $89 to $109; lower off-season rates. Major credit cards. TV movies, room phones and refrigerators; pool, spa, gift shop, free cooked-to-order breakfast. **Gregory's on the Reef Restaurant** with beef and seafood menu, dinner $10 to $20, mountain view, non-smoking areas, full bar service.

Hampton Inn • ∆∆∆ $$$ ∅
8101 N. Black Canyon Hwy. (Northern Avenue, east of I-17), Phoenix, AZ 85021; (602) 864-6233. Doubles $41 to $61, singles $39 to $56; lower off-season rates. Major credit cards. TV movies, room phones; pool, spa, free continental breakfast.

Hotel Desert Sun • ∆∆ $$ ∅
1325 Grand Ave. (15th Avenue), Phoenix, AZ 85007; (602) 258-8971 or (800) 227-0301 outside Arizona. Doubles $35 to $50, singles $35 to $40, suites $50 to $100; lower off-season rates. Major credit cards. Downtown location, spacious grounds. TV movies, room phones; coin laundry, exercise room. **Desert Sun Restaurant** open 24 hours, American, home-made soups, "killer chili", dinners $3.50 to $12, full bar service.

Hyatt Regency Phoenix • ∆∆∆∆ $$$$$ ∅
122 N. Second St. (Monroe), Phoenix, AZ 85004; (602) 252-1234 or (800) 233-1234. Doubles $144 to $164, singles $119 to $139, suites $250 to $750. Major credit cards. Striking atrium hotel with pool, spa, exercise room, other resort amenities. Stereo/TV movies, room phones, refrigerators. **Compass**

revolving rooftop restaurant serves from 11 a.m. to 11 p.m., Continental, dinners $12 to $25. Informal **Terrace Theatre Cafe** serves from 6 a.m. to midnight. Both have non-smoking areas and full bar service.

La Mancha Hotel and Athletic Club • △△△ $$$ ∅

100 W. Clarendon Ave. (two blocks north of Park Central Mall), Phoenix, AZ 85013; (602) 279-9811 or (800) 422-6444. Doubles and singles $65 to $85, kitchenettes and suites $95 to $125; lower off-season rates. Major credit cards. TV movies, room phones, two floors of non-smoking rooms; pool, spa; adjacent athletic club free to guests. **Brass Helmet Restaurant** and Lounge, open 24 hours with "social gambling", dinners $4 to $11, non-smoking areas, full bar service.

Les Jardins Hotel • △△△ $$$$ ∅

401 W. Clarendon (mid-town area), Phoenix, AZ 85013; (602) 234-2464 or (800) JARDINS. Doubles and singles $85 to $135, suites $105 to $135; lower off-season rates. Major credit cards. TV, room phones, honor bars in stylish, oversized rooms. **Fourth Avenue Cafe** serves 6 a.m. to 10 p.m. (from 7 a.m. Sundays), mixed menu, dinners $14 to $19, non-smoking areas, full bar service.

Park Central Motor Hotel • △△ $$$ ∅

3033 N. Seventh Ave. (Thomas Road exit from I-17), Phoenix, AZ 85013; (602) 277-2621 or (800) 528-0368. All kitchenettes; studios $57 to $66, suites $63 to $72; lower off-season rates. Major credit cards. TV movies, room phones; pool. **Gaslight Restaurant** serves 6 a.m. to 9 p.m., mixed menu, dinners to $10, mini-cocktails or beer and wine.

The Ritz-Carlton Phoenix • △△△△△ $$$$$ ∅

2401 Camelback Rd. (24th Street), Phoenix, AZ 85016; (602) 468-0700 or (800) 241-3333. Doubles $135 to $180, singles $125 to $170, suites $325 to $550; lower off-season rates. Major credit cards. European elegance in a new cosmopolitan resort with opulently-furnished, beautifully-decorated over-sized rooms. TV/stereo radios, several room phones, honor bars; pool, sauna, spa, complimentary fitness center, tennis courts. Two **restaurants** featuring Continental cuisine, dinners $22 to $35, non-smoking areas, full bar service.

Royal Palms Inn • △△△ $$$$$ ∅

5200 E. Camelback Rd. (44th Street), Phoenix, AZ 85018; (602) 840-3610. Doubles $140 to $210, singles $110 to $170, kitchen units and suites $145 to $200; lower off-season rates. Major credit cards. Room rates include free golf and tennis; spacious rooms with TV, phones, refrigerators. Landscaped grounds with tennis courts, nine-hole golf course, two swimming pools, coin laundry. **Orange Tree Dining Room** serves from 7 a.m. to 9 p.m., Continental cuisine, dinners $12 to $19, non-smoking areas, full bar service.

Sheraton Greenway Inn • △△△△ $$$$$

2510 W. Greenway Rd. (Greenway exit from I-17), Phoenix, AZ 85023; (602) 993-0800 or (800) 325-3535. Doubles from $99, singles from $89; lower off-season rates. Major credit cards. Mini-bars, complimentary breakfast and cocktails, room phones, TV movies; pool, children's pool, spa, sauna, lighted tennis courts; beautifully landscaped grounds. **Daisy Restaurant** serves from 6:30 a.m. to 10 p.m., American, dinners $10.50 to $14.50, non-smoking areas, full bar service.

RESORTS

Arizona Biltmore ● △△△△△ $$$$$ ∅
24th Street and Missouri, Phoenix, AZ 85016; (602) 955-6600 or (800)
228-3000. Doubles $210 to $290, suites $550 to $1,300; lower off-season
rates. Major credit cards. Arizona's historic, award-winning "jewel of the
desert," designed in collaboration with Frank Lloyd Wright more than 50
years ago. Now surrounded by Phoenix but still secluded on 200 lushly
landscaped acres. TV movies, room phones, elegant furnishings. Three swimming pools, 17 tennis courts, fitness center, cabanas, boutiques, hair salon,
massage salons; bicycling, jogging paths, two 18-hole golf courses, lawn
games, fitness programs. Southwestern architecture with textured block
walls, artworks in rooms and public areas. Several award-winning **restaurants**; see Orangerie listing under "Where to Dine" above.

Marriott's Mountain Shadows ● △△△△ $$$$$ ∅
5641 E. Lincoln Dr. (east of Tatum), Phoenix, AZ 85023; (602) 948-7111
or (800) 228-9290. Doubles $210 to $410, singles $190 to $410; lower off-
season rates. Major credit cards. TV movies, room phones, elegantly furnished
rooms. Extensive grounds with golf, three swimming pools, spas, lighted
tennis courts, pro shops, fitness center, game room, activities program,
guided hikes. **Shells** and **Cactus Flower** restaurants serve from 6 a.m. to
10 p.m., American and Southwestern, dinners $13 to $25, non-smoking
areas, full bar service.

The Pointe on South Mountain ● △△△△ $$$$$ ∅
7777 S. Pointe Parkway (west off I-10 at Baseline Road), Phoenix, AZ
85044; (602) 438-9000 or (800) 528-0428. All suites; doubles $120 to $235,
singles $110 to $225; lower off-season rates. Major credit cards. Luxurious,
handsomely landscaped resort in South Mountain foothills; six pools, spas,
saunas, putting green, 18-hole golf course, lighted tennis courts, racquetball,
health club. Units have living room, den and bedroom; two TVs, VCR with
rentals, desks with dual-line phones, wet bars, refrigerators, balconies. Many
rooms have city views. Four **restaurants**: Another Pointe in Tyme
(American, listed above), Aunt Chilada's (Mexican), Sport Club (Mexican)
and Rustler's Rooste (Western)—dinners $11 to $29, non-smoking areas,
full bar service.

The Pointe at Squaw Peak ● △△△△△ $$$$$ ∅
7677 N. 16th St. (half mile east of Northern Avenue), Phoenix, AZ 85020;
(602) 997-2626 or (800) 528-0428. Double and single studios $185 to $195,
double and single suites $195 to $235, villas $275 to $287, larger suites to
$1,000; lower off-season rates. Major credit cards. Opulent Spanish colonial-
style resort in the Squaw Peak foothills; six pools, spas, saunas, 18-hole golf
course, lighted tennis courts, racquetball, fitness center, equestrian center.
Rooms and suites have stocked refrigerators, honor bars, TVs with VCR rentals, desks with dual-line phones, private balconies—some with city views.
Three **restaurants**: Beside the Pointe serving Caribbean, South Pacific and
Southwest cuisine, with an adjacent sports lounge, 6 a.m. to 11 p.m.; Hole
in the Wall serving mesquite grill, with Western decor and music, 7 a.m. to
10 p.m. and Aunt Chilada's, Mexican food and decor, 11 a.m. to 11:30 p.m.
All have non-smoking areas and full bar service.

WHERE TO CAMP

Covered Wagon RV Park ● *6540 N. Black Canyon Hwy. (Glendale Avenue exit from I-17, then half mile south), Phoenix, AZ 87017. RV and tent sites, full hookups $18, no hookups $15. No credit cards.* Flush potties, showers, coin laundry, pool and patio; shaded grassy sites; near shopping areas.

Desert's Edge RV Park ● *22623 N. Black Canyon Hwy. (East Deer Valley Road exit from I-10, then half mile north on frontage road), Phoenix, AZ 85027; (602) 869-7021. RV sites, full hookups $15. No credit cards.* Flush potties, showers, coin laundry, Propane, dump station. Pull-throughs, shaded sites, swimming pool and spa, recreation hall with planned activities.

North Phoenix Campground ● *2550 W. Louise Drive (northwest side of Deer Valley Road I-10 exit), Phoenix, AZ 85027; (602) 869-8189. RV and tent sites; full hookups $17, tents $15, cabins $23. Reservations accepted; MC/VISA, AMEX.* Flush potties, showers, convenience store and gift shop, playground, RV and car wash, recreation room with planned activities, kids rec room and playground, pool and spa, outdoor games. Camping cabins and trailers for rent.

Phoenix West Citrus Grove KOA ● *1440 N. Citrus (west of Phoenix, off I-10), Goodyear, AZ 85326; (602) 853-0537. RV and tent sites; full hookups $16, water and electric $15, no hookups $13, tents $10. Reservations accepted; MC/VISA.* Tidy new RV park with pull-throughs; flush potties, showers, coin laundry, groceries, Propane, dump station, snack bar, recreation room, pool and spa, playground.

Pioneer Travel Trailer Park ● *P.O. Box 1674 (Pioneer Road exit 225 from I-17, 30 miles north), Phoenix, AZ 85027; (602) 229-8000 or (800) 658-5895. RV sites, full hookups $13. Reservations accepted.* Flush potties, showers, coin laundry, pool and spa, rec center with live bands and planned activities, billiards, shuffleboard, horseshoes, TV hookups. Located adjacent to (but not affiliated with) the Arizona Pioneer Living History Museum.

Scottsdale, Carefree & Cave Creek

Scottsdale elevation: 1,260 feet   Population: 121,000

Good grief, Scottsdale, what happened to you? When we first visited the mountainous desert area northeast of Phoenix 20 years ago, Scottsdale was a quiet, upscale Western-style hamlet. As we explored the town's Western wear stores, art galleries and curio shops, words like "quaint" and "charming" came to mind.

Those shops still exist, but they're surrounded by a burgeoning suburban sprawl. In the past decade, Phoenix has spilled northward and threatened to engulf Scottsdale. In self defense, the little town went on an annexation binge and promptly covered the pretty desert landscape with its own suburban scatter.

Has Scottsdale diluted its charm? We'll leave that to the eye of the beholder. It certainly is an attractive—if sprawling—community, with lots of red tile roofs and white stucco walls. And it is host to some of the Valley of the Sun's most opulent resorts, offering pampered escape from the suburban scatter. Scottsdale is on the outer edge of the Valley of the Sun megalopolis, so a drive north takes you into countryside that is still free of subdivisions and service stations.

The craggy Camelback Mountain, so named because it resembles a kneeling camel, offers a dramatic backdrop. Most of the posh resorts are tucked into these foothills. Others share cactus country with luxurious Southwestern-style homes in the rock-rimmed Paradise Valley, north of Scottsdale.

Folks at the **Scottsdale Chamber of Commerce** at 7333 Scottsdale Mall (945-8481) will give you a walking map of the old downtown area, which is centered around Main Street and Brown Avenue. Chamber hours are 8:30 to 5 weekdays. Two blocks of Main have been converted into a landscaped pedestrian walk, which merges into the large Scottsdale Mall shopping complex.

The chamber is housed in "The Little Red Schoolhouse," one of the town's oldest surviving structures. Built in 1909, it was Scottsdale's first school, then it served as the city hall, justice court and library.

As you follow the walking tour, which covers about 12 blocks, you'll learn how Scottsdale came to be. In 1894, Rhode Island Banker Albert G. Utley came to this spot, subdivided 40 acres of desert and sold off lots. Utleydale or Urleyburg didn't sound right, so he named the new town for former Army Chaplain Winfield Scott, an early resident who did much to encourage settlement.

Through the years, it became famous as a charming little Western town, way out in the desert beyond Phoenix. Horses had the right-of-way and hitchin' rails stood before false-front stores. Scottsdale prided itself in being one of America's most Western towns.

Today, with its fashionable shopping centers and expensive desert homes, it more resembles Palm Springs with a Stetson, which isn't necessarily bad. The Old West still lurks nearby—in Rawhide, Pinnacle Peak and Cave Creek.

Carefree and Cave Creek are a joined pair of desert hamlets about 20 miles north of Scottsdale. Although neighbors, they come from different backgrounds. Carefree is a planned community, begun in 1959 as a vacation retreat. Cave Creek is a deliberately funky Western town, populated with false-front stores, cowboy saloons and steakhouses. It dates back to the 1870s, when gold was discovered in the rough surrounding hills.

Both communities are in dramatic settings, tucked among desert gardens, giant boulders and redrock ramparts. They're more than a thousand feet higher than Phoenix, offering some respite from summer heat. The **Cave Creek Ranger Station** of Tonto National Forest is on the main highway, between the two communities.

If you like country cooking in a Western atmosphere, plan to invest a dinner hour in Cave Creek. Its rustic main street is lined with cowboy steakhouses. Choose from among these: **Horny Toad Restaurant, Mine Shaft Restaurant and Bar, Treehouse Restaurant** and **Cave Creek Corral**. They're all pretty much the same in funky atmosphere and steak-chops-ribs menus. You can bend elbows with Charley Daniels look-alikes at **Buffalo Chips Saloon**.

Carefree consists mostly of boutique shopping centers with Southwesterny names like Spanish Village, Sundial Plaza and Carefree Plaza. Make it a point to check out **El Pedrigal** shopping complex and **The Boulders** luxury resort on the southern edge of town (listed below).

THE BEST ATTRACTIONS

Taliesin West ● *108th Street (East Shea Boulevard), Scottsdale, AZ 85261; (602) 860-2700. Tours daily, on the hour 10 to 4 (at 9, 10 and 11 in summer). Adults $6, kids 5 to 12, $2.50.* The winter home and studio of America's foremost architect, Taliesin West is an intriguing mix of concrete and stone that seems fused into the desert instead of rising from it. Frank Lloyd Wright came here from Wisconsin in the 1930s to create a teaching center for his concept of "organic architecture." The complex sits on a 600-acre alluvial fan, sweeping down from the McDowell Mountains.

Wright's designs involved the repeated play of geometric forms. Natural materials were used to embody nature, man and architecture. Taliesin West is mostly triangular, with red sandstone and concrete wedges and desert stone sculpted into the sloping hill. The 45-minute tours begin hourly— more often if crowds warrant. Usually led by students expounding Wright's philosophy, the tours take you over landscaped terraces and courtyards and past a drafting studio where students are learning the Wright stuff. In the "Kiva" conference center, you see architectural drawings and models by Wright and his followers.

After the master's death in 1959, the Frank Lloyd Wright Foundation was created to continue his architectural school. Students first become "one with the earth," retreating to the desert to build and occupy a shelter, as they did in Wright's day. Then they live at the school (some stay in the desert), working communally, sharing chores, energies and ideas. The program still includes those elegant touches that Wright treasured, like formal dinners, art shows and musicales.

There are no rigid prerequisites for admission, other than a proclivity to create architectural beauty. New students range from high school graduates to adults seeking mid-life career switches. After they pass written and oral admissions exams, they often must wait a year or more for an opening.

The foundation also sponsors public programs, including seminars on art, architecture and Wright's philosophy, plus half-day tours, evenings of music and dancing, and buffet suppers.

Nights are beautiful here, with the lights of the Valley of the Sun sparkling like scattered diamonds. But the master didn't like this intrusion. He once told his wife, long before Phoenix-Scottsdale had spread this far: "It's time to move Taliesin. I can see a light in the valley."

Cosanti ● *6433 Doubletree Ranch Road (Invergorden), Scottsdale, AZ 85253; (602) 948-61454. Daily 9 to 5; $1 donation.* If aren't skipping ahead in this guide and you've read our Sedona-Prescott chapter, you know that Paolo Soleri is an architectural visionary working on an environmental city called Arcosanti, 68 miles north of Phoenix.

Cosanti is his home, workshop and art studio in Paradise Valley, north of Scottsdale. Here, he and his students create the famous Soleri bronze and ceramic bells and wind chimes. Like Arcosanti, his Cosanti studio has an extra-terrestrial look with pre-cast concrete free-form shapes. It sort of resembles melted geometry, with a kind of doughy primitive look. Yoda would feel right at home here.

The complex includes a gallery of sculptures and other artworks by Soleri and his students, a sales shop and a small foundry. On weekdays, you can watch the artists at work.

Rawhide • *23023 N. Scottsdale Rd. (Pinnacle Peak Rd.), Scottsdale, AZ 85261; (602) 563-5600. October to May—5 to 10 p.m. weekdays and noon to 10 weekends; June to September—5 to 10 daily. Free; museum admission $1.* "How the West was fun," says the sign out front. Rawhide is the largest and probably the best of several wanna-be cowboy towns in the area, with a couple dozen false-front stores standing along its main street. They house boutiques, curio shops, saloons and restaurants.

Visitors can catch a stagecoach, witness a shoot-out, feed goats in a petting zoo and watch a "meller-drammer" in the Moonshine Theatre. An Old West museum boasts 5,000 items—from high-button shoes to antiques; it's easily worth the dollar admission.

You can have a friend arrested for $3, and hung for another $2. Or you can just clump along the boardwalks, feeling Western. Rawhide's Steakhouse offers such rural fare as hickory-broiled steak, barbecued ribs or chicken and even fried rattlesnake, plus live country music. (See "Where to Dine" listing.)

The last time we were there, the streets were busy with Japanese visitors looking a little silly in cowboy hats and red neckerchiefs. Rawhide obviously is the darling of the tour bus set.

Scottsdale-Cave Creek Scenic Drive • *About 70 miles round-trip.* You'll encounter a mix of luxury resorts, fancy Paradise Valley homes, rugged desert-mountain scenery and slices of the Old West in this drive north from Scottsdale.

From Old Town, go north briefly on Scottsdale Road, then west on Camelback Road. You'll travel along the foothills of Camelback Mountain, haven for upscale desert living. At 44th Street, turn right (north) and follow it around the edge of Camelback. It blends into McDonald Drive in a sweeping 90 degree turn. At the next major intersection, turn left (north) onto Tatum Boulevard and follow this through the town of Paradise Valley.

Stay on Tatum for about two miles, then turn right onto Mockingbird Lane, which makes a series of square turns past the Valley's posh Southwestern-style homes. You may get lost, but eventually, you'll bump into Scottsdale Road. Follow this north toward Carefree and Cave Creek. You soon break free of the Phoenix-Scottsdale sprawl and find yourself in open desert. Scottsdale Road becomes Cave Creek Road at some point.

After you've explored Carefree and Cave Creek, return on this route. At Pinnacle Peak Road (next to Rawhide), turn east and wind up into the rock-strewn ramparts of Riata Pass. The road shifts in several places, so keep a watch for Riata Pass signs. At the top, you'll have an impressive view of the Valley of the Sun. It's a good spot to watch the sunset. Two rustic cowboy cafes are up here—**Pinnacle Peak Patio** and **Riata Pass Steakhouse**.

THE REST

Cave Creek Museum • *Basin and Skyline (to the right, off Cave Creek Road), Cave Creek, AZ 85331; (602) 488-2764. Thursday-Sunday 1:30 to 4:30; closed in summer. Free; donations appreciated.* This typically small-town historical museum displays relics of Cave Creek's past as a mining and ranching center. A model pit house and Indian artifacts trace the early Native American cultures in the area.

El Pedrigal Festival Marketplace • *Cave Creek Road at Tom Darlington Road, Carefree.* Watch for this strange-looking shopping center on the right

El Pedrigal Festival Marketplace near Carefree.

as you approach the edge of Carefree. Built into the base of an impressive mountain of boulders, it looks like a cross between Frank Lloyd Wright architecture and Tune Town. The building material might have been multi-colored play dough.

Most of the shops in this gaudy complex are upscale boutiques, Western art galleries and jewelry stores. The quality and prices obviously are intended for guests at the posh Boulders resort, just up Darlington Road. We hope they have an architectural sense of humor.

Hoo-hoogam Ki Museum • *10,000 E. Osborn Rd. (Longmore Rd.), Scottsdale, AZ 85256; (602) 941-7379. Tuesday-Friday 10 to 4, Saturday 10 to 2. Adults $1, kids 50 cents.* The Pima-Maricopa Indians of the Salt River Reservation operate this small museum in an historically authentic structure of adobe, stone and desert plants.

Exhibits—photos, pottery, baskets and other artifacts—reflect lifestyles of the early Hohokam and present-day Pima and Maricopa Indians. Visitors can purchase Indian fry bread and other typical Native American foods at an outdoor dining area.

McCormick Railroad Park • *7301 E. Indian Bend Rd. (Scottsdale Rd.) Scottsdale, AZ 85253; (602) 994-2312. Daily 11 to 5:30. Park admission is free; train rides 50 cents.* Half-pints and adults can ride a half-scale train around this 30-acre park devoted to railroad buffs. Gift shops housed in old railway stations sell choo-choo memorabilia, books and model train supplies. Exhibits include a full-size Mogul Baldwin steam engine and several cars.

If you're a model train nut, drop by on Sunday afternoons, when local clubs set up and run their mini-railroading layouts.

Mouse House Museum • *3634 Civic Center Plaza (Second Street), Scottsdale, AZ 85251; (602) 990-2481. Monday-Thursday 10 to 4.* More than 3,000 mousy reproductions occupy this busy museum, which started as a private collection in the 1920s.

"Enter the mouse house and you'll squeak with delight!" promises the brochure. Perhaps not, but you'll enjoy visiting this menagerie of early Mickey Mouses, church mice, foreign mice, domestic mice, *kachina* mice and lovable rodents of every description. Focal point is a nine-room Victorian doll house that's just—forgive the expression—crawling with mice.

Scottsdale Center for the Arts • *Scottsdale Mall (between the Little Red Schoolhouse and the library), Scottsdale, AZ 85251; (602) 994-ARTS. Tuesday-Friday 10 to 8, Saturday noon to 8 and Sunday noon to 5. Free; fees for stage shows, concerts and films.* Scottsdale's cultural mecca, the city-owned center hosts performing arts in its 830-seat theater, art exhibits and sales, classic movies and other things cultural. Statuary decorates an outdoor sculpture garden. Works of local artists can be purchased in the gift shop.

Scottsdale Historical Museum • *7272 E. Indian School Road (Suite 110 in the Scottsdale Financial Center at Brown Avenue), Scottsdale, AZ 85252; (602) 945-6650. Wednesday-Friday 11 to 3. Free; donations appreciated.* Temporarily housed in the Scottsdale Financial Center, the historical society museum exhibits original furniture of the the town's founders, along with artifacts and photos of the early days. A statue of the town's namesake is in a nearby courtyard.

WHERE TO SHOP

Scottsdale is a-brim with shops featuring cowboy art, Western wear and Indian crafts. Most are in old town near Civic Center Plaza, along Brown Avenue between Main and Second Streets. The largest—with a busy curio shop atmosphere—is **Bischoff's Shades of the West**, at Brown and Main. A good place for Navajo turquoise, silver and blankets is **Atkinson's Indian Trading Post** at 3957 N. Brown, near Old Town just off Indian School Road. Four Scottsdale branches of **Gilbert Ortega's** offer a good selection of Mexican and Indian crafts.

Several modern malls lure shoppers as well. **Scottsdale Mall** is immediately east of Old Town; the upscale **Scottsdale Fashion Square** is at Scottsdale Road and Camelback. The posh **Borgata of Scottsdale,** fashioned after Italy's San Gimignano towers, is on Scottsdale Road, a quarter mile south of Lincoln Drive. Several malls are along Indian School Road, west of Old Town; they're listed in our Phoenix section. Then there's **El Pedrigal Marketplace** in Carefree, more interesting for its architecture than its shops (listed under "The Rest," above).

WHERE TO DINE

American

The American Grill • △△△ $$$ ∅
6113 N. Scottsdale Rd. (Hilton Village Center near Lincoln), Scottsdale; (602) 949-9907. American regional; dinners $15 to $20; full bar. Lunch Monday-Friday 11:15 to 3:30, dinner Monday-Friday 5 to 11 and Sunday 5 to 10. Reservations accepted; major credit cards. Regional American cuisine with emphasis on fresh fish; menu changed monthly. Piano bar Tuesday-Saturday.

Crazy Ed's Satisfied Frog • △△ $$
6245 E. Cave Creek Rd. (in Frontier Town), Cave Creek; (602) 253-6293. Western-style; dinners $5 to $14; full bar. Daily 11 a.m. to 11 p.m. Reservations accepted; MC/VISA, AMEX. Rustic dining room featuring "giant portions" of country American, Mexican and barbecue. Brewery adjacent; 50s and 60s music on weekends.

8700 ● ΔΔΔΔ $$$$ ∅
8700 E. Pinnacle Peak Rd. (Puma), Scottsdale; (602) 994-8700. South-western; dinners $19 to $35; full bar. Daily 6 to 10 p.m. Reservations advised; major credit cards. Luxurious Southwestern setting with fireplaces and a valley view. Menu features mesquite grilled steaks, chops and poultry. Live piano Tuesday through Sunday in adjoining lounge.

El Chorro Lodge ● ΔΔΔΔ $$$ ∅
5550 E. Lincoln Dr. (across from Mountain Shadows), Scottsdale; (602) 948-5170. American; dinners $14 to $39; full bar. Lunch Monday-Friday 11 to 3 and Saturday-Sunday 9 to 3, dinner nightly 6 to 11. Reservations advised; major credit cards. Historic lodge on 22 acres in Paradise Valley; Western-style dining room with original art. American-Continental menu with chateaubriand, rack of lamb, French fried lobster tails and steaks.

LuluBelle's ● ΔΔΔ $$ ∅
7212 E. Main St. (Scottsdale Road in Old Town), Scottsdale; (602) 990-2787. Mexican-American; dinners $9 to $13; full bar. Sunday-Thursday 11 a.m. to 10 p.m., Friday-Saturday 11 to 11. MC/VISA. A Scottsdale landmark since the turn of the century, it features a mix of Mexican and American dishes, from fajitas and red snapper Veracruz to steaks and ribs.

Oaxaca Restaurant ● ΔΔΔ $$$ ∅
8711 E. Pinnacle Peak Rd. (Pinnacle Peak Village), Scottsdale; (602) 998-2222. American; dinners $11 to $28; full bar. Daily from 5 p.m. Reservations advised; major credit cards. Handsome Southwest-style restaurant with "all-American" menu featuring prime rib, baby-back ribs and fresh seafood. Valley view; live entertainment and dancing nightly in adjoining nightclub.

Rawhide Steakhouse ● ΔΔΔ $$ ∅
23023 N. Scottsdale (in Rawhide theme park), Scottsdale; (602) 563-5600. Western-style menu; dinners $8.50 to $18; full bar. Weekdays 5 to 10, weekends 11 to 10 (shorter hours in summer). Reservations for nine or more only; MC/VISA, AMEX. Rustic old West restaurant with country and Western band in the restaurant and live entertainment in adjoining saloon. Mesquite broiled steaks, ribs and chicken.

Continental
Chaparral ● ΔΔΔΔ $$$ ∅
At Marriott's Camelback Resort, 402 E. Lincoln Dr. (off Scottsdale Road), Scottsdale, AZ 85253; (602) 948-1700. Continental; dinners $15 to $26; full bar. 6 p.m. to 10 p.m. (to 11 Friday-Saturday). Reservations essential; major credit cards. Stylishly casual award-winning restaurant in one of Arizona's premiere desert resorts (see listing below).

Mancuso's ● ΔΔΔ $$$ ∅
6166 N. Scottsdale Rd. (in Borgata center), Scottsdale; (602) 948-9988. Italian-French; dinners $11.50 to $22; full bar. Daily 5 p.m. to 10:30. Reservations advised; major credit cards. A local favorite, featuring veal, pasta, fowl and seafood; live entertainment.

Marche Gourmet ● ΔΔ $$ ∅
4121 N. Marshall Way, Scottsdale; (602) 994-4568. French-Continental; dinners $7 to $16; wine and beer. Daily 7:30 a.m. to 10 p.m. Reservations advised; MC/VISA, AMEX. Popular with locals; Continental-Mediterranean mix, including some vegetarian dishes. A non-smoking restaurant.

Mexican

Los Olivos Mexican Patio • ΔΔ $$

7328 Second St. (at Scottsdale Road), Scottsdale. Dinners $3.75 to $12.50; full bar. Sunday-Thursday 11 to 10:30, Friday-Saturday 11 to 1 a.m. Major credit cards. Long-time local favorite, featuring sour cream enchiladas, chimichangas and fajitas. Live music Fridays and Saturdays in adjoining cocktail lounge.

WHERE TO SLEEP

Cave Creek Tumbleweed Hotel • ΔΔ $$$

6333 E. Cave Creek Rd. (at Schoolhouse Road), Cave Creek, AZ 85331; (602) 488-3668. Doubles and singles $53 to $58, kitchenettes $58 to $63, suites $90. MC/VISA. TV, room phones, pool. **Longbranch Saloon** serves 10 a.m. to 1 a.m., Western-style (mesquite grilled steaks, fish, pork, chicken), dinners $9 to $18, full bar service.

Best Western Papago Inn • ΔΔ $$$ ∅

7017 E. McDowell Rd. (70th Street), Scottsdale, AZ 85257; (602) 947-7335 or (800) 528-1234. Doubles and singles $68 to $88; lower off-season rates. Major credit cards. TV, room phones, room refrigerators; pool, spa, exercise room. **CoWah Restaurant** serves 7 a.m. to 1 p.m. and 5 to 9 p.m., Chinese-American, dinners $7 to $12, non-smoking areas, full bar service.

Days Inn Scottsdale • ΔΔ $$$ ∅

4710 N. Scottsdale Rd. (Camelback), Scottsdale, AZ 85251; (602) 947-5411 or (800) 325-2525. Doubles $45 to $104, singles $39 to $104, kitchenettes $50 to $114, suites $65 to $124; lower off-season rates. Major credit cards. TV movies, room phones; free continental breakfast, free van transportation to nearby areas. **Charlie Brown's** and **Coco's** restaurants serve from 6:30 a.m. to midnight, American steak and seafood, dinners $7 to $13, non-smoking areas, full bar service.

Holiday Inn Scottsdale • ΔΔΔ $$$$ ∅

5101 N. Scottsdale Rd. (Chaparral Road), Scottsdale, AZ 85250; (602) 945-4392 or (800) HOLIDAY. Doubles $81 to $108, singles $71 to $108; lower off-season rates. Major credit cards. TV movies, room phones. Attractive grounds with heated pool and spa; lounge, complimentary champagne. **Flamingo Room Restaurant** serves from 6:30 a.m. to 10 p.m., American, dinners from $10 to $20, non-smoking areas, full bar service.

Marriott Suites-Scottsdale • ΔΔΔ $$$ ∅

7325 E. Third Ave. (near Indian School and Scottsdale Road intersection), Scottsdale, AZ 85251; (602) 945-1550 or (800) 228-9290. All suites; doubles and singles $65 to $169; lower off-season rates. Major credit cards. TV movies, room phones, refrigerators, wet bars. Pool, spa and health club; sundry shop, meeting facilities. **Windows Restaurant** serves from 6 a.m. to 10 p.m., American (seafood and lighter fare), dinners $7 to $19, attractive Southwestern decor, non-smoking areas, full bar service.

The Safari Resort • ΔΔΔ $$$$ ∅

4611 N. Scottsdale Rd. (north of Camelback, opposite Scottsdale Fashion Square), Scottsdale, AZ 85251; (602) 945-0721 or (800) 824-4356. Doubles $42 to $114, singles $42 to $104, kitchenettes $60 to $135, suites $75 to $145; lower prices are off-season rates. Major credit cards. TV movies, room phones, refrigerators; two swimming pools; free passes to nearby Seeker's

Comedy Club. The **Brown Derby** restaurant serves 11 a.m. to 10 p.m., American-Continental; coffee shop serves 24 hours, American; dinners $5.25 to $15, non-smoking areas, full bar service. Happy hour, complimentary snacks and live music in adjacent lounge.

Shangrila Resort ● △△ $$$
6237 N. 59th Place (Lincoln Drive), Scottsdale, AZ 85253; (602) 948-5930. Doubles and singles $60 to $75, kitchenettes and suites $70 to $75; lower off-season rates. MC/VISA, AMEX and DC. Small motel with TV, room phones, private patios; pool, citrus trees on landscaped grounds.

RESORTS

The Boulders ● △△△△ $$$$$
P.O. Box 2090 (34631 N. Tom Darlington Rd.), Carefree, AZ 85377; (602) 488-9009. Doubles $325 to $395 including two meals; lower off-season rates. Major credit cards. Posh adobe-style resort with over-sized rooms in a stunning boulder-desert setting with dramatic architecture to match. Rooms have fireplaces, patios, TV movies, phones, refrigerators and other amenities. Swimming pools, spa, tennis courts, exercise room, 27 holes of golf. **Dining room** serves 7 to 10 a.m., 11:30 to 2:30 p.m. and 6 to 9:30, dinners $15 to $38, full bar service.

Hyatt Regency Scottsdale ● △△△△ $$$$$ ∅
7500 E. Doubletree Ranch Rd. (Paradise Valley), Scottsdale, AZ 85258; (602) 991-3388. Doubles and singles $100 to $275, suites and casitas with kitchens $200 to $1,550; lower off-season rates. Major credit cards. Expansive, palm shaded desert garden resort with 27 holes of golf, half-acre "water playground" lake with beach and water slide, fitness center, art objects, pools and saunas. Beautifully styled rooms with TV movies, phones and all amenities. **Three restaurants**—Squash Blossom (Southwestern), Golden Swan (American-Continental) and Sandolo (Italian), service from 6:30 a.m. to 10:30 p.m., dinners $9 to $48, non-smoking areas, full bar service.

Marriott's Camelback Inn ● △△△△△ $$$$$
5402 E. Lincoln Dr. (off Scottsdale Road), Scottsdale, AZ 85253; (602) 948-1700 or (800) 242-2635. Doubles and singles $180 to $225, suites $250 to $1,200; lower off-season rates. Major credit cards. Historic world-class resort on lushly landscaped grounds; 36 holes of golf, putting green, indoor and outdoor pools, spa, lighted tennis courts, playground, rental bicycles, health club with massage studio, coin laundry. Cabana rooms with full amenities including TV/stereo radio, movies, balconies or patios, refrigerators; some fireplaces and private pools; beautiful mountain views. **Restaurants** include Chaparral (see listing above) and Navajo, serving from 6:30 a.m. to 10 p.m., American regional, dinners $8 to $15, non-smoking areas, full bar service.

Orange Tree Golf Resort ● △△△△ $$$$$ ∅
10601 N. 56th St. (Shea), Scottsdale, AZ 85254; (602) 948-6100 or (800) 228-03886. All mini-suites; doubles $100 to $210, singles $90 to $190; lower off-season rates. MC/VISA, AMEX. New resort with 18-hole golf course, pool, sauna, health club with massage studios. Rooms with wet bars, oversized TV/stereo/VCRs, spa tubs. **Joe's at Orange Tree** serves 6 a.m. to 10 p.m., regional American, dinners $11 to $40, attractive dining room overlooking 18th fairway, non-smoking areas, full bar service.

The Phoenician Resort ● △△△△△ $$$$$ ⌀

6000 East Camelback Rd. (60th Street), Scottsdale, AZ 85251; (602) 941-8200 or (800) 423-4127. Doubles and singles $125 to $390; kitchen units and suites $400 to $1,250; lower off-season rates. Major credit cards. The Valley of the Sun's most luxurious new resort set into the foothills of Camelback Mountain; desert-garden grounds with city views. Rooms have three phones, remote-control TV/stereo and all amenities. Tennis courts, 18-hole golf course, seven swimming pools, spas, health clubs; supervised children's activities. **Four restaurants**—Mary Elaine's, the Terrace, Windows on the Green and the Oasis—serve French, Italian, Southwestern and American fare; service from 6 a.m. to 11 p.m. Dinners from $4 to $39, non-smoking areas, full bar service. Some restaurants offer impressive valley views.

Scottsdale Princess Resort ● △△△△ $$$$$

7575 Princess Dr. (near Bell Road and Scottsdale Road), Scottsdale, AZ 85255; (602) 585-4848. Doubles and singles $90 to $260, suites $180 to $1,500; lower off-season rates. Major credit cards. Elegant resort with handsome Mexican colonial architecture, set in the McDowell foothills. Guest rooms, suites and casitas on 450 acres. Luxuriously furnished oversized rooms with TV movies, phones, wet bars, refrigerators, terraces, some with fireplaces. Two 18-hole golf courses, nine tennis courts, racquet and squash court, health club, spa with saunas, steam bath and beauty salon; "Horseworld" adjacent with polo field and stables. **Several restaurants**, including La Hacienda (upscale Mexican), Marquesa (Continental), Las Ventanas (casual American), Cabana Cafe (casual pool-side dining) and Champions Bar & Grill (steaks, seafood and oyster bar).

Tempe

Elevation: 1,105 feet   **Population: 150,000**

Arizona State University dominates both the cultural and economic life of this fast-growing suburb of Phoenix. More than 70 percent of Tempe's residents are college-educated, and the large ASU campus functions as the area's cultural center.

The town began life in 1872 when Charles Trumbull Hayden opened a general store and flour mill on the banks of the Salt River in 1872. He called the place Hayden's Ferry. In 1878, Phoenix' Darrel Duppa—who obviously had a talent for naming towns—commented that the area resembled the Vale of Tempe in Thessaly, Greece.

Many of the town's early buildings, including Hayden's home, have been preserved in the Old Town section near the ASU campus. The look is a pleasant mix of contemporary and Western rustic, with palm-lined streets and shaded sidewalks.

ATTRACTIONS

Arizona State University Campus ● *Apache Boulevard curves around the large campus, with access at various points. Call (602) 965-5728 to find out what's happening on campus.* Green lawns and palms create a park-like setting for ASU's handsome gathering of brick buildings. The centerpiece is Frank Lloyd Wright's Gammage Center for the Performing Arts, a dramatic sandstone pink structure of circles within circles. The effect is a bit like a masonry circus tent.

Get a campus map at the information desk in the Memorial Union, which will direct you to parking areas as well as campus attractions. The Memorial Union also offers nine places to eat, plus a campus shop, lounge and even a bowling alley and movie theater. The open-air University Tram will scoot you around. Four information booths are spotted about the campus, in addition to the one in the Memorial Union. Most of ASU's museums are around Matthews Center.

Anthropology Museum, *965-6213; weekdays 8 to 5; free.* Prehistoric and modern Indian cultures are the focus here.

Arizona University Art Collections, *965-2874; weekdays 8 to 5, Sunday 1 to 5.* On the second floor of Matthews Center, the ASU art museum displays paintings, ceramics, statuary and other artworks from the Americas and Europe.

College of Architecture and Environmental Design, *965-3216; weekdays 8 to 5; free.* The Gallery of Design has drawings and scale models of current architectural trends.

Geology Museum, *965-5081; 10 to 1 during the school year; closed in summer; free.* Exhibits include sundry rocks and minerals, a seismograph and six-story Foucault Pendulum.

Grady Gammage Center for the Performing Arts *(965-3434)* was one of the last buildings designed by Frank Lloyd Wright. Tours of the dramatic structure are scheduled periodically; call for times.

Harry Wood Gallery, *965-3468; weekdays 8 to 5; free.* Student artists display their work in this School Arts Building gallery.

Northlight Gallery, *965-5667; Sunday-Thursday 10:30 to 4:30, closed in summer; free.* In Matthews Hall behind Matthews Center, it features changing photo exhibits.

Planetarium, *965-6891; $1.* Public star shows are held Tuesday and Thursday nights during the school year; it's in the Physical Sciences Center. The **Center for Meteorite Studies** here exhibits rocky visitors from outer space.

Niels Peterson House ● *1414 W. Southern Ave. (Priest Drive), Tempe, AZ 85282; (602) 829-1392. Monday-Friday 10 to 2; free.* This is a Queen Anne Victorian built in 1892, although the interior is furnished in 1930s style. It's partly restored and open to visitors.

Tempe Arts Center ● *Tempe Beach Park (Mill Avenue and First Street), Tempe, AZ 85282; (602) 968-0888. Tuesday-Sunday, noon to 5; free.* Works of local artists are displayed here. Most of the paintings, ceramics, sculptures, photographs and other artworks are for sale. You also can buy creative snacks. Modernistic shapes inhabit a sculpture garden.

Tempe Historical Museum ● *Tempe Community Center (3500 S. Rural Road at Southern Avenue), Tempe, AZ 85282; (602) 731-8842. Tuesday-Saturday 10 to 4:30; free.* Tempe's early days are preserved in this collection of farm implements, historical photos, kitchen utensils, toys, furniture and clothing. Exhibits include a Model-T fire truck, post office and prairie schooner.

WHERE TO SHOP

Old Town Tempe, a four-block stretch of Mill Avenue between Third and Seventh Streets, has several curio, Indian handicraft and Western shops.

WHERE TO DINE

Garcia's ● △△ $ ∅

1604 S. Southern Ave. (McClintock); (602) 820-0400. Mexican; dinners $5 to $8; full bar service. Sunday-Thursday 11 to 10, Friday-Saturday 11 to 11. Reservations accepted; major credit cards. Cheerful Latin place with strolling mariachis; typical Mexican menu.

Jasmine Cafe ● △△ $ ∅

1805 E. Elliot (McClintick and Elliott, suite 104 in Royal Palms Plaza); (602) 491-0797. Pan-Asian; dinners $4 to $6.45; full bar service. Monday-Thursday 11 a.m. to 9:30, Friday-Saturday 11 to 10, dinner only on Sunday. Reservations for 6 or more only; MC/VISA, AMEX, DC. Trendy neon-trimmed cafe, eclectic health-oriented menu; live entertainment on weekends from folk to classical flutist.

Manuel's Mexican Food △△ $ ∅

1123 W. Broadway; (602) 968-4437. Mexican; dinners $5 to $8. Daily 11 a.m. to 11 p.m. MC/VISA, AMEX, DC. Family-owned business serving authentic Mexican food for 25 years.

Ming's Restaurant △△ $

3300 S. Mill Ave. (Southern Avenue), (602) 966-6464. Chinese; dinners $6 to $9.50. Daily 11:30 a.m. to 10 p.m. Reservations accepted; MC/VISA, AMEX, DC. A mix of Cantonese and Mandarin styles; specials include Peking duck, lemon chicken and garlic shrimp.

WHERE TO SLEEP

Budget Host Motel ● △△ $$

947 E. Apache Blvd., Tempe, AZ 85281; (602) 894-0909 or (800) 283-6732. Doubles $35 to $65, singles $25 to $45; lower off-season rates. Major credit cards. TV movies, phones, free coffee, pool.

Comfort Inn Tempe ● △△ $$ ∅

5300 S. 56th St. (Baseline Road), Tempe, AZ 85283; (602) 820-7500 or (800) 221-2222. Doubles $40 to $55, singles $30 to $50; lower off-season rates. Major credit cards. TV movies, room phones, pool, some room refrigerators; free continental breakfast.

Fiesta Inn ● △△△ $$$ ∅

3100 S. Priest Dr. (Broadway exit from I-10), Tempe, AZ 85383; (602) 967-1441 or (800) 528-6481. Doubles $48 to $105, singles $45 to $98, suites $85 to $175; lower off-season rates. MC/VISA, AMEX, DC. TV movies, room phones, room refrigerators and hair dryers; pool, spa, sauna, tennis, lighted golf practice range, exercise room. **Dale Anderson's Other Place** restaurant serves 6:30 a.m. to 10 p.m.; American (salad bar, fresh fish, prime rib), dinners $10 to $26, Southwestern decor, non-smoking areas, full bar service.

Holiday Inn ● △△△ $$$ ∅

915 E. Apache Blvd. (Scottsdale Road), Tempe, AZ 85281; (602) 968-3451 or (800) HOLIDAY. Doubles and singles $59 to $67, kitchen units $69, suites $95; lower off-season rates. Major credit cards. TV movies, phones, pool, stocked refrigerators, fitness center, hot tub. **Ducks Sports Lounge & Grill** serves from 6 a.m. to 10 p.m., American (ribs featured), dinners $6 to $13, non-smoking areas, full bar service.

Ramada Hotel Airport East ● △△△ $$$ ∅
1600 S. 52nd St. (Broadway exit off I-10), Tempe, AZ 85283; (602) 967-6600. Doubles $49 to $79, singles $49 to $69; lower off-season rates. MC/VISA, AMEX, DC. TV movies, free newspapers and coffee; pool. **C.W. Dandy's Restaurant** serves 6 a.m. to 2 p.m. and 5 to 10 p.m., American, non-smoking areas, full bar service.

Westcourt in the Buttes ● △△△△ $$$$$ ∅
2000 Westcourt Way (south of 48th and Broadway), Tempe, AZ 85281; (602) 225-9000 or (800) 843-1986. Doubles $175 to $195, singles $165 to $185, suites $375 to $575; lower off-season rates. Major credit cards. Strikingly modern resort built onto a 25-acre mountaintop site; some rooms and dining rooms have panoramic views of the Valley of the Sun. TV movies, VCRs, stocked refrigerators, hair dryers and other amenities. Pool, spa, saunas, health club, tennis courts, hiking trails; golf nearby. Concierge level with free food and beverages. Two **restaurants** serving nouvelle Southwestern and American; breakfast, lunch and dinner, $11.50 to $27, non-smoking areas, full bar service; exhibition kitchen, valley views, indoor pond with rock waterfall.

WHERE TO CAMP

Green Acres RV Park III ● *1890 E. Apache Blvd. (two miles north on McClintock from Highway 360), Tempe, AZ 85281; (602) 829-0106. RV sites, full hookups $13.50; no credit cards.* Pull-throughs; flush potties, showers, coin laundry, dump station; RV supply and repair nearby.

Mesa, Fountain Hills & Chandler

Mesa elevation: 1,225 feet   **Population: 250,000**

A group of Mormons settled on a bluff above the Salt River in 1877 and named their village after the Spanish word for plateau—*mesa*. Like the pioneers of neighboring Phoenix, they cleaned out old Hohokam canals and soon had a thriving farming community.

But they had no idea how *much* it would thrive.

Today's Mesa is Arizona's third largest city, with a population topping a quarter of a million. During the Valley of the Sun's feverish surge from 1983 to 1987, it was one of the fastest growing cities in America. It's an attractive residential community with Spanish colonnaded sidewalks and brick crosswalks downtown. Orange trees and palms line its streets. Although not noted for tourism, it does have a few interesting visitor lures.

The **Mesa Convention and Visitors Bureau,** downtown at 120 N. Center St., will help you find your way around this growing community.

Fountain Hills is a planned community of 8,000 in the McDowell Mountain foothills north of Mesa. It's all carefully laid out with shopping centers and upscale homes. Centerpiece is the world's highest fountain, a Swiss-made spigot that shoots water 560 feet into the air.

Chandler, one of the Valley of the Sun's mushrooming communities with a population of 65,000, is essentially a Phoenix bedroom. It was rated in the mid-1980s as the fastest-growing city in America. Although not a tourist area, it offers some lodgings with handy freeway access.

Rising to the east of this swelling Phoenix suburbia are the craggy Superstition Mountains, home to the legendary Lost Dutchman Mine. We'll discuss that strange tale in the next chapter.

THE BEST ATTRACTIONS

Mesa Southwest Museum ● *53 N. MacDonald St. (First Street), Mesa, AZ 85201 (602) 644-2230 or 644-2169. Tuesday-Saturday 10 to 5, Sunday 1 to 5. Adults $2.50, kids under 13, $1.* This fine City of Mesa museum effectively captures the area's history, from the mysteries of the vanished Hohokam Indians to the legend of the Lost Dutchman Mine. It's housed in an attractive Spanish-style structure surrounded by landscaped gardens

Among the professionally-rendered exhibits are memorabilia of Mesa's early days, Indian artifacts and reconstructions of Indian dwellings using native materials. The garden shelters several outdoor exhibits, including an adobe schoolhouse, 1890s territorial jail, covered wagon and a stagecoach.

You can pan for gold outside and shop for books and souvenirs in the gift shop. Kids have fun trying to break the code and find the Lost Dutchman mine.

Champlin Fighter Museum ● *4636 Fighter Aces Dr. (at Falcon Field, off McKellips Road, seven miles from downtown), Mesa, AZ 85205; (602) 830-4540. Daily 10 to 5. Adults $5, kids 14 and under, $2.50.* Snoopy would love this place. You can fantasize dogfights with the Red Baron and other aces at this impressive gathering of World War I and II fighter planes. They're housed in two hangars on the edge of Mesa's airport.

Twenty-eight planes, either restored originals or airworthy replicas, seem ready to take off into the wild blue yonder. Our favorite is the world's first combat aircraft—a 1914 German Rumpler Taub fabric-winged observation plane. It streaked along at 74 miles an hour and carried only four hours of fuel. (Sounds like Ickybod, our VW camper). The pilot's only weapons were hand-lobbed grenades.

Others in the collection are a rare Fokker tri-plane, a Sopwith Camel, a Russian MIG-17, the world's only airworthy F6F Hellcat, and one of those legendary Nationalist Chinese P-40 Flying Tigers with shark's teeth painted on its cowling. Most of the World War I versions are replicas; all of the World War II planes are restored originals.

The museum has thousands of other bits of aviation memorabilia—weapons, flight gear, medals and oil paintings of fighters in action. More than 700 autographed photos paper the "Hall of Aces," honoring the world's top fighter pilots. Combat films recall those dangerously romantic days when men with flying scarves and nerves of steel fought to the death in the heavens.

It also exhibits the world's largest private collection of combat firearms—more than 200 items ranging from early machine guns to anti-aircraft weapons. Visitors can buy memorabilia and model planes in a large gift shop.

Out of Africa ● *Two S. Fort McDowell Rd. (near Beeline Highway), Fountain Hills, AZ 85269; (602) 837-7779 or 837-7677. Tuesday-Sunday 10:30 to 4:30. Adults $5.95, kids 4 to 12, $2.95.* Two animal enthusiasts intrigued with people-big cat relationships have turned their research project into a public attraction. Visitors can see lions, tigers and panthers and an assortment of other critters and watch animal handlers work with the big felines. These aren't training sessions, they say, but animal-human encounters. Often, visitors have a chance to cuddle with a new cub or two.

Food is available at the Ring-Tail Safari Cafe, and the Mombassa Trading Company offers gifts with an animal angle. There's also a kid's playground.

Best time to go is Friday through Sunday, when shows are presented at 11, 2 and 4:30. Visitors are taken on guided tours of the park's animal habitats Tuesday through Thursday, but there are no shows.

THE REST

Arizona Museum for Youth • *35 N. Robson St. (Main Street), Mesa, AZ 85201; (602) 644-2647. Summer—Tuesday-Saturday, 10 to 5 and Sunday, 1 to 5; rest of the year—Tuesday-Friday and Sunday, 1 to 5 and Saturday 10 to 5.* Aimed at the grade school set, this museum is a touch-and-feel, crawl-through, scramble-over place with displays that are changed several times a year. (It's sometimes temporarily closed for new exhibit installation, so call first.) It also features child-oriented art exhibits and hobbycraft classes.

Arizona Temple and Visitor Center • *525 E. Main St. (near Mesa Drive), Tempe, AZ 85203; (602) 964-7164. Daily 9 to 9; one-hour tours on the hour and half-hour. Free.* Mesa's Mormon founders built this striking temple in a landscaped park in 1927. It's still the town's most noted landmark—a low-rise granite structure that more resembles a government center than a religious bastion.

Tours take you through the visitor center and beautifully landscaped grounds. Only the faithful can enter the temple itself. A frankly religious pitch is delivered through movies and animated displays. If you want to learn more, the good brothers and sisters will haul out more movies and videos.

Buckhorn Mineral Wells • *5900 E. Main St. (Recker Road), Mesa, AZ 85205; (602) 832-1111. Museum and baths open Tuesday-Saturday 9 to 5; museum—adults $2, kids under 12, $1.* You can soak your cares away in hot mineral pools, then wander through a museum of 400 stuffed animals in this health spa, seven miles east of downtown Mesa. Fees are $12 for a whirlpool mineral bath and $20 for a Swedish massage. Also, you can spend the night in rustic housekeeping units for $35 ($25 in the off-season). Built in the 1930s, it's a bit weathered and showing its age.

Mesa Historical and Archaeological Society Museum • *2345 N. Horne St. (Lehi Road), Mesa, AZ 85201; (602) 835-7358.* Four historic sites are under the protective hand of the Mesa Historical and Archaeological Society. **Crimson's Arizona Farm and Heritage Museum** at 2345 N. Horne was opened just recently as a museum with furnished turn of the century rooms, a tack room and early farm implements. **Park of the Canals** at 1710 N. Horne (McKellips) preserves some of the original Hohokam canals. **"Teaching Children,"** the nation's first monument to education, stands at 200 S. Center (Broadway). The **Sirrine House** is a typical small turn-of-the-century Victorian home at 160 N. Center (University), currently being restored.

WHERE TO SHOP

Fiesta Mall in southwest Mesa at Alma School Road (off Freeway 360) is the area's largest shopping center. It houses several major department stores, restaurants and specialty shops.

WHERE TO DINE

The Landmark Restaurant • ▵▵▵ $$ ∅

809 W. Main St. (Extension Street), Mesa; (602) 962-4652. Midwestern American; dinners $9 to $15, full bar service. Lunch Monday-Friday 11:30 to 2, dinner Monday-Saturday 5 to 9 and Sunday noon to 7; full bar service.

MC/VISA, AMEX, DC. Oldstyle restaurant furnished with Victorian antiques, serving home-style fare with an over-sized salad bar. Dinner theater in summer.

The Olive Garden ● ∆∆ $$ ∅
1261 W. Southern (west of Alma School Road, near Fiesta Mall), Mesa; (602) 890-0440. Italian; dinners $5.50 to $12.50, full bar service. Sunday-Thursday 11 a.m. to 10 p.m., Friday-Saturday 11 to 11. Typical Italian entrees plus four combination platters; free refills on soup, salad and beverages.

The Other Place ● ∆∆ $$ ∅
1644 S. Dobson Rd. (Superstition Freeway), Mesa; (602) 831-8877. American; dinners $10 to $19, full bar service. Breakfast, lunch and dinner, Sunday brunch; reservations accepted. MC/VISA, AMEX, DC. Breakfast buffet $3.95, large salad bar; dinner specials include prime rib, fried chicken and fresh fish. Lively place with deejay and big-screen TV.

Rockin' R Ranch ● ∆∆ $$ ∅
6136 E. Baseline Rd. (half mile west of Power Rd.), Mesa; (602) 832-1539. "Chuck wagon" supper with Western stage show; adults $12.95, kids $7.95; no alcohol. Scheduled dinner and show, so call for times. MC/VISA, AMEX, DC. Western style cookout with sliced beef, baked potato, beans, biscuits and dessert; cowboy music and entertainment follows. Also, a "frontier town" with gift and Western shops.

WHERE TO SLEEP

Arizona Golf Resort ● ∆∆∆∆ $$$$$
425 S. Power Rd. (a mile north of Freeway 360), Mesa, AZ 85206; (602) 832-3202 or (800) 528-8282. Doubles $114 to $124, singles $70 to $110, kitchenettes $60 to $125; suites $75 to $150; lower off-season rates; golf packages. Major credit cards. TV, room phones, refrigerators, coffee makers, private patios; pool, spa, golf course, barbecue grills. **Annabelle's Restaurant** serves 6 a.m. to midnight daily, Continental and prime rib, dinners from $7, non-smoking areas, full bar service; happy hour *hors d'oeuvres*, breakfast buffet.

Hilton Pavilion ● ∆∆∆∆ $$$$ ∅
1011 W. Holmes Ave. (off Freeway 360, near Alma School Road), Mesa, AZ 85202; (602) 833-5555 or (800) 445-8667. Doubles $71 to $109, singles $61 to $99, suites $89 to $139; off-season rates are the lower rates. Major credit cards. Striking courtyard-style architecture; TV movies, phones, some room refrigerators; pool, night club, gift shop, styling salon; golf adjacent. **Imperial Restaurant** serves 6:30 a.m. to 10 p.m., Continental and Southwestern fare, fresh seafood, European-style decor, non-smoking areas, full bar service.

Holiday Inn Mesa ● ∆∆∆ $$$ ∅
1600 S. Country Club Dr. (Off Freeway 360), Mesa, AZ 85210; (602) 964-7000 or (800) 999-MESA. Doubles $69 to $99, singles $59 to $89, suites $79 to $109; lower off-season rates. MC/VISA, AMEX, DC. TV movies, phones, wet bars and mini bars, refrigerators; indoor-outdoor pool, sauna, spa, lounge with entertainment. **Michelles Restaurant** serves 6 a.m. to 10 p.m., Continental, dinners from $13 to $17, non-smoking areas, full bar service.

Mesa Courtyard Hotel ● ∆∆∆ $$$$ ∅
1221 Westwood Ave. (just east of Fiesta Mall), Mesa, AZ 85201; (602) 461-3000 or (800) 321-2211. Doubles $72 to $90, singles $62 to $80, suites

$78 to $96; lower off-season rates. Major credit cards. Attractive courtyard design; TV movies, phones, in-room boiling water for coffee and tea; pool and spa, weight room. **Courtyard Restaurant** serves weekdays from 6:30 a.m. to 10 p.m. and weekends 7 to 10, Continental, dinners $5.25 to $12, non-smoking areas, full bar service.

Mesa Days Inn • △△△ $$ ∅
333 W. Juanita (Country Club and I-10), Mesa, AZ 85210; (602) 844-8900 or (800) 325-2525. Doubles $39 to $80, singles $29 to $80; major credit cards. TV, room phones, refrigerators; free continental breakfast, pool and spa, weight room.

New Ramada Inn • △△△ $$$ ∅
7475 W. Chandler Blvd. (exit 160 off I-10), Chandler, AZ 85226; (602) 961-4444 or (800) 228-2828. Doubles $59 to $99, singles $49 to $89, suites $75 to $125; lower off-season rates. MC/VISA, AMEX, DC. TV, rental movies, phones; pool, spa, fitness room, coin laundry, hearthside lounge. **Cafe Fennel** serves 6:30 a.m. to 10 p.m., American, dinners $8 to $20 with daily specials, non-smoking areas, full bar service.

Ramada Renaissance • △△△△ $$$$ ∅
200 N. Centennial Way (downtown area), Mesa, AZ 85201; (602) 898-8300 or (800) 456-6372. Doubles $90 to $100, singles $80 to $90, suites $105 to $120; lower off-season rates. MC/VISA, AMEX, DC. TV movies, phones; pool in courtyard lagoon; masseuse; concierge floor. **Encore Restaurant** serves 6 a.m. to 2 p.m. and 5 to 10 p.m., Continental, dinners $7 to $20 with early-bird specials, breakfast buffet and Sunday brunch, non-smoking areas, full bar service.

Sheraton San Marcos Golf Resort • △△△△ $$$$$ ∅
One San Marcos Place (seven miles south of I-10 on State Highway 87), Chandler, AZ 85224; (602) 963-6655 or (800) 325-3535. Doubles $150 to $165, singles $140 to $155; lower off-season rates. Major credit cards. A restored 1912 resort on 123 acres with an 18-hole golf course, tennis courts, swimming pools and spas, exercise rooms, par course, **three restaurants** and two lounges. Dinners $6 to $11 at A.J.'s Cafe, Nineteen Twelve and Mulligan's; service from 6 a.m. to 10 p.m., non-smoking areas, full bar service.

WHERE TO CAMP

Green Acres RV Park I • 2055 W. Main St. (Dobson), Mesa, AZ 85201; (602) 964-5058. RV sites, full hookups $13.50; no credit cards. Flush potties, showers, coin laundry, dump station. Family and adult sections available; pool and spa. RV supply and repair nearby.

Green Acres RV Park II • 1836 E. Apache Blvd. (McClintock), Mesa, AZ 85281; (602) 966-7399. RV sites, full hookups $13.50; no credit cards. Flush potties, showers, coin laundry, dump station. Pool and spa; RV supply and repair nearby.

Chapter 8

THE PHOENIX NEIGHBORS

And in death he still is laughing,
For the grave his secret holds,
And the mighty Superstition
Keeps the Dutchman's yellow gold
—from The Dutchman's Gold

THE PHOENIX SUBURBS stretch to the edges of the Salt River Valley, then give way to open desert and rocky, low hills. Driving east of Mesa on Freeway 360 or State Highway 60/89, you climb into the rough lowlands of the Superstition Mountains, home to the legendary Lost Dutchman Mine.

Interstate 10 south is Arizona's busiest corridor, linking the major metropolitan centers of Phoenix and Tucson. That monumental pueblo ruin called Casa Grande is worth a diversion; it's 15 miles east of the freeway.

If you take Horace Greeley's advice and go west—well, northwest—you'll encounter that most Western town of all, Wickenburg.

EAST OF PHOENIX

Beyond Tempe and Mesa, the seemingly endless metropolitan sprawl dissolves into desert gardens, steep river canyons and those foreboding Superstitions.

Apache Junction

Elevation: 1,715 feet   **Population: 17,500**

This scattered town has come of age in the last decade as a Snowbird retreat, as well as a bedroom community for the Valley of the Sun. Sitting at the junction of the Apache Trail (State Highway 88) and U.S. 60, it's the gateway to the Salt River Canyon and Tonto National Forest.

The "Trail" was carved through the rough canyon early in this century as a construction road for the Theodore Roosevelt Dam. Completed in 1911, the dam is the cornerstone of the Salt River Project, which provides water to the Valley of the Sun. In the 1920s, Highway 60 was cut through the Pinal Mountains to the south, linking Phoenix with the silver and copper mines of Globe.

Apache Junction was born in 1922 when entrepreneur George Cleveland Curtis put up a tent and started peddling sandwiches and water to travelers along the two routes. Sitting on the outer fringe of the Valley of the Sun, the town has more of a rural look and feel than neighboring Mesa and Tempe. The business district is enhanced by the dramatic backdrop of the Superstition Mountains.

Apache Junction Chamber of Commerce at the Civic Center, 1001 N. Idaho Road (near the Highway 88-60 junction), can provide data on eating and sleeping places and material on the Superstitions and Salt River Canyon. It's open weekdays from 9 to 5.

ANNUAL EVENTS
Lost Dutchman Days, the last full week of February, and **Fall Fiesta** the third Saturday in November.

THINGS TO KNOW BEFORE YOU GO

Best time to go ● Like Phoenix, most nearby communities are primarily spring-winter-fall destinations. To the east, Apache Junction attracts around 35,000 Snowbirds each winter. Wickenburg to the northwest is famous for its dude ranches. Get reservations early during peak season for both areas. Casa Grande, named for a huge pueblo that's closer to Coolidge, is a handy provisioning stop between Phoenix and Tucson.

Climate ● Warm to hot summers; cool winters. **Apache Junction:** July average—high 105, low 74; January average—high 65, low 36; rainfall—7.5 inches; snowfall—none. **Casa Grande:** July average—high 106, low 74; January average—high 67, low 36; rainfall—8 inches; snowfall—none. **Wickenburg:** July average—high 104, low 70; January average—high 63, low 30; rainfall—11 inches; snowfall—trace.

Useful contacts

> Apache Junction Chamber of Commerce, P.O. Box 1747, Apache Junction, AZ 85217; (602) 982-3141.
> Florence Chamber of Commerce, P.O. Box 929, Florence, AZ 85232; (602) 868-5889.
> Gila River Indian Community, P.O. Box 457, Sacaton, AZ 85247; (602) 963-3981.
> Greater Casa Grande Chamber of Commerce, 575 N. Marshall, Casa Grande, AZ 85222; (602) 836-2125.
> Tonto National Forest, 2324 E. McDowell Rd., Phoenix, AZ 85010; (602) 225-5200.
> Wickenburg Chamber of Commerce, P.O. Drawer CC, Wickenburg, AZ 85358' (602) 684-5479.

Area radio stations

> KTIM-AM, 1250, Wickenburg—Big band sounds
> KTIM-FM, 105.3, Wickenburg—Big band sounds
> Also see Phoenix listings in previous chapter.

WHERE TO DINE

Mining Camp Restaurant ● ΔΔ $$ ∅
6100 E. Mining Camp Rd. (four miles north on Highway 88); 982-3181. American; dinners $11 to $14; no alcohol. Tuesday-Saturday 4 to 9:30, Sunday noon to 9:30. Reservations accepted; MC/VISA. Western-style all-you-can-eat restaurant with cowboy singers and comedy Western shoot-outs.

Sundancer Restaurant ● ΔΔ $$
1535 E. Highway 60 (corner of Tomahawk); (602) 982-6474. American; dinners $6 to $12; full bar service. Daily from 6 a.m. to 1 a.m.; no credit cards. Popular western-style restaurant and saloon serving steaks, chicken, seafood and barbecued ribs; homemade desserts. Live country and Western music Friday, Saturday and Sunday.

WHERE TO SLEEP

Gold Canyon Resort ● ΔΔΔ $$$
6100 Kings Ranch Rd., Apache Junction, AZ 85219; (602) 982-9090. Doubles, singles, kitchenettes and suites $65 to $130; lower range is the off-season rate. MC/VISA, AMEX. An attractive resort in the Superstition foothills with impressive mountain views. TV, room phones, fireplaces, refrigerators, private patios; many rooms with tub spas. Restaurant serves from 7 a.m. to 10 p.m., American, dinners $9 to $18, non-smoking areas, full bar service.

Palm Springs Motel ● ΔΔ $$
709 E. Ninth Ave. (Royal Palm Road), Apache Junction, AZ 85219; (602) 982-7055. Doubles $25 to $36, singles $20 to $28, kitchenettes $32 to $42; lower off-season rates. MC/VISA. TV, refrigerators and free coffee in all rooms. Small family-operated motel.

Superstition Grand Hotel ● ΔΔΔ $$$
201 W. Apache Trail, Apache Junction, AZ 85220; (602) 982-3500 or (800) 847-6575. Doubles $58 to $72, singles $48 to $58, kitchenettes $60 to $75, suites $68 to $88; lower off-season rates. Major credit cards. Spanish-style resort hotel with tennis, shuffleboard; golf and shopping nearby. TV, room phones, free morning coffee. **Superstition Grand Dining Room** serves from 6 a.m. to 9 p.m. Monday-Saturday and 8 to 7 Sunday, Italian-American, dinners $5 to $12, non-smoking areas, full bar service.

WHERE TO CAMP

Apache Trail KOA ● *1540 S. Tomahawk Rd. (Highway 60), Apache Junction, AZ 85219; (602) 982-4015. RV and tent sites; full hookups $16 to $19, water and electric $14 to $16, no hookups $10 to $14. Reservations accepted; MC/VISA.* Pull-through sites; flush potties, showers, coin laundry, groceries, Propane, dump station, snack bar. Heated pool, recreation building, TV lounge, pool table, shuffleboard and horseshoes.

Cactus Gardens RV Park ● *1024 S. Cedar (near Meridian and Broadway), Apache Junction, AZ 85220; (602) 983-6528 or 982-9278. RV sites; full hookups $12. No credit cards; reservations accepted.* Flush potties, no showers. Adults-only park with horseshoes, rec room and planned activities.

Rock Shadows Travel Trailer Resort ● *600 S. Idaho (U.S. 60), Apache Junction, AZ 85290; (602) 982-0450 or (800) 521-7096. RV sites; full hookups $20. Reservations accepted; MC/VISA.* Flush potties, showers, coin laundry. Adult park with many planned activities.

APACHE TRAIL-HIGHWAY 60 LOOP

If you're willing to subject your car to some gravelly bumps, we recommend one of the state's most interesting and varied loop trips. It takes you along the Apache Trail, up the Salt River Canyon, past Tortilla Flat to the old copper town of Globe, then back to Florence Junction on Highway 60.

The route basically wraps around the Superstition Mountains, or Superstition *Mountain*, the reference preferred by old-timers. Glowering on the skyline, looking appropriately sinister—particularly during a storm—they provide the proper setting for the strange saga of the Lost Dutchman Mine (see box). This mystery mine, which probably doesn't exist, has been heralded in book, film and TV documentary.

Driving east from Apache Junction on the Apache Trail, you see the rugged southwestern face of the Superstitions, filling the horizon like a giant Roman temple. You also encounter a ghost town that—having failed as a mining center—is succeeding as a rustic tourist attraction.

Goldfield Ghost Town • *About four miles north of Apache Junction; (602) 983-0333. Daily 10 a.m. to 6 p.m. Museum open daily 10 a.m. to 5 p.m.; adults $3, kids $1.* Goldfield was established in 1892 when a sizable vein was found at the base of the nearby Superstitions. Today, its weathered old buildings attract tourists, who eat cowboy grub, tour an underground mine and browse through an antique shop. The grounds are scattered with a rusting museum of old mining and railroad equipment.

An indoor museum offers interesting exhibits on the geology, mining history and folklore of the area, including a good gathering of artifacts and an historic audio-visual presentation on the Superstitions.

Lost Dutchman State Park • *6109 N. Apache Trail (five miles north) Apache Junction, AZ 85219; (602) 982-4485. Park office open 8 a.m. to 5 p.m. Day use $3, camping $5, no hookups.* Located just beyond Goldfield, Lost Dutchman State Park preserves 292 acres of foothill desert gardens at the base of the mountains. Ranger hikes and talks are conducted from October to April. Nature trails wind about the gardens of saguaro, paloverde and other desert fauna, and longer trails lead into the Superstitions. For a nice day hike, take the **Siphon Draw Trail** from a trailhead above the campground and follow it toward the rugged escarpment of the mountains. The area presents a particularly striking setting from early to mid-March when poppies bloom among the cactus and paloverde.

The campground, set amidst thick desert foliage, offers barbecues, tables, pit toilets and a dump station. The views are worth much more than the $5 fee and the place fills up early. There's also a picnic area.

Continuing eastward, the Apache Trail enters **Tonto National Forest** and picks its way through tumbled foothills that suggest gray-green waves of a petrified sea. A turnout offers a view of Weaver's Needle in the distance; it's a huge, tapered monolith named for trail-blazer Pauline Weaver. This is an area of heavy off-road vehicle use. You may be disturbed by the threadbare landscape, stripped clean by the angry tread of macho four-wheel high-riders. We certainly were.

Along the highway, trailheads offer hiking access into the Superstition Wilderness. After a few miles, the Apache Trail leaves thick saguaro forests and enters steep-walled Salt River Canyon, a favorite playground for heat-fleeing Phoenicians.

Canyon Lake and Marina ● The first of a chain of Salt River Project reservoirs, Canyon Lake—behind Mormon Flat Dam—is popular for fishing, swimming and boating. The marina has boat moorage, a launch ramp, picnic areas and swimming beaches. Day-use is $7 per vehicle. A pretend

THE MYSTERY OF THE DUTCHMAN'S GOLD

The story of the Lost Dutchman Mine is an intriguing chapter in the treasure trove of Western folklore. It's the kind of tale old-timers like to spin as they sit around a pot-bellied stove, pausing now and then to spit into the ash box.

Some dismiss the story as hogwash, yet scores of people who have entered the Superstitions in search of the mine have been found dead—sometimes beheaded. The most recent mystery death occurred in 1979 when the skeletal remains of a missing hiker were discovered in a rugged canyon.

What started all this?

Jacob Waltz, gold-seeker and chicken farmer, was born around 1810 in Oberschwandorf, Germany. He came to America in 1841 and was lured west by the 1849 California Gold Rush. Later, he drifted to Arizona, seeking gold in the Prescott mining regions. Finding none, he settled on 160 acres near Phoenix in 1868 and began chicken farming. But he still wandered in the nearby mountains, seeking that elusive treasure trove.

He did find small amounts of gold—he wouldn't say where—and sold it to augment his meager chicken income. In 1878, sick and aging, he signed his homestead and possessions over to a German friend, Andrew Starar, with the agreement that Starar would care for him until he died.

Waltz continued prospecting when he felt able, and he began spinning tales of a rich mine he'd found in the Superstitions. Some say it was the mine of a Mexican family named Peralta that was massacred by Apaches in 1848. Supposedly, one of the Peraltas escaped with a map, and that document fell into Waltz' hands. Stories began circulating about the mystery mine of the "Dutchman" (a common mispronunciation of *Deutschman,* or German).

Jacob's death was rather bizarre. He caught pneumonia after being chased up a tree by a flood in early 1891. He never fully recovered and expired seven months later—broke and homeless—at the house of a neighbor, Mrs. Julia Thomas.

Shortly after his death, the story of the Lost Dutchman gained momentum. A Phoenix newspaper reported in 1892 that a "Mrs. Julia Thomas has traveled by wagon to the western end of Superstition Mountains in search of a gold mine and she has returned unsuccessfully." Had Jacob given her his map?

Julia never did find gold, nor have the thousands who followed her into the Superstitions. For a few years, con men did a brisk business peddling "authentic" maps, but the quest for the Dutchman's gold has lost its luster in recent years.

Today, these mystic mountains are part of the Superstition Wilderness. Thousands of hikers tramp its trails in search of solitude—and perhaps gold. They emerge unscathed.

Maybe geologists and Tonto National Forest officials have the final chuckle. They say the Superstitions are mostly made of igneous dacite and andacite—an unlikely repository for gold.

But what about those killings? Perhaps it is the ghosts of the Peraltas and Jacob Waltz who are laughing last.

steamboat, *Dolly II,* offers 90-minute cruises around the shoreline daily at noon and 2 p.m.; $9.50 per adult and $7.40 per child. Two-hour dinner cruises are $23.25 and $15.95.

Tortilla Flat Campground ● *Two miles beyond Canyon Lake Marina; RV and tent sites; full hookups $6.* Sites in this Tonto National Forest campground are terraced above the canyon, with barbecues, tables, flush potties and a dump station.

Tortilla Flat ● *Monday-Thursday 9 a.m. to 6 p.m., Friday 9 to 7, Saturday 8 to 8 and Sunday 8 to 6. MC/VISA in restaurant and gift shop.* Boasting a population of six, Tortilla Flat is a deliberately funky collection of buildings that appear to be leaning against one another for support. They house a post office, grocery store, gift shop, a restaurant serving rural American fare, and a saloon.

A sign makes joking references about the "Dutchman" Jacob Waltz enjoying Tortilla Flat's home cookin', but of course his soul departed long before the hamlet was founded. Tortilla Flat started as a road camp for work crews on the Salt River Project in 1904. It has since survived as a watering hole and tourist stop for travelers along the Apache Trail, which is now paved up to this point, but not much beyond.

The pavement gives up about five and a half miles east of Tortilla Flat. The dirt and graveled road bumps up over Fish Creek Hill, providing impressive views of the canyon. It twists through the narrow chasm, brushes past Apache Lake and finally arrives—after 22 miles of dirt—at the keystone of the Salt River Project.

Theodore Roosevelt Dam and Lake ● If a dam can look rustic, it's the Theodore Roosevelt. This unusual cut-stone structure is the largest masonry dam in the world, a 280-foot high wedge in Salt River Canyon.

The superlatives were even greater when it was completed in 1911. It was the world's highest dam of any sort, and it created the globe's largest manmade lake, covering 17,335 acres. Since every scrap of material had to be hauled by high-wheeled wagon over the bumpy, corkscrew Apache Trail, it was a remarkable engineering accomplishment. And it gave thirsty

Goldfield—an appropriately scruffy old mining town near Apache Junction.

Superstition Mountains rugged escarpment above Lost Dutchman State Park.

Phoenix a much-needed drink, starting it on its way as one of the Southwest's largest cities.

The lake's sloping shorelines are popular with swimmers, sunners and boaters. A marina offers moorage, a boat launch, boat rentals, groceries, a snack shop and other essentials. A Tonto National Forest ranger station is located at Roosevelt Lake Marina, and several basic campsites are available, with pit toilets, barbecues and picnic tables.

Two concessionaires provide lodgings:

Roosevelt Lake Marina ● *P.O. Box 458, Roosevelt, AZ 85545; (602) 467-2245. Doubles $40, kitchenettes $45.* Basic accommodations with no phones, TV or utensils.

Roosevelt Lake Resort ● *c/o HC-02, Globe, AZ 85501; (602) 467-2276. Doubles $32; kitchenette cabins $36.* This small resort complex also offers a steak house, cocktail lounge and trailer park.

At Roosevelt Lake, you re-discover pavement and head southeast on Highway 88 toward the copper-mining center of Globe-Miami. You shortly encounter, on the right, one of the state's better-preserved Indian ruins.

Tonto National Monument ● *P.O. Box 707 (a mile off Highway 88), Roosevelt, AZ 85545; (602) 467-2241. Daily 8 to 5, Lower Ruins trail closes at 4; $3 per car.* A small prehistoric tribe called the Salado built two cave-sheltered adobes in brushy cliffs above the Salt River around the 14th century. These cliff dwellings are now protected within a 1,120-acre national monument.

A half-mile trail takes you to the first of these pueblos, simply called the Lower Ruin (although it's an uphill climb from the visitor center). The more extensive Upper Ruin, a 40-room complex, can be reached only by ranger-led hikes, which depart at 9 a.m. daily, from mid-October through April. Reservations are needed for these three-hour treks; make them at least two days in advance.

A small museum displays fragments of cotton cloth, tools, attractive polychrome pottery and other implements found at the sites. The Salado ("salt" in Spanish) were among the more advanced of Arizona's early tribes. Farmers, hunters and gatherers, they diverted water from the Salt River to irrigate their food and cotton patches. They were excellent potters and weavers. They abandoned these dwellings around the 15th century.

From Tonto National Monument, the route drops down out of the national forest to Globe and Miami, two rustic towns sitting on the brink of tailing dumps and terraced copper pits. We'll explore these historic mining centers in Chapter 12. Between Globe and Miami, you pick up Highway 60 and head west, back toward Phoenix. After passing through the copper mining town of **Superior,** take a break at an elaborate desert garden.

Boyce Thompson Southwestern Arboretum ● *P.O. Box AB, Superior, AZ 85273; (602) 689-2811. Daily 8 to 5; adults $2, kids 5 to 17, $1.* Say hello to a boojum tree and listen to a cactus wren in this large desert arboretum. It's operated jointly by a foundation set up by the late copper baron William Boyce Thompson, Arizona State Parks and the University of Arizona.

More than 1,500 species of desert plants from around the world are crowded into this "Noah's Ark" of a semi-arid garden. The visitor center, a 1920s cut-stone mansion listed on the National Register of Historic Places, houses an information desk and a gift shop selling books, cacti and sundry other succulents. Adjacent greenhouses display hundreds of varieties of semi-arid plants, and nature trails wind through 35 acres of landscaped grounds. Picnic tables invite lunching among the flora.

At Florence Junction, you can complete your loop back to Apache Junction along a four-lane highway at the foot of the Superstitions, or head south toward Tucson.

SOUTH TO TUCSON VIA CASA GRANDE

Interstate 10 between Phoenix and Tucson is noted mostly for semi-monotonous desert rimmed with ragged mountains. It's also noted for dust storms, so try to avoid it on windy days. Call 279-2000 and punch R-O-A-D to learn about driving conditions.

The corridor offers a few worthy attractions, so you might want to set aside the better part of a day to make the crossing. A few miles south of Chandler, you enter the Gila River Indian Reservation, which offers an excellent Native American arts and craft center.

Gila Indian Community

Unnoticed by many Phoenix-Tucson travelers, this 337,000 acre Pima-Maricopa reservation is one of Arizona's most progressive Indian communities. It boasts 32 industries, a 15,000-acre community farm and a modern hospital. Tribal headquarters are at **Sacaton,** eight miles southeast of I-10, off exit 175.

Gila River Arts and Crafts Center ● *Casa Blanca Road (I-10 exit 175, then a half mile west), P.O. Box 457, Sacaton, AZ 85247; (602) 963-3981. Daily 9 to 5 (shorter hours in summer); free.* More than 30 different tribes and 2,000 years of Native American history are represented in this modern cultural center. It's actually a blend of four facilities—the Gila River Museum, with historical exhibits; the Arts and Crafts Center; Heritage Park, with reconstructions of Indian dwellings; and a restaurant serving fry bread and other typical Indian fare.

Museum exhibits include old photos and examples of Pima and Maricopa basketry, pottery, weapons and other artifacts. In Heritage Park, you can poke through traditional dwellings of Pima, Maricopa, Tohono O'odham and Apache tribes. The handiwork of more than a dozen Southwestern tribes is on display in the Arts and Crafts Center; much of it is for sale in the gift shop. Items include *kachinas*, basketry, paintings, jewelry, sculptures, pottery and hand-woven rugs. Both traditional and modern artworks are represented.

Craft demonstrations, traditional dances and other activities are held periodically—particularly during the fall-winter-spring tourist season.

ANNUAL EVENTS

The Gila Indian Community is one of the best places in Arizona to sample both modern and traditional cultural activities. Annual events include the **St. John's Indian School Festival** with dances, crafts and a carnival, the first Sunday in March; **Native American Festivities and Crafts Sale,** the second weekend of March, **"Gathering of the People"** tribal fair with a rodeo, parade, arts and music, the second weekend of April, **Pima-Maricopa Arts Festival,** the second weekend of November, and the **Native American Dance Festival,** the fourth weekend of November.

WHERE TO CAMP

Casa Blanca RV Park • *Half-mile west of I-10 (P.O. Box 176), Sacaton, AZ 85247; (602) 562-3205. RV and tent sites, full hookups $12.50 with discounts for subsequent days, no hookups $5.50. Reservations accepted; no credit cards.* Flush potties, showers, laundromat, convenience store nearby, Propane, dump station, TV cable. New park with all pull-throughs.

Casa Grande

Elevation: 1,398 feet   **Population: 16,000**

Once a wide spot in the road, Casa Grande has grown in the last couple decades to a fair-sized residential community. It offers visitors a provisioning pause between Phoenix and Tucson. Although it is named for the Casa Grande pueblo ruin, that structure is northeast of here, near Coolidge.

Casa Grande Ruins National Monument • *P.O. Box 518 (off Highway 87), Coolidge, AZ 85228; (602) 723-3172. Daily 7 a.m. to 6 p.m.; $3 per family, $1 per person; kids 17 and under free.* It looks odd, standing there with its sheltering metal roof supported by tall pylons—like a blend of adobe ruin and Chinese pagoda. But the modern roof over Casa Grande is necessary to keep this massive, multi-storied structure from melting back into the earth.

Casa Grande is the tallest and perhaps the most mysterious of Arizona's pueblos. It's four stories high with four-foot thick walls at the base to support its 2,800-ton mass. Six hundred wooden beams were needed to hold up its ceilings. The structure was the centerpiece of a Hohokam village, occupied for about a century, until 1450 A.D. Archaeologists don't know why Casa Grande was built, nor why it was abandoned. The towering structure may have been used for ceremonies or even astronomical observations.

Visitors can observe it only from the ground, for it is too fragile to be entered. National Park rangers conduct frequent tours around its perimeter, discussing its construction methods and its long-vanished inhabitants. Fragments of the village wall and smaller buildings rim the great structure.

The visitor center contains fine example of large, fully intact pots and exhibits concerning irrigation, tool-making and other crafts of the Hohokam.

Casa Grande Valley Historical Museum ● *110 W. Florence Blvd., Casa Grande, AZ 85222; (602) 836-2223. Tuesday-Sunday 1 to 5 from mid-September to mid-June; free.* Furnished rooms of the town's early days, a turn-of-the-century store and historical diorama are features of this museum. Other exhibits focus on the area's Indian cultures, mining and agricultural development.

WHERE TO SLEEP

Francisco Grande Resort & Golf Club ● △△△△ $$

26000 Gila Bend Hwy. (five miles west), Casa Grande, AZ 85222; (602) 836-6444 or (800) 237-4238 in Arizona and (800) 782-2887 outside. Doubles and singles $45 to $85, kitchenettes $139 to $159, suites $83 to $159; lower off-season rates. MC/VISA, AMEX and DC. Full-service resort with 18-hole golf course, tennis courts, croquet, volleyball, horseshoes and conference facilities. TV movies, phones, pool and spa. **Palo Verde Dining Room** serves from 6:30 a.m. to 10 p.m.; American menu, casual atmosphere, outdoor dining; private dining in the Gourmet Room; dinners $9 to $16, full bar service.

Florence

Elevation: 1,493 feet   **Population: 6,300**

One of Arizona's first American settlements, Florence dates back to 1866, when one Levi Ruggles laid out a townsite near a ford in the Gila River. It was named for the sister of Territorial Governor Richard McCormick. Although smaller than Casa Grande, it's the seat of Pinal County.

It's a handsome old town, with several 19th century homes in the Florence Townsite National Historic District. More than 100 of these structures are listed on the National Register of Historic Places. Styles range from Sonoran to Victorian to Arizona territorial. The Western-flavor downtown with false front stores and sidewalk overhangs looks right out of a cowboy movie set. In fact, it's often used by Hollywood film makers.

The Pinal County Courthouse on Butte Avenue near Main Street is the town's architectural gem—an 1891 yellow brick structure with gingerbread trim and a hexagonal clock tower.

Florence also is home to Arizona State Prison, built in 1909 to replace the notorious Yuma Territorial Prison. Signs near the lockup advise you not to pick up hitchhikers.

The **Florence Chamber of Commerce** operates the Pinal County Visitor Center in the historic Jacob Suter House at 270 Bailey St.; phone (602) 868-4331. Nearby Jaques Square is a prettily landscaped park with brick walkways, oldstyle street lamps and wrought iron benches.

THE ATTRACTIONS

McFarland State Historic Park ● *Main and Ruggles streets (P.O. Box 109), Florence, AZ 85631; (602) 868-5216. Thursday-Monday 8 to 5. Adults $2, kids under 17 free.* Pinal County got its start here; this adobe functioned as the courthouse, sheriff's office and jail from 1878 to 1891. It spent another half century as a county hospital. One side of the structure houses the old courtroom with its jury box, wooden pews and judge's bench, while the other contains early 20th century hospital exhibits.

A special display focuses on local boy-makes-good Ernest W. McFarland, author of the G.I. Bill of Rights and chief justice of the Arizona Supreme Court. Arriving in the state in 1919 with $10 in his pocket, he climbed the political staircase from a local irrigation district counsel to county attorney to state governor. He was sent to Washington as a U.S. Senator, became Senate Majority Leader and finally wound up on the state's high court. McFarland never lived in this structure; he purchased it as a gift to the state in 1974, thus earning the right to have his name attached.

Pinal County Historical Museum ● *715 S. Main St., Florence, AZ 85631; (602) 868-4382. Wednesday-Sunday 1 to 5; closed in January; free.* A typical county history center, it also has some untypical exhibits. They include a hundred varieties of barbed wire, a large bullet display, antique woodworking tools and some gruesome photos of hanging victims, a gas chamber chair and hang nooses from Arizona prisons. Exhibits of Southwest Indians are quite extensive. Newspaper clippings report the sad news of the death of cowboy star Tom Mix. He rolled his high-speed Cord sports car into a nearby ditch on October 12, 1940.

ANNUAL EVENTS

Historic homes tours, first Saturday of February; **Founders' Day,** first Saturday of March; **Spring Festival,** second Saturday of April; **Junior Parada (Rodeo),** Thanksgiving weekend.

After exploring Casa Grande National Monument and Florence, you can head south on State Highway 87 and re-join I-10. You'll shortly see a rather dramatic monolith that looks like a giant tiger's fang.

Picacho Peak State Park ● *P.O. Box 275, Picacho, AZ 85241; (602) 466-3183. Day use $3, RV and tent sites with hookups for $8. No reservations or credit cards.* The park offers picnic areas and hiking trails, including a path to the 1,400-foot summit of this stone upcropping. The campground has flush potties, showers, picnic tables and barbecue facilities.

Confederate and Union forces clashed near here on April 15, 1862, in the westernmost battle of the Civil War. These weren't regular troops, but members of the Confederacy's Texas Volunteers and the Union-supporting California Volunteers. The Californians routed the Texans in the brief skirmish.

Another campground is nearby:

Picacho KOA ● *P.O. Box 368, Picacho, AZ 85241; (602) 466-7401. RV and tent sites, hookups $11; "Kamping Kabins" $20. Reservations accepted; MC/VISA.* Some pull-throughs; flush potties, showers, coin laundry, pool and spa, recreation room, groceries and Propane, disposal station.

Pinal Pioneer Parkway

An alternate route between Phoenix and Tucson—which we prefer—is Highway 89, the Pinal Pioneer Parkway. It becomes the Tucson-Florence Highway as you continue south. It's much prettier and less subject to dust storms than I-10.

South of Florence, the highway passes through thick desert gardens marked with signs identifying the flora—cat claw, prickly pear, paloverde, saguaro and such. Think of it as a 55-mile-an-hour nature trail. There are occasional turn-outs and picnic tables.

Tom Mix Monument, 17 miles south of Florence, marks the spot where the 1930s movie cowboy met his Maker. A stone marker with a rider-less, sad-looking horse is inscribed: *In memory of Tom Mix, whose spirit left his body on this spot, and whose characterization and portrayals in life served to better fix memories of the Old West in the minds of living men.* There's a parking area and picnic tables here, if you want to spend a few moments with the famous star's memory. Expect your kids to ask: "Tom who?"

Approaching Tucson, the route dips into the foothills of the Santa Catalina Mountains, which are sprinkled with upscale subdivisions, includ-ing the newest Del Webb retirement community, **Rancho Vistoso.** After passing through the hamlet of Catalina—which is little more than a roadside traffic hindrance—the highway becomes four-lane Oracle Road, which takes you into the heart of Tucson.

OUT WICKENBURG WAY

U.S. 89/60 runs northwest out of Phoenix at an odd angle. It brushes past the growing communities of Glendale, Peoria, Sun City and Youngtown, then heads into the desert. Some people think Del Webb invented the retire-ment community with the creation of Sun City. But Youngtown came first, opening in October, 1954. Sun City started six years later. It's now the largest, with a population topping 46,000. Nearby Sun City West has about 14,500, and a third Webb Corporation pension farm, Sun City Vistoso near Tucson, opened in 1987.

Beyond Sun City West, the last of the metro Phoenix suburbs surrenders to creosote-bush desert. Then the highway gains altitude as it climbs into the saguaro-studded Vulture Mountains. Shortly, the traveler is greeted by a sign exclaiming: "Howdy! You're Out Wickenburg Way!"

Wickenburg

Elevation: 2,100 feet   **Population: 4,500**

I'll be danged if this ain't the cutest little cowboy town in Arizona. Wick-enburg works at being Western, with balconied store fronts, boardwalks and a friendly down-home attitude. "Tie up, come in and swap stories," invites a sign outside Ben's Saddlery. The town calls itself the dude ranch capital of the world, and real cowboys still ride herd in the surrounding high desert.

THE WAY IT WAS • Gold, not beef, put the town on the map. In 1862, an Austrian named Henry Wickenburg hitched his hopes to an onery burro and began prospecting in the nearby hills. He struck it rich with the Vulture Mine. Some say he picked up a rock to throw at a vulture, or at his stubborn mule—and the rock was veined with gold.

Either version of the story sounds like campfire talk. But one truth is un-deniable: Gold mines in the area yielded $30 million between the 1860s and 1900. Miners needed water to wash their diggin's, so they settled along the Hassayampa River and Wickenburg was born.

Ore from 80 mines poured into town, along with the usual ration of drifters, rascals and fallen angels. At its prime, Wickenburg was the third largest city in Arizona, and one of the wildest. Folks were too busy seeking gold to build a jail, so they simply chained the bad guys to a large mesquite tree. During visiting hours, prisoners' relatives would come out and have a picnic. The tree still stands, behind the Circle K mini-mart at Tegner Street and Wickenburg Way.

As the mines played out, cattlemen began running their herds in the brushy desert. Easterners, reading newspaper reports and dime novels about the Wild West, came out to see what all the excitement was about. Dude ranching, born in Montana, quickly spread to Arizona. Wickenburg and Tucson were early dude ranch centers, and they still are. Nowadays, of course, folks call them guest ranches.

THE WAY IT IS • There isn't much to downtown Wickenburg; only a few city blocks. But it's all charmingly Western. False-front stores tempt visitors with cowboy clothing, Indian crafts and curios. Seven galleries sell paintings, sculptures and ceramics; most have Western themes.

Tourism has replaced gold and cattle as the town's reason for being. Indeed, 80 percent of Wickenburg's jobs are directly tied to visitor services. Thus, you will find a surprisingly large assortment of restaurants and motels for such a small town.

Wickenburg Chamber of Commerce, in the restored 1895 Santa Fe Railway depot at 215 N. Frontier Street, has an impressive selection of brochures on the town's attractions, lodgings and restaurants. You can pick up a walking tour map and stroll past an assortment of turn-of-the-century homes and stores.

The depot itself, listed on the National Register of Historic Places, is worth a look. Another point of interest is the **Old Wishing Well** near the highway bridge crossing the Hassayampa River. The funny name is Apache for "up-side down river," since most of the flow through here is beneath its dry sands.

A sign warns that anyone drinking from the well will never be able to tell the truth. Why? During Wickenburg's wicked mining era when fiction flew thick and fast, a tall story was called a "Hassayamper." The idea seems far-fetched, but since we strive for the truth in our guidebooks, we chose not to to take a sip.

Wickenburg's premier attraction is merely the best small community museum in Arizona.

ATTRACTIONS

Desert Caballeros Western Museum • *20 N. Frontier St. (at Wickenburg Way), Wickenburg, AZ 85358; (602) 684-2272. Monday-Saturday 10 to 5, Sunday 1 to 4. Adults $2; kids free.* The local branch of the Maricopa County Historical Society has done an outstanding job of preserving the past. Instead of a clutter of high-button shoes and butter churns, the Desert Caballeros Museum features a full-scale turn-of-the-century street scene to capture that yesterday feeling.

In the museum's Hall of History, dioramas and artifacts recall the area's development from the Paleozoic to the present. Other exhibits include a mineral collection, Indian arts and crafts, and rooms with period furnishings. An adjoining gallery, with Western art by such notables as Russell, Remington and Catlin, would be the envy of a major metropolitan museum. The gallery—like the rest of the museum—is spacious, uncluttered and professionally done.

There's more to see outside. A stagecoach sits on the porch of this handsome adobe-sandstone structure. Bits of Arizona history are captured in bas relief wall plaques. A large bronze statue of a kneeling cowboy and his horse, entitled "Thanks for the rain," occupies a landscaped cactus garden.

Hassayampa River Preserve ● *West side of Highway 60/93, six miles from town (P.O. Box 1162), Wickenburg, AZ 85358; (602) 684-2772. Open Wednesday-Sunday: Mid-September to mid-May, 8 to 5; mid-May to mid-September, noon to 5. Free.* This is a fine example of a riparian woodland along the course of the Hassayampa, with hiking trails and picnic areas. Once a stage stop and guest ranch, it was opened as a preserve in 1987 by the Nature Conservancy. The old ranch house is now a natural history museum, library and bookstore.

Self-guided nature trails take you along the lush riverbottom. The Hassayampa, which usually flows *above* the sand in this area, supports a rich plant and animal habitat. It's a great place for bird-watching. Free guided nature walks are conducted periodically; call for dates and times.

Hiking ● *See "Guide to Hiking in the Wickenburg Area" brochure, available at the Chamber of Commerce.* This brochure, prepared by a naturalist,

---

WHAT IN TARNATION IS A COWBOY, ANYHOW?

Nothing has captured the world's fancy quite so much as the American cowboy. Folks from around the country—and the globe—are lured to Arizona guest ranches to stuff themselves into blue denims, sit tall in the saddle and eat beef and beans around a campfire. Of course, most ranches offer swimming pools and other amenities, so greenhorns can play cowboy in comfort.

Although he's considered an American institution, the cowboy has his roots in Mexico. And the "cowboy era"—which endures in books, movies, TV shows and in romantic hearts—lasted less than 25 years.

Gold, not cattle, lured the first flood of Americans West. When California's Forty-niners and Arizona's argonauts arrived in the mid-1800s, they'd never heard of ten-gallon hats, lassos or blue denims.

As gold played out in the 1870s, some pioneers began running cattle and sheep. Those early ranchers marveled at the skill of Mexico's *vaqueros*, who could catch a running steer with a length of braided rawhide called a *riata*. Their saddles had high backs to help them keep their seats, and snubbing horns for their rawhide ropes. The *vaqueros* wore broad-brimmed *sombreros* for sun shelter and leather leggings—or "chaps"—as protection from scratchy chaparral. These outfits made sense, so the gringos adopted them.

To reach Eastern markets, livestock had to be herded to northern railheads, and the romance of the great cattle drives was born. Yes, they *did* sing to calm the spooky critters at night—and they were probably terribly off-key.

Spreading railroads soon eliminated the need for cattle drives, and straight-shooting marshals eliminated most of the bad guys in rowdy Western towns. Settlers fenced in much of the open range. By the 1890s, the era of cattle drives and range wars was over. The beef you barbecue today probably came from a feedlot.

What about those blue denims, which are *de rigueur* for every cowboy from Tucson to Tinseltown? Well, dang my britches, they weren't even produced until 1874, after the "cowboy period" had begun. Levi Strauss made his famous jeans from gray tent canvas, and they were for California gold miners, not Arizona cowpokes.

directs you to four hikes in the area. You can walk the extensive grounds of the venerable Wickenburg Inn and visit its nature center, explore the Hassayampa River Preserve, trek into Box Canyon northwest of town and walk about the Vulture Peak area where old Henry struck it rich.

Ghost town prowling • *See "Out Wickenburg Way" booklet published by the Chamber of Commerce.* Remnants of four ghost towns survive in the rough hills around Wickenburg. A chamber of commerce booklet tells you about them: **Weaver**, first a mining camp and then a hangout for bad guys; **Stanton**, now a privately owned town, once run by a notorious defrocked priest; **Octave**, which yielded $8 million from its deep pit quartz vein; and **Congress**, with only a tailing dump surviving from its glory years, when it yielded $1 million in gold.

The Vulture Mine headframe and outbuildings still stand outside of Wickenburg, but it's privately-owned and off limits to visitors.

Some geologists say only 10 percent of the area's gold has been mined; the rest lies hidden underground. Recreational panning is still popular. The best place to find gold is in an alluvial fan at the base of a hillside ravine. Like the miners of old, you'll have to carry your diggin's to water to separate the gold.

Joshua Forest Parkway • *Twenty-four miles northwest on U.S. 93.* Great stands of Joshua trees, those strange fuzzy-armed desert plants, line the highway northwest of Wickenburg. They earned their odd name because Mormon settlers said they resembled Joshua praying to Heaven. (Joshua must have had very hairy arms). They can reach heights of 30 feet or more. But they aren't trees; they're members of the lily family.

ANNUAL EVENTS

Gold Rush Days, second weekend of February; **High Desert Sports Festival,** first weekend of August; **Four-Corner States Bluegrass Festival and Fiddle Championship,** second weekend in November; **Cowboy Christmas Poets' Gathering**, first weekend in December.

WHERE TO DINE

Charley's Steakhouse • △△ $$
1187 W. Wickenburg Way (California Highway); (602) 684-2413. American; dinners $4.50 to $14.50; full bar. Daily 5 to 10 p.m. Reservations accepted; MC/VISA. Assorted char-broiled steaks, plus chicken and seafood dishes.

Frontier Inn • △△ $$
430 E. Wickenburg Way; (602) 684-2183. Western-style fare; dinners $6.50 to $14; wine and beer. Monday 6 a.m. to 11 a.m., Tuesday-Saturday 6 a.m. to 9 p.m., Sunday 8 a.m. to 8 p.m. Reservations accepted; MC/VISA. Mesquite-cooked meats in a Chinese oven; homemade soups, sauces and pies.

Gold Nugget Restaurant • △△ $$ ∅
222 E. Wickenburg Way (adjacent to Best Western Rancho Grande); (602) 684-2858. American-Continental; dinners $6 to $15; full bar. Daily 6 a.m. to 10 p.m. Reservations accepted; Major credit cards. Victorian decor; American, Italian and other European dishes.

Wickenburg Inn • △△△△ $$$
Prescott Highway between Wickenburg and Congress; (602) 684-7811. American; dinners $16.50; full bar. Open daily; breakfast 7:30 to 9:30, lunch

noon to 2, dinner 6:30 to 9. Reservations required. MC/VISA. This Western-style dining room at Wickenburg Inn guest ranch is open to the public by reservation. American menu, with theme night variations such as Mexican buffets. Saturday night cookouts with hayrides. Cocktail lounge; live music periodically.

WHERE TO SLEEP

AmericInn Motel ● ΔΔ $$$ ∅
850 E. Wickenburg Way (just east of downtown), Wickenburg, AZ 85358; (602) 684-5461. Doubles $55 to $65, singles $49 to $55, suites $65 to $75; lower off-season rates. Major credit cards. TV, room phones, pool, spa. **Willows Restaurant** is open Tuesday-Sunday 7 a.m. to 1:30 and Tuesday-Saturday 5 to 8:30 p.m., American, dinners $4 to $20, non-smoking areas, full bar service.

Best Western Rancho Grande ● ΔΔΔ $$
293 E. Wickenburg Way (P.O. Box 1328), Wickenburg, AZ 85358; (602) 684-5445 or (800) 528-1234. Doubles and kitchenettes $45 to $67, singles $42 to $56, suites $60 to $74. Major credit cards. Room phones, TV, some refrigerators; pool, spa, tennis courts, playground. Gold Nugget Restaurant (listed above).

Garden City Resort ● ΔΔ $$
Highway 60 at Garden City Road (P.O. Box 70), Wickenburg, AZ 85358; (602) 684-2334. Doubles and singles $35 to $40. No credit cards. Room phones; some fully-furnished units with complete kitchens; weekly and monthly rates.

Joshua tree doesn't look much like a lily.

Mecca Motel • △ $$
163 E. Wickenburg Way (downtown), Wickenburg, AZ 85358; (602) 684-2753. Doubles $26.50 to $31.30, singles $23.50 to $26.50. Major credit cards. TV, room refrigerators.

Westerner Motel • △ $$
680 W. Wickenburg Way, P.O. Box 1682 (near downtown), Wickenburg, AZ 85358; (602) 684-2493. Doubles $35 to $50, singles $25 to $35. MC/VISA, DISC. Coffee pots in rooms; refrigerators in some.

WHERE TO CAMP

Hospitality RV Park • *51802 Highway 60 (two miles south; P.O. Box 2525), Wickenburg, AZ 85358; (602) 684-2519. RV sites, full hookups $12, water and electric $10. Reservations accepted; MC/VISA.* Pull-throughs; flush potties, showers, coin laundry, snack bar.

North Ranch RV Park • *10 miles north on U.S. 89 (P.O. Box 1604), Wickenburg, AZ 85358; (602) 427-6335. RV sites, full hookups $12. Reservations accepted.* Flush potties, showers, coin laundry, rec room with pool table and crafts, horseshoe pits.

WHERE TO PLAY COWBOY

These five guest ranches are within a short drive of Wickenburg, earning it the title of "the dude ranch capital of the world."

Flying E Ranch • *P.O. Box EEE (four miles west of town on U.S. 60), Wickenburg, AZ 85358; (602) 684-2690. From $165 to $210 per couple, including all meals. No credit cards; checks OK.* Small, family-run working ranch on a 2,400-foot mesa near Vulture Peak. Breakfast and lunch rides, chuckwagon cookouts, hay rides, square-dancing, swimming pool, spa, sauna, shuffleboard, ping pong, horseshoes, tennis; golf nearby.

Kay El Dar Ranoh • *P.O. Box 3180 (Rincon Road, off N Highway 89-93), Wickenburg, AZ 85358; (602) 684-7593. From $165 to $185 per couple, including all meals.* An 80-year-old historic landmark ranch. Lodge rooms and cottages; pool, full bar, hiking, riding, outdoor games.

Rancho Casitas • *P.O. Drawer A-3 (five miles north, off U.S. 89), Wickenburg, AZ 85358; (602) 684-2628. From $350 to $450 per week, without meals. No credit cards.* A small national historic site guest ranch with old adobe buildings; casual and cozy. Riding, shuffleboard, horseshoes, volleyball, pool, laundry. Units are one and two-bedroom apartments with full kitchens; Spanish and Mediterranean decor.

Rancho de los Caballeros • *P.O. Box 1148 (two miles west on U.S. 60, then two miles south on Vulture Mine Road), Wickenburg, AZ 85358; (602) 684-5484. From $208 to $250 per couple, including all meals. No credit cards.* A large, resort-style guest ranch with golf course, pool, spa, skeet and trap, tennis, cookouts, trail rides, lunch rides. TV in rooms on request.

Wickenburg Inn Guest and Tennis Ranch • *P.O. Box P (Highway 89 between Wickenburg and Congress), Wickenburg, AZ 85358; (602) 684-7811 or (800) 528-4227. From $150 to $280 per couple, including all meals. MC/VISA.* Noted guest ranch on a 4,700-acre desert nature preserve. TV, room phones; most rooms have fireplaces, refrigerators and other amenities. Swimming pool and spa, arts and crafts studio, tennis (with clinics), trail rides and other ranch activities, archery, wildlife study and nature walks with a resident naturalist. Restaurant (listed above) and cocktail lounge.

Chapter 9

TUCSON AND FRIENDS

*Tucson's climate in winter is finer than that of Italy. It
would scarcely be possible to suggest an improvement.*
—Tucson visitor in the 1860s

 IF AMERICA HAS AN IDEAL city, it might be Tucson. It's large
enough to provide all the cosmopolitan essentials, yet small
enough to negotiate easily. It offers a wonderful mix of indoor
culture and outdoor recreation. During most of the year—except for mid-summer's heat—it boasts a temperate climate with sunny,
wind-free days.

It's our favorite city in the Southwest.

Tucsonans—smiling smugly in the direction of Phoenix—boast that it's
the only Arizona city with a major university, plus a professional symphony,
theater company, ballet and opera. A *Wall Street Journal* article called it "a
mini-mecca for the arts." Modern high-rises sprout from the heart of
downtown, casting today's shadows over yesterday's El Presidio Historic District. Here, the Old Pueblo planted its Spanish roots while America was still
a British colony.

Occupying the northeastern rim of the Sonoran Desert, Tucson sits in a
virtual cactus garden, surrounded by five mountain ranges. In winter, you
can work on your suntan at poolside, then drive to the Mount Lemmon ski
area in about an hour and strap on the sticks.

Tucson, then, is an intriguing blend of the cosmopolitan, the old pueblo
and the great outdoors.

Tucson

Elevation 2,389 feet **Population 664,000**

THE WAY IT WAS ● If it weren't for the Mormons and the Gadsden Purchase, we might need a Mexican tourist card to visit Tucson. When the American-Mexican border was set by the Treaty of Guadalupe Hidalgo in 1848, the southern third of Arizona—including Tucson—was on the Mexican side.

However, Tucson was occupied by members of the Mormon Battalion. They had grabbed it two years earlier during the Mexican War, and they weren't about to give it up. Then in 1854, the 30,000-square-mile Gadsden Purchase was negotiated and the American flag remained over the Old Pueblo.

Tucson goes well beyond that period, of course. When mission-builder Eusebio Kino visited in 1687, he found Tohono O'odham Indians living in a village they called *Stjukshon* (Stook-shon). It means "blue water at the base of a black mountain," referring to springs in the now-dry Santa Cruz River and Sentinel Peak. The Spanish altered it to *Tucson*, which initially was pronounced "TUK-son."

Local historians, possibly stretching a point, say Stjukshon-cum-Tucson is the oldest continuously inhabited settlement in America. (The same claim is made about Oraibi on the Hopi Reservation to the north.)

Father Kino returned in 1700 to build Mission San Xavier in the Indian village of Bac. Tucson itself was established in 1775 by a wandering Irishman who was scouting for the Spanish crown. Settlers began moving into the Tucson Basin and the original inhabitants naturally objected. They went on the warpath and a walled presidio was built to protect the intruders. This was the first walled city in America—except that it was still part of Spain.

After the Gadsden Purchase put Tucson on our side of the border, it continued growing as a ranching and provisioning center. A Butterfield Stage stop was opened in 1857 and Tucson's cantinas became notorious hangouts for drifters, outlaws and lonesome cowpokes. Folks said the outpost was so primitive that stage passengers who spent the night had to sleep in a "Tucson bed"—using their stomach for a mattress and their back for a blanket.

The pueblo suffered the indignity of capture by Rebel troops during the Civil War. Union forces sent them scattering in the Battle of Picacho Pass in 1862—the war's westernmost conflict. Tucson lured the territorial capital from Prescott in 1867, only to have it taken away ten years later.

By the turn of the century, Tucson was a busy if still somewhat remote town of 10,000. World War II brought thousands of servicemen to Davis-Monthan Army Air Corps Base. Many of them liked the idea of January suntans and returned.

THE WAY IT IS ● You may question our notion that Tucson is small enough to negotiate easily. Viewed from Sentinel Peak (the one with the "A" on it) or Mount Lemmon, it spreads as a vast carpet of commerce over the high desert. Indeed, greater Tucson covers 500 square miles.

However, wide thoroughfares get you quickly from one end of Tucson to the other. Interstate 10 cuts a northwest-southeast diagonal, providing quick access to the town's opposite corners. I-19 whisks you down south. In fifteen minutes, you can be in your own personal patch of uncrowded desert.

Surprisingly, Tucson suffers little commuter congestion; traffic-watchers get excited over a ten-minute delay on I-10. The only areas we'd recommend avoiding during the rush hour are the northeast foothills, which have attracted most of Tucson's new subdivisions.

Today's Tucson wears its Spanish heritage rather handsomely. Red-tile and flat-roofed pueblo architecture predominates. The town has more good Mexican restaurants than you can shake a tortilla at. Mexican arts and crafts add color to curio shops. Many signs are bilingual, since 26 percent of Pima County's citizens are Hispanic.

THINGS TO KNOW BEFORE YOU GO

Best time to go • Tucson's best weather is fall and spring; lodgings get crowded just after Christmas, when the snowbird crowds hit. Some hotels and most RV parks book up by mid-January.

Climate • Sunny! Tucson has more days of sunshine than any other American city. Winters are cool to warm; summers warm to hot. Although farther south than Phoenix, Tucson is nearly 1,500 feet higher and therefore slightly cooler. July average—high 101, low 73; January average—high 66, low 37; rainfall—11 inches; snowfall—less than an inch.

Useful contacts

Metropolitan Tucson Convention & Visitor's Bureau, 130 S. Scott Ave., Tucson, AZ 85701; (602) 624-1889.

NOTE: The Tucson CVB can assist with long-term as well as short-term lodgings. The office at 130 S. Scott Avenue has an apartment locator service.

Sun Tran (Tucson bus system schedules): 792-9222.

Tucson Airport Authority (airline schedules): 573-8000.

City arts line (for cultural activities): 642-0595.

Road and weather information: 294-3113.

Emergencies: 911.

Coronado National Forest, 300 W. Congress, Tucson, AZ 85701; (602) 670-6483. Mount Lemmon information—(602) 576-1542; Sabino Canyon information—749-8700 or 629-5101.

Nogales-Santa Cruz County Chamber of Commerce, Kino Park, Nogales, AZ 85621; (602) 287-3685.

Tubac Chamber of Commerce, P.O. Box 1866, Tubac, AZ 85646; (602) 938-2704.

Area radio stations

KAWV-FM, 103.1—New wave

KCEE-AM, 790—Oldies, easy listening

KIIM-AM, 1290—Country and Western

KIIM-FM, 99.5—Country and Western

KKLD-FM, 95—Contemporary adult music

KMRR-AM, 1330—Nostalgia, easy listening

KNST-AM, 940—News, sports, talk

KPLX-FM, 96—Rock

KRQQ-FM, 93.7—Contemporary hits

KWFM-FM, 92.9—Oldies, easy listening

FINDING YOUR WAY ● Tucson's attractions are widespread, so get a rental car with unlimited mileage if you've flown in. Downtown is easy to reach; just take the Broadway-Congress exit from I-10 and go east. Broadway and Congress are parallel one-way streets cutting through the heart of the small downtown area. Streets take some funny angles here, so it's best to park and walk to downtown attractions. You can pick up a walking tour map at the **Visitors Bureau** at 130 S. Scott Avenue.

Motels are clustered around downtown I-10 off-ramps. Others, including some budget ones, are strung along Broadway, just east of downtown.

THE BEST ATTRACTIONS

The Arizona-Sonora Desert Museum ● *2021 N. Kinney Rd. (in Tucson Mountain Park), Tucson, AZ 85743; (602) 883-2702. Daily 7:30 to 6 in summer, 8:30 to 5 the rest of the year (ticket sales end at 4). Adults $6, kids 6 through 12, $1.* Planners re-invented the museum when they created this indoor-outdoor complex. The *New York Times* called it "the most distinctive zoo in the United States." Certainly, it is the finest exhibit center in Arizona, and it is Tucson's most-visited attraction.

The museum takes its name from the states of Arizona, USA, and Sonora, Mexico. Its primary focus is the ecology, geology and climatology of the Sonoran Desert that covers much of these two states. Plan most of a day to walk its paths, viewing desert creatures in typical habitats, learning about desert flora and strolling through a bird-busy aviary. Over-under exhibits allow you to watch beavers and river otters at play above and below the surface of streams. Inside several exhibit buildings, state-of-the-art displays explain what makes a desert happen; rattlesnakes and scorpions snooze behind glass enclosures.

The newest—and perhaps the best—exhibit is the Earth Sciences Center. This elaborate grotto features a realistic limestone cave, a jewel-like mineral display and a graphic, step-by-step explanation of the formation of our four-billion-year-old planet. You see the earth's transition from a meteor-impacted chunk of rock to the cloud-sworled globe so familiar to us from space photos.

Arizona Historical Society Museum ● *949 E. Second St. (Park Avenue), Tucson, AZ 85719; (602) 628-5774. Monday-Saturday 10 to 4, Sunday noon to 4; free.* Located just outside the University of Arizona campus, it picks up where the Indians left off, covering the state's settlement from the arrival of the Spanish through the development of modern Arizona.

Uncluttered, informative exhibits tell the state's story with cattle brands, Bull Durham pouches, high-wheeled bicycles and period costumes. In a full-sized mock-up mine, you learn about copper mining methods before the days of the open pit. An excellent film traces Arizona's transportation development from stagecoaches to Colorado River steamers to Lieutenant Beale's strange camel corps. Appropriately, one display concerns the development of air conditioning, so essential to southern Arizona's existence.

Arizona State Museum ● *University Avenue at Park Avenue (c/o University of Arizona, Tucson, AZ 85721); (602) 621-6302. Monday-Saturday 9 to 5, Sunday 2 to 5; free.* Occupying two buildings just inside UA's main gate, this museum focuses on prehistoric and modern Indian cultures of the Southwest.

GREATER TUCSON AREA

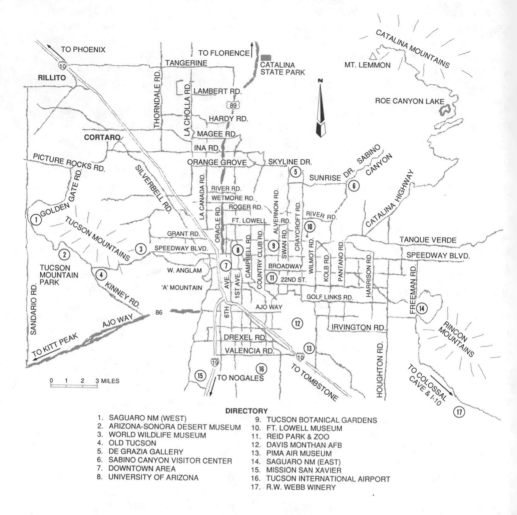

DIRECTORY

1. SAGUARO NM (WEST)
2. ARIZONA-SONORA DESERT MUSEUM
3. WORLD WILDLIFE MUSEUM
4. OLD TUCSON
5. DE GRAZIA GALLERY
6. SABINO CANYON VISITOR CENTER
7. DOWNTOWN AREA
8. UNIVERSITY OF ARIZONA

9. TUCSON BOTANICAL GARDENS
10. FT. LOWELL MUSEUM
11. REID PARK & ZOO
12. DAVIS MONTHAN AFB
13. PIMA AIR MUSEUM
14. SAGUARO NM (EAST)
15. MISSION SAN XAVIER
16. TUCSON INTERNATIONAL AIRPORT
17. R.W. WEBB WINERY

In the main exhibit building (on the right as you enter the campus), a new display offers an excellent view of the lifestyle of the Apache, past and present. Another intriguing exhibit discusses cave archaeology—how both prehistoric and modern societies have used earth recesses for shelter. A mezzanine is stuffed with stuffed animals from the state, along with a gemstone and Hohokam exhibit.

The museum's administration building across the street is used primarily for changing exhibits, covering a wide range of subjects.

De Grazia Gallery in the Sun ● *6300 N. Swan Rd. (Skyline Drive), Tucson, AZ 85718; (602) 299-9191. Daily 10 to 4; free.* The late Ted De Grazia developed a large following for his impressionistic, whimsical style of painting. Simple, quick brush strokes created color-splashed Indians, Mexicans, roadrunners and other Southwestern subjects. An earthy individual, he used local adobe and other materials to build his studio and adjacent chapel called "Mission in the Sun."

After his death, a foundation was created to continue operating his rustic gallery and gift shop. Exhibits are changed periodically, drawn from his extensive collection. Ceramics, wind chimes, enamel work and reproductions of De Grazia's art can be purchased.

De Grazia did not shy from commercialism. In the gift shop here and throughout Arizona, you will see his style emblazoned on everything from greeting cards to refrigerator magnets.

Several years ago, we had the good fortune to meet the artist. We spent an afternoon discussing his gentle philosophy and dickering over the price of a large pastel serigraph he called *Prancing Horse*. Like any true artist—commercialized or not—he would not budge from his price.

Prancing Horse now hangs above our fireplace.

El Presidio Historic District ● *Bounded by Pennington, Church, Washington and Main.* Although its adobe walls have long since melted back into the sand, El Presidio retains some of its yesterday flavor. Many of its 19th century adobes house galleries and restaurants. Signposts and plaques relate the history of homes dating back more than a century.

Old Town Artisans *at 186 N. Meyer (Telles); (602) 623-6024. Monday-Saturday 9:30 to 5:30 and Sundays noon to 5.* It's the largest arts and crafts shopping complex in El Presidio. This 13-room marketplace features handcrafted Southwestern art, Indian tribal arts, Latin American imports and sundry other giftwares and souvenirs. More than 150 local artists are represented.

Fort Lowell Museum ● *Craycroft and Fort Lowell (mailing address: 949 E. Second St., Tucson, AZ 85719); (602) 885-3832. Wednesday-Saturday 10 to 4; free.* Part of a large city park and recreation center, Fort Lowell Museum is a reconstruction of a military camp established in 1873. Like most Arizona forts, it was not a stockade, but a garrison from which troops set forth to do battle with the Indians.

When they weren't chasing Apaches, they were socializing with the citizens of Tucson, attending dances, fielding sports teams and raising a little Saturday night hell.

"The boys in blue raked over the dry embers of the town in pursuit of life and sport," the *Tucson Citizen* reported in a May, 1874, issue.

Museum structures include the commanding officers quarters with period furnishings and historical displays, and the "kitchen building," with exhibits concerning the fort's development and early Indian digs. The crumbling adobe ruins of the fort hospital stand nearby.

Grace H. Flandrau Planetarium ● *University of Arizona campus at University and Cherry; (602) 621-STAR. Museum and astronomy store open Monday 1 to 4, Tuesday-Thursday 10 to 4, weekends 1 to 5. Public telescope viewing Tuesday through Saturday, 8:30 p.m. to 10 p.m. in summer and 7 to 10 p.m. in winter. Museum free; planetarium shows $3.75 for adults and $3 for kids 3 to 12, U of A students and seniors.*

This is a science museum as well as a planetarium. Push assorted buttons and levers to learn about lasers, radio waves and Light Amplification by Stimulated Emission Radiation. A holographic lady blows you a kiss as you walk by and a star projector in a mini-dome introduces you to the constellations. Our only complaint was that many of the hands-on scientific gadgets

TUCSON

DIRECTORY
1. WORLD WILDLIFE MUSEUM
2. OLD PUEBLO MUSEUM
   (IN FOOTHILLS MALL)
3. TOHONO CHUL PARK
4. EL PRESIDIO HISTORIC DISTRICT
   & TUCSON MUSEUM OF ART
5. ARIZONA HISTORICAL SOCIETY
   MUSEUM
6. ARIZONA STATE MUSEUM
7. TUCSON BOTANICAL GARDENS
8. DE GRAZIA GALLERY
9. FT. LOWELL MUSEUM
10. REID PARK ZOO
11. PIMA AIR MUSEUM

didn't work. The museum seems long on innovation but short on maintenance.

Star shows in the planetarium change periodically, usually with the seasons.

International Wildlife Museum ● *4800 W. Gates Pass Rd. (Camino de Oeste), Tucson, AZ 85745; (602) 629-0100 or (602) 624-4024 (recording). Open Wednesday-Sunday; Labor Day to Memorial Day 9 to 5:30 and Memorial Day to Labor Day 8:30 to 6. Adults $4; seniors, students and military $3.50; kids 6 to 12, $1.50.* Talk about strange. The wildlife museum is enclosed in an architectural blend of feudal castle and Arabian desert fort. Exhibits, including more than 300 varieties of stuffed animals, are intended to "promote wildlife appreciation in a multitude of ways."

Indeed, many displays do just that. Several videos focus on wildlife conservation; graphics tell of the threat to the world's rain forests. Yet one large room—the C.J. McElroy Hall—is filled with hunting trophies. Exhibits even include slugs taken from some of the victims! A bronze figure of McElroy stands at the museum entrance, brandishing his rifle, looking hungry for his next kill.

If you have an appetite for this curiosity, there's a snack bar in one wing of the museum, along with a gift shop.

In fairness, we should stress that the museum is *very* well done, and a good zoological teaching tool for kids. Particularly impressive is a 30-foot mountain occupied by stuffed wild goats and sheep. It's surrounded by 22 dioramas with critters of North America, Europe and Africa in natural settings. The museum was opened in 1986 by the World Safari Club.

—Arizona Department of Archives photo

Mission San Xavier at the turn of the century; Indian women shelling corn in the foreground.

Mission San Xavier del Bac ● *San Xavier Road (9 miles south, off I-19); (602) 294-2624. Church, museum and gift shop open daily 9 to 5:30; Mass Saturday at 5:30 and Sunday at 8, 9:30, 11 and noon. Free; contributions appreciated.* In simplicity, someone once said, there is grace and beauty. The "White Dove of the Desert," with its Spanish-colonial architecture, gleaming white walls and brown facade, is perhaps Arizona's most beautiful structure.

It is the symbol of Arizona. Its roots reach back to the earliest days, when Father Kino ministered to the people of the village of Bac. Located on the San Xavier Reservation, it still serves Native Americans, who comprise an important segment of the state's population. Its architecture is typical of the Southwest look; its surrounding gardens are of the Arizona desert. It certainly belongs on the cover of this book.

In the sanctuary, the elaborate alter—with its busy columns and saintly niches—offers contrast to the simple exterior. There is even whimsy in this hallowed place. Comical lions wearing wide grins guard the altar. Above the main door, a plaster-cast cat and mouse eye one another warily.

On weekends, members of the Tohono O'odham tribe set up a market on the mission grounds, selling crafts and tasty Indian fry bread. Inside the sanctuary, a recording disturbs the quiet with a recitation of the mission's history and architecture. A gift shop occupies one end of the building and a nearby path leads to a hilltop cross with a fine view of the surrounding countryside.

It is fortunate that the mission occupies Native American ground, for the Indians have kept development from its doors. In Tucson, it would be surrounded by subdivisions or high-rises. The White Dove of the Desert gleams—alone but not forlorn—from an open desert basin.

The Tohono O'odham mission dates from Father Kino's arrival in 1700. The present church was constructed around 1778 by later Franciscans. Its architecture is a splendid curiosity. Lacking materials but wanting a church as elegant as those in Spain, the builders used Indian-made paints and dyes to simulate marble, tile and even chandeliers. These features have been faithfully preserved. Two mysteries surround the old church: Who designed it, and why was the second bell tower never finished? A fanciful story is that the Spanish Crown would tax a building only after it was completed, so the wily padres never finished the second tower. A less interesting but more logical theory is that they simply ran out of funds.

Mission San Xavier should be visited at least three times. Go on a busy weekend to catch the Indian market and to hear that recording. Return again when it is empty; listen to the silent flicker of candles in the sanctuary's shadows. Then bid farewell to the White Dove at night, when it glows like a gentle beacon in the desert.

Mount Lemmon ● *Reached via the Catalina Highway from northeast Tucson. For information: Coronado National Forest, (602) 576-1542.* The Catalina Highway spirals quickly from the saguaro-thick foothills of the Catalina Mountains to the piney forests of Mount Lemmon. Along the way, you'll see fantastic roadside rock formations that look like misplaced Easter Island statues or broken columns of Greek temples.

Several viewpoints offer impressive vistas of the Tucson Basin's vast carpet of civilization. Plan this drive in the afternoon, then return at night to watch Tucson twinkle like an upside-down universe.

Mount Lemmon rock formations along Catalina Highway; plaque honors highway-creator Frank Harris Hitchcock.

In winter, you can hit the slopes at Mount Lemmon Ski Valley. The small facility offers two lifts and a dozen runs. Nearby Summerhaven is an alpine community with shops, a couple of restaurants and a general store. A-frame homes tucked among the ponderosas provide summer escape for desert dwellers.

It's all part of Coronado National Forest, with the typical recreational opportunities of camping, picnicking, hiking, backpacking and fishing. And it's only an hour from poolside in downtown Tucson.

Old Pueblo Museum • *In Foothills Shopping Mall (On La Cholla Boulevard, just north of Ina Road), Tucson, AZ 85741; (602) 742-2355. Monday-Friday 10 to 9, Saturday 10 to 6 and Sunday noon to 5; free.* Most everything else in Tucson has moved into air-conditioned shopping centers, so why not a museum? This small but handsome $3 million facility features a realistic reproduction of a Paleo-Indian rock shelter, mammoth bones and minerals and other displays relating to the history, culture, arts and natural sciences of Tucson and the Southwest. Major exhibits change periodically and range from Ansel Adams photos to carousel horses to textiles to cactus portrayed in various art mediums.

The museum itself is a work of art—a dramatic Southwest style creation in salmon and turquoise, with an art deco waterfall cascading down a stairstep creek. After browsing through the latest exhibits, you might catch a science or art film in the theater, then peruse the small museum gift shop.

Old Tucson • *201 S. Kinney Rd. (Tucson Mountain Park), Tucson, AZ 85746; (602) 883-6457 or 883-0100. Daily 9 to 9. Adults $8.95, kids 4 to 11*

$4.95. The first thing you learn, upon entering this Western-movie-set-turned-theme park, is that former President Ronald Reagan performed here in a 1950 horse opera called *The Last Outpost.*

From there, it just keeps getting better—or worse, if you're not a fan of Westerns.

Old Tucson is Universal Studios with hay bales—a working memorial to all those shoot-outs that have blazed across the Arizona landscape. It began in 1939 when Columbia Pictures produced one of the first multi-million dollar movie epics, based on Saturday Evening Post story called *Arizona.* Seeking authenticity, producers built a life-sized model of early-day Tucson, complete with adobe buildings, corrals and hitchin' rails. The star was a young actor named William Holden; Jean Arthur was his leading lady. When the shooting was completed (no pun intended), the company left Old Tucson to wither in the desert sun.

Twenty years later, entrepreneur Bob Sheldon bought the crumbling ruin, added more weather-worn buildings and created a permanent set for Western movies. Since then, more than 150 oat-baggers have been filmed here. Logic dictated that it be used as a tourist attraction as well.

Today, you can watch shoot-outs on Main Street, tour a giant sound stage and survive an Indian attack in the Royal Oak Saloon. You can buy a margarita to go or a John Wayne memorial clock. A Cowboy Breakfast will set you back $3.95.

Since I grew up on Westerns, my favorite pastime here is simply reading the placards announcing what film was shot where. They read like a horse opera honor roll: *McClintock, Gunfight at the O.K. Corral* and *Rio Lobo,* along with television's *Little House on the Prairie* and *The High Chaparral.*

HOW TO SPEND YOUR TUCSON DAYS

First day ● Head west out Speedway Boulevard; it becomes Gates Pass Road and takes you to Tucson Mountain Park. There, the Arizona-Sonora Desert Museum, Old Tucson theme park and Saguaro National Monument will keep you occupied for most of a day. (Trailers aren't permitted on Gates Pass and lengthy RVs are discouraged; take Highway 86 west, then Kinney Road north.) If you have just one day, save time for the hauntingly beautiful "White Dove of the Desert"—Mission San Xavier.

Second day ● Head east to the Santa Catalina Mountains, stopping at the University of Arizona campus with its many museums. After lunch, explore Sabino Canyon, then take the scenic drive up Mount Lemmon to catch the sunset.

Third day ● Drive southeast to Pima Air Museum and the Rincon Mountain branch of Saguaro National Monument. After lunch, drive south on I-19 to Mission San Xavier.

Fourth day ● Get to know downtown Tucson. Stop at the Visitor's Center (130 S. Scott Ave.) for a walking tour map. It'll take you through the town's compact metropolitan core and El Presidio Historic Area. Then drive northeast on the Old Spanish Trail along the Santa Catalina foothills. Visit Fort Lowell Museum and Tohono Chul Park.

Fifth day ● Make a run for the border to Nogales, Mexico, stopping along the way at the Titan Missile Museum in Green Valley, historic Tubac and Tumacacori National Monument.

Titillating "nose art" on a Consolidated B-24 at Pima Air Museum.

Hollywood still uses Old Tucson. When we visited, "hot set" signs were posted around the deliberately dusty Mexican plaza, where *The Young Guns* was being filmed.

Pima Air Museum ● *6000 E. Valencia Rd. (Wilmot), Tucson, AZ 85706; (602) 574-0462 or (602) 574-9658 (recorded message). Daily 9 to 5 (doors close at 4). Adults $4, seniors and military personnel $3, kids 10 to 17 $2.* If you've ever wanted to soar on fanciful wings of eagles, you'll love this place. More than 150 aircraft are on display, from a realistic full-scale model of the Wright brothers craft to recently retired Air Force jet fighters.

A large building is filled with old planes, gliders, aircraft engines, flight suits and other airborne regalia. Exhibits here trace the development of aviation from pre-Wright brothers attempts to space flight. Out on the tarmac, a hundred or so planes glisten in the sun. Most are post World War II vintage.

Of particular interest is a four-engine DC-6 that served as Air Force One for Presidents Kennedy and Johnson. You can tour the President's quarters, press and Secret Service compartments and full-sized kitchen. You'll see the desk and leather chair, where our leaders contemplated the missiles of October and other frustrations as they flitted about the country.

Reid Park Zoo ● *1100 S. Randolph Way (enter Lakeshore Drive off 22nd Street), Tucson, AZ 85716; (602) 791-4022. Daily 9:30 a.m. to 5 p.m. Adults $2, seniors $1.50, kids 5 to 14, 50 cents.* This is a small but very attractive zoo landscaped with green lawns shaded by eucalyptus and palm trees. It offers a typical collection of giraffes, lions, tigers, hippos, and simians. Some of its critters are housed in modern open-air enclosures; birds flit around a large aviary.

The zoo shares large Reid Park with a baseball and soccer field, rose garden, duck pond, fishing and paddleboat lake, playground, picnic areas. Hi

Corbett Field here is spring training camp for the **Cleveland Indians.** (See "Activities and Entertainment" listing below.)

Sabino Canyon • *Sabino Canyon Road; (602) 749-2861 for tram schedules or (602) 749-8700 for canyon information. From December through May, trams run every half hour, daily from 9 to 4:30; the rest of the year, they run hourly 9 to 4 on weekdays and 9 to 4:30 weekends. Adults $5, kids 3 to 12, $2. Bear Canyon tram runs less frequently; adults $3, kids 3 to 12, $1.25. Sabino Canyon Visitor Center open 8 to 4:30.*

Sabino Canyon is a prime example of Tucson's delightful contrast. Just minutes from downtown, this steep-walled chasm cuts deeply into the flanks of the Santa Catalina Mountains. Forests of saguaro cactus march from the banks of Sabino Creek up rugged canyon walls. Ultimately, they give way to forests of pines. Hiking trails lead into the more remote heights.

Because of congestion on the narrow canyon road, vehicle access is limited to a tram. It takes visitors on a 45-minute round trip, with stops at picnic areas and trailheads along the way. The driver offers description of the canyon's geology, flora and fauna as the tram trundles along.

On summer weekends, the canyon is wall-to-wall as residents come to splash in what's left of Sabino Creek, seeking relief from valley heat.

Bear Canyon is less crowded but equally rugged. Shuttles from the same tram station take visitors to Silver Falls Trailhead for a 2.2-mile hike to the falls.

A **Coronado National Forest** visitor center near the tram station offers interpretive exhibits of the geology, plant life and critters of the Santa Catalina Mountains and their craggy canyons.

Saguaro National Monument • *Rincon Mountain section off Old Spanish Trail east of Tucson; (602) 296-8576; 7 a.m. to 6 p.m., visitor center open 8 to 5; $3 per vehicle, $1 per hiker or biker. Tucson Mountain section off Sandario Road in Tucson Mountain Park; (602) 883-6366; open 24 hours, Red Hills visitor center open daily 8 to 5; free.* The two sections of Saguaro National Monument serve the same function—to preserve and exhibit their giant cactus namesake. Yet the areas have different personalities.

Saguaro East is the larger of the two, covering 62,499 acres. It climbs through five climate zones from the desert to the conifer ramparts of the Rincon Mountains. Its saguaro forests are older and thinner than those of its smaller satellite, Saguaro West.

At the visitor center, you learn more than you probably ever wanted to know about this strange plant. It grows only in the Sonoran Desert of Arizona and Mexico—lopping slightly into California. It can reach a height of 50 feet but it takes its time getting there. A seedling grows only a quarter of an inch the first year and it takes 15 years to reach a foot; those familiar arms don't appear until it's more than 50 years old.

A desert garden in front of the visitor center helps you tell a pincushion cactus from a prickly pear. The best way to experience the monument is to purchase a $1 driving guide and follow the eight-mile Cactus Forest Drive through the Rincon foothills. There are picnic areas and hiking trails along the way.

Saguaro West, covering 21,152 acres, doesn't have the elevation range of its eastern counterpart, but if offers more bountiful cactus gardens. Its small visitor center is primarily a natural sciences book shop. Wall graphics describe the geology, flora and fauna of the Sonoran Desert. A photo exhibit depicts a harvest of saguaro fruit, conducted annually in the park by local Indians.

The six-mile Bajada Loop Drive will take you through a dense saguaro thicket, scattered over the rough surfaces of Tucson Mountain. Several 200-year-old giants line the road. Some are turning brown with age and drooping their arms, like tired old men. A rich cactus garden stands at their feet.

Tohono Chul Park • *7366 N. Paseo del Norte (northwest corner of Ina and Oracle), Tucson, AZ 85704; (602) 742-6455. Daily 7 a.m. to sunset; exhibit hall, gift gallery and Tea Room open Monday-Saturday 8 a.m. to 5 p.m. and Sunday 11 to 5. Free; contributions accepted.* Perhaps Arizona's finest privately-endowed park, Tohono Chul preserves a patch of desert landscape in the middle of Tucson. Nature trails, patios, shade ramadas, two gift shops, and exhibit center and a wonderful Southwest-style tea room offer refuge from the growing city.

Fashioned from two estates, the park was created by Richard and Jean Wilson, owners of the adjacent Haunted Bookshop. They purchased the land to rescue it from development, then formed a non-profit foundation to operate the park. Their bookshop, named because people are "haunted by the books they haven't gotten around to reading," offers an excellent section on Arizona plus a good selection of general reading material.

A park exhibit center offers changing displays focusing on Arizona arts, crafts and lifestyles. Two attractive gift shops—one in the exhibit center and another in the tea room—sell crafts, curios, artworks and Indian handicrafts. Tohono Chul Tea Room, set in a handsome courtyard, is reviewed in our dining section below.

Tucson Mountain Park • *Eight miles west (take either Speedway west from downtown or Kinney Road northwest from State Highway 86); (602) 883-4200. Day use from 7 a.m. to 10 p.m.; overnight camping (see listing under "Where to Camp").* This huge Pima County park sprawls over 17,000 acres of rough-hewn Tucson Mountain foothills. It provides "instant desert wilderness" to residents of the city, just eight miles away. Within the park's boundaries are three other attractions: the Tucson Mountain section of Saguaro National Monument, Arizona-Sonora Desert Museum and Old Tucson (all listed separately).

Park facilities include picnic areas, hiking and riding trails and the Gilbert Ray Campground. As in state and national preserves, shooting and disturbing flora and fauna are *verboten*. A viewpoint at the top of Gates Pass (an extension of Speedway Boulevard) is a great place to watch the sunset. Several hiking trails extend from there into the rugged, cactus-covered Tucson Mountains.

Tucson Museum of Art • *140 N. Main Ave. (Alameda, next to El Presidio Historic District), Tucson, AZ 85701; (602) 624-2333. Sunday 12 to 4, Tuesday-Saturday 10 to 4; docent tours Tuesday-Friday at 11 a.m. and Sunday at 2 p.m. Adults $2, seniors $1, children free; Tuesday is free day for everyone. Historic Block tours Tuesday and Thursday at 10 a.m. and Sunday at 1 p.m.* Galleries are laid out along downward spiraling ramps in this modern museum on the edge of Tucson's oldest district. The complex also includes the Historic Block, containing five houses built between 1850 and 1907.

Galleries feature a large collection of Western art, pre-Columbian artifacts and special changing exhibits. Contemporary sculpture enhances the museum grounds. Original works and prints by Southwestern artisans are on sale in the museum gift shop—everything from dazzling glassworks to whimsical ceramics of camels and cows on wheels.

University of Arizona campus • *Campus Visitor Center open Monday-Friday 8 to 5 and Saturday 9 to 2; (602) 621-5130.* The university's expansive campus, located in the heart of Tucson, is a major cultural resource as well as important learning center. Eight museums and galleries occupy its sturdy red-brick buildings.

U of A caters to tourists as well as students. The Campus Visitor Center at Cherry and University offers maps, brochures, activity lists, university catalogues and even a selection of brochures on Tucson's other attractions.

You can grab a snack or a substantial meal at the Student Union. Visitor parking is available in the Second Street garage (corner of Highland). Campers won't fit so you'll have to try your luck in metered lots or on street meters. These are scarce on school weekdays but plentiful on weekends.

Here's a list of on-campus attractions and activities:

Arizona Historical Society Museum and **Arizona State Museum,** see separate listings above.

Campus Tours, *(602) 621-3641. During the academic year—weekdays at 10 a.m. and 2 p.m. and Saturday at 10; during the summer—Monday-Saturday at 10 a.m.* These tours are given by student volunteers. Meet in the lobby of the Nugent Building across the main walkway from the student union.

Center for Creative Photography, *(602) 621-7968. Weekdays 10 to 5 and Sunday noon to 5; free.* One of America's largest collections of Ansel Adams photos is displayed in the center's new gallery, along with rotating exhibits.

Mineral Museum *(602) 621-4227. Weekdays 8 a.m. to 3 p.m.; free.* Rock and gem specimens from the Southwest and around the world are on display.

University of Arizona Museum of Art, *(602) 621-7567. Monday-Friday 9 to 5 and Sunday noon to 4 during the school year; Monday-Friday 10 to 3:30 and Saturday noon to 4 in summer; free.* Rated as one of the finest university museums between Houston and Los Angeles, it has large collections of Middle Ages and 20th Century art.

Wildcat Heritage Gallery, *(602) 621-2411. Weekdays 8 to 5; free.* It's an essential stop for University of Arizona alumni, with photos and other memorabilia of U of A teams dating back to 1897.

THE REST

Catalina State Park • *Nine miles north on U.S. 89 (P.O. Box 36986), Tucson, AZ 85740; (602) 628-5798. Day use $3, camping $6 (see listing under "Where to Camp").* More than 5,500 acres of Santa Catalina Mountain foothills have been set aside in this state park. In the upper reaches of the Sonoran Desert, the park has picnicking, hiking and horseback riding. A trailhead offers access to adjacent Coronado National Forest hiking trails.

Colossal Cave • *Old Spanish Trail (20 miles southeast on I-10, then six miles north) P.O. Box D-7, Vail, AZ 85641; (602) 791-7677. April to September—Monday-Saturday 8 to 6, Sundays and holidays 8 to 7; the rest of the year—Monday-Saturday 9 to 5, Sundays and holidays 9 to 6. Adults $4.75; kids 11 to 16, $3.50; 6 to 10, $2. MC/VISA.*

Colossal Cave isn't very. It might have been, but past decades of vandalizing ruined many of its formations. One early operator would break off stalactites and stalagmites and sell them to his customers for $2 each. The cave is still privately owned and the present operators are much more conscientious, of course.

Guides conduct one-hour tours past the formations of this dry limestone cavern. Our guide, who sounded like a high-pitched recording, warped history a bit with her tales of bad guys who stashed booty here from a stagecoach robbery. It may still be hidden in the cave, she speculated. However, historical sources tell us that the outlaws paused here only briefly, emptied their mail sacks of loot and continued on their way.

Actually, there's more here than meets the eye—literally. Colossal is thought to be the world's largest dry cave, with more than 40 miles of corridors. In fact, the end still hasn't been found. The public tour covers only about a mile.

John C. Fremont House ● *Near the Community Center downtown, off Granada (P.O. Box 2588), Tucson, AZ 85702; (602) 622-0956. Wednesday-Saturday 10 to 4; free.* John C. Fremont was one busy fellow. In a single lifetime he was a Western explorer and pathfinder, military commandant of California during the Mexican War, civil governor of California, U.S. senator from California, commander of the U.S. Army's Western Military Department and governor of the Arizona Territory.

During his stint as Arizona's governor, he occupied homes in Prescott and Tucson. This one is an 1858 adobe brick house, squatting almost timidly among the bold new structures of the Tucson Community Center. Now a museum operated by the Arizona Historical Society, it's furnished with Victorian, early American and early Southwestern antiques. Note the unusual ceilings, held up by heavy beams interlaced with spiny ocotillo or saguaro ribs.

Tucson Botanical Gardens ● *2150 N. Alvernon Way (Grant), Tucson, AZ 85712; (602) 326-9255. Monday-Friday 9 to 4, Saturday 10 to 4 and Sunday noon to 4. Adults $2, seniors $1.50, kids under 12 free.* Our first impression was that this botanical garden resembled someone's oversized back yard. Once the estate of a local nurseryman, it's heavily planted and rather rambling.

More interesting than the main garden is the "Xeriscape Demonstration Garden" which exhibits water-conservation methods essential to a desert environment. Solar energy is used to irrigate and illuminate this water-sipping state-of-the-art garden.

The Botanical Garden gift shop is particularly cute. In addition to gardening books, it has a clever assortment of gift items, many with gardening and chili-pepper themes.

Tucson Children's Museum ● *300 E. University Ave. (Fifth Avenue), Tucson, AZ 85705; (602) 792-9985. Tuesday-Saturday 10 to 5, Sunday 1 to 5. Adults $3, kids 2 to 18 and seniors $1.50.* Directed mostly to primary school children, this small museum encourages kids to learn by doing. Exhibits include a "pedal your own image" exercycle that generates enough electricity to put you on TV, a gallery of optical illusions, and an animated see-through mannequin. Computer health quizzes will interest adults.

Tucson Plaza with Moorish-domed county courthouse contrasting modern office building.

Walking tours of downtown ● Self-guided tours: *Brochures available at the Visitors Bureau, 130 S. Scott Avenue.* **Guided tours:** *Meet at the Fremont house; tours start at 10 a.m. Saturdays, October through March and at 9:30 Saturdays during April; $3 per person, less for children and seniors. For information, call (602) 622-0956.*

Whether you prefer to go it alone with a Visitors Bureau brochure, or join a tour led by an Arizona Historical Society docent, these walks will teach you much about downtown Tucson's yesterdays. The route takes you through El Presidio Historic Area, to the Moorish-domed Pima County Courthouse and adjacent plaza, and to St. Augustine Cathedral which is a near twin to Mission San Xavier.

Unfortunately, many of downtown's adobes have been replaced or covered and modernized. You'll see a lot of plaques along the way, telling you where things were, instead of where they are. The docent-led tour is more interesting; skilled historians help you envision those days when almond-eyed senoritas swirled their bright skirts in dimly-lit cantinas.

R.W. Webb Winery ● *13605 E. Benson Highway (14 miles southeast, off I-10), P.O. Box 130, Vail, AZ 85641; (602) 629-9911. Tours and tastings Monday-Saturday 10 to 5, Sunday noon to 5 (last tour starts at 4 each day). Admission $1, applied against purchase.* Premium wine grapes among the cactus? The R.W. Webb Winery is the first in Arizona, producing and marketing an assortment of varietal wines. Tours cover the modern 10,000-square-foot facility, followed by sips of the product.

ACTIVITIES & ENTERTAINMENT

Arizona Opera Company ● *3501 N. Mountain Ave., Tucson, AZ 85719; 293-4336.* Four professional productions presented from October through March.

Arizona Theatre Company ● *330 S. Scott St., Tucson, AZ 85701; (602) 622-2823; tickets $9.50 to $18.50; less for seniors and students. Major credit cards.* Professional thespians perform Tuesday-Sunday from October through April at the Tucson Convention Center theater.

Bobby McGee's Conglomeration ● *6464 E. Tanque Verde Rd., Tucson, AZ 85715; (602) 886-5551.* This is a combination restaurant and nightclub with singing, dancing and variety acts.

CCC Chuckwagon Suppers ● *8900 Bopp Rd. (eight miles west; Ajo Way to Kinney Road, then left on Bopp Road), Tucson, AZ 85746; (602) 883-2333 or (800) 446-1798. Adults $15, kids 12 and under $10 for dinner and show. Tuesday-Saturday, gates open at 5, dinner served at 7; extra shows late December through early May.* A cowboy band descended from the Sons of the Pioneers sings trail-riding songs and a few modern country and Western numbers at this chuckwagon feed. Dinner includes baked beans, a hunk of beef and biscuits and honey.

Gaslight Theatre ● *7000 E. Tanque Verde Rd. (near Sabino Canyon Rd., in Gaslight Square); (602) 886-9428. Adults $10; seniors, students and military $9; kids under 12, $5.50. Major credit cards.* Oldstyle melodramas are performed Wednesday-Thursday at 8, Friday-Saturday at 7 and 9:30 and Sunday at 7. Hiss the hero and boo the villain; stomp your feet to banjo and honky-tonk piano music. Adjacent Little Anthony's Diner serves steaks, chicken and sandwiches; meals from $4 to $9.

Gray Line Tours ● *P.O. Box 1991, Tucson, AZ 85702; 622-8811.* Guided tours around Tucson and elsewhere in Arizona.

Western Tours ● *P.O. Box 31831, Tucson, AZ 85751; (602) 721-0980.* Guided tours of Tucson and southern Arizona.

Greyhound racing ● *Tucson Greyhound Park, 2601 S. Third Ave., Tucson, AZ 85713; (602) 884-7576.* The mutts gallop the year-around; pari-mutuel betting, clubhouse dining.

Orts Theatre of Dance ● *328 E. Seventh St., Tucson, AZ 85705; (602) 624-3799.* Professional repertory dance company presents four programs each year.

Professional baseball—Tucson Toros AAA League ● *P.O. Box 27045, Tucson, AZ 85726; (602) 325-2621* They play at Hi Corbett Field from April through August.

Professional baseball—Cactus League ● *Cleveland Indians; for tickets, call Dillard's box office at 293-1008.* Cactus League games at Hi Corbett Field (East Broadway at Randolph Way) in March.

Sunshine Jeep Tours ● *641 E. Windward Circle, Tucson, AZ 85704; 742-1943.* Trips into the Sonoran Desert in four-wheel-drive, open air jeeps.

Tucson Symphony Orchestra ● *443 S. Stone Ave., Tucson, AZ 85701; (602) 882-8585 or 792-9155.* Tucson's professional symphony presents five programs of classics, pops and chamber concerts from October through April.

Ultimate Fitness and Hiking ● *9222 E. Indio Place, Tucson, AZ 85749; (602) 749-5712.* Conducted scenic fitness hikes in the surrounding mountains. Outings include nature study and meals.

University of Arizona Cultural Affairs Department ● *800 E. University Blvd., #110, Tucson, AZ 85719; (602) 621-3364 pr 621-3341.* The University hosts a variety of professional artists and attractions, ranging from contemporary and classic music to live theater and dance.

ANNUAL EVENTS

Tucson Open golf tournament, first weekend of January; **Two Flags International Art Festival,** third weekend of January; **Indian Arts Benefit Fair**, first weekend of February; **Festival in the Sun,** cultural program at University of Arizona, late February to early March; **Tucson Balloon Festival,** mid-February; *Fiesta de los Vaqueros* Rodeo, third weekend of February; **Southern Arizona International Livestock Show,** second weekend of March; **Mount Lemmon Ski Carnival,** second weekend of March; **Aerospace and Arizona** air show, mid-March; **Pima County Fair,** early to mid-April; **Tohono O'Odham Indian Arts Festival** and **Fiesta del Presidio,** first weekend of April; **Tucson Summer Arts Festival,** June-August; **Tucson International Film Festival,** late October to early November.

WHERE TO SHOP

Tucson offers a rich mix of Indian and Mexican handicraft shops and modern malls. One complex, **El Mercado del Boutiques** (Broadway and Wilmot, east of downtown) is a blend of both; it's a collection of ethnic Southwestern shops. Another good place to find Southwest arts and crafts is **Old Town Artisans,** 186 N. Meyer in El Presidio, which we mentioned above. The Mexican-style **Many Hands Courtyard**, 3054 First Ave. (between Ft. Lowell and Grant), also features Southwestern boutiques. For a Western-style shopping center, try **Trail Dust Town** at 6541 E. Tanque Verde Rd. (east of downtown near Wilmot).

Several enclosed shopping malls are worth of a visit by your credit cards. They include large **Tucson Mall** at Oracle and Wetmore; **El Con Mall**, just east of downtown on Broadway (between Country Club and Alvernon); **Park Mall**, east of El Con on Broadway (between Craycroft and Wilmot); and **Foothills Center**, 7401 N. La Cholla Blvd. (northeast of town, near Ina Road). Among Tucson's boutique malls are **The Plaza at Williams Center,** 5420 E. Broadway (Craycroft); **St. Philip's Plaza** at 4330 N. Campbell Ave. (River Road); and **Plaza Palomino** at 2920 N. Swan Ave. (Ft. Lowell).

Downtown shopping is focused on Fourth Avenue between Fourth and Seventh streets, with a mix of apparel shops, boutiques, antique shops and galleries.

If you like used book stores, you'll love **Bookman's** at 1930 E. Grant Ave. (Campbell); phone 325-5767. It's a monster of a used book store—one of the largest in the Southwest. And it's intelligently laid out. Fliers available at the front counter will direct you to your areas of interest. It has an extensive children's book selection, and it also deals in used records, tapes and CD's. If you tend to over-spend in book stores—as we do—you'll be glad to learn that Bookman's takes VISA and MasterCard.

WHERE TO DINE

American

Anthony's in the Catalinas ● △△△ $$$ ∅

6440 N. Campbell Ave. (Skyline); (602) 299-1771. Southwestern, Continental, Italian; dinners $11 to $23; full bar. Lunch Monday-Saturday noon to 3, dinner daily 5:30 to 10. Reservations advised; MC/VISA, AMEX. Indoor and outdoor dining with views of Catalina Mountains and the city; varied menu; extensive wine list. Pianist nightly in the cocktail lounge.

Cafe Terra Cotta ● △△△△ $$$ ∅
4310 N. Campbell Ave. (St. Philip's Plaza at River Street); (602) 577-8100. Southwestern; dinners $15 to $25; full bar. Daily from 11 a.m. Reservations advised; Major credit cards. One of Arizona's leading contemporary Southwestern restaurants; menu specialties include prawns with goat cheese, roasted duckling with prickly pear and black pepper glaze, smoked pork loin with white bean chili and creative pizzas. Extensive wine selection by the glass; excellent desserts.

Janos ● △△△△ $$$ ∅
150 N. Main Ave. (in El Presidio Historic District); (602) 884-9426. American nouvelle; dinners $15.50 to $27; full bar service. Monday-Saturday from 5:30 p.m. (closed Monday from June to January). MC/VISA, AMEX. One of Tucson's finer upscale restaurants; nouvelle menu with a Southwestern slant; constantly-changing menu. Janos occupies an historic landmark adobe.

Joe's Oyster Bar ● △△ $$$
6310 E. Broadway (Wilmot, in El Mercado Shopping Center), (602) 748-9060. Seafood; dinners $10 to $35; full bar. Monday-Thursday 11 a.m. to 10 p.m., Friday-Saturday 11 to midnight, Sunday 2 to 10. Reservations advised on weekends; MC/VISA, AMEX. Fresh shellfish and other seafood dishes; patio dining. Cocktail lounge adjacent.

Iron Mask Restaurant ● △ $$ ∅
2464 E. Grant Rd. (Tucson Boulevard); (602) 327-6649. American-Continental; dinners $10.25 to $15.50; full bar service. Lunch Tuesday-Friday 11:30 to 2, dinner Tuesday-Saturday 5:30 to 9:30, closed Sunday-Monday. Major credit cards. Chef-owned restaurant featuring Beef Wellington, Shrimp Wellington, roast duck, veal and fresh fish.

La Villa Restaurant ● △△△ $$$ ∅
In Westin La Paloma at 3800 E. Sunrise; (602) 577-5806. American; dinners $12.50 to $19; full bar. Daily 5 to 10:30 p.m. Reservations advised; Major credit cards. Casual dining in a Southwestern-style restaurant with a fireplace; city views. Fresh fish, steaks and chops. Disco with deejay, nightly dancing in the adjoining Cactus Club.

Pinnacle Peak Steakhouse ● △△△ $$ ∅
6541 E. Tanque Verde Rd. (Wilmot); (602) 886-5012. Western; dinners $7 to $12; full bar service. Daily 5 to 10 p.m. Reservations accepted; Major credit cards. Remarkably tasty yet inexpensive mesquite-grilled steaks served in an Old West atmosphere. The open rafters are festooned with ties, snipped off by waitresses to insure the informality of this place. Located in Trail Dust Town, a Western-style shopping complex with boutiques, galleries and other restaurants. Look for the full-sized prairie schooner sitting atop a stack of balanced boulders.

PoFolks ● △△ $ ∅
5632 E. Speedway Blvd. (Craycroft); (602) 748-2700. American; dinners $4 to $8; no alcohol. Sunday-Thursday 11 a.m. to 9 p.m., Friday-Saturday 11 to 10. No credit cards. Very inexpensive "down-home" cooking, including chicken and dumplings, catfish, pork chops and other rural fare. Voted "Tucson's Best Family Restaurant" by a local restaurant guide.

Solarium ● △△△ $$ ∅
6444 E. Tanque Verde; (602) 886-8186. American; dinners $8 to $16; full bar service. Lunch weekdays 11:30 to 2:30, dinner nightly from 5. Reservations

advised; Major credit cards. Airy restaurant under glass, in modern architec-tually-distinctive building; culinary emphasis is on seafood.

Saguaro Corners Restaurant ● △△△△ $$$
3750 S. Old Spanish Trail (opposite Saguaro National Monument entrance); (602) 886-5424. American; dinners $8 to $28; full bar service. Lunch Tuesday-Saturday noon to 2:30, Sunday service noon to 9:30, dinner Tuesday-Sunday 5 to 9:30. Reservations advised, MC/VISA, AMEX. Charmingly rustic restaurant in the desert; windows look out on desert wildlife attracted by evening lights. American-Southwestern menu.

The Tack Room ● △△△△△ $$$$ ∅
2800 N. Sabino Canyon Rd. (half mile north of Tanque Verde Road), (602) 722-2800. Southwestern; dinners $24.50 to $34.50; full bar service. Daily from 6 p.m.; reservations strongly advised. Major credit cards. Five-star Mobil restaurant in a rustically elegant half-century old adobe hacienda; stone fireplace, cozy living room atmosphere. Specialties include rack of lamb with mesquite honey and lime and other innovative Southwestern dishes.

Tohono Chul Park Tearoom ● △△△ $
7366 N. Paseo del Norte (in Tohono Chul Park, northwest corner of Ina and Oracle); (602) 797-1711. American; meals $7 to $10; wine and beer. Daily 8 to 5, high tea 2:30 to 4:30. MC/VISA, AMEX. Beautiful little cafe in a brick Southwest style home; outdoor dining in a central courtyard and serene landscaped patio. Light meals of sandwiches and soups, breakfast croissants. Tasty desserts; high tea with scones and pastries.

Continental

Arizona Inn Restaurant ● △△△△ $$$ ∅
2200 E. Elm St. (Campbell Avenue, near U of A); (602) 325-1541. Dinners $12 to $23; full bar service. Daily; breakfast 7 to 10, lunch 11:30 to 2, dinner 6 to 9, Sunday brunch 11 to 2; reservations advised. MC/VISA, AMEX. Located in an attractively-landscaped resort complex (listed below), this European-style dining room features fresh fish and rack of lamb. Pianist offers dinner music Tuesday through Saturday evenings.

Charles Restaurant ● △△△ $$$ ∅
6400 E. Eldorado Circle (Speedway and Wilmot); (602) 296-7173. Dinners $10 to $20; full bar service. Monday-Saturday from 5:30 p.m.; reservations advised. MC/VISA, AMEX, DC. An attractive restaurant in a stately stone mansion; veal, Steak Diane, roast duckling and fresh fish. Piano bar Friday and Saturday evenings.

Daniel's Restaurant ● △△△ $$$ ∅
2930 N. Swan Road (in Plaza Palomino Center, off Ft. Lowell); (602) 742-3200. Italian-French; dinners $16 to $24; full bar service. Daily 5 p.m. to 11 p.m.; reservations advised. Major credit cards. This handsome restaurant fea-tures Northern Italian and regional French entrees on a weekly-changing menu. Its large wine cellar has 160 varieties.

The Gold Room ● △△△ $$$
Westward Look Resort (245 E. Ina Road east of Oracle), (602) 297-1151. Dinners $17 to $23; full bar service. Breakfast 7 to 10:30, lunch 11:30 to 2, dinner 5:30 to 10. Reservations essential. Major credit cards. Continental menu with Southwestern accents; fresh seafood, veal, rack of lamb. City view; live music in adjacent cocktail lounge.

Le Rendez-Vous ● ▵▵▵ $$$ ⊘
3844 E. Ft. Lowell Rd. (Alvernon); (602) 323-7373. French; dinners $14 to $18; full bar service. Tuesday-Sunday; lunch 11 to 2, dinner 6 to 10; reservations advised. Major credit cards. Menu specials in this cozy French restaurant include rack of lamb, mussels and salmon.

Palomino Restaurant ● ▵▵ $$$ ⊘
2959 N. Swan Rd.; (602) 325-0413. Continental, some American dishes; dinners $12 to $17. Daily 4:30 to 12:30 p.m.; reservations recommended. MC/VISA, AMEX, DC. Small family-owned cafe with Mediterranean decor; featuring bouillabaisse, veal, seafood, broiled steaks, sweetbreads.

Penelope's Restaurant Francais ● ▵▵▵▵ $$$$ ⊘
3619 E. Speedway Blvd. (2.5 blocks west of Alvernon); (602) 325-5080. French; prix fixe dinner $27.50, with wines $39.50; wine and beer. Lunch Tuesday-Friday 11:30 to 2, dinner Tuesday-Sunday from 5:30; reservations advised. MC/VISA. An intimate French restaurant serving both classic and country styles in a six-course prix fixe dinner. Changing menu offers three to four entrees. In an old adobe farmhouse; decorated with works of local artists.

Scordato's Restaurant ● ▵▵ $$ ⊘
4405 W. Speedway Blvd.; (602) 792-3055. Italian-American; dinners $11 to $20; full bar service. Sunday from 4 p.m., Tuesday-Saturday from 5; reservations accepted. Major credit cards. Veal is a feature of the Italian menu; the American side of the menu includes chicken, steaks, chops and seafood.

Mexican

Courtyard Cafe ● ▵▵ $
186 N. Meyer (Telles, in patio of Old Town Artisans); (602) 622-0351. Mexican-American; meals $5 to $10; wine and beer. Open daily for lunch. A pleasant little cafe in the landscaped patio of a large Mexican arts and crafts market in El Presidio Historic District.

El Charro Cafe ● ▵▵ $ ⊘
311 N. Court Street (at Franklin, in El Presidio Historic District); (602) 622-5465. Dinner $5 to $10; wine and beer. Sunday-Thursday 11 a.m. to 9 p.m., Friday Saturday 11 to 10; reservations accepted. MC/VISA, AMEX. In business since 1922, El Charro is Tucson's oldest Mexican restaurant. Present owners are seventh generation members of a pioneer Tucson family. The food is excellent—all made from scratch. *Carne seca,* a chewy, almost sweet sun-dried beef, is a special menu item. A gift shop occupies the cellar of the 1880 stone building.

La Fuente Restaurant ● ▵ $ ⊘
1749 N. Oracle Rd. (south of Grant Road); (602) 623-8659. Dinners $5 to $11. Daily 11 a.m. to midnight; reservations accepted for dinner. MC/VISA, AMEX. Cheerful little place with nightly mariachi music, starting at 6:30.

La Parilla Suiza ● ▵▵ $ ⊘
5602 E. Speedway; (602) 747-4838. Dinner $5 to $12; full bar service. Monday-Thursday 11 a.m. to 10 p.m., Friday-Saturday 11 to 11, Sunday 1 to 10; reservations advised. Major credit cards. A cut above typical smashed beans and rice places, La Parilla Suiza specializes in Mexico City-style fare. A menu feature is an open-faced "taco", with meat, fish or poultry stir-fried with chilies, onions and other veggies. The taco soup is excellent.

WHERE TO SLEEP

The Alpine Inn ● ΔΔ $$$

12925 Sabino Canyon Parkway (in Summerhaven; P.O. Box 789), Mount Lemmon, AZ 85619; (602) 576-1500. Doubles $65 to $75; discount for two or more nights. MC/VISA. Mountain-style six-room inn tucked among the pines of Mount Lemmon above Tucson; near ski area. Free breakfast. **Restaurant** serves breakfast, lunch and dinner—until 6 p.m. Monday-Thursday, 8 p.m. Friday, 9 p.m. Saturday and 7 p.m. Sunday; Continental-Southwestern (noted for fondue, chili, cornbread), dinners $9 to $14, non-smoking areas. Full bar, weekend entertainment.

Best Western Executive Inn ● ΔΔΔ $$$

333 W. Drachman (Speedway exit off I-10), Tucson, AZ 85705; (602) 791-7551 or (800) 528-1234. Doubles $40 to $85, singles $36 to $85, suites $65 to $125; lower off-season rates. Major credit cards. Large rooms with TV, rental movies, room phones; swimming pool, wading pool, spa. **La Fiesta Restaurant** serves from 6:30 a.m. to 2 p.m. and 5 to 10 p.m., American, dinners $6 to $15, full bar service.

Chateau Apartment-Hotels ● ΔΔ $$ to $$$ ∅

1402 N. Alvernon (Speedway), Tucson, AZ 85712; (602) 323-7121. All kitchen units, $39 to $99. MC/VISA, AMEX. Pool, spa, tennis courts.

Cliff Manor Inn ● ΔΔΔ $$

5900 N. Oracle Rd. (six miles north of downtown), Tucson, AZ 85704; (602) 887-4000 or (800) 999-4440. Doubles and suites $35 to $55, singles $32 to $48, kitchenettes $38 to $58; lower off-season rates. Major credit cards. TV movies, phones; pool, spa, golf, game room with live entertainment, beauty parlor. **Cliff Manor Restaurant** open 24 hours, American (steaks, seafood), dinners $7 to $15, non-smoking areas, full bar service; panoramic views from dining room.

Courtyard by Marriott ● ΔΔΔ $$$ ∅

2505 E. Executive Dr. (Tucson Boulevard and Valencia), Tucson, AZ 85706; (602) 573-0000 or (800) 321-2211. Doubles $54 to $82, singles $44 to $72; lower off-season rates. Major credit cards. TV movies, phones, in-room coffee service, desk; rooms have separate seating areas. Indoor and outdoor pool, hot tub, exercise room, laundry, lounge, enclosed terrace courtyard. **Restaurant** serves daily 6:30 to 2 and 5 to 10, American, dinners $8 to $15, non-smoking areas, full bar service; Southwestern decor.

Doubletree at Randolph Park ● ΔΔΔ $$$ ∅

445 S. Alvernon Way (between Broadway and 22nd), Tucson, AZ 85711; (602) 881-4200 or (800) 528-0444. Doubles $59 to $125, singles $49 to $115; lower off-season rates. Major credit cards. TV movies, phones, attractively furnished rooms; pool, spa, exercise room, tennis courts. Adjacent to Randolph Park with two golf courses, tennis, jogging track and zoo. **Cactus Rose** (Continental) and **Javelina Cantina** (Mexican) restaurants; service from 6 a.m. to 11 p.m., dinners $6 to $15, non-smoking areas, full bar service.

Embassy Suites ● ΔΔΔ $$$ ∅

5335 E. Broadway (Craycroft, near downtown), Tucson, AZ 85711; (602) 745-2700 or (602) EMBASSY. All two-room suites, doubles and singles $59 to $114, kitchen units $55 to $104; lower off-season rates. Major credit cards. TV in each room, phones, living room with sofa, chair and work—dining area, wet bar, refrigerator; free breakfast and cocktails. Units open onto atrium courtyard with landscaping and a fountain. **Jason's Deli** adjacent.

Holiday Inn Broadway • ΔΔΔ $$$$ ∅

181 W. Broadway (Congress Street, downtown), Tucson, AZ 85701; (602) 624-8700 or (800) HOLIDAY. Doubles $75 to $95, singles $65 to $85, suites from $150; lower off-season rates. Major credit cards. Attractively decorated rooms with TV movies, phones, other amenities; pool, lounge. **Lilies Restaurant** serves 6:30 a.m. to 2 and 5 to 10, American and Mexican, dinners $9 to $12, non-smoking areas, full bar service.

Hotel Congress • Δ $$

311 E. Congress (downtown, near train station), Tucson, AZ 85701; (602) 622-8848. Doubles $35 to $49, singles $30 to $38. MC/VISA, AMEX, DC. Older refurbished hotel with TV, rental movies, pool. **Bowen and Bailey Cafe** is a European style deli with sidewalk dining; meals from $6 to $8, non-smoking areas, full bar service.

La Quinta Motor Inn • ΔΔΔ $$$ ∅

665 N. Freeway (St. Mary's exit from I-10), Tucson, AZ 85705; (602) 622-6491. Doubles $53 to $58, singles $45 to $40; lower off-season rates. Major credit cards. Located just off the freeway, downtown; TV movies, room phones, pool. Coffee shop nearby.

Lexington Hotel Suites • ΔΔ $$$ ∅

7411 N. Oracle Rd. (Ina Road), Tucson, AZ 85704; (602) 575-9255. Studios, one and two-bedroom suites $59 to $124; lower off-season rates. Major credit cards. Kitchens, TV movies, phones; free breakfast and free Wednesday cookout, pool, spa, putting green; nice views.

Lodge in the Desert • ΔΔΔΔ $$$$ ∅

306 N. Alvernon Way (P.O. Box 42500), Tucson, AZ 85733; (602) 325-3366. Doubles $78 to $163, singles $66 to $151, kitchenettes $113, suites $92 to $125; lower off-season rates. Major credit cards. A beautifully-maintained 50-year-old garden lodge with adobe-style casitas, pool, shuffleboard, croquet, ping pong, lounge and library. Large guest rooms with beam ceilings, ceramic tile accents, TV, phones, many rooms with fireplaces, some with refrigerators; free breakfast, semi-private patios. The **Lodge Restaurant** serves daily 7 to 9:30 a.m., noon to 1:30 and 6 to 8:30, American-Continental, dinners $7 to $18, non-smoking areas, full bar service.

Paul's Hide-Away Lodge • ΔΔ $$

255 W. Flores St. (near Grant and Oracle), Tucson, AZ 85705; (602) 624-2221. Doubles $25 to $30, singles $20 to $24, kitchenettes $24 to $28, suites $95 to $140; lower off-season rates. No credit cards. Small lodge with TV, room refrigerators and phones; pool, carports.

Pueblo Inn • ΔΔΔ $$$ ∅

350 S. Freeway (Congress off-ramp from I-10), Tucson, AZ 85745; (602) 622-6611 or (800) 533-6838. Doubles $68 to $78, singles $56 to $66, suites $85 to $135; various special rates. Major credit cards. TV movies, phones, pool, spa, tennis, shuffleboard, landscaped courtyard, weight room; some lanais. **Cactus Flower Cafe** serves 7 a.m. to 2 p.m., American and Mexican, non-smoking areas, full bar service.

Quality Inn Tucson Airport • ΔΔ $$$ ∅

6801 S. Tucson Blvd. (near Tucson International Airport), Tucson, AZ 85706; (602) 746-3932 or (800) 526-0550. Doubles $59 to $99, singles $49 *to $89, suites $69 to $125; lower off-season rates. MC/VISA, AMEX, DC.* TV movies, phones, free breakfast, cocktails and late-night snacks; landscaped courtyard, pool, spa, airport shuttle. **Quincy's Restaurant** serves from 6 a.m. to 10 p.m., Continental, dinners $6 to $13, non-smoking areas, full bar service.

Quality Inn University • △ $$$ ∅
1601 N. Oracle Rd. (Grant), Tucson, AZ 85705; (602) 623-6666 or (800) 777-2999. Doubles $51 to $59, singles $46 to $54, kitchenettes $105, suites $64 to $105; lower off-season rates. Major credit cards. TV movies, phones; guest rooms around landscaped courtyard with rose garden, cactus garden and pool. **Cafe Adobe** serves from 6:30 a.m. to 10 p.m., American-Mexican, dinners from $8 to $13, non-smoking areas, full bar.

Radisson Suite Hotel • △△△ $$$ ∅
6555 E. Speedway (Wilmot), Tucson, AZ 85710; (602) 721-7100 or (800) 333-3333. All suites, $54 to $120; lower off-season rates. MC/VISA, AMEX, DC. Two TV sets with movies, phones, refrigerators, private balconies or patios overlooking central courtyard; free buffet breakfast and cocktails. **Cafe Dorado** serves 11 a.m. to 11 p.m., American-Continental, dinners $12 to $17, non-smoking area, full bar service.

Ramada Downtown • △△△ $$$ ∅
475 N. Granada (St. Mary's exit from I-10), Tucson, AZ 85701; (602) 622-3000 or (800) 228-2828. Doubles $89 to $99, singles $70 to $80, suites from $125; lower off-season rates. Major credit cards. TV movies, phones; pool, putting green, mini-mall and gift shop. **Cafe Classic** serves from 6:30 a.m. to 10 p.m., American and Southwestern (soup and salad bar), dinners $7 to $13, non-smoking areas, full bar service.

Ramada Inn • △△△ $$$ ∅
404 N. Freeway (St. Mary's exit from I-10), Tucson, AZ 85705; (602) 624-8341 or (800) 2-RAMADA. Doubles $63 to $73, singles $53 to $63; lower off-season rates. Major credit cards. Just off the freeway, downtown; TV movies, room phones, pool, kids' pool. **Dining room** and coffee shop 6:30 a.m. to 10 p.m., dinners $6 to $15; full bar service.

Ramada Inn Foothills • △△△ $$$ ∅
6944 E. Tanque Verde (near Sabino Canyon), Tucson, AZ 85715; (602) 886-9595 or (800) 272-6232. Doubles $54 to $70, singles $48 to $60, kitchen units and suites $56 to $85; lower off-season rates. Major credit cards. TV movies, phones, some refrigerators; free breakfast buffet and happy hour. Pool, spa, sauna; free passes to health club.

Regal Inn • △△ $$
1222 S. Freeway (22nd Street exit from I-10), Tucson, AZ 85713; (602) 624-2516 or (800) 851-8888. Doubles $39 to $46, singles $29 to $36; lower off-season rates. MC/VISA. TV, room phones, pool.

Residence Inn by Marriott • △△△ $$$$ ∅
6477 E. Speedway Blvd. (east side, a mile from Park Mall Shopping Center), Tucson, AZ 85710; (602) 721-0991 or (800) 331-3131. Doubles and singles $69 to $107, suites $69 to $137; lower prices are off-season rates. Major credit cards. Kitchen units in all rooms with microwaves, TV movies, VCR, phones, some fireplaces; pool, spa, sports court; free breakfast and afternoon social hour; free passes to nearby athletic club.

Rodeway Inn • ∆∆ $$ ∅
810 E. Benson Hwy. (I-10 exit 262), Tucson, AZ 85713; (602) 884-5800 or (800) 228-2000. Doubles $30 to $70, singles $28 to $65; lower off-season rates. Major credit cards. TV movies, phones, free Continental breakfast, some refrigerators; pool in landscaped courtyard.

Sunny 9 Motor Inn • ∆∆ $$
1500 E. Santa Fe (near Speedway and Stone), Tucson, AZ 85705; (602) 622-6446. Doubles $25 to $65, kitchenettes $28 to $75; lower off-season rates. MC/VISA, AMEX. TV movies, room phones, pool.

Tanque Verde Inn • ∆∆∆ $$$ ∅
7007 E. Tanque Verde Rd. (east of Kolb and Wilmot) Tucson, AZ 85715; (602) 298-2300 or (800) 882-8484. Doubles and singles $39 to $72, kitchen units $49 to $90, suites $88 to $120; lower prices are off-season rates. MC/VISA, AMEX, DC. Hacienda-style inn with rooms open to a landscaped courtyard with Spanish-style fountains and tropical foliage; pool, spa, health club privileges. TV movies, phones, in-room coffee makers, free breakfast, daily cocktail parties.

Tucson Desert Inn • ∆∆ $$ ∅
#1 North Freeway (Congress off-ramp from I-10), Tucson, AZ 85745; (602) 624-8151 or (800) 7-DESERT. Doubles $30 to $45, singles $24 to $38, suites $45 to $75; lower off-season rates. MC/VISA, AMEX, DC. TV movies, phones, pool. **Foxy's Cafe** serves 6 a.m. to 9 p.m., American, dinners $5 to $15; desert-Western decor, full bar service.

RESORTS

Arizona Inn • ∆∆∆∆ $$$
2200 E. Elm Street (off Campbell Avenue near U of A), Tucson, AZ 85719; (602) 325-1541 or (800) 421-1093. Doubles $62 to $130, singles $52 to $120, suites $105 to $120; lower off-season rates. MC/VISA, AMEX. Luxurious old world-style resort, sheltered from the surrounding city in a 14-acre garden setting. Handsomely decorated guest rooms feature fireplaces, antique furnishings, TV/stereo/radio, phones; some have patios. Pool, clay tennis courts, cocktail lounge, gift shop, library-lounge. It offers typical resort amenities, yet it's close to downtown Tucson. **Arizona Inn Restaurant** (listed above).

Loews Ventana Canyon Resort • ∆∆∆∆ $$$$$
7000 N. Resort Dr. (near Sunrise and Kolb), Tucson, AZ 85715; (602) 299-2020. Doubles $200 to $220, singles $190 to $210; lower off-season rates. Major credit cards. Opulent resort in desert foothills. Rooms feature TV movies, phones, refrigerators, luxury furnishings. Two golf courses, pools, sauna, steam room, health club, expansive grounds. Noted for its dining with **four restaurants**: Ventana Room, serving American nouvelle; Canyon Cafe, casual with luncheon buffets and Sunday brunch; Bill's Grill, American fare at pool side; and Flying V Bar and Grill, a steakhouse and disco.

Sheraton Tucson El Conquistador • ∆∆∆∆ $$$$$ ∅
10,000 N. Oracle Rd. (north of Ina Road), Tucson, AZ 85737; (602) 742-7000 or (800) 325-3535. Doubles and singles $150 to $225; lower off-season rates. Major credit cards. Large full-service resort set against a dramatic backdrop of rugged desert mountains. Elegant guest rooms with South-

western decor and private patios or balconies; TV movies, phones, some rooms with fireplaces; 45 holes of golf, tennis, biking, hiking, horseback rides, racquetball, volleyball, swimming pools, spa, saunas, health club with masseur. **Five restaurants** serving Western-style, American, Continental and Mexican fare. All have non-smoking areas and full bar service.

Ventana Canyon Golf & Racquet Club • △△△△ $$$$$
6200 N. Clubhouse Lane (near Sunrise and Kolb), Tucson, AZ 85715; (602) 577-1400 or (800) 233-4569 in Arizona and (800) 828-5701 outside. All suites, from $190 to $400; lower off-season rates. MC/VISA, AMEX. Elegantly-appointed resort in the Santa Catalina foothills; extensive grounds with two golf courses, lighted tennis courts, pools, spas, saunas, full men's and women's health club facilities and exercise rooms. One and two-bedroom suites have kitchen and living-dining areas, TV movies, phones and other amenities. **Clubhouse Dining Room** and the **Terrace Lounge and Patio** serve 7 a.m. to 10 p.m.; Continental, Southwestern and American fare; dinners $10 to $35, full bar service.

Westward Look Resort • △△△△ $$$$$ ∅
245 E. Ina Rd. (half mile east or Oracle), Tucson, AZ 85704; (602) 297-1151 or (800) 722-2500. Doubles and singles $110 to $175; lower off-season rates. MC/VISA, AMEX, DC. In pleasant desert setting with three pools, spas, saunas, health club, jogging track, tennis. Attractive rooms with balconies or patios, TV movies, phones, in-room coffee, refrigerators, separate sitting areas. **Gold Room** and **Lobby Cafe** restaurants; service from 7 a.m. to 10 p.m., American and Continental (veal, fresh seafood, Southwestern cuisine), dinners $15 to $27, full bar service. Also pool-side cabana dining.

BED & BREAKFAST INNS

The Desert Yankee • *1615 N. Norton (off Elm, near U of A), Tucson, AZ 85719; (602) 795-8295. Couples $65; lower off-season rates. Private baths; Continental breakfast; no credit cards.* New England-style cottage with Southwest furnishings; pool, landscaped courtyard; afternoon snacks served between 4 and 6. Smoking outside only.

El Presidio Bed & Breakfast Inn • *297 N. Main Ave. (in El Presidio Historic District), Tucson, AZ 85701; (602) 623-6151. From $80 to $95 per couple. Private baths; full breakfasts; no credit cards.* An 1870s American territorial Victorian; lush gardens, courtyards and fountains. Victorian and early American antiques in rooms. Complimentary wine and juices. Two suites with private entrances and kitchens. Smoking outside only.

June's Bed & Breakfast • *3212 W. Holladay St. (Ajo Way off-ramp from I-190), Tucson, AZ 85746; (602) 578-0857. Doubles $40, singles $30. Some private, some shared baths; Continental breakfast; no credit cards.* A Western ranch-style home with modern furnishings. Located near Tucson Mountain Park; excellent mountain views. Smoking outside only.

La Posada del Valle • *1640 N. Campbell Ave. (Elm, near the university), Tucson, AZ 85719; (602) 795-3840. Doubles $85 to $105; lower off-season rates. Private baths; Continental breakfast on weekdays, full breakfast on weekends; MC/VISA.* A 1929 Southwest adobe surrounded by a garden and orange trees; rooms furnished with early 20th century antiques. Afternoon tea served in courtyard patio. Smoking outside only.

The Peppertrees • *724 E. University Blvd. (near U of A between Euclid and First Avenue), Tucson, AZ 85719; (602) 622-7167. Doubles $65 to $100.*

Full breakfasts; shared bath. No credit cards. A turn-of-the-century territorial home, elegantly furnished with English and early American antiques. Two guest rooms inside; two modern guest houses on grounds. Complimentary sherry, afternoon English-style tea, off-street parking; picnic baskets prepared for day excursions.

Triangle L Ranch Bed & Breakfast ● *P.O. Box 900 (35 miles north on Highway 77), Oracle, AZ 85623; (602) 896-2804. From $55 to $65 per couple. Private baths; full breakfasts.* An 1880s adobe homestead on a former cattle ranch and guest ranch in the Santa Catalina foothills. All private cottages in desert gardens; farm animals; bird-watching, hikes.

WHERE TO PLAY COWBOY
Including guest ranches outside Tucson

Circle Z Ranch ● *P.O. Box 194 (off Highway 82), Patagonia, AZ 85624; (602) 287-2091. From $196 to $245 per couple, including all meals. No credit cards.* Trail rides, all-day rides with picnics, spring roundups, pool, tennis, target shooting, birding, hiking. A 5,000-acre working cattle ranch surrounded by federal and state lands.

Hacienda del Sol Guest Ranch ● *5601 Hacienda del Sol Rd. (in Santa Catalina foothills), Tucson, AZ 85718; (602) 299-1501 or (800) 444-3999. Doubles $75 to $250, without meals. MC/VISA, AMEX, DISC.* Trail rides, cookouts, swimming pool, spa, tennis, croquet, nature tours, cowboy barbecues, Mexican fiestas; lobby with library, bridge tables and fireplace. Housed in a 1929 pueblo-style adobe that originally was a girls' prep school.

Lazy K Bar Guest Ranch ● *8401 N. Scenic Dr. (16 miles from downtown), Tucson, AZ 85743; (602) 744-3050. From $160 to $190 per couple, including all meals. MC/VISA, AMEX.* Modern guest ranch on 160 acres in the Tucson Mountain foothills. Trail rides, hay rides, cookouts, square dances, tennis, swimming pool and spa. Lounge, library, patio, barbecue area with ten-foot waterfall; miles of riding and hiking trails.

Rancho de la Osa ● *P.O. Box 1 (66 miles southwest, on Mexican border), Sasabe, AZ 85633; (602) 823-4257. Rates from $80 per person, including meals. MC/VISA.* An 80-year-old guest ranch with riding, pool and spa, nature strolls and bird-watching in the surrounding desert. Guest rooms are adobe brick, set about a 250-year-old cantina-restaurant-lounge originally built as a mission.

Tanque Verde Guest Ranch ● *14301 E. Speedway (Route 8, Box 66), Tucson, AZ 85748; (602) 296-6275. From $210 to $295 per couple, including all meals and ranch activities; lower off-season rates. MC/VISA.* One of America's oldest guest ranches on 640 acres between Coronado National Forest and Saguaro National Monument. Casita-style rooms with fireplaces, antiques and original art. Riding, breakfast rides, nature programs, children's program, tennis, nature rides, walks and talks. Indoor and outdoor pools, sauna, spa, tennis courts, outdoor games, health club.

White Stallion Ranch ● *9251 Twin Peaks Rd. (17 miles northwest, near Tucson Mountain Park), Tucson, AZ 85743; (602) 297-0252. From $180 to $206 per couple, including all meals. No credit cards.* A semi-working ranch with a few longhorns and quarter horses. Pool, spa, tennis, pool tables, ping-pong, shuffleboard, volleyball, basketball, horseshoes, breakfast rides, trail rides into the desert and mountains; hayride with cookout, bonfire and entertainment; steak barbecues and Indian oven dinners. Rodeo and petting zoo.

Wild Horse Ranch ● *6801 Camino Verde (I-10 exit at Ina Road, then 1.8 miles west), Tucson, AZ 85743; (602) 744-1012. From $55 to $95 per couple; meals extra. No credit cards.* A 20-acre ranch resort near Tucson Mountain Park. Pool, tennis, horseback riding, hayrides, volleyball, ping-pong, cookouts, nature walks, horseshoes, volleyball, badminton, dances. Dining facilities with full bar service.

WHERE TO CAMP

Cactus Country RV Park ● *10195 S. Houghton Rd. (Route 7, Box 840; 19 miles south on I-10, then north on Houghton Road exit 275), Tucson, AZ 85747; (602) 574-3000. RV and tent sites; hookups $14.50, no hookups $10.50. Reservations accepted; MC/VISA.* Shaded pull-through sites; flush potties, showers, coin laundry, pool, whirlpool, recreation room, planned activities, horseshoes, shuffleboard; Propane, disposal station.

Catalina State Park ● *P.O. Box 36986 (9 miles north on U.S. 89), Tucson, AZ 85470; (602) 628-5798. RV and tent sites; no hookups $6. No reservations or credit cards.* Picnic and barbecue areas, flush potties. Nature trails, hiking into adjacent Coronado National Forest. In desert foothills of Santa Catalina Mountains.

Crazy Horse Campground ● *6660 S. Craycroft Rd. (seven miles east, off I-10), Tucson, AZ 85706; (602) 574-0157. RV and ten sites; full hookups, $14.50. Reservations accepted; MC/VISA.* Picnic tables, flush potties, showers, swimming pool and spa, coin laundry, small store, recreation center, dump station. Also RV repair facilities.

Desert Shores RV & Mobile Home Park ● *1067 W. Miracle Mile (a mile east of I-10 Miracle Mile off-ramp), Tucson, AZ 85705; (602) 622-4332. RV sites; Full hookups $13.72. Reservations accepted; no credit cards.* Older but well-maintained RV park with rec hall, shuffleboard, horseshoes, swimming pool, lake and picnic area, showers, coin laundry, Propane.

Gilbert Ray Campground ● *In Tucson Mountain Park (Route 13, Box 977), Tucson, AZ 85713; (602) 883-4200. Hookups $7, no hookup and tent camping $5. No reservations, no credit cards.* Picnic tables, barbecues, flush potties, hot water, no showers. Dump station. Attractive desert campsites in Tucson Mountain Park, close to Old Tucson, Arizona-Sonora Desert Museum and Saguaro National Monument. Get there by noon during the busy winter season.

Rincon Country West RV Resort ● *4555 S. Mission Rd. (half mile south of Ajo Way exit from I-10), Tucson, AZ 85714; (602) 294-5608 or (800) RV-2PARK (outside Arizona only). RV sites, full hookups $17. No credit cards.* Large complex with showers, coin laundry, RV resort amenities.

Rose Canyon ● *On Mount Lemmon in Coronado National Forest, just off Catalina Highway, 33 miles from Tucson. RV and tent sites; no hookups $5. No reservations or credit cards.* Picnic and barbecue areas, water, pit potties. Fishing, nature trails.

Spencer Canyon ● *On Mount Lemmon in Coronado National Forest, just off Catalina Highway 39 miles from Tucson; (602) 629-5101. RV and tent sites; no hookups $5. Reservations required; no credit cards.* Picnic and barbecue areas, flush potties, National Forest visitor center, nature trails.

Tratel Tucson RV Park ● *2070 W. Fort Lowell Rd. (four miles west from I-10 Prince Road exit, then south on Ft. Lowell Road), Tucson, AZ 85705; (602) 888-5401. RV sites, full hookups $13.95. Reservations accepted; MC/VISA.* Flush potties, pool, coin laundry, recreation room.

Whispering Palms Travel Trailer Park ● *3445 Romero Rd. (Prince Road exit from I-10, then half mile east), Tucson, AZ 85705; (602) 888-2500. RV and tent sites; hookups $12.50. Reservations accepted.* Flush potties, showers, coin laundry, pool, recreation room.

WEST TO KITT PEAK

State Highway 86 heads west through the huge Tohono O'odham Indian Reservation, curves north above Organ Pipe Cactus National Monument and links with I-10 at Gila Bend. It's all desert country, ranging from saguaro forests to boring stretches of mesquite and creosote bush.

Tohono O'odham is America's second largest Indian reservation, after the huge Navajo nation. The state of Connecticut would fit within its three million acres. San Xavier Indian Reservation just south of Tucson is a spur of the Tohono O'odham nation.

Most maps still show this as the Papago Reservation, for that was the tribal name until a few years ago. Seeking links to their past, they adopted their ancestral name, which means "desert dwellers who emerged from the earth." That's a considerable improvement over Papago, which means "bean people."

Better an earthly spirit than a bean counter.

This swatch of Arizona and Organ Pipe Cactus National Monument are covered in the next chapter. However, we'll list an important attraction here, for it's generally visited as a day trip from Tucson.

Kitt Peak National Observatory ● *P.O. Box 26732, Tucson, AZ 85726-6732 (40 miles west on Highway 86, then 12 miles south on Highway 386); (602) 620-5350. Daily 10 to 4; 30-minute film and lecture at 10:30 and 1:30; on weekends and some holidays, a tour follows the 1:30 film. Free; donations accepted for new a visitor center.* The world's largest astronomical observatory, Kitt Peak scatters its gleaming white domes over the upper reaches of the Quinlan Mountains, high above the Tohono O'odham Reservation.

This busy complex provides extensive visitor facilities; a new reception center and theater are planned. Self-guided tours take you into structures housing three of the observatory's 13 telescopes. A highlight attraction is the monster McMath solar telescope, built into a 500-foot angular shaft thrusting 300 feet into the earth. From a platform inside, you seem to be peering down the shaft of an ultra-modern mine. But there's a huge mirror—not an ore vein—at the bottom. This giant telescope tracks the sun and projects its image onto a 30-inch surface. There, scientists can study its flares, spots and other quirks.

You can ride an elevator to the Mayall telescope observation deck for a panorama of the Arizona desert and Quinlan Mountains. The Burrell-Schmidt telescope, which takes wide-angle photographs of the heavens, also is open to visitors.

These aren't the kinds of telescopes that one uses to peer at the moon—or into their neighbor's bedroom window. Some don't even have eyepieces, but feed their images into computers or fan them out as spectrographs. A complex instrument called the Very Long Baseline Array Radio Telescope studies the stars by gathering their radio waves.

Funded by the National Science Foundation, Kitt Peak is operated by a consortium of 20 universities. Eager astronomers and astronomy students take turns at the instruments, which have produced some of America's most impressive galactic discoveries. Observers here have measured the most distant galaxies known, about 12 billion light years away. Recently, they found the largest objects ever seen—colossal luminous arcs near clusters of faraway galaxies.

The visitor center features heavenly exhibits and diagrams of several telescopes. The gift shop sells things astronomical (no pun intended), along with crafts of the Tohono O'odham Indians. A nearby picnic area offers a nice desert view. There's no food sold at the gift shop, so bring a lunch. Bring your jacket, too; the elevation here is 7,000 feet.

SOUTH TO THE BORDER

Interstate 19 provides a fast link between Tucson and the twin border cities of Nogales, Arizona and the Mexican state of Sonora. The first community you'll encounter, other than dusty little Sahuarita, is Green Valley.

Unkindly referred to as Wrinkle City by Tucsonans, it's a retirement town of 14,000. It started as an adult community in 1964 and has since blossomed into a full-scale town with shopping centers, four golf courses, heated swimming pools and other amenities that make the desert a pleasant place to live. It's also the site of a grimly fascinating reminder of the Cold War.

Titan Missile Museum • *Green Valley Road (Exit 69, then west), Green Valley, AZ 85614; (602) 625-7736. Open from 9 to 5 Wednesday-Sunday from May through October and daily from November through April. One-hour tours; last tour at 4 p.m. Adults $4, seniors and military $3, kids 10 to 17 $2.* Standing in the command center, deep underground, you hear the deadly countdown as the crew prepares to launch a Titan II missile. In seconds, its 430,000 pounds of thrust will blast it from its silo. In less than an hour, its nuclear warhead will detonate above a computer-selected target more than 8,000 miles away. As you listen to the countdown, your palms begin to sweat.

Fortunately, it's just a recording from a movie soundtrack, being played in the world's only public underground missile complex. When the SALT Treaty called for de-activation of the 18 Titan missile silos that ring Tucson, folks at the Pima Air Museum asked if one could be retained for public tours. After much negotiation, including additional talks with SALT officials, the Green Valley complex of the 390th Strategic Missile Wing was opened to the public. Of course, it was rendered inoperable.

This is one of the most fascinating tours in Arizona. After watching a video about the history of the Titan and its deadly nuclear delivery capability, you're taken deep into the "hardened" command center. Here, essential equipment—indeed the center itself—is mounted on springs to withstand anything but a direct hit. Then you pass through a couple of 6,000-pound blast doors and walk along a space-age corridor to the silo itself. The 110-foot-tall missile weighed 170 tons when it was fueled and ready to fly. It's empty and harmless now, but it still looks deadly, crouched on its launch pad.

Topside, you can peek down into the silo, half-covered by its cemented-in-place lid. Nearby are the missile's jet engine and an empty nuclear warhead the size of a Mercury space capsule.

You learn that launching the missile required a complicated—although speedy—procedure. Two sets of keys and two combination locks had to be operated by two different officers to retrieve launch codes and start the

Titan II missile posing ominously in its silo.

wicked process. There were 16 million possible code combinations, so it was unlikely that someone could launch a missile without authority.

Still, we're glad that business is done with. We'll take *Glasnost* any day.

Looking east from Green Valley, you'll see an island of mountains called the Santa Ritas, topped by 9,543-foot Mount Wrightson. The Santa Ritas are an extension of Coronado National Forest, with miles of hiking trails and three campgrounds.

Madera Canyon, reached from I-19 via exit 63, is a pretty chasm noted for the brightly-colored Mexican trogon bird, which spends its summers here. Bird-watchers have counted about 200 other winged species in Madera Canyon, as well.

If you're a serious bird-watcher, or you just want to spend more time in this forested chasm, you can stay over at **Santa Rita Lodge** (P.O. Box 444, Amado, AZ 85640; 625-8746), which has small kitchenette units. Nearby **Bog Springs** national forest campground offers RV and tent sites for $6 per night, with barbecues, picnic tables, water and pit toilets; no hookups. Several hiking trails reach into the mountains from here, including a 4.5 mile round-trip to Bog Springs.

Quality Inn Green Valley ΔΔ $$$ ∅
111 S. La Canada (west of Esperanza exit from I-19), Green Valley, AZ 85614; (602) 625-2250 or (800) 344-1441. Doubles $55 to $83, singles $45 to $73; lower prices are off-season rates. Major credit cards. TV movies, phones, free morning coffee and paper; guest laundry; landscaped courtyard with pool and spa. **Palms Restaurant** serves from 7 a.m. to 2 p.m. and 5 to 8 p.m., Continental-Southwestern (pork chops, chicken dijon, mesquite broiled steak), dinners $8 to $10, non-smoking areas, full bar service.

Tubac

Elevation: Approx. 3,000 feet   **Population: 600**

Twenty miles south of Green Valley, Tubac is Arizona's oldest non-Indian settlement, established as a Spanish presidio in 1752. The year before, Pima Chief Oacpicagigua had led a revolt against missionaries and settlers, who had gained virtual control over the Indians' land—and their lives. The army was called to quell the uprising, then the troops stayed around to build a fort.

Tubac commander Juan Bautista de Anza left here in 1776 on his historic overland trek to establish the pueblos of San Francisco and San Jose in California. After Mexico won its independence from Spain in 1821, troops were pulled from Tubac and the settlement—harassed by Apache raids—was abandoned. The Gadsden Purchase brought the community under America's protection and it was re-settled. In 1860, it was Arizona's largest town. But the Civil War pulled American troops away, and hostile Apaches again forced its abandonment. Resettlement came after the Apaches finally were subdued late in the 19th century.

Today, slightly scruffy little Tubac is a major art colony, with more than 50 galleries housed in a mix of old and new adobe and brick buildings. This is where "art and history meet," proclaims a sign at the edge of town. A dozen or more boutiques, import and curio shops also line its quiet streets, selling Indian and Arizona crafts and assorted giftwares.

If you like things spicy, check out the **Chili Pepper** on Tubac Road; it features a variety of chili-based products, along with Southwest cookbooks, herbs and spices, coffees and light snacks. **Tubac Center of the Arts** on Plaza Road exhibits works of local artisans; many can be purchased at its gift shop. **Mercado de Baca** on Tubac Road is a small shopping center with assorted boutiques, galleries and restaurants.

Tubac Presidio State Historic Park ● *P.O. Box 1296, Tubac, AZ 85646; (602) 398-2252. Daily 8 to 5; adults $1, kids free.* Little remains of the presidio, but an exhibit center effectively traces its history. Displays take you from Tubac's days as a 17th century Pima Indian village through its Spanish, Mexican and American periods. Exhibits include a set of wrist irons tied to a post that served as the town's jail, plus period weapons and friars' frocks.

A volunteer docent might crank off a copy of the *Weekly Arizonan*, the state's first newspaper, on the original 1859 flatbed printing press. Outside the museum, paths lead through the presidio grounds where archaeological digs have been continuing on and off since 1974. Of particular interest is the "Stairway to the Past," which leads you down into an excavation. Artifacts found at different levels are displayed in place behind protective windows in this cut-away dig.

Tumacacori National Monument ● *P.O. Box 67, Tumacacori, AZ 85640; (602) 398-2341. Daily 8 to 5; $3 per family or $1 per individual.* "At the rancheria of San Cayetano de Tumacacori, we found people so docile and so friendly. Such lovely and such fertile and delightful valleys inhabited by industrious Indians."

Thus, Father Kino described a small village he visited in 1691. He erected an earth-roofed adobe house and began preaching to the Indians. Half a century later, other missionaries built a small church, followed by a more elaborate structure in the 1790s.

Tumacacori Mission ruins, framed through arched window of the visitor center.

Today, Tumacacori Mission is a noble ruin, standing forlornly on a grassy field three miles south of Tubac. The excellent interpretive center features a diorama of the mission in its heyday, relics from the old church and an artistically-produced video of missionaries ministering to the Indians.

The ruined church is short distance away—a time-stained shell of its former glory. Inside its darkened, weathered walls, you can still see traces of lime plaster and paint used to emulate the marble, carved woods and other fineries of Spain's great cathedrals.

WHERE TO DINE & RECLINE

Sgt. Grijalva's Restaurante & Cantina ● ΔΔ $$

255 Camino Otero (Chavez Road siding), Tubac; (602) 398-2263. Mexican-Continental; dinners $10 to $15; full bar service. Daily 11 a.m. to 9 p.m.; reservations advised. MC/VISA. Southwest style restaurant with patio dining; Misty Mountain Art Gallery adjoining.

Rio Rico Resort and Country Club ● ΔΔΔ $$$$ ∅

1550 Camino a la Posada (just south of Tumacacori, off I-19), Rio Rico, AZ 85621; (602) 281-1901 or (800) 288-4746. Doubles $78, singles $68, suites $125 to $200; lower off-season rates. MC/VISA, AMEX, DC. Resort in desert setting with Olympic-sized pool, spa, sauna, tennis and 18-hole golf course. TV movies, phones and other amenities in rooms. **La Cima Restaurant** serves from 6:30 a.m. to 9:30 p.m., Southwestern and Continental, dinners $6 to $19, Southwestern decor, non-smoking areas, full bar service.

Rancho Santa Cruz ● ΔΔΔ $$$ ∅

P.O. Box 8 (off I-19 exit 29), Tumacacori, AZ 85640; (602) 281-8383. Doubles $50, singles $30, suites $90 to $125; lower off-season rates. MC/VISA. Small resort-style guest ranch (meals not included) with horseback riding, swimming pool, lawn games and walking trails. In original adobe ranch buildings with Southwestern decor. **Restaurant**—open to the public—serves daily from 8 a.m. to 9 p.m., American (mesquite broiled ribs, steaks and chops), dinners $8 to $15, non-smoking areas, full bar service.

South of Tumacacori, we encounter the twin towns of Nogales, or *Ambos Nogales,* as our Mexican neighbors would say. Nogales, incidentally, means "walnuts."

Nogales

Elevation: 3,865 feet   **Population: 20,000**

Like the Walnuts they were named for, the two towns are scattered over the foothills of the Patagonia Mountains. It's a pretty setting for buildings that are often less than pretty.

Ethnically, there is little distinction between the two dusty communities, and only a border fence separates them. However, if you assume (as we did) that they were a single town before the Gadsden Purchase, you are incorrect. The towns were established separately, long after the 1854 land deal that brought southern Arizona into the Union. A Mexican roadhouse was established on the Latin side of Nogales Pass in 1880 by Juan Jose Vasquez. In the same year, Jacob Isaacson started a trading post on the Arizona territory side.

The two towns grew up as good neighbors, even during the unsettling years when Pancho Villa was creating border havoc during this century's teens. Nogales, Mexico, grew much faster than its northern twin and now has ten times the population. The largest of the Arizona-Mexico border towns, it offers the best shopping—which we discuss in more detail in the next chapter.

The **Nogales-Santa Cruz County Chamber of Commerce** visitor center is in Kino Park near the junction of highways 89 and 82, just over a mile north of the border.

Primeria Alta Historical Society Museum ● *Grand Avenue and Crawford Street (P.O. Box 2281), Nogales, AZ 85621; (602) 287-5402. Monday-Friday 9 to 5, Saturday 10 to 4 and Sunday 1 to 4. Free; donations encouraged.* Housed in the former city hall, this museum personifies the close ties between *Los Nogales.* Photos, documents and pioneer artifacts trace the history of both communities. Even the brochure—like many signs in Nogales, Arizona—is bi-lingual.

Although not professionally done, the museum is quite interesting, offering exhibits such as a hand-drawn fire pumper, mantle clocks, old sewing machines and a branding iron collection. The old iron-barred jail is still in place; gringos and their Mexican buddies slept off their hangovers in this grim-looking lock-up until it was retired in 1978.

The museum is easy to spot; look for the Spanish colonial building with the conical-roofed clock tower at the point where the highway swings right to enter Mexico. It's just two blocks from the border.

ANNUAL EVENTS

Tubac Arts Festival in Tubac, the first full week of February; **Bed Race** in Nogales, Arizona, the last Saturday of March; **Fiestas de las Flores** in Nogales, Mexico, from mid-April through the first week of May. *Cinco de Mayo,* marking the Mexican victory over Napoleon III in 1862, is celebrated on both sides of the border May 5 and usually extending into the nearest weekend. **Bullfights** are held Sunday afternoons on the Mexican side at Guadalupe Plaza de Toros; the American-side Chamber of Commerce can provide details.

WHERE TO DINE

Mr. C's Supper Club ● ∆∆∆ $$$ ∅

302 W. Mariposa Rd. (three miles north of town), Nogales; (602) 281-9000. American; dinners $12 to $20. Monday-Saturday 11:30 a.m. to midnight; reservations advised. MC/VISA, AMEX. Crowning a hill north of town, this large, rather elegant restaurant features fresh seafood, steaks and other American specialties. Live music for dancing in an adjoining lounge.

Molina's PK Outpost ● ∆∆ $$

Highway 89 frontage road (five miles north), Nogales; (602) 281-9946. Mexican-Southwestern; dinners $6 to $15. Daily from 11:30 a.m. MC/VISA. The kitchen of the historic Pete Kitchen adobe ranch house produces tasty Sonoran and American Southwestern fare.

Two restaurants in Sonora, Mexico, are worthy of mention. (See the next chapter about dining, shopping and traveling in Mexico.)

El Cid ● ∆∆ $$

124 Avenida Obregon; (52) 2-64-00. Mexican-Continental; dinners $5 to $11. Daily from noon. MC/VISA. Seafoods are the specialty in this large tiled restaurant with an unusual domed ceiling; the menu focuses on classic Mexico City-style entrees.

La Roca ● ∆∆∆ $$$

91 Calle Elias; (52) 2-07-60. Mexican-Continental; dinners $10 to $20. Daily from noon. Major credit cards. This is where you dine if you're a wealthy Mexican or an American taking advantage of the favorable exchange rate. Candle-lit tables, formal waiters, a fireplace and courtyard fountain accent excellent Mexican and European seafood and beef dishes.

WHERE TO SLEEP

Best Western Motel Time ● ∆∆ $$ ∅

1200 Grand Ave. (highways 89 and 93), Nogales, AZ 85621; (602) 287-4627 or (800) 528-1234. Doubles $36 to $40, singles $32 to $38; lower off-season rates. Major credit cards. TV movies, phones, pool and spa; coffee shop adjacent.

Best Western Siesta Motel ● ∆∆ $$ ∅

910 Grand Ave. (near highways 89 and 93), Nogales, AZ 85621; (602) 287-4671 or (800) 528-1234. Doubles $36 to $40, singles $30 to $34; lower off-season rates. Major credit cards. TV movies, phones, pool; coffee shop nearby.

Chapter 10

THE SOUTHERN EDGE

The deserts are not worthless wastes. They are the breathing spaces of the west and should be preserved forever.
— John C. VanDyke, 1901

 THE SONORAN DESERT'S great cactus garden extends along much of the 350-mile border between Arizona and the Mexican state of Sonora. If you like desert wilderness, you'll love exploring these remote reaches—particularly from March to early May when the cacti offer their spring flower show.

We'll cover the western two-thirds of the border in this chapter, then we'll dip into Mexico to explore its friendly, pastel border towns.

Yuma

Elevation: 138 feet   **Population: 50,000**

If you've already experienced the mighty Colorado River upstream, you'll be startled by what's left of it at Yuma Crossing. Tamed and sometimes reduced to a trickle, it flows meekly between desert bluffs marking the California-Arizona border. It enters Mexico 25 miles south at San Luis, then dribbles into the Gulf of California.

The first attempts at taming the Colorado began here in 1901 with the diversion of water into California's Imperial Valley. Resisting man's tampering, the river washed the project away in 1905. In the 1930s, the Hoover Dam upstream put an end to Rio Colorado's willfulness.

Today, Yuma is surrounded by thousands of acres of rich farmland. Billions of gallons of water are diverted into Arizona and California to grow winter lettuce and other salad fixin's.

THE WAY IT WAS • Yuma earned its place in Arizona's historical sun early. In 1540, Spanish naval Captain Hernando de Alarcon sailed up the Gulf of California and into the mouth of the Colorado River. He probably got as far north as Yuma before turning back.

Father Eusebio Kino, seeking a land route to California in 1699, found a suitable place to cross the Colorado at its junction with the Gila, in present-day Yuma. He is credited with naming the river for its reddish, silt-laden waters. In his diary, he commented on the area's value as a river crossing, but decades passed before anyone followed his advise.

Finally, in 1779, Father Francisco Tomas Garces established two missions along the river. A presidio was built to protect Mission la Purisima Concepcion, on what is now the California side. The entire settlement—including the good padre—was wiped out in a bloody Quechan Indian uprising two years later. That finished things for the Spanish at Yuma Crossing.

In 1846, Colonel Stephen Watts Kearny and frontier scout Kit Carson forded the river here. They were headed west to snatch California lands from Mexico. The Mormon Battalion of Colonel Philip Cooke followed in Kearny's path, carving the first rough wagon road into California.

When gold was discovered in northern California in 1848, many argonauts used Cooke's southern route through Yuma Crossing. They were reluctant to tackle the rugged east face of the Sierra Nevada range farther north. A few returned to this area, attracted by nearby gold strikes and the agricultural potential along the Colorado's bottomlands.

The army built an encampment on the California side in 1851 to keep an eye on the still-restless Quechans. Small paddlewheel steamers churned upstream from the Gulf of California, supplying new riverside settlements.

THINGS TO KNOW BEFORE YOU GO

Best time to go • The Arizona-Sonora border, like the Colorado River corridor, is a fall-winter-spring place. Yuma's population is nearly doubled by Snowbirds each winter. Great expanses of desert lie to the east, particularly on the Mexico side. It's not cool to submit your car and yourselves to these remote areas during the summer.

Climate • Borderland summers are, in a word—HOT. Winters are warm to cool. Yuma July average—high 107, low 74; January average—high 68, low 37; rainfall—3 inches; snowfall—none

Useful contacts

Ajo District Chamber of Commerce, 2050 N. Highway 85 (P.O. Box 507), Ajo, AZ 85321.

Superintendent, Organ Pipe Cactus National Monument, Route 1, Box 100, Ajo, AZ 85321; (602) 387-6849.

Yuma County Chamber of Commerce, 377 S. Main St. (P.O. Box 6468), Yuma, AZ 85366; (602) 344-3800.

Area radio stations

KBLU-AM, 560, Yuma—Oldies of the 50s, 60s and 70s.

KEZC-AM, 1400, Yuma—Country, network news.

KJOK-FM, 93.1, Yuma—Rock.

KTTI-FM, 95.1, Yuma—Country.

KYXI-FM, 100.9, Yuma—Light rock.

One of these was Colorado City, founded on the Arizona side in 1854. Historians tell us—with a sly grin—that the town's first permanent resident was a shady lady named Sarah Bowman, who ran a combined restaurant, bar and bawdy house.

The river flexed its muscles in 1862, washing Colorado City into the Gulf of California, bordello and all. Another community, called Arizona City, was built on higher ground. Later, the name was changed to Yuma, after the local Indians, who were a blend of Quechans, Cocopahs and Mohaves.

In the 1870s, Governor Anson P. Safford sought construction of a territorial prison in Yuma to replace a scattering of local jails. "No provisions can be made for employing the prisoners (in county jails)," he complained. "Close confinement and idleness often result injuriously to health, with scarcely a possibility for moral improvement."

Were they any better off in the notorious Yuma prison? As we shall see, it was Hollywood—not brutal conditions and nasty prison guards—that gave the place its bad name.

THE WAY IT IS ● Yuma Territorial Prison State Park, on a bluff overlooking Rio Colorado, is the main drawing card for passing tourists. For Snowbirds, however, it's the climate. Yuma's population nearly doubles every winter as 40,000 retirees flock to mobile home parks on both sides of the stream.

Yuma continues its long role as a strategic provisioning center and rest stop for travelers. Motorists hopping off Interstate 8 have a good selection of motels and restaurants. Most are scattered along Business I-8. Coming from the west, it follows Fourth Avenue, passes through old downtown Yuma, executes an abrupt left turn called "The Big Curve" and follows 32nd Street east. Most of the town's shopping malls are along 32nd.

If you approach Yuma from California, you'll pass through a sand dune area right out of *Lawerence of Arabia*. In fact, several films have been shot here, including desert scenes from *Star Wars*. From fall through spring, hundreds of RVers camp along a frontage road and run their dune buggies over this slice of California Sahara. We usually fuss about off-road vehicles in fragile desert areas, but the tracks here will be erased by the first wind. And it looks like fun!

The Yuma County Chamber of Commerce at 377 S. Main Street (off Giss, near the central freeway off-ramp) offers the usual assortment of area brochures and maps. It's open Monday through Thursday from 8:30 to 5 and Friday from 9 to 5. A walk-up window is open Saturday from 10 to 2.

The military was attracted by Yuma's cloud-free days and wide open spaces during World War II. Two outfits are still here—a Marine Corps Air Station and the U.S. Army Yuma Proving Ground. Folks who were stationed here in years past—including a couple of our friends and relatives—used to complain that there wasn't much to do. They should see Yuma now.

THE BEST ATTRACTIONS
Yuma Territorial Prison State Historic Park ● *Prison Hill Road (P.O. Box 10792), Yuma, AZ 85366-8792; (602) 783-4771. Daily 8 to 5. Adults $2, kids under 17 free.* Thick adobe walls and rusty bars over darkened cells are certainly grim enough to give the old prison its notorious reputation as "the hell-hole of Arizona." But that's merely the stuff of which Hollywood movies

Yuma Territorial Prison watchtower, built over reservoir.

were made. In truth, it was regarded as a model prison for its day with a library, schooling for the convicts and—good grief!—even crafts classes. The men crocheted lace and sold it at a crafts mart. Some rather delicate examples are on display.

The prison still wasn't a pleasant place to pass the time. Temperatures in the adobe cells hit 120 in the summer, and men who broke the rules wound up in a windowless dungeon—sometimes sharing it with scorpions and rattlesnakes.

Although the prison had its hardened criminals—including a lady named "Heartless" Pearl Hart—most of its guests were merely convicted burglars. Among offenses that would land you in the slammer in those days were obstructing a railroad, seduction, polygamy and adultery. One of the oldest inmates was a 77-year-old man who got a year for selling liquor to Indians. Most prisoners didn't serve out their terms; early paroles and pardons were easy to come by. No one was ever executed here, although eight were killed trying to escape.

Prisoners themselves built the place. When it was completed on July 1, 1876, they were herded inside and locked up. It was overcrowded by 1907 with no room for expansion on Prison Hill, so the inmates built a new lock-up near Florence; the Yuma slammer closed two years later. It served as Yuma High School from 1910 until 1914, then it sheltered homeless families during the Depression.

Through the years, residents helped themselves to most of the building materials. What remains in the present-day state park are the cell block, the "new yard" where cells were dug into the hillside to relieve overcrowding, and the main guard tower built atop a water tank. These can be explored on self-guided tours.

A museum was built over part of the mess hall foundation in 1940. Exhibits include prison artifacts, scowling photos of inmates and interesting graphics about prison life. And yes, prisoners in those days did wear funny striped uniforms.

Century House Museum • *240 Madison Ave. (Giss), Yuma, AZ 85364; (602) 782-1841. Tuesday-Saturday 10 to 4. Free; donations encouraged.* Italian pioneer E.F. Sanguinetti made his fortune as a Yuma merchant and developer, and he spent a lot of it on this spacious 19th century mansion and gardens.

Today, the 1870 adobe is a fine museum operated by the Rio Colorado branch of the Arizona Historical Society. Exhibits focus on early Colorado River sternwheelers, period furnishings contributed by local pioneer families and early Indian cultures. The lush garden out back is alive with plants and birds, just as it was a century ago when Sanguinetti turned it into a virtual bird park. Caged macaws, parrots, parakeets and mynah birds offer their comments as you explore the extensive grounds.

The adjacent **Adobe Annex** at 2150 Madison houses a gift shop styled after a turn-of-the-century drygoods store. Several boutiques and the **Garden Cafe and Spice Company** are behind the annex. You can dine on a palm shaded patio, next to the museum's backyard aviary. The cafe is open weekdays from 10 to 3 and weekends from 8 to 3; phone 783-1491. (See restaurant listing below.)

Fort Yuma Quechan Museum • *Fort Yuma (Picacho Road to Indian Hill Road on the California side), c/o Quechan Tribal Council, P.O. Box 1352, Yuma, AZ 85364; (619) 572-0661 or (619) 572-0213. Weekdays 8 to 12 and 1 to 5. Adults 50 cents.* It's historically ironic that this fort, established to protect settlers from the Indians, is now part of the Fort Yuma Indian Reservation. It occupies a bluff on the California side of the Colorado River, directly across from Yuma Territorial Prison. The small tribal museum, in an old pink adobe, traces the history of the Quechan people. They were one of eight Colorado River tribes sharing a common Yuman language.

The web-work of roads among the fort buildings may confuse you, but anyone on the hill can point you toward the museum. Exhibits cover both the Indian and military history of the area. Particularly interesting are clay figurines that suggest an ancestral tie between the Quechans and ancient Hohokam. More contemporary Indian crafts can be purchased at a gift shop.

St. Thomas Mission Church, a classic of Spanish colonial architecture, is just below the museum. It was built in 1923 on the site of Mission La Purisima Concepcion, which was founded by Father Garces and destroyed by the Quechans in 1781.

Yuma Crossing Park • *Along the riverfront, extending from the Yuma Quartermaster Depot to the territorial prison; (602) 329-0471.* By the time you read this, there may or may not be something new to see at Yuma Crossing. The area along the waterfront has been declared a National Historic Landmark. Ambitious plans are afoot to create a major living history center covering more than 100 acres. Costumed docents will recapture the days when Yuma Crossing was one of the leading gateways to California. It's set for completion in 1995.

THE REST

Arizona City Doll Company ● *54 W. Third St. (off the downtown mall); Yuma, AZ 85364; (602) 783-5544. Tuesday-Saturday 11 to 6.* This small shop exhibits and sells antique dolls.

Erlich's Date Garden ● *868 Avenue B (Eighth Street), Yuma, AZ 85364; (602) 783-4778. Daily 9 to 5.* Learn how the fruit of the desert grows in this date garden near downtown Yuma. You can nibble free samples of khadrawis, medjools, halawis and zahadis and buy gift packs to take home. No credit cards but they take out-of-town checks. Best time to buy is in winter, when you can get tasty fresh dates that are too fragile for shipping and storage.

The Peanut Patch ● *4322 E. County 13th St. (Avenue 4E), Yuma, AZ 85365; (602) 726-6292. Daily from 9 to 6.* Ever wonder where peanuts come from? You can watch the harvest from October to December, and tour the processing facility the year around. A gift shop sells all sorts of peanutty things, plus citrus, dates and candies.

Yuma Art Center ● *281 Gila St. (Second Street), Yuma, AZ 85364; (602) 783-2314. Tuesday-Saturday 10 to 5, Sunday 1 to 5; free.* Housed in the old Southern Pacific Railroad Depot, the center displays works of local artists, along with historical and science exhibits. A small theater is host to plays, dances and things musical.

Yuma County Fairgrounds ● *2520 E. 32nd St. (Pacific Avenue), Yuma, AZ 85365; (602) 726-4420.* Normally, fairgrounds are only interesting during the county fair, but this one has a modest botanical garden, duck pond and a scatter of old farm machinery. What makes it more interesting is its position at the end of the Marine Corps Air Station runway. People often gather here to watch powerful jet fighters blast into the wild blue wherever.

Yuma Quartermaster Depot State Historic Park ● *At the foot of Second Avenue, behind city hall (P.O. Box 10792), Yuma AZ 85366 8792; (602) 343-2500. Tuesday-Saturday 10 to 4; free.* This site is more interesting for what it represents than for what it offers. Several buildings—most of them empty—survive from this depot near Yuma Crossing, where supplies were stored for military posts throughout the Southwest. From 1864 until 1883, it kept six months worth of Army goods on hand, along with 900 mules for pulling overland freight wagons to distant posts.

A storehouse, office, reservoir, commanding officers quarters and kitchen survive. Exhibits in the storehouse—mostly photographs and a few artifacts—recall the days when the lower Colorado teemed with sternwheelers.

Yuma River Tours ● *1920 Arizona Ave. (in the DuraShield building), Yuma, AZ 85364. Boat tours along the lower Colorado (including refreshments)—two hours, $17.50, half-day, $32 (including lunch); full day, $49 (including lunch). MC/VISA.* Narrated jetboat tours cover old mining camps, petroglyphs, steamboat landings and pioneer sites along the Colorado.

ANNUAL EVENTS

Square Dance Festival, second weekend of February; **Silver Spur Rodeo,** second weekend of February; **American Indian and Western Art Show,** fourth weekend of February; **Yuma Crossing Day,** first weekend of March; **Old Town Yuma Desert Festival,** second weekend of March; **Yuma County Fair,** five days in early April; **Air Show** at the Marine Corps Air Station, second Sunday in November; **Main Street Arts and Crafts Festival,** third weekend in December.

WHERE TO DINE

Garden Cafe and Spice Co. • ΔΔ $
250 Madison Ave. (behind Century House Museum); (602) 783-1491. American; breakfasts and lunches to $8. Weekdays 10 to 3, weekends 8 to 3. MC/VISA. Indoor and outdoor dining in a pleasant garden setting beside the Mission House Museum's landscaped aviary.

The Crossing • ΔΔ $ ∅
2690 S. Fourth Ave. (27th Street); (602) 726-5551. American; dinners $6 to $15; wine and beer. Daily 11 a.m. to 10 p.m.; reservations suggested. MC/VISA, AMEX. Steaks, seafood, chicken; specialties include catfish and prime rib.

Chretin's Mexican Food • ΔΔΔ $ ∅
485 15th Ave. (corner of Fifth Street); (602) 782-1291. Mexican; dinners $4.50 to $8.75; full bar service. Monday-Saturday 11 a.m. to 11 p.m. MC/VISA. Long-time popular favorite noted for its home-cooking, nachos and margaritas; cheerfully decorated interior. All ingredients made from scratch.

El Charro Cafe • ΔΔ $
601 W. Eighth St. (near Fourth Avenue); (602) 783-9790. Mexican-American; dinners $4 to $7; full bar service. Tuesday-Sunday 11 a.m. to 9 p.m. MC/VISA. Family-run cafe since 1949; traditional Mexican fare plus some American items; bright Latin decor.

Hensley's Beef, Beans & Beer • ΔΔΔ$$
2855 Fourth Ave. (downtown); (602) 344-1345. American; dinners $8 to $12.50; wine and beer. Daily 11 a.m. to 10 p.m. MC/VISA. Lively Western-style cafe specializing in beef; hickory and mesquite grilled steaks, hamburgers and ribs; also prime rib, fish and chicken.

Mandarin Palace • ΔΔΔ $$ ∅
350 E. 32nd St. (Arizona Avenue); (602) 344-2805. Mandarin, Szechuan and American; dinners $6 to $15; full bar service. Weekdays 11:30 a.m. to 10 p.m., weekends 11:30 to 11:30. MC/VISA, AMEX. Large, attractive restaurant with sunken bar and elaborate Oriental decor; divided dining areas. Extensive Chinese and American menu.

WHERE TO SLEEP

Best Western Coronado Motor Hotel • ΔΔΔ $$ ∅
233 Fourth Ave. (downtown, near Giss Parkway), Yuma, AZ 85364; (602) 783-4453 or (800) 528-1234. Doubles $35 to $75, singles $45 to $79; kitchenettes $45 to $79, suites $39 to $85; lower prices are off-season rates. Major credit cards. TV movies, phones, room refrigerators, hair dryers, VCRs available, some in-room spas; free Continental breakfast, swimming pool and spa. Adjacent **restaurant** serves from 8 a.m. to 10 p.m., Chinese-American, dinners $4 to $25, full bar service.

Desert Grove Motel • ΔΔ $$
3500 S. Fourth Ave. (half mile of south 32nd Street), Yuma, AZ 85365; (602) 344-1921. All kitchen units, doubles $40 to $42, singles $38 to $40. Major credit cards. Full kitchens, TV, radios, phones; pool, spa, coin laundry; nicely landscaped grounds.

Royal Motor Inn ● ∆∆∆ $$$ ∅
*2941 S. Fourth Ave. (Catalina Drive), Yuma, AZ 85364; (602) 344-0550
or (800) 729-0550. Doubles $50 to $64, singles $40 to $50; lower off-season
rates. Major credit cards.* TV movies, phones, refrigerators, microwaves; pool,
spa, sauna. **Bobby's Restaurant** serves from 6 a.m. to 9 p.m., American-
Mexican, dinners $5 to $20, no alcohol, non-smoking areas.

Shilo Inn ● ∆∆∆ $$$$ ∅
*1550 S. Castle Dome Rd. (I-8 and Highway 95 junction), Yuma, AZ 85365;
(602) 782-9511 or (800) 222-2244. Doubles $79 to $108, singles $69 to
$102. Major credit cards.* TV movies, radios, phones, room refrigerators,
some kitchen units; coin laundry, pool, spa, sauna, steam room and exercise
room. **Restaurant** serves from 6 a.m. to 10 p.m., American, dinners $10 to
$20, non-smoking areas, full bar service.

Stardust Resort Motor Inn ∆∆ $$$
*2350 S. Fourth Ave. (P.O. Box 5028), Yuma, AZ 85364; (602) 783-8861.
Doubles $42 to $49, singles $36 to $43. Major credit cards.* Large, older resort
motel located between downtown and eastside shopping areas. TV movies,
radios, phones, some kitchen units; pool, spa, putting green, playground,
coin laundry. **Dining room** and coffee shop open 6 a.m. to 10 p.m.,
American, dinners $5 to $16, full bar service.

WHERE TO CAMP

Araby Acres Travel Trailer Park ● *6649 E. Highway 80 (I-8 exit 7, six
miles east), Yuma, AZ 85365; (602) 344-8666. RV sites, full hookups $19.
Reservations accepted; MC/VISA.* Some pull-throughs; flush potties, showers,
coin laundry, Propane. Adults park—55 and older, with recreation room,
landscaped grounds, putting green, horseshoes, shuffleboard, gym, swimming pool and hydro pool.

Bonita Mesa RV Resort ● *9400 N. Frontage Rd. (I-8 exit 12, ten miles
east), Yuma, AZ 85365; (602) 342-2999. RV sites, full hookups $16.* Flush
potties, showers, coin laundry, Propane.

Roger's RV Resort ● *9797 E. Highway 80, Yuma, AZ 85365; (602) 342-
2992. RV sites, full hookups $16. Reservations accepted; MC/VISA.* Flush pot-
ties, showers, coin laundry, dump station, snack bar; shuffleboard, billiards,
golf course, swimming pool, horseshoes, hot tub, gymnasium; activity center
with cards, square-dancing and other planned functions.

Spring Gardens Trailer Park ● *3550 W. Eighth St. (Two blocks before
Avenue C), Yuma, AZ 85364; (602) 783-1526. RV sites, full hookups $13 and
up.* Recreational hall, spa, horseshoes, shuffleboard, pool table, planned activities; landscaped area with grass and shade trees.

Sundancer RV Park ● *13502 N. Frontage Rd. (I-8 exit 14), Yuma, AZ
85365; (602) 342-9333. RV sites, full hookups $15. No credit cards.* Flush pot-
ties, showers, coin laundry, Propane, dump station; two rec halls, billiards,
planned activities, swimming pool, hot tubs, shuffleboard and horseshoes.

YUMA TO ORGAN PIPE CACTUS

Although several RV parks occupy both sides of the Colorado River
around Yuma, you'll see even more of them as you drive east on I-8. Your
route takes you past great fields of glistening RVs, then through green fields
in a pretty little irrigated valley.

Shortly, these signs of civilization surrender to creosote bush, and you
don't see much life again until you enter **Gila Bend**. This community of

2,000 started life as a Butterfield Stage stop back in the 1850s, and not much has happened here since. It's a provisioning center for surrounding ranches and a handy rest stop for travelers on this long strip of I-8. Since it's a 116-mile haul between Yuma and Gila Bend, you may want to stop and stretch your legs. The town offers half a dozen motels and a similar number of restaurants.

Short of Gila Bend, you can drive 16 miles north of I-8 to a state park in the rough-hewn Painted Rocks Mountains.

Painted Rocks State Park ● *Painted Rocks Rd. (P.O. Box 273), c/o Gila Bend, AZ 85337; (602) 683-2151. Tent and RV sites; no hookups $6; day use $3. No reservations or credit cards.* This park comes in two sections. Prehistoric graffiti marks several boulders in one area. The main section, four miles north, borders a small lake below Painted Rocks Dam. That's right: below. You're likely to find more water in a lower basin that was excavated for the earth-fill dam than in the reservoir above it. Swimming, boating, fishing and water skiing are available here.

The desert is not terribly inspiring around Gila Bend, but as you head south on Highway 85 toward Organ Pipe Cactus National Monument, you begin climbing into higher Sonoran desert gardens.

Ajo

Elevation: 1,798 feet   **Population: 5,200**

Ajo is a cute little community that seems quite content to be sitting in the middle of nowhere. Actually, this Spanish-style hamlet is a company town, built to house workers at the nearby New Cornelia open pit mine. Ajo's economic fates rest on the mine, which may be shut down by the Phelps Dodge Corporation when copper prices drop. So it isn't always that content. But it is cute, with a neat Spanish plaza in its center.

New Cornelia Mine south of town can be viewed from a rim lookout. It's an impressive sight—nearly a mile and a half across. You'll find copper mining exhibits in a nearby ramada. A former Catholic church serves as the Ajo Historical Museum; open from September to mid-July from 1 to 4:30 daily.

WHERE TO SLEEP

Guest House Inn Bed & Breakfast ● *Three Guest House Rd. (right at the Plaza traffic light), Ajo, AZ 85321; (602) 387-6133. Doubles $49 to $59 including full breakfasts; private baths. Major credit cards.* Built in 1925 by the Phelps Dodge Corporation for company officials. Southwestern and Victorian decor; patio with desert views; full breakfasts, afternoon tea.

Managers House Inn ● *One Greenway Dr., Ajo, AZ 85321; (602) 387-6505. Doubles $49 to $99 including full breakfast; lower off-season rates. Private baths. MC/VISA.* A 1919 Craftsman bungalow built for the copper mine manager, on a hilltop with a town view; period furnishings. Afternoon wine and cheese, evening snacks, spa and patio.

South from Ajo, the highway passes through a wide spot in the road called Why. It's named for the "Y" junction where State Highway 86 heads east from 85. Shortly, you'll begin climbing into rugged terrain with some of the richest botanical bounty of the Sonoran Desert. Here, you meet a cactus that earns its name from its spiny arms, said to resemble pipes on an organ.

Organ Pipe Cactus National Monument ● *Route 1, Box 100, Ajo, AZ 85321; (602) 387-6849. Open 24 hours; visitor center open daily 8 to 5; $3*

Organ pipe cactus casts web-like shadow at sundown.

per vehicle. RV and tent sites in campgrounds, no hookups $6; flush potties, water, picnic tables and barbecues.

Arizona's largest and most remote national monument preserves some of the world's most striking desert wilderness. It's named for a large cactus which is common in northern Mexico but rare in the United States. The organ pipe approaches the saguaro in size, but it's quite different, with multiple arms reaching upward from a common base. Of course, it is but one resident of this mountainous rock garden, which is busy with giant saguaro and hundreds of other desert plants.

Far from civilization's pollution, Organ Pipe has been designated by the United Nations as an International Biosphere Preserve. It's one of our favorite corners of Arizona—a peaceful place with unending panoramas of rock-strewn hills and a virtual showcase of desert flora. Twenty-nine species of cacti have been identified here. During springtime after a wet winter, the blooms of cactus, poppies, lupine and other flowers can be absolutely dazzling.

Less conspicuous are the desert animals, most of whom prefer to come out at night. Take a flashlight hike and you're likely to encounter kangaroo rats with silly-looking pom-poms on their tails, along with jackrabbits and perhaps an owl or three. Rattlesnakes loves this desert, too, so step lightly.

Abrupt elevation changes create three distinct plant communities here. You can drive or hike into the hot and dry Lower Colorado division, with creosote bush and mixed scrub; the Arizona Upland section with its mixed cactus and paloverde; and into rare pockets of the Central Gulf Coast division, where you'll see elephant trees and senita cactus, normally found only in Mexico.

This remote corner can be a busy place, if you choose. Rangers conduct guided walks, talks and slide programs to teach you everything you thought you needed to know about the Sonoran Desert. The visitor center offers fine exhibits on the flora, fauna, geology and history of the area. Several hiking trails take you into surrounding desert gardens.

The best way to discover this 330,690-acre national monument is to take the two scenic drives. The 21-mile **Ajo Mountain Drive** winds through the foothills of the highest range in the area. The **Puerto Blanco Drive**, 53 miles long, circles the Puerto Blanco Mountains, offering scenic variety. Both drives are over dirt roads that are generally graded, but they can get a bit bumpy. Any passenger car can make it, but don't hurry; there's too much to see and the washboard road surface gets too rough.

The hamlet of **Lukeville** is wedged between the southern edge of the monument and the Mexican border. Its Gringo Pass complex offers a trailer park, motel, service station, laundromat and Mexican insurance, if you want to drive on into Mexico. Lukeville also has a post office and cafe. A couple of miles over the line is **Sonoita**, which we will visit in our upcoming South of the Border section.

EXPLORING SOUTH OF THE BORDER

Arizona shares a long border and many ethnic ties with Mexico. Indeed, Southwestern cooking, architecture and even cowboying are heavily influenced by our friendly neighbor to the south. One out of six Arizonans trace their roots to Mexico.

Visiting the Mexican state of Sonora through any of the six border crossings is a simple matter. At most points, you can merely walk across the international boundary to nearby shopping areas, restaurants and cantinas. If your visit is less than 72 hours and you don't go beyond the border town, no formalities are required.

Bear in mind that these aren't typical Mexican cities, any more than Arizona border towns are typically American. Each is influenced by the presence of the other. Mexican border towns cater heavily to tourists, with an inordinate number of curio shops and restaurants.

While you won't experience a typical slice of Mexico, you'll enjoy meeting its friendly people and browsing through shops with bewildering selections of leather goods, ceramics, costume jewelry, turquoise and silver, onyx and wood carvings, embroidered clothing and glassware. Some of the Mexican Indian handicrafts are particularly nice.

Since most towns have shopping areas right next to the border, we recommend parking and walking across. U.S. Customs officials are more picky than their Mexican counterparts, and you might get stuck in a long line of cars, trying to get back into Arizona.

Here's a run-down of what you need to know before making a run for the border.

Entry formalities ● If you're an American or Canadian citizen, you need only to declare your citizenship for visits of 72 hours or less, if you aren't going beyond a border town. If you plan to stay longer and go deeper, you'll need a Mexican Tourist Card and an automobile permit. These can be obtained quickly at the border, or from the Mexico Tourist Office at 2744 E. Broadway in Tucson. You'll need proof of citizenship such as a birth certificate, passport, voter's registration certificate or military ID. A driver's license won't work. For a vehicle permit, you'll need proof of ownership.

Incidentally, if you're a Mexican-American, take some evidence of U.S. residency for re-entry.

If you aren't an American citizen, check with border officials before entering Mexico.

Auto insurance ● Do not drive anywhere in Mexico without Mexican auto insurance. Although insurance isn't mandated by law, your vehicle might be impounded if you're involved in an accident. Few American insurance policies extend coverage to Mexico and even if they do, Mexican officials won't recognize them. If you have a rental car, make sure your rental agreement permits driving into Mexico, and get the proper insurance coverage.

Mexican auto insurance is available on both sides of the border. Rates are comparable with American premiums. For instance, if your car is worth $10,000, the premium would be about $34 for five days or $725 a year. Don't bother shopping around because rates are set by the government.

We recommend Sandborn's, an American-owned company with offices at most border towns. In addition to insurance coverage, the firm provides a question-and-answer leaflet, Mexican milepost guides, camping directories and other helpful stuff. You can contact the Nogales office at P.O. Box 1584 (3420 Tucson Highway), Nogales, AZ 85621.

Shopping ● American money is widely accepted in border towns, so don't bother with currency exchanges. Expect to haggle over prices in curio shops. The rule of thumb is to offer a third what they ask, then meet somewhere in the middle. Don't embarrass the poor shopkeeper and take all the fun out of bargaining by paying full price.

Because of lower labor costs and a favorable exchange rate, you'll find good buys south of the border. Booze is cheap because of the lack of tax, and Mexican-made liquor such as tequila and brandy are less than half the price that they are in the States.

Se habla Ingles ● You won't have to resort to your high school Spanish in the border towns; English is spoken at virtually every shop, motel and restaurant.

Health measures ● We've traveled extensively in Mexico without getting anything worse that diarrhea, but that's awfully unpleasant, so take precautions. Even in the finest restaurants, we routinely avoid drinking unbottled water or eating fresh vegetables that have been washed in tap water. Those nasty little bugs that commit Montezuma's revenge can be killed by heat, so the best precaution is to eat hot food while it's still hot.

We like Mexico and its friendly people and these health precautions aren't meant as an insult. But it's a simple fact that through the decades, their digestive systems have developed an immunity to critters that raise havoc with ours. Mexican citizens visiting the U.S. often experience digestive discomfort.

There's a simple solution to avoiding contaminated water. When in doubt, remember that our Mexican friends make great beer!

Driving in the interior ● It's as safe as driving across Arizona, but there's a major difference. Once you get away from the border, service facilities are scarce and car parts even scarcer. For an extended trip into Mexico, take spare parts such as fan belts, water pumps and such—things that might likely conk out. And don't forget plenty of bottled water in case you're stranded for a while.

Paved Mexican roads are generally good, although they're often narrower than ours. And watch out for potholes, tractors and livestock. Because of open ranges in the state of Sonora and elsewhere, we make it a rule never to drive after dark.

Unleaded gasoline is plentiful in border towns, less so as you travel south. You may want to filter your gasoline through a fine sieve or cloth, particularly if you have a fuel-injected vehicle.

Returning to Arizona ● You can bring back $400 worth of duty-free goods per family member, plus one quart of liquor per adult. Also, Mexico enjoys favored nation status with the U.S., and certain handicrafts can be imported in excess of the $400 limit. Check with a U.S. Customs office to see what's currently on the list.

Bear in mind that some items can't be imported from *any* country, including ivory and certain animal skins and sea turtle oil. Customs can advise you what not to buy when you shop across the border.

The Border Towns

While none of the border towns are cool in summer, Nogales and Agua Prieta—at nearly 4,000 feet elevation—are a bit more livable. San Luis, below Yuma, is near sea level; expect to sizzle if you plan a summertime visit.

Nogales ● Opposite Nogales, Arizona, it's the largest of the six border towns, with a population exceeding 200,000. Predictably, it's also the best place to shop. Scores of curio and liquor stores are crowded into the Calle Obregon, a shopping area that starts just a block from the border. Narrow arcades are stuffed with stalls, some specializing in leather goods, fabric, glassware and other products.

The town also offers several good restaurants, including two which we reviewed in the Nogales, Arizona, section of the previous chapter. There are inexpensive parking lots on the Arizona side and—except on some weekends—plenty of street parking in American Nogales.

San Luis ● South of Yuma, San Luis is an agricultural community of 50,000 or so. It offers several shops within two blocks of the border, in the weathered old business district. Selections aren't large; it's a distant second to Nogales for shopping variety. You can park free in Friendship Park on the American side; the lot closes at 9 p.m.

Sonoita ● Opposite Lukeville below Organ Pipe Cactus National Monument, Sonoita about three miles from the border. However there are a few shops within walking distance of Lukeville. Neither area has extensive selections. You might like to drive 63 miles south to **Rocky Point** (*Puerto Penasco*), where you can swim, snorkel and fish in the clear waters of the Gulf of California. Remember that you need a Mexican Tourist Card and vehicle permit to go south of Sonoita. Incidentally, the Sonoita-Lukeville border station is closed between midnight and 8 a.m.

Sasabe ● At the bottom of Highway 286 southwest of Tucson, this is the smallest, least crowded and most typically Mexican of all the border towns. A handful of residents occupy its weathered buildings and its matching Arizona twin. Only dirt roads lead south from here, so Sasabe obviously gets very little through traffic. Like Sonoita, the border is closed between midnight and 8 a.m.

Naco ● A hamlet south of Bisbee, Naco is one of our favorite border towns. If there's such a thing as scruffily cute, this is it. Naco is more like an interior village—uncrowded, with little Mexican shops behind dusty pastel store fronts. You won't find much of a shopping selection here, but there's one good-sized liquor store. The wide (although pot-holed) streets with center planters give the place a nice colonial charm.

Agua Prieta ● This is Mexico's twin to Douglas. Like Nogales/Nogales, the two towns rub shoulders at the border, and shops are less than a block from the boundary. With about 70,000 inhabitants—ten times as many as Douglas—it offers a fair variety for shoppers. They're not as abundant as those in Nogales or San Luis, however. Downtown here is more of a conventional mix, with gift shops tucked among department stores, *farmacias* and professional offices.

Paved highways lead from here into the interior; it's the most direct driving route to Mexico City.

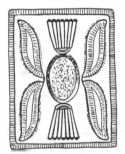

HISTORICAL-SCENIC DRIVE THROUGH COCHISE COUNTY

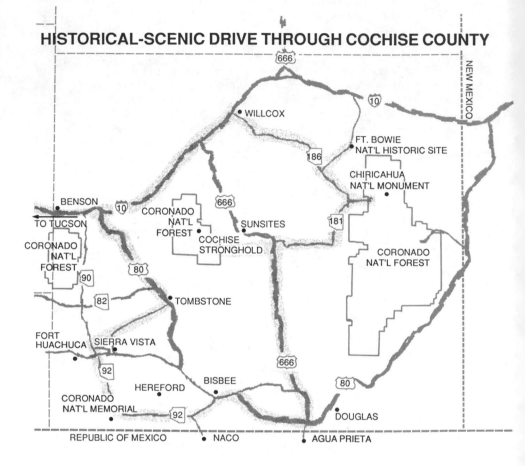

NEW MEXICO

666

10

WILLCOX

FT. BOWIE
NAT'L HISTORIC SITE

186

CHIRICAHUA
NAT'L MONUMENT

BENSON

10

TO TUCSON

CORONADO
NAT'L
FOREST

666

CORONADO
NAT'L
FOREST

SUNSITES

181

COCHISE
STRONGHOLD

90

80

CORONADO
NAT'L FOREST

82

TOMBSTONE

FORT
HUACHUCA

SIERRA VISTA

92

666

92

BISBEE

80

HEREFORD

CORONADO
NAT'L MEMORIAL

92

DOUGLAS

REPUBLIC OF MEXICO

NACO

AGUA PRIETA

Chapter 11

THE COWBOY CORNER

*The 26th of October, 1881, will always be marked as one
of the crimson days in the annals of Tombstone—a day always to be remembered as witnessing the bloodiest and dead
liest street fight that ever occurred in this place, or probably
in the territory.*
— Tombstone *Nugget*, October, 1881

 WHAT WE'VE CHOSEN to call the Cowboy Corner is Cochise
County, a 90 by 75-mile history-laden rectangle that occupies
Arizona's southeastern edge. It could as easily be called the
Cochise Corner in honor of the Chiricahua Apache warrior
chief, or the Copper Corner, for the great copper mines around Bisbee.

Some of Arizona's most intriguing historical pageants were played out
here. Francisco Vasquez de Coronado passed through in 1540 during his
quest for the seven golden cities. Cochise made a futile stand against the in-
truding whites from 1858 to 1869, then Geronimo took up the lance of resistance. In a dusty ally in Tombstone, three men died on October 26, 1881, in
the most celebrated gun battle of Western history.

Then the dust settled and the southeastern corner dozed contentedly
while Tucson, Phoenix and the Colorado River corridor lured hundreds of
thousands of settlers and tourists.

In recent years, Cochise County has re-awaked as an important tourist
destination and burgeoning new retirement haven. Its high altitude tempers
the summer sun and its southern location moderates winter cold.
Climatologists say it offers some of the most temperate climate in America.
The county's mountain ranges—like ships on a desert sea—attract hikers
and campers.

Since Cochise County's tourist lures are somewhat scattered, we've put
together a scenic-historic drive with an accompanying map, to guide you to
the high spots. It roughly follows a route that tourist promoters call the
Cochise Trail.

We approach from Tucson on Interstate 10, then turn south on State Highway 90 at **Benson**, a former cowboy town and Butterfield Stage stop. It now offers a few motels and restaurants and a small museum.

San Pedro Valley Arts and Historical Museum ● *180 S. San Pedro St. (near Main), Benson, AZ 85602; (602) 586-3070. Tuesday-Friday 10 to 4, Saturday 10 to 2, shorter hours in summer. Free; donations accepted.* The small museum has an art gallery and gift shop, along with displays of the usual pioneer and Indian artifacts. Exhibits focus on the Butterfield Stage, early railroad and ranching days.

Tombstone

Elevation: 2,389 feet   Population: 1,700

From Benson, we head south on Highway 80 to the "town too tough to die." Tombstone couldn't die even if it wanted to; Hollywood would never permit it.

THE WAY IT WAS ● Ed Schieffelin hadn't had much luck, prospecting around Arizona. In 1877, he decided to try the rocky hills southeast of Tucson, although the Chiricahua Apaches were still on the warpath.

"All you'll find out there is your tombstone," a friend warned.

THINGS TO KNOW BEFORE YOU GO

Best time to go ● Arizona's southeastern corner is an all-year place. The desert basins that cradle the towns of Sierra Vista, Tombstone, Bisbee and Willcox are nearly a mile high, easing summer temperatures.

Climate ● Balmy summers; cool winters with occasional light snowfall. July average in Sierra Vista—high 85 to 90; low 65 to 70. January average—high 55 to 60; low 35 to 40. Rainfall—15 inches; snowfall—10 inches.

Useful contacts

Coronado National Forest, Sierra Vista Ranger District, 769 N. Highway 90, Sierra Vista, AZ 85635; (602) 455-5530; and Douglas Ranger District, Route 1, Box 228-R, Douglas, AZ 85607; (602) 364-3468.

Greater Bisbee Chamber of Commerce, P.O. Box BA, Bisbee, AZ 85603; (602) 432-2141.

Douglas Chamber of Commerce, 1125 Pan American Ave., Douglas, AZ 85607; (602) 364-2477.

Sierra Vista Chamber of Commerce, 77 Calle Portal, Suite A-140, Sierra Vista, AZ 85635; (602) 458-6940.

City of Tombstone Tourist Information Office, P.O. Box 339, Tombstone, AZ 85638; (602) 457-2202; or Tombstone Tourist Association, P.O. Box 917, Tombstone, AZ 85638.

Willcox Chamber of Commerce and Agriculture, 1500 N. Circle I Rd., Willcox, AZ 85643; (602) 384-2272.

Area radio stations

KCUV-AM, 1490, Safford—Light rock and pop
KFMN-FM, 99.1, Safford—Light rock, pop and oldies
KHIL-AM, 1250, Willcox—Country
KKRK-FM, 95.3, Douglas—Rock
KMFI-AM, 1470, Sierra Vista—Nostalgia, oldies
KZMK-FM, 92.1, Bisbee—Rock

Ed found a big silver strike instead, and called it—appropriately—the Lucky Cuss. Word spread and other argonauts poured in. A town was staked out two years later, in Goose Flat, two miles from Schieffelin's hillside mine. Soon, it was one of the largest, wildest and wickedest mining camps in the Southwest. It attracted such characters as Doc Holliday, Johnny Ringo, Bat Masterson and—of course—the Earp brothers. Wyatt was co-owner of the Oriental Saloon, where gunslinger Luke Short was a faro dealer.

By 1881, Tombstone boasted about 10,000 citizens, and it became the seat of Cochise County. In that same year, the Earps shot it out with the Clantons and McLaurys (spelled McLowry by some sources) near the O.K. Corral. Actually, it was more of a blood feud than a police action. The Earps had accused the Clantons and McLaurys of cattle thievery and sheltering stage robbers at their ranches. The cowboys boasted openly that they would kill the Earps for besmirching their reputations.

"They tried to pick a fuss out of me," Wyatt testified at the hearing following the corral shoot-out. But he admitted that earlier on the day of the shooting, he and his brother Morgan had tried to goad Ike Clanton into a fight.

After the excitement from the West's most publicized gun battle had died down, Tombstone faced other problems. Most of the downtown area burned in 1882. A few years later, water began seeping into its mines. Falling silver prices and labor problems closed the last of the mines early in this century. The county seat was moved to Bisbee in 1931 and the town too tough to die was on the verge of doing it. The population dropped to 150.

Then tourists began trickling in, lured by stories of the Earp brothers and the shoot-out. The town's old Western look, unchanged because nobody could afford to modernize, became an asset.

THE WAY IT IS • When we began researching this book, I hadn't been to Tombstone for 20 years. I feared that it might have become an artificial tourist gimmick by now, like Old Tucson. We were pleased to find it just as real and corny as ever—a mix of history and hokum.

Visitors clunk along boardwalks shaded by overhangs from false front stores. They buy snow cones and John Wayne posters and visit museums that are mostly fronts for souvenir shops. They browse through boutiques called Big-Nose Kate's Gifts and Collectibles and "Madame Mustache, Purveyor of Pleasure." A sign above the O.K. Corral entrance invites tourists to "Walk where they fell."

Most of the shops and quasi-museums are housed in century-old buildings along three blocks of Allen Street, a block south of—and parallel to— Highway 80 (Fremont Street). Some vacant lots have been cleared away to provide visitor parking.

The **Tombstone Information Center** is at Allen and Fourth streets. It's staffed by volunteers, so hours tend to be unpredictable. When you find it open, you can pick up a walking map that will guide you past such structures as the century-old **St. Paul's Episcopal Church, Tombstone City Hall** with its elaborate facade, the site of the **Oriental Saloon** and the 1888 **Wells Fargo office.** A more detailed *Tombstone Map and Guide* is available at museums and curio shops for 50 cents.

A mule-drawn surrey, stagecoach rides and Sunday afternoon gunplay— either in the O.K. Corral or on Allen Street—recall the days when newly-rich silver barons and steely-eyed gunfighters swaggered about Tombstone. Downtown has been declared a national historic landmark and the 1882 courthouse is now an Arizona state historic park.

THE BEST ATTRACTIONS

Tombstone Courthouse State Historic Park • *219 E. Toughnut St. (Third Street), Tombstone, AZ 85638; (602) 457-3311. Daily 8 to 5; adults $1, kids free.* This imposing brick structure with Greek pediments and a witch's hat tower served as the Cochise County Courthouse from 1882 until neighboring Bisbee snatched away the county seat in 1931. It's now a museum of Cochise County yesterdays with a restored sheriff's office, courtroom and various exhibits. A gift shop run by the Tombstone Restoration Commission has a good selection of books on local and Arizona history.

Assorted versions of the O.K. Corral shoot-out hang on the courthouse walls. An exhibit case contains Wyatt Earp memorabilia, including his razor. Among other displays are photos of town founder Schieffelin, an assay office, mining paraphernalia, a mock-up saloon and cowboy gear. The reconstructed gallows is out back, where seven men did a rope-dance.

Boothill Cemetery and Gift Shop • *Highway 80 (half mile north of town); (602) 457-3348. Daily 7:30 to 6; free.* You don't often find cemeteries that accept Visa and MasterCard. Of course, that's only in the gift shop,

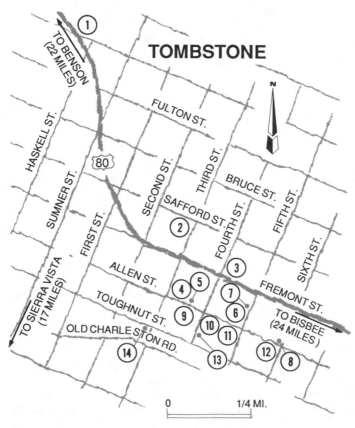

TOMBSTONE

DIRECTORY

1. BOOT HILL GRAVEYARD
2. ST. PAUL'S EPISCOPAL CHURCH
3. SCHIEFFELIN HALL
4. OK CORRAL
5. "HISTORAMA" SHOW
6. CRYSTAL PALACE SALO
7. TOMBSTONE EPITAPH
8. SILVER NUGGET MUSEU
9. CHAMBER OF COMMER
10. ARIZONA TERRITORIAL MUSEUM
11. BIG NOSE KATE'S SALO
12. BIRD CAGE THEATRE
13. ROSE TREE INN AND MUSEUM
14. TOMBSTONE COURTHO STATE HISTORIC PARK

—**Arizona Department of Archives photo**
*Wyatt Earp during his Tombstone days in 1886, and in a more
sedate guise in 1920.*

through which you pass to view the graves of Tombstone's fallen. As the
sound of cash registers rings in your ears, you read the sign over the
graveyard entrance:

This is a cemetery. Please treat it and the graves with respect. Thank you.

Frank and Tom McLaury and Billy Clanton lie side by side, near the parking lot fence. The marker says they were "murdered in the streets of
Tombstone." More than 250 other citizens are buried here and grave signs
remind you that life was often short and death was quick in the Wild West:

"Tom Waters. Shot, 1880"—"Dick Toby. Shot by Sheriff Behan"—"Two
Cowboys. Drowned"—"Charley Storms. Shot by Luke Short, 1880"—
"Teamster, 1881. Killed by Apaches"—"Della William, 1881. Suicide"—
"Thos. Harper. Hanged, 1881" and "Geo. Johnson. Hanged by mistake."

Some mistake.

The original wooden markers, either weathered away or taken by
souvenir hunters, have been replaced by steel nameplates mounted on pipes.
This supposedly was the first cemetery to be called "boothill"—a term inspired by the unfortunate fact that many of its occupants died with their
boots on.

Crystal Palace Saloon ● *Allen Street at Fifth; (602) 457-3611.* We like
the Crystal Palace because it's not an "attraction" but a functioning saloon.
It has been faithfully restored to its 1880's glitter, with American eagle
wallpaper, hurricane lamp chandeliers and a handsome oversized back bar.
You can get an honest schooner of Coors for $1.25, listen to live Western
music and watch wanna-be gunslingers and their ladies do the cowboy two-
step.

The O.K. Corral and Camillus Fly Photo Studio ● *Allen Street (between
Third and Fourth); (602) 457-3456. Daily 8:30 to 5. Admission $1, shoot-out
re-enactment $2.* The O.K. Corral has been corralled into a tourist attraction
which also includes frontier photographer Camillus S. Fly's photo studio,
and 19th century rigs including a hearse that once toted unfortunate cowboys to Boothill.

Bad guys bite the dust in re-enactment of the O.K. Corral shoot-out.

A movie poster reminds us that *The Gunfight at the O.K. Corral* hit the big screen with Burt Lancaster as Wyatt and Kirk Douglas as Doc. It was filmed not at the original site but in the make-believe Western town of Old Tucson.

Near the scene of the shoot-out, beside Fly's studio, poorly-done mannequins mark the position of the eight combatants when their guns started blazing. However, they're farther apart than newspaper accounts reported. The fight took place in a 15-foot-wide alley between two buildings, and the first shots were fired at nearly point-blank range. Fly's studio contains some fine example of his frontier photography, including photos taken at the surrender of Geronimo to the U.S. Army in 1886.

A group of volunteer actors called the Wild Bunch re-enacts the shoot-out on the first and third Sundays of each month at 2 p.m. It takes place in another part of the corral, before a small grandstand. On the second, fourth and fifth Sundays, another outfit—the Vigilantes—stages gunfights (not the Earp-Clanton shoot-out) on Allen Street.

The Wild Bunch's shoot-out, obviously well-researched, is startlingly realistic. You come away almost sensing that you just witnessed that violent 30 seconds of history when 34 shots were fired and three men died. It's the climax of a half-hour show that includes a couple of allegedly funny skits and some other gunplay. Unfortunately, the skits are poorly done; they diminish the talents of the performers and the impact of the shoot-out itself.

Silver Nugget Museum ● *Allen Street at Sixth; (602) 457-3310. Daily 9 to 5; adults $1.* This rather large museum behind a gift shop has an extensive exhibit of early day documents, including papers relating to the Earps and Clantons, plus mining gear and old photos. Attractive carved wooden display cases contain Indian beadwork and arrowheads, early Chinese artifacts, dishware and other pioneer stuff. Other exhibits include a mock-up gambling room with a roulette wheel and faro table, Motel-T and Model-A Fords and a tack room.

Tombstone Historama ● *Allen Street near Third, adjacent to the O.K. Corral; (602) 457-3456. Admission $1; shows on the hour from 9 a.m. to 4 p.m.* While not as awesome and unique as its promotion suggests, Historama is a nicely-done audio-visual presentation. Vincent Price narrates while five dioramas revolve. The animation is pretty simplistic, but you learn a lot about Tombstone. A screen drops occasionally to show films and slides to augment this history lesson.

"DON'T SHOOT ANYMORE. YOU HAVE KILLED ME!"

It was like a scene from a low-budget Western, with stilted dialogue to match. But it was frighteningly real. Tombstone Police Chief Virgil Earp, his deputized brothers Wyatt and Morgan, and Doc Holliday advanced upon five cowboys, standing in a narrow alley.

Word around town was that—brothers Frank and Tom McLaury and Ike and Billy Clanton—had threatened to kill the Earps. They'd been feuding for weeks, after the Earps accused them of cattle rustling and stealing six army mules. With the four was Billy "The Kid" Claiborne, a town tough who had recently killed a man over a drink.

Sheriff Johnny Behan failed to disarm the glowering cowboys, then he tried to stop the Earps and Holliday. "For God's sake don't go down there or you'll get murdered," he pleaded.

The four brushed past him and kept walking. They stopped within ten feet of the cowboys, who were between Camillus C. Fly's photo studio and the O.K. Corral. Frank McLaury stood beside his horse; a Winchester rifle was in a saddle scabbard.

"You sons of bitches, you've been looking for a fight, and now you have it!" Wyatt growled.

"Throw up your hands!" Virgil ordered.

Claiborne—not so tough when facing the Earps—ran for cover.

"Don't shoot me! I don't want to fight!" Billy Clanton pleaded, raising his hands.

In a split second, two shots were fired, followed by a wild volley. Frank McLaury fell first. Billy Clanton was hit in the chest at point-blank range; he lurched into a wall and slid to the ground. Tom McLaury clawed at the rifle scabbard on his brother's horse but the animal bolted. He started running and Morgan fired at him; McLaury pitched forward.

"I got him!" Morgan shouted. Then he spun and fell as a bullet smashed through both shoulders.

Ike Clanton grabbed Wyatt's left arm; the deputy gave him a rude shove. "Go to fighting or get away!" Earp yelled.

Clanton fled into Fly's studio.

Virgil sagged to one knee as a bullet pierced his right calf. Billy Clanton struggled to sit up and fire, but he was too weak; the life was draining out of him. He slumped back against the wall.

"Don't shoot me anymore!" he begged. "You have killed me!"

Then, silence. The McLaurys and Billy Clanton lay dying. Doc Holliday winced from a bullet that had smashed into his holster and grazed his hip. Wyatt was unscathed. He and Doc and had stood and fired "as cool as cucumbers," an onlooker said. Virgil and Morgan would survive their wounds.

A hearing was held to determine of the Earps and Holliday should be tried for murder. They were cleared, even though some witnesses—including the sheriff—said they had fired first.

Hundreds of gun battles echoed through the Old West, but none caught the public's fancy like the gunfight at the O.K. Corral. It has been played out thousands of times since, in movies and books, on TV and at the corral itself by actors before camera-clicking tourists. It seems ironic that—in the "town too tough to die"—it was thirty seconds of death that put it on the map.

Two men on opposite sides of Arizona's history: Tombstone founder Ed Schieffelin and Apache resistance leader Geronimo.

World's Largest Rosebush Museum ● *Fourth and Toughnut streets; (602) 457-3326. Daily 9 to 5; adults $1, under 14 free.* What's a rose bush got to do with Arizona history? Nothing, but it's an impressive thing, crawling over 8,000 square feet of a lattice-roofed patio. A white-blossoming *Lady Banksia*, it started as a cutting sent from Scotland in 1885. Owners claim it's the world's oldest as well as the largest.

The adjoining Victorian-style Rose Tree Inn houses a gift shop and one of Tombstone's nicer museums, with plush wallpaper, Victorian and early American antiques. It features an interesting lock exhibit, a cut-away of the Schieffelin's Lucky Cuss Mine and—of course—a diorama of The Shoot-out.

THE REST

Arizona Territorial Museum ● *Allen Street (near Fourth); (602) 457-3344. Free, donations accepted.* This U-shaped museum surrounding Casa de Mexico Gift Shop offers several historic tableaux. They're interesting, although rather scruffy-looking. You'll see a Mexican couple all dressed up for a fandango, a blacksmith shop, general store with old package goods and a miner looking properly startled as a bear invades his mining supply room. Both the bear and mannequin miner have seen better days; it looks like they both lost the fight.

Bird Cage Theater ● *Sixth and Allen streets; (602) 457-3421. Daily 8 to 7 (shorter hours in the off-season); adults $2; teens 13-18, $1; kids 50 cents.* This should be one of Tombstone's finer attractions, for it's the town's only original, fully-intact gambling hall-theater-saloon. Unfortunately, the museum is cluttered and ratty-looking—a thrown-together jumble of old pianos, sewing machines and other dusty junk totally unrelated to the theater's lively history. However, you can see dusty four-by-six foot bird-cage "cribs" suspended from upper walls, where fallen angels entertained their gents. These cubicles inspired the song, *She's only a bird in a gilted cage.* During performances, curtains were opened and the cribs functioned as box seats.

The most interesting thing about the Bird Cage is the lively—if sometimes exaggerated—historical spiel that's delivered in the lobby before you enter the main museum. You learn that Tombstone had 106 bars and 3,700 working girls who fattened the city's coffers with a $10 monthly tax. The lobby itself is nicely restored with a beautifully-carved bar and back-bar with French mirrors. If you carefully examine a nine-foot nude portrait of Lady Fatima, hanging in the same spot since 1881, you'll see six patched bullet holes.

Schieffelin Hall • *Fourth and Fremont streets.* Built by a Schieffelin relative, this imposing two-story structure is one of the largest adobe buildings in the West. It was the town's social and theatrical center where John Sullivan and traveling Shakespearean troupes appeared. Although still intact, it was closed to the public at this writing.

Schieffelin Monument • *Three miles west at the end of Allen Street.* A monument patterned after a miner's claim marks the final resting place of the father of Tombstone. Although he scored a major silver strike and founded one of the west's most famous mining towns, Schieffelin eventually lost his fortune. He left Tombstone after a few years and died in a simple cabin near Canyonville, Oregon, on May 12, 1897.

Tombstone *Epitaph* • *Nine S. Fifth St. (P.O. Box 1880), Tombstone, AZ 85638 (602) 457-2211.* The *Epitaph* was founded by Tombstone pioneer John P. Clum in 1880. A history-oriented version is still being published. You can order a year's subscription for $10, or buy souvenir editions containing accounts of the O.K. Corral shoot-out. The shop also sells books and pamphlets on local history.

Displays include old type cases and the original Washington hand-operated printing press on which Clum published his first edition. Supposedly the paper earned its name when Schieffelin told Clum that his town of Tombstone should have an *Epitaph*.

ANNUAL EVENTS

Territorial Days, first weekend in March; **Wyatt Earp Days,** Memorial Day weekend; **Vigilante Days,** second weekend of August; **Rendezvous of Gunfighters,** Labor Day weekend; **Helldorado Days** Old West celebration with shoot-outs, Indian dancers and parade, third weekend of October.

WHERE TO DINE

Nellie Cashman's Boarding House Restaurant • ΔΔ $$

Fifth Street near Toughnut; (602) 457-3950. American-Mexican, dinners $6 to $16, wine and beer. Daily 7 a.m. to 9 p.m. MC/VISA, AMEX. Mexican and American entrees, omelets, sandwiches. In an 1879 Spanish-style building with Western-style wainscoting, lamps, historic posters and photos.

Gallows behind Tombstone courthouse, where seven men were dispatched to Boothill.

Wagon Wheel Restaurant ● △△ $$

401 E. Fremont (Highway 80, at Fourth Street); (602) 457-3656. American, dinners $6 to $12, full bar. Daily 6 a.m. to 9 p.m.; reservations accepted. Major credit cards. Steaks, chops and seafood; prime rib a specialty. Housed in the old Tombstone post office; antique guns and other memorabilia on the walls. Western saloon up front.

Longhorn Restaurant ● △ $$

Allen at Fifth Street; (602) 457-3405. American, dinners $7 to $12, full bar. Daily 7 a.m. to 8 p.m. MC/VISA. Family-style fare; semi-cowboy decor, Western saloon.

WHERE TO SLEEP

Adobe Lodge Motel ● △ $$

505 E. Fremont St. (Fifth Street), Tombstone, AZ 85638; (602) 457-2241. Doubles $32 to $35, singles $25 to $30. MC/VISA. TV; downtown, near Tombstone attractions.

Best Western Lookout Lodge ● △△ $$ ∅

P.O. Box 787 (a mile northwest on Highway 80), Tombstone, AZ 85638; (602) 457-2223 or (800) 528-1234. Doubles $45 to $54, singles $35 to $45. Major credit cards. TV, phones, heated pool, free coffee.

The Larian Motel ● △ $$ ∅

410 Fremont St. (Fourth Street) Tombstone, AZ 85638; (602) 457-2272. Doubles $33 to $39, singles $26 to $31; lower off-season rates. MC/VISA. TV; downtown, near Tombstone attractions.

BED & BREAKFAST INNS

Tombstone Boarding House Bed & Breakfast ● *108 N. Fourth St. (P.O. Box 906), Tombstone, AZ 85638; (602) 457-3716. Doubles $39 to $44,*

singles $32, including full breakfast. Period furnishings in converted century-old adobe home; private baths.

WHERE TO CAMP

Tombstone Hills KOA ● *P.O. Box 99 (Highway 80, two miles northwest), Tombstone, AZ 85638; (602) 457-3829. RV and tent sites, full hookups $15.95, no hookups $13.95, "Kamping Kabins" $21.95. Reservations accepted; MC/VISA.* Some pull-throughs; flush potties, showers, coin laundry, groceries and souvenir shop, Propane, dump station. Large shaded sites; playground, swimming pool, horseshoes and shuffleboard; free shuttle to town.

Wells Fargo RV Park ● *Fremont (Highway 80) and Third streets, P.O. Box 1076, Tombstone, AZ 85638; (602) 457-3966. RV and tent sites, full hookups $15.50, water and electric $14.50, no hookups $13.50.* Flush potties, showers, cable TV; downtown, close to Tombstone attractions.

Tombstone wasn't the only mining camp that flourished in and about the Dragoon Mountains, but it was the only one that survived. Several ghost towns now dot the hills and hide in the ravines. You might want to visit **Watervale,** on a dirt road, leading to the right from the west end of Allen Street; **Charleston** and **Millville,** nine miles southwest, toward Sierra Vista on Charleston Road; and **Gleeson,** 15 miles east on a dirt extension of Fremont Street.

Having had our moment with history, we follow Charleston Road southwest of Tombstone to a town that started only yesterday.

Sierra Vista-Fort Huachuca

Elevation: 4,623 feet   **Population: 34,000**

Started in 1956 as a retirement and vacation retreat, Sierra Vista has mushroomed to become the largest city in Cochise County; more than one out of three residents live here. It's no wonder. Surrounding mountains provide an impressive backdrop. Climate experts say its one of the most temperate regions in the nation, with an average maximum high of 75 and low of 50. It's almost a room temperature community.

Rivaling neighbor Tucson in total land area, it looks more like a well-planned suburb than a town—an extensive spread of shopping centers, subdivisions and stoplights. The **Sierra Vista Chamber of Commerce** is at 77 Calle Portal, in the Southern Arizona Financial Center at the corner of Fry Boulevard; hours are 8 a.m. to 5 p.m. weekdays. The chamber immodestly boasts that Sierra Vista is "the nicest little town under the sun" with 800 rooms and 30 restaurants.

Coronado National Forest's Sierra Vista Ranger District office is at 769 N. Highway 90; (602) 455-5530. You can buy a map for $2 and get free camping and hiking guides to surrounding forest lands. It's open weekdays from 8 to 5.

The area's main attraction is next-door Fort Huachuca, a still-active 1877 army base with an excellent museum. To reach it, drive west on Fry Boulevard (Highway 90) which leads right into the fort. You must first stop at the Visitor Center to get a car pass and directions to the museum.

Set against the dry, brushy Huachuca Mountains, the fort played a pivotal role in the settlement of the southwest. A drive around the extensive grounds and past austere wooden buildings lining the old parade field takes you back to the days of the Pony Soldiers. The only Southwestern military post still active, the fort has been declared a national historic landmark.

Fort Huachuca Museum • *c/o U.S. Army Garrison, Fort Huachuca, AZ 85613-6000; (602) 533-2714. Weekdays from 9 to 6 and weekends from 1 to 6; free.* This is one of Arizona's great surprises—an outstanding museum sitting among the barracks buildings of an old Army fort. It has a dual focus: the history of the Southwest and the history of the fort—which are frequently linked.

The museum comes in two parts. The main building is an 1892 structure that housed the post chapel and later the officers' club. It offers exhibits concerning the fort's role in various conflicts, from the Apache uprisings to Pancho Villa's border skirmishes to World War II. Among the displays are a fine collection of period uniforms, a special exhibit on the black "Buffalo Soldiers" who fought with the Army of the West, models of military wagons and typically furnished rooms of military families, representing various historical periods.

The annex is our favorite part. The focal point is a large open exhibit portraying a patrol at evening's rest, somewhere on the desert. Tents are pitched, a campfire crackles and a soldier strums a guitar. Watching the dimly-lit scene, you can almost hear a coyote howling on a distant ridge. And that movement in the brush; is an Apache sneaking up on the camp?

This life-sized scene is surrounded by western storefront facades with tableaux set in window casings. They tell the story of the Army of the West as it wrestled Arizona, New Mexico and California from the Mexicans, then tried to keep the settlers and Indians out of one another's scalps.

Ramsey Canyon Preserve • *Six miles south on Highway 92, then four miles west on Ramsey Canyon Road; (602) 378-2785; trails open 8 to 5.* This Nature Conservancy Preserve shelters 280 acres of a protected, wooded gorge in the Huachuca Mountains. Its a favorite haunt of hummingbirds; more than a dozen species have been counted here. The Mile Hi/Ramsey Canyon Bird Observation Station and a nature trail are free to the public. Vehicle space is limited, so you should call the above number for parking reservations on weekends and holidays; it can't accommodate trailers, or RVs over 20 feet.

If you want to spend more time in this peaceful, pristine setting, you can rent rustic cabins at Mile Hi by the day or week. For lodging, contact Mile Hi Preserve: Route 1, Box 84, Hereford, AZ 85615; (602) 378-2785.Ramsey Canyon Inn Bed & Breakfast (listed below) is near the preserve.

WHERE TO DINE

Apache Pointe Ranch Steakhouse • △△ $$

Ramsey Canyon Road (P.O. Box 1713), Sierra Vista; (602) 378-6800. American, dinners $5 to $21; full bar service. Tuesday-Sunday 5 to 9; full bar service. MC/VISA. Ranch house style dining room serving mesquite broiled bison steaks and other Western grub; Friday night fish fry; country and western dance in adjoining saloon.

G&M Stronghold Steakhouse • △△ $$ ∅

332 N. Garden Ave. (near Fort Huachuca gate), Sierra Vista; (602) 458-2575. American, dinners $6 to $22, full bar service. Monday-Thursday 11 a.m. to 9 p.m., Friday-Saturday 11 to 10, Sunday 11 to 8; reservations accepted. MC/VISA. Mesquite-grilled steaks, ribs, seafood, chicken; located in an 1880 trading post; western decor.

The Mesquite Tree ● △△ $$
South Highway 92 at Carr Canyon Rd., Sierra Vista; (602) 378-2758. American, dinners $7 to $15; full bar service. Tuesday-Saturday 11 to 3 and 5 to 9, Sunday 5 to 8.; reservations accepted. MC/VISA, DISC. An attractive restaurant with old Southwest decor, specializing in steaks, barbecued ribs, prime rib and seafood.

Thunder Mountain Inn Restaurant ● △△△ $$ ∅
1631 S. Highway 92 (a mile south of Highway 90 junction), Sierra Vista; (602) 458-7900. American, dinners $10 to $20; full bar service. Daily from 6:30 a.m. to 9 p.m.; reservations accepted. MC/VISA, AMEX, DC. Attractive, modern restaurant featuring ribs, steak, calves liver and onions, lamb chops, grilled chicken and seafood. Live entertainment in adjacent cocktail lounge.

WHERE TO SLEEP

Bella Vista Motel ● △ $$
1101 E. Fry Blvd., Sierra Vista, AZ 85635; (602) 458-7593. Doubles $25 to $27, singles $23, kitchenettes $23 to $25. MC/VISA, DISC. TV, room phones. The **Coffee Cup** restaurant serves from 5 a.m. to 2 p.m., American and Mexican, meals from $3 to $6, non-smoking areas; no alcohol.

Ramada Inn ● △△ $$$ ∅
2047 S. Highway 92, Sierra Vista, AZ 85635; (602) 459-5900 or (800) 825-4656. Doubles $55 to $73, singles $55 to $69. Major credit cards. TV, phones, refrigerators, microwaves; pool, spa. **Brass Eagle** restaurant serves from 6 to 9 a.m., 11 to 2 and 5 to 9, American (German specialties on Wednesdays), dinners $7 to $16, non-smoking areas, full bar service.

Sierra Vista InnSuites ● △△ $$$ ∅
391 E. Fry Blvd. (2.5 miles west of Highway 90-92 junction), Sierra Vista, AZ 85635; (602) 459-4221. Mini-suites; doubles $56 to $89, singles $49 to $89. MC/VISA, AMEX, DC. TV, phones, some refrigerators; pool, spa, free Continental breakfast and beverages.

Super 8 Motel ● △△ $$ ∅
100 Fab Ave. (off Fry Boulevard, west of 90-92 junction), Sierra Vista, AZ 85635; (602) 459-5380 or (800) 843-1991. Doubles $40 to $42, singles $36. Major credit cards. TV movies, radios, phones; pool.

Thunder Mountain Inn ● △△△ $$ ∅
1631 S. Highway 92 (a mile south of Highway 90 junction), Sierra Vista, AZ 85635; (602) 458-7900 or (800) 222-5811. Doubles $44, singles $39, suites $100 to $150. MC/VISA, AMEX, DC. Spacious rooms, some with a view of the Huachuca Mountains; TV movies, phones, some refrigerators; pool, spa. **Restaurant** serves daily from 6:30 a.m. to 9 p.m. (listed above).

BED & BREAKFAST INN

Ramsey Canyon Inn ● *P.O. Box 85 (Ramsey Canyon Road, off Highway 92), Hereford, AZ 85615; (602) 378-3010. Doubles $55 to $85, full breakfast. No credit cards.* A country-style inn located at creekside in a wooded canyon; hiking trails, nature walks. Rooms furnished with antiques; some shared, some private baths; homemade pies served in the afternoons. Smoking outside only.

WHERE TO CAMP

Sun Country RV Resort ● *Highways 82 and 90 (P.O. Box 4585), Huachuca City, AZ 85616; (602) 456-9301. RV and tent sites; full hookups $12, water and electric $9, no hookups $9. Advance reservations accepted;*

MC/VISA. Some pull-throughs; Flush potties, showers, coin laundry, Propane, dump station. Clubhouse for social activities; horseshoe pits; birdwatching.

TO CORONADO, BISBEE & DOUGLAS

From Fort Huachuca, we return east on Fry Boulevard, then head south on Highway 92 along the foothills of the Huachuca Mountains. Then we follow signs to a memorial honoring someone who visited this region long before the Army of the West arrived.

Coronado National Memorial • *Route 2, Box 126, Hereford, AZ 85615. Visitor center open daily 8 to 5; free.* Have you ever seen one of those gag signs that reads: "On April 22, 1934, nothing happened here." This could be said of Coronado National Memorial, a 4,976-acre preserve in the wooded flanks of the Huachuca Mountains.

The memorial was established to mark Francisco Vasquez de Coronado's entry into present-day Arizona in 1540 to search for the Seven Cities of Cibola. However, he passed about ten miles to the east, wisely choosing the San Pedro River Valley instead of the rugged Huachuca Mountains. National parks officials had hoped to establish an international memorial at the Mexican border. But old Frank Coronado isn't exactly loved by our neighbors, so Mexico demurred. But we still wanted to honor him and—what the hey—this land in Montezuma Canyon happened to be available.

It's certainly a pretty site, tucked into a hillside oak and pine woodland. If you're willing to follow an awfully narrow and bumpy road a few miles beyond the small visitor center, you'll be rewarded by an awesome view of the surrounding desert and mountains. A short hike takes you even higher, to the top of Coronado Peak. Along the way, signposts with quotes from journals of the Coronado party give you an excuse to stop and catch your breath.

The visitor center exhibits armor and weapons of Spanish soldiers of the era. Nicely done paintings and graphics detail Coronado's trek, which extended as far north as Kansas. We learn that he was only 30 years old at the time of his commission as "Captain General of the Provinces of Cibola." He left with a grand entourage of 339 soldiers, wives, servants and 1,500 head of horses, cows, goats and sheep. He staggered back two years later, footsore and dejected, having found nothing but a lot of open space and a few mud pueblos.

The national monument has no campground or services, but it does offer picnic areas, and trails through the pretty wooded slopes of Montezuma Canyon.

Moving with much more ease than Coronado's troupe, we follow Highway 92 east to one of early Arizona's great copper camps.

Bisbee

Elevation: 5,490 feet   **Population: 7,300**

Bisbee is another delightful Arizona surprise—a sturdy old mining town cantilevered into the steep flanks of Mule Pass Gulch. Like Jerome, this is the sort of place where your neighbor above can look down your chimney. The post office department complains that its too steep for mail delivery.

Bisbee copper mining town crawling up the steep slopes of Mule Mountain.

Headframes and tailing dumps mark the hillsides; corrugated buildings shelter smelters and stamp mills. Hillsides have been ripped away to expose orange, rust and gray-green wounds. You *know* this is mining country. Driving east beyond the sturdy Victorian downtown area, you encounter something even more dramatic—the great terraced cavity of the Lavender Pit Mine. It's so close it appears ready to swallow up the town.

THE WAY IT WAS ● Bisbee didn't burst into glory overnight, in the style of Tombstone. It grew steadily and sturdily as big corporations gouged deep into the earth for copper, gold, silver, lead and zinc. Army Scout Jack Dunn filed a claim in the area in 1877, then brought in one George Warren as a partner. Warren cheated Dunn out of his share, found some investors, then eventually sold to a conglomerate headed by Judge DeWitt Bisbee of San Francisco. They formed the Copper Queen Mine Company and eventually merged with the large Phelps Dodge Corporation.

In, around, and under Bisbee, more than $2 billion worth of ore was pulled from miles of shafts and deep open pit mines. Reveling in this wealth, the town grew as a sort of vertical San Francisco, with plush Victorian homes, fine restaurants and—of course—bordellos. Brewery Gulch was Bisbee's version of San Francisco's Barbary Coast, with more than 50 drinking, gambling and whoring establishments.

At its peak, Bisbee was the world's largest copper-mining town, with a population of 20,000. Phelps Dodge operated the underground Queen Mine and the Lavender open pit mine until 1975 when diminishing returns and falling copper prices forced the operation to shut down.

THE WAY IT IS ● Logic says the town should have withered and died, but retirees and tourists began coming here, drawn by the mild climate and sturdy charm of the old town. Boutiques, galleries and antique shops were opened in the red brick and tufa buildings. Bed and breakfast inns are proliferating. The great Queen Mine, unable to process copper economically, began mining tourists by offering underground tours.

The town even attracts a few movie companies, since the hillside buildings can become—with a little creative camera work—a bit of Old Spain, Greece or Mexico.

To begin your Bisbee exploration, pick up a walking map (perhaps we should say hiking map) of historic downtown buildings. They're available at the **Chamber of Commerce** at 10 OK St. (Naco Road), open weekdays from 9 to 5 and Saturdays from 9 to 2.

THE BEST ATTRACTIONS

Queen Mine Tour • *Opposite downtown Bisbee, across Highway 80; (602) 432-2071. Mine tours depart daily at 10:30, noon and 3:30, $5; Lavender Pit tour at noon daily, $4; historic city tour at 10:30, 2 and 3:30, $4.* This was just plain fun! We were rigged up in slickers, hard-hats, lights and battery packs. Then we trundled deep into a copper mine, sitting astraddle a rattly, clunky shuttle called a miner's mule. Actually, we traveled horizontally into the face of the mountain, going slightly uphill.

Our lamps darted about like fat fireflies as we studied the walls, still marbled with veins of copper, lead, zinc and manganese. The guide, a former miner, explained drilling and blasting techniques—a process of setting rows of dynamite to loosen the stubborn rock.

"Our drills had no reverse and they could really get stuck in seven feet of rock," he said. "I used to wish the damned thing was alive so I could kill it."

Mules were used deep in the mines before the days of electric ore carts. Some never saw daylight, living within the earth for as long as 17 years. We learned that miners befriended rats by sharing their lunches because the varmints could sense the vibration of a coming cave-in. They'd be the first to give the alarm and head for cover. And we learned that more than 2,500 miles of tunnels and shafts riddle the mountains around Bisbee.

Incidentally, the mine stays at 47 degrees, so take a warm jacket. The company also offers tours of the town and visits to the edge of Lavender Pit.

Bisbee Mining & Historical Museum • *Five Copper Queen Plaza (near Brewery Gulch), P.O. Box 14, Bisbee, AZ 85603; (602) 432-7071. Monday-Saturday 10 to 4, Sunday 1 to 4. Adults $2, kids free.* The former Phelps Dodge headquarters, this large red brick building is probably the first structure to catch your eye. Inside, you'll see photos of early mining days, equipment and a make-believe shaft with cutaways of mining methods as they evolved through the years. Other exhibits feature the Slavs, Mexicans and English from the Isle of Man who were the dominant ethnic groups in the mines.

The founder's room, richly paneled in oak, with a coffered ceiling and period office furniture, is quite handsome. You can imagine cigar-chewing copper magnates swapping lies and talking million dollar deals. Although not professionally done, the museum is well organized and worth an hour or so.

Lavender Pit • *Adjacent to Highway 80, immediately south of town.* Tours aren't necessary to visit this gigantic rusty brown, yellow and pale green hole in the ground. You can simply park and walk to the fenced-off edge. A sign advises you that the great terraced pit is more than a mile long,

Lavender Pit copper mine left a giant, terraced hole in the ground.

three-fourths of a mile wide and 950 feet deep. More than 280 million *tons* of material came out of this hole, yielding 94 million tons of copper ore.

THE REST

Bisbee Restoration Association Museum ● *37 Main Street (Subway Street). Monday-Saturday 10 to 3; free.* Located in the old Fair mercantile building, this museum looks more like an overstocked antique shop. One gets the impression that the curators managed to find a spot to display whatever anyone wanted to donate. If you like clutter, you'll love this collection of old magazines, historic photos, spinning wheels, typewriters, period costumes, china, lace and the list goes on.

Brewery Gulch ● *Downtown, off Howell Avenue.* A stroll up a side canyon on elevated sidewalks takes you past century-old brick and stone buildings that once housed saloons and bawdy houses. They now contain restaurants, boutiques and galleries.

Copper Queen Hotel ● *Howell Avenue near Brewery Gulch.* This opulent mix of Mediterranean and Spanish colonial architecture was one of the grandest hotels in the Southwest when it was built at the turn of the century. "Black Jack" Pershing and Teddy Roosevelt tested its beds and many a wealthy miner came here to sleep off a night in Brewery Gulch around the corner. Even if you aren't staying here, stroll the lofty lobby and visit the old-fashioned saloon with its requisite nude portrait and elaborate bar, then lounge with a drink at an umbrella table on a patio elevated over Howell Avenue.

Muheim Heritage House ● *207B Youngblood Hill (a mile north of downtown); 432-7071 or 432-4461. Friday-Monday 1 to 4.* This elegant 1902 home above Bisbee is on the National Register of Historic Places. Tours through its furnished rooms are conducted by the Bisbee Arts and Humanities Council.

WHERE TO DINE

Brewery Steakhouse ● ΔΔΔ $$

Brewery Gulch (Howell Avenue), Bisbee; (602) 432-3457. American, dinners $7.50 to $16.50; full bar. Lunch Monday-Friday 11:30 to 2:30, dinner nightly 5 to 9. No credit cards. Oldstyle steakhouse in the basement of the historic Muheim Block brewery building. Menu features steaks, ribs, chicken and fresh fish of the day.

Copper Queen Restaurant ● ΔΔΔ $$

In the Copper Queen Hotel, 11 Howell Avenue (Brewery Gulch), Bisbee; (602) 432-2216. American-Continental, dinners $8 to $17, full bar service. Monday-Thursday 7 a.m. to 9 p.m, Friday-Saturday 7 a.m. to 10 p.m.; reservations accepted. MC/VISA, AMEX. Mixed menu with American and Continental fare, tilted toward Italian; veal, prime rib and lamb specialties; large wine list. Victorian decor with Tiffany-style lamps.

The Wine Gallery Bistro ● ΔΔΔ $$

Four Main Street, Bisbee; (602) 432-3447. American-Northern Italian, dinners $8 to $13, wine and beer. Monday-Saturday 11:30 to 8:30. Major credit cards. Lively "gourmet bistro" with period decor, in a weathered brick building. Innovative entrees such as salmon tarragon, sausage creole and tequila shrimp; unusual pastas and soups.

WHERE TO SLEEP

Copper Queen Hotel ● ΔΔΔ $$$

11 Howell Avenue (P.O. Drawer CQ), Bisbee, AZ 85603; (602) 432-2216 or (800) 247-5829 (Arizona only). Doubles and singles $45 to $70; special package rates. MC/VISA. Restoration is bringing this old hotel back to its former glory. Many of the rooms—all with private baths—have period furnishings. Attractive turn-of-the-century dining room (listed above).

Jonquil Motel ● Δ $ ∅

317 Tombstone Canyon (downtown), Bisbee, AZ 85603; (602) 432-7371. Doubles $26.50 to $28.50, singles $22.50. MC/VISA. TV, free coffee in office.

BED & BREAKFAST INNS

The Bisbee Inn ● *45 OK St. (P.O. Box 1855), Bisbee, AZ 85603; (602) 432-5131. Doubles $34 to $39, singles $29 including all-you-can-eat breakfast. MC/VISA.* Housed in a restored 1917 hotel; period furnishings and an elegant breakfast dining room; share baths. A non-smoking establishment.

The Greenway House ● *401 Cole Ave. (off Bisbee Road, south of town), Bisbee, AZ 85603; (602) 432-7170. Doubles and singles $75 to $125, including Continental breakfast. MC/VISA, AMEX.* Nicely restored 1906 Craftsman-style home; rooms furnished with antiques. Private baths. All rooms have kitchenettes and refrigerators stocked with drinks and breakfast fixings. Robes, flowers, candy, complimentary wine and other amenities. All are non-smoking rooms.

The Inn at Castle Rock ● *112 Tombstone Canyon Rd. (near downtown), P.O. Box 1161, Bisbee, AZ 85603; (602) 432-7195. Doubles $45 to $50, includes fruit-and-cereal breakfast. MC/VISA.* A restored 1895 miners' boarding house with Victorian and early American furnishings. Private baths, free wine, large garden. Smoking permitted.

Park Place Bed & Breakfast ● *200 E. Vista (south of downtown, off Ruppe), Bisbee, AZ 85603; (602) 458-4388 or (602) 432-3054. Doubles $50 to $70, full breakfast. MC/VISA.* A two-story 1920s Mediterranean-style home in nearby Warren. Private baths; large bedrooms with balconies or terraces. Library and sun room. Smoking outside only.

WHERE TO CAMP

Queen Mine RV Park ● *One Dart Ave. (above Queen Mine), P.O. Box 488, Bisbee, AZ 85603; (602) 432-5006. RV sites, full hookups $12, no hookups $9. Reservations accepted; MC/VISA.* Graveled sites on a hill with impressive views of the city on one side and Lavender Pit Mine on the other. Flush potties, showers, coin laundry, dump station.

From Bisbee, we recommend that you drop south to visit the affable little Mexican border town of Naco, which we describe in more detail under "Exploring South of the Border" in the previous chapter. Then return to Bisbee, pick up highway 80 and follow it east to another copper town.

Douglas

Elevation: 3990 feet   Population: 14,135

Douglas does not offer the dramatic canyon setting of Bisbee; it's more of a working town than a tourist stop. It enjoys modest success as a manufacturing center, and ranches and farms dot the surrounding Sulphur Springs Valley.

Douglas began life in 1901 when a large smelter was built here by the Phelps Dodge Corporation to process copper from company mines in Mexico. It was named for company boss James Douglas. The Mexican revolution nearly disrupted the work-a-day life in Douglas when Pancho Villa and Mexican federal troops clashed just across the border in Agua Prieta in 1915.

In recent years, as copper prices fell, civic leaders sought a way to keep Douglas afloat. Cheap labor across the border provided the solution. By the time the giant Phelps Dodge smelter belched its last puff of smoke in 1987, Douglas and Agua Prieta had about 40 manufacturing plants going. They use a "twin plant" concept, in which Mexican nationals assemble American products in factories on both sides of the border. They work for about 68 cents and hour. While Douglas gained only about one percent population in the last decade, its Mexican neighbor boomed from 18,000 to 70,000.

Coronado National Forest operates a Douglas Ranger District office at Highway 80 and Leslie Canyon Road, north of town; (602) 364-3468. You can buy a map for $2 and get free camping and hiking guides to surrounding forest lands. It's open weekdays from 8 to 5.

Life in Douglas is closely allied with Agua Prieta. The **Douglas Chamber of Commerce** tourist maps and brochures tell you what to see on both sides of the border. The office is at 1125 Pan American Avenue, a few blocks from the boundary; it's open from 9 to 5 weekdays. There's not really a a lot to see in Douglas. The old but tidy-looking downtown is a good provisioning center, however, and Agua Prieta has the usual curio shops. Douglas does offer one grand jewel:

The Gadsden Hotel ● *G Avenue and 11th Street.* This imposing five-story structure was built in 1907 by copper barons to provide suitable lodgings for visiting dignitaries. It was rebuilt in 1928 after a fire, and has undergone recent restoration. Particularly impressive is the atrium lobby with a grand curving Italian marble staircase. The ceiling, held up by rose marble columns with ornate gold-leaf capitals, contains barrel-arched stained glass skylights. A genuine Tiffany stained glass mural stretches 42 feet across the mezzanine.

Arizona cattle brands are burned into the walls of its oldstyle saloon. Not surprisingly, the Grand old Gadsden is a national historic monument.

Douglas Wildlife Park ● *Plantation Road, 1.5 miles north of Highway 80 (northwest of Douglas); (602) 364-2515. Open daily 10 to 5; adults $2.25, kids 3 to 12, 75 cents.* This small zoo adjacent to a pet shop has a few big cats, deer, monkeys, llamas and those funny-looking pot-bellied Vietnamese pigs. There's also a kids' petting zoo.

ANNUAL EVENTS

Two Flags International Arts Festival, third weekend of January; **Gun Show,** second weekend of February; **Great American Bed Race,** first weekend of June; **Douglas Fiestas Celebration,** marking Mexico's independence, second weekend of September; **Cochise County Fair,** third week of September.

WHERE TO RECLINE & DINE

The Gadsden Hotel ● ΔΔΔ $$

1046 G Ave. (11th Street), Douglas, AZ 85607; (602) 364-4481. Doubles $26 to $85, singles $24 to $80. Major credit cards. Refurbished rooms in grand old hotel (described above) with lobby lounge, restaurant, coffee shop and oldstyle saloon. TV, VCR, rental movies, phones; some suites, apartments and kitchenettes. **El Conquistador Dining Room** serves from 5:30 to 9 Sunday-Wednesday and 5:30 to 10 Thursday-Saturday; adjacent coffee shop serves breakfast and lunch. American-Mexican menu, dinners $7 to $25. Handsome Spanish-style dining room with outdoor terrace; full bar service.

Motel 6 ● ΔΔ $$ ∅

111 16th St. (Highway 80), Douglas, AZ 85607; (602) 364-2457. Doubles $28, singles $22. MC/VISA, AMEX, DC. TV movies, phones, pool.

WHERE TO CAMP

Saddle Gap RV Park ● *Highway 80 at Washington Avenue (Route 1, Box 241), Douglas, AZ 85607. RV sites, full hookups $10. Reservations accepted; major credit cards.* Flush potties; showers and laundry under construction at press time; Propane, dump station. Large gravel sites with picnic tables; TV hookups.

Douglas Golf and Social Club ● *Off Leslie Canyon Road, north from U.S. 80 (P.O. Box 1220) Douglas, AZ 85608; (602) 364-3722. RV sites, full hookups $10, golf $6, golf carts $9. Reservations accepted; MC/VISA.* An unusual combination of RV park and golf course with paved sites, flush potties, showers, laundry and pool. Golf clubhouse, nine-hole course with double tee markers.

GUEST RANCH

Price Canyon Ranch ● *P.O. Box 1065 (42 miles northeast on U.S. 80), Douglas, AZ 85607; (602) 558-2383. Doubles $150 per day including all meals. No credit cards; personal checks accepted.* Daily riding, hiking, rockhounding, birdwatching. Rowing and fishing in catfish pond. Lounge with TV, books and games. A century-old working cattle ranch where guests can help with the chores or relax. Also an apartment with kitchen, and RV hookups.

TO CHIRICAHUA, BOWIE & WILLCOX

Highway 666 takes you north from Douglas into the rolling Sulphur Springs Valley, flanked by mountainous islands of Coronado National Forest. You pass from ranching country into the high desert.

If you want to brave 21 miles of dusty and often bumpy road, you can turn east onto Rucker Canyon Road (about 21 miles north of Douglas) and explore **Camp Rucker** in the foothills of the Chiricahua Mountains. It's a little-known late 18th century army post with several remarkably intact buildings.

At the junction of Highway 666 and 181, you can visit two attractions— one in each direction. Each was a haven for the Chiricahua Apaches, among the last of the American Indians to resist intrusion by outsiders (see box).

Cochise Stronghold • *In the Dragoon Mountains west of Highway 666, c/o Douglas Ranger District, Route 1, Box 228-R, Douglas, AZ 85607; (602) 364-3468. RV and tent camping $5; picnic tables and barbecues, water (shut off in winter), pit toilets.* These rocky upcroppings in the Dragoon Mountain foothills served as Cochise's fortress during his 11-year battle the U.S. Army and with settlers in the valley below.

It's now a U.S. Forest Service recreation area with a self-guided nature trail and hiking trails into the surrounding mountains. To reach it, follow Highway 666 to a turnoff just north of the planned community of Sunsites. The road is dirt and sometimes bumpy but navigable by the family sedan.

Leaving Cochise Stronghold, retrace your route briefly on U.S. 666, cross Sulphur Springs Valley, then take State Highway 181 to another Apache hideout.

Chiricahua National Monument • *Dos Cabezas Route, Box 6500, Willcox, AZ 85643; (602) 824-3560. Admission $3 per family, $1 per hiker or biker. Camping $6 per night; shaded spots with barbecues and picnic tables, water and flush potties. Visitor center open daily 8 to 5.* This pocket-sized preserve is one of the little jewels of the national park system. Covering only 12,000 acres, it shelters some incredibly complex rock formations and five of the seven North American life zones.

Wind and rain have eroded a 25-million-year-old volcanic rhyolite deposit into fantastic shapes. Wander with your eyes and your camera and take your pick of descriptions: remnants of Greco-Roman temples, crowds of Easter Island statues, colonnades. Some formations, shrouded in trees, suggest jungle-clad Mayan ruins. The Apaches called this the "Land of standing-up rocks," which may be the best description of all. Some are precariously balanced, as if ready to fall at the slightest breath. But they have held that pose for tens of thousands of years.

A steeply winding eight-mile drive takes you up through Bonita Canyon—and through those five climate zones—to Massai Point at the crest of the Chiricahua Mountains. From here, you can take in a grand expanse of the Chiricahuan Desert sweeping southeast into Mexico and the Sonoran Desert to the west.

The best way to see the park is afoot. Hiking trails lead deep into the rock formations and up to vista points. A free shuttle leaves the visitor's center at 8:30 each morning to take hikers up to Massai Point. From there, you can follow a complex of trails, leisurely working your way back to the center. More than 20 miles of trails wind through the park.

—Arizona Department of Archives photo

The last warrior Apaches (from left): Yanozha, Geromino's son Chappo, Yanozha's half-brother Fun and Geromino. Photo taken by C.S. Fly just before their surrender.

Ranger hikes and talks at the amphitheater near the campground are scheduled periodically. Exhibits at the visitor center museum cover the area's flora, fauna and geology. Some fine Chiricahua Apache artifacts are on display, including buckskin leggings, a pitch basket, war club and arrows.

These rocky ramparts were the refuge of the Chiricahuas during the 25-year war with the U.S. Army. Only when Geronimo reluctantly surrendered in 1886 did settlement begin in earnest. One of the original homesteads, Faraway Ranch, is still intact, sitting in a pretty wooded glen of Bonita Canyon, near the park entrance. It was established in 1887 by a Swedish immigrant couple, Neil and Emma Erickson. A second generation turned it into a guest ranch in the 1920s. It remained in the family until it was purchased by the park service in 1979.

Tours through the ranch house, furnished in a rustic 1920s style, are conducted at 2 and 4 p.m., daily in spring and summer, and weekends only the rest of the year. At other times, you can can view ranch historical exhibits in a nearby outbuilding and prowl the grounds of the old homestead. The cabin of another pioneer family—the Staffords—is just above the ranch; it's one of the oldest log structures in Arizona.

From Chiricahua National Monument, turn north onto State Highway 186 at its junction with 181 and head for Willcox. But before getting back into cowboy country, you have one more date with Indian history. Nine miles from the junction, a dirt road takes you to one of the most remote preserves in the national park system.

THE LAST WARRIOR APACHES

The Chiricahua Apaches were a fierce semi-nomadic warrior clan, pillaging, raiding and resisting white intrusion. "In all the wars for the North American continent, the European invader encountered no more formidable adversary than the Apache warrior," wrote Robert M. Utley in *A Clash of Cultures.*

From the ranks of these ferocious people emerged two leaders whose names would be known to every American school child—and every Hollywood script writer. Cochise was chief of a band of Chiricahuas that hunted, gathered and raided in the rough, thorny high desert below the mountains that now bear their tribal name. Geronimo, although equally famous, was not a Chiricahua by birth and never wore the mantle of chief.

The Chiricahuas had been battling Spanish intruders since the 1700s, but it was white settlement a century later that pushed Cochise and his followers to their limits. Initially, he was friendly with the Americans. He even allowed the Butterfield Overland Mail Company to build a way station in 1858 in Apache Pass. This low saddle in the Chiricahua Mountains, with a year-around spring, was a critical link to east-west migration.

In 1861, Cochise came upon an army patrol camped at the pass. The unit's leader, young Lt. George N. Bascom, accused the chief of stealing livestock and abducting the stepson of a nearby rancher. The chief denied the charges but Bascom ordered his arrest. In a scene right out of a movie script, Cochise slit the wall of Bascom's tent with his knife and escaped.

The incident evolved into a bloody conflict that didn't end until 1872. Then, with assurances that his people could remain in the Apache Pass area, Cochise signed a peace treaty.

"Hereafter, the white man and the Indian are to drink of the same water, eat of the same bread, and be at peace," he said.

Cochise died less than two years later, still at peace with the whites. But peace was short-lived. The government wanted all Apaches moved the San Carlos reservation to the north. In 1876, a brave named Pionsenay got drunk and killed a whiskey seller. That gave officials an excuse to declare all Chiricahuas as renegades and order them to San Carlos.

Some went in peace but others escaped into Mexico. There, they joined with the Nednhi Chiricahuas and resumed raiding white settlements. Their chief was a man named Juh, but the Indians began rallying around a scowling, fierce Nednhi warrior named Geronimo, already admired for his terrorist raids in Mexico.

Juh and Geronimo raided settlements and clashed with the army for four years. Then, seeing that their fight was futile, they agreed to surrender and move their band to San Carlos. But it was a hot, miserable, disease-ridden place. Corrupt agents kept rations intended for the Indians and unrest grew. Geronimo and Juh fled the reservation in 1881 with about 70 followers. They took refuge in Mexico's Sierra Madre range and the war resumed.

Two years later, Geronimo agreed to return to the reservation, but he bolted again, in 1885. After more bloody skirmishes, he yielded to unconditional surrender in September of 1886. He and his entire band were loaded onto a train and shipped to Florida. Even those who had remained peacefully on the reservation and Apache scouts who had served with the army where shipped east. Treated like prisoners instead of reservation Indians, the men and women were separated and sent to different camps.

Generals O.O. Howard and George Crook, who had fought the Apaches, now pleaded with authorities to re-unite them with their families. It was finally done after a year's separation. Then in 1894, the tribe was moved to Oklahoma, where they remain today.

Geronimo—the last warrior Apache—died there on February 17, 1909.

Chiricahua National Monument's wonderland of rocks; this formation is called Organ Pipe.

Fort Bowie National Historic Site ● *P.O. Box 158, Bowie, AZ 85605; (602) 847-2500. Visitor center open 8 to 4:30; free.* It requires an eight-mile drive on a dirt road, then a 1.5 mile hike to reach what's left of one of the West's most vital army posts. We think it's worth it.

Fort Bowie was built in 1862 to protect the vital Apache Pass during the army's war with the Chiricahuas (see box). Patrols were launched from here to pursue the elusive Cochise and later Geronimo. When Geronimo surrendered, he and his band were brought to Bowie, then shipped in exile to Florida. Peace finally settled onto this lonely outpost. In fact, things were so peaceful that it was abandoned in 1894.

All that remains now are weathered ridges of adobe and stone walls—and a lot of history. The hike to the fort is a pleasant one—from a parking area up a gentle, winding incline to a remote high desert valley. Along the way, you pass the ruins of the old Butterfield stage stop, the fort cemetery and Apache Springs, still seeping water from the rough mountainside.

Once at the fort, you can chat with the ranger on duty and wander among the ruins, reading signs that describe the spartan life at a frontier army post. Books and pamphlets concerning the fort and the Apache wars are on sale in the small visitor kiosk.

You have two choices for continuing on to Willcox, the last stop in this circle tour of Cochise County. Either retrace your dusty route to Highway 186 and head northwest, or continue 12 miles north on the Fort Bowie road until it intersects with Interstate 10. Both routes are equally dusty; the first one is shorter.

Willcox

Elevation: 4,167 feet   **Population: 3,300**

Willcox began life in 1880 as a construction supply camp for the Southern Pacific Railroad, then it evolved into a small cowtown. It still is a small cowtown, although it has become a major cattle shipping center, as well as a stopover for travelers on busy I-10.

Townspeople like to brag about their native son, Rex Allen, a real cowboy who became a Hollywood cowboy. They've opened a museum to their sequinned hero, who lives in Sonoita, southeast of Tucson. The downtown area retains an Old West look with false front stores and narrow brick and masonry buildings.

The **Chamber of Commerce** shares a modern structure with the Museum of the Southwest, on a frontage road beside I-10. Take the Rex Allen Drive off-ramp, cross to the north side and travel northeast alongside the freeway. It's open Monday-Saturday from 8 to 5 and Sunday from 1 to 5. You can pick up area maps and brochures, including a walking map identifying century-old structures in the Willcox Historic District.

Stout's Cider Mill, adjacent to the museum, is your kind of place if you love the cinnamon aroma of fresh-baked apple pies. You can buy them by the slice or by the pie, along with fresh squeezed cider, a wonderful applesauce and other things applish. The smell will draw you in and the sight of all those goodies will have you reaching for you wallet or purse. It's open daily from 9 to 6.

Museum of the Southwest ● *1500 N. Circle I Rd., Willcox, AZ 85643; (602) 384-2272. Monday-Saturday 9 to 5, Sunday 1 to 5; free.* Exhibits discuss both the early Indian and cowboy life in this corner of Cochise County. The museum offers a fine display of Indian artifacts, graphics on Apache migration patterns and details of the Cochise-Apache Pass incident that started the 25-year Chiricahua war. A wall graphic quoting Cochise is particularly memorable:

How was it, when I was young, I walked all over this country, east and west and saw no other people other than the Apaches. After many summers, I walked again and found another race of people had come to take it. How is it?

A "Cowboy Hall of Fame" displays portraits of prominent local cattlemen. Other exhibits include gems and minerals, army regalia and weapons, an old buggy and a horse-drawn sleigh. Overall, it's a nicely-done museum.

Rex Allen Arizona Cowboy Museum ● *Railroad Avenue at Malley Street (P.O. Box 995), Willcox, AZ 85644; (602) 384-4583. Monday-Saturday 10 to 4; adults $3, families $5.* They call him the "Arizona Cowboy," and he was that before he became a movie, TV and rodeo star. Rex Allen was born on a homestead ranch near Willcox. When he was 11, his father bought him a Sears and Roebuck mail-order guitar, and the rest is a press agent's dream. If you're too young to remember his many Republic Pictures horse operas, you surely recall his fine resonant voice as narrator of nature films by Disney and other producers.

The Rex Allen Museum opened in late 1989 in a storefront in the Willcox Historic District. Exhibits trace his rise to stardom, with movie posters, some of his gaudy sequinned boots and cowboy clothes, sheet music and even a badly-done oil painting done by Rex. Other displays trace the settling of the west by Spanish, Anglo and black cowboys.

The next-door Rex Allen Theater, sporting an old-fashioned marquee, shows Western films—including some of Rex's, of course. It's also used for live entertainment.

*Rex Allen's yesterdays are
preserved in a new Willcox museum.*

WHERE TO DINE

Peking Express ● △△△ $$
*130 E. Maley (Railroad Avenue), Willcox; (602) 384-4400. Chinese; din-
ners $8 to $13; wine and beer. Daily 11 to 9; MC/VISA.* Housed in a bright
red vintage railroad car with a cheerful interior of red and gold Chinese
trim. The large menu features Szechuan and Mandarin cuisine as well as
some American dishes.

Robin's Nest Restaurant ● △△ $$
*622 N. Haskell (I-10 exit 340, then a mile east), Willcox, (602) 384-3844.
American-Mexican; dinners $5 to $13; full bar service. Daily 11 to 9.* Popular
local place with Western decor; steaks, chops and chicken, plus Mexican
entrees. Live country-Western music in adjoining bar on Friday and Saturday nights.

WHERE TO SLEEP

Best Western Plaza Inn ● △△△ $$$ ∅
*1100 W. Rex Allen Dr. (I-10 exit 340), Willcox, AZ 85644; (602) 384-3556
or (800) 528-1234. Doubles and singles $45 to $80. Major credit cards.* TV
movies, radios, phones, some refrigerators, some whirlpool tubs; pool, spa,
coin laundry. **Restaurant** serves from 6 a.m. to 10 p.m., American, dinners
$6 to $13, non-smoking areas, full bar service.

Comfort Inn ● △△ $$ ∅
*724 N. Bisbee Ave. (I-10 exit 340), Willcox, AZ 85644; (602) 384-4222
(800) 221-2222. Doubles $44 to $46, singles $35. Major credit cards.* TV
movies, phones, pool.

Motel 6 ● △△ $$ ∅
*921 N. Bisbee Ave. (I-10 exit 340, then southeast two blocks), Willcox, AZ
85644; (602) 384-2201. Doubles $32 to $40, singles $25 to $32. Major credit
cards.* TV movies, room phones, pool.

WHERE TO CAMP

Willcox KOA ● *700 N. Virginia Ave. (I-10 exit 340, then half mile northwest on Fort Grant Road), Willcox, AZ 85644; (602) 384-3212. RV sites, full hookups $14.75, no hookups $11.* Flush potties, showers, coin laundry, groceries, Propane, dump station, kids playground, pool.

GUEST RANCH

Grapevine Canyon Ranch ● *Highland Road (P.O. Box 302), Pearce, AZ 85625. Doubles $70 to $90 including all meals. MC/VISA, DISC.* A working cattle ranch with a swimming pool; cookouts, overnight pack trips. Pearce is just south of Sunsites, off Highway 66.

Heading back toward Tucson on I-10, we encounter an excellent Native American archaeological museum, 22 miles west of Willcox.

The Amerind Foundation Museum ● *I-10 exit 318, then southeast one mile, Dragoon, AZ 85609; (602) 586-3666. Daily 10 to 4 September to May, shorter hours in summer; adults $2, seniors and kids 12 to 18, $1.* This fine museum, housed in Spanish Colonial buildings set into a rocky canyon, is a treasure trove of early American Indian lore. Exhibits focus on Southwestern and Mexican archaeology, featuring pottery, basketry, projectile points and other implements unearthed in various digs.

Other displays center on Northwest and Arctic bands and the highly-developed Indian cultures of Mexico, Central and South America. More than 25,000 objects covering 10,000 years of Native American cultures are in the collection. Paintings and sculptures of past and contemporary Native American artists are exhibited in an adjacent gallery.

The "Amerind" (for American Indian) foundation was established in 1937 by amateur archaeologist William Fulton, who was intrigued by native cultures. The facility was opened to the public in 1986. A picnic area is on the grounds.

Chapter 12

THE MID-EAST

*I love to get high on a promontory and gaze for hours out
over a vast open desert reach, lonely and grand, with its far-
flung distances and its colors. I love the great pine and spruce
forests, with their spicy tang and dreamy peace.*

—Zane Grey

MIDEASTERN ARIZONA is a sampler of the rest of the state:
high desert, piney mountains, sculpted badlands, a large Indian reservation and craggy canyons—everything but a slice of
the Sonoran Desert. Climate varies from the dry, hot Gila River
Valley around Safford to cold and snowy winters of Show Low and the
White Mountains.

With few major tourist attractions, it is one of the state's least-visited
areas by outsiders. However, it's popular with sun belt Arizonans who seek
relief from summer heat while enjoying the trout streams, campgrounds and
hiking trails of Coronado, Tonto and Apache-Sitgreaves national forests.

Having finished prowling southeastern Arizona, we'll begin in the south
and work our way northward toward the area's best-known attraction,
Petrified Forest National Park.

Safford

Elevation: 2,920 feet   **Population: 7,710**

The seat of Graham County, Safford is the centerpiece of a broad agricultural valley between the Pinaleno Mountains to the southeast and the Gila
Mountains to the northwest. Sheltered from rainfall and sitting below 3,000
feet, it has a dry climate more akin to the desert than the mountains surrounding it. Hot summers provide the proper environment for cotton, one of
the area's major crops.

Although not a tourist town, Safford is a handy provisioning center and a
stepping-off point for outdoor recreation in the Coronado National Forest

that encloses the Pinaleno range. The town serves a trade area of 50,000 people, extending from mideastern Arizona into midwestern New Mexico. Modern shopping centers rim Safford, while the downtown area is country old-fashion. With its oldstyle wood frame and brick buildings and surrounding agricultural fields, it has rather a Midwestern look.

The **Safford-Graham County Chamber of Commerce,** sits in a brick structure beside a small park on Highway 70 (1111 Thatcher Boulevard), just west of the 70-66 junction. It's open Monday-Saturday from 9 to 5; (602) 428-2511.

THINGS TO KNOW BEFORE YOU GO

Best time to go • The high deserts and higher mountains of eastern Arizona are primarily summer havens. Show Low and Pinetop in the White Mountains are popular retreats for Valley of the Sun folks seeking heat relief.

Climate • Warm to hot summers; cool to cold winters. **Safford:** July average—high 95 to 100; low 65 to 70. January average—high 60 to 65; low 25 to 30. Rainfall—8 inches; snowfall—1 inch. **Show Low:** July average—high 85 to 90; low 55 to 60. January average—high 40 to 45; low 17 to 20. Rainfall—21 inches; snowfall—38 inches. **Globe-Miami:** July average—high 95 to 100; low 70 to 75; January average—high 55 to 60; low 30 to 35. Rainfall—18 inches; snowfall 4 inches. **Holbrook:** July average—high 95 to 100; low 60 to 65. January average—high 45 to 50; low 15 to 20. Rainfall 7 inches; snowfall 5 inches.

Useful contacts

Greater Globe-Miami Chamber of Commerce, P.O. Box 2539, Globe, AZ 85502; (602) 425-4495 or (800) 448-8983.

Greenlee County Chamber of Commerce, P.O. Box 1237, Clifton, AZ 85533; (602) 865-3313.

Holbrook-Petrified Forest Chamber of Commerce, 100 E. Arizona St., Holbrook, AZ 86025; (602) 524-6558.

Payson Chamber of Commerce, P.O. Box 1380, Payson, AZ 85547; (602) 474-1515.

Safford-Graham County Chamber of Commerce, 1111 Thatcher Blvd., Safford, AZ 85546; (602) 428-2511.

Show Low Chamber of Commerce, P.O. Box 1080, Show Low, AZ 85901; (602) 537-2326.

Apache-Sitgreaves National Forest, P.O. Box 640, Springerville, AZ 85938; (602) 333-4301.

Petrified Forest National Park, c/o Painted Desert Visitor Center, Petrified Forest, AZ 86028.

San Carlos Apache Recreation and Wildlife Department, P.O. Box 97, San Carlos, AZ 85550.

White Mountain Apache Enterprises, P.O. Box 220, Whiteriver, AZ 85941; (602) 338-4385 or 338-4386.

Area radio stations

KGRX-FM, 100.3, Phoenix-Globe—New wave, light rock & jazz.

KMOG-AM, 1420, Payson—Country and Western

KNNB-FM, 88.1, Whiteriver (Apache station)—Country, pop.

KRFM-FM, 96.5, Show Low-Holbrook—Rock.

KVSL-AM, 1450, Show Low-Springerville—Country.

KXKQ-FM, 94.1, Safford—Country rock

AREA ATTRACTIONS

Mount Graham • *In the Pinaleno range, Coronado National Forest.* At 10,720 feet, Mount Graham is one of Arizona's highest peaks. It's the centerpiece of an alpine recreation area popular with hikers and campers; fisherpersons angle for trout in Riggs Lake. Dramatic Mount Graham Drive—paved until you hit the heights—takes you through five climate zones to the 10,000 foot level. It's known locally as the Swift Trail. You'll pass several national forest campgrounds along the route. Hiking map and such are available at the **district ranger office** in the Safford post office building on Thatcher Boulevard, just west of the Highway 666 junction; (602) 428-4150.

Eastern Arizona Museum • *Highway 70 at Main Street in Pima, seven miles northwest of Safford on Highway 70; (602) 485-2288. Wednesday-Friday 2 to 4 and Saturday 1 to 5.* This small museum of pioneer and Indian artifacts is housed in an old turn-of-the-century masonry building.

Graham County Historical Society Museum • *Second floor of the library, 808 Eighth Ave.; (602) 428-1531. Monday-Tuesday 1 to 4; free.* It offers a limited exhibit of pioneer and Indian relics and photos of Graham County.

Museum of Anthropology • *On the campus of Eastern Arizona College, 400 College Ave., Thatcher, northwest of Safford on Highway 70; (602) 428-1133, ext. 310. Open weekdays during the school year, 9 to 4; free.* Anthropology-oriented displays feature area Indian artifacts such as projectile points, pottery and jewelry, plus a hands-on area where kids can try chipping arrowheads and making a fire with rubbing-sticks.

Museum of Discovery • *Proposed at Mt. Graham International Observatory; c/o Mt. Graham International Science and Culture Foundation, 1111 Thatcher Blvd., Safford, AZ 85546; (602) 428-2511.* Scheduled for completion in 1992, a new observatory on Mount Graham will house the world's largest binocular telescope. The museum, planned in conjunction with the observatory, will feature exhibits on both modern and ancient astronomy and cosmology. Check with the chamber to see it it has been opened.

Roper Lake State Park • *Four miles south of Safford off Highway 666; (602) 428-6760. Day use $3, camping with hookups $6.* The state park encompasses two small reservoirs. Roper Lake offers a campground, picnic area, boat launch, swimming beach, shower and flush potties, a dump station and nature trails. Dankworth Lake is a day-use area with fishing and nature trails.

Aravaipa Canyon • *30 miles west of Safford.* A year-around creek, unusual in a desert climate, weaves through the bottom of rock-ribbed Aravaipa Canyon. Wilderness hikers are drawn to this area, particularly in the spring and fall. It's reached by the 24-mile dirt Klondyke Road, off Highway 70, about 15 miles north of Safford. Primitive campsites are available in this wooded riparian oasis. All hiking and camping requires a permit from the **Bureau of Land Management** office at 425 E. Fourth St., Safford; (602) 428-4040.

WHERE TO DINE & RECLINE

El Charro Restaurant • △ $ ∅
628 Main St. (a block from the courthouse), Safford; (602) 428-4134. Mexican-American, dinners $4 to $7; no alcohol. Reservations accepted.

MC/VISA. Mexican fare, with a few American dishes, including chicken specialties. Old-time fiddlers entertain on Wednesday nights.

Budget Host Sandia Motel ● ∆∆ $$ ∅
520 E. Highway 70 (near downtown), Safford, AZ 85546; (602) 428-1621 or (800) 950-SAND. Doubles $36 to $42, singles $30 to $33. MC/VISA, AMEX, DC. TV movies, phones, refrigerators and microwaves in some rooms, free Continental breakfast; pool, hot tub.

Country Manor Motel ● ∆∆ $$
420 E. Highway 70 (near downtown), Safford, AZ 85546; (602) 428-2451 or (800) 321-6550 (Arizona only). Doubles $38 to $45, singles $30 to $33. Major credit cards. TV, phones, refrigerators, in-room coffee, free breakfast; pool, barbecue facilities. **Restaurant** serves 24 hours, American and Mexican, dinners $6 to $15, full bar service, country-style decor.

You have a choice of two northbound routes through mideastern Arizona from Safford. One takes you east and then north into Apache-Sitgreaves National Forest; the other goes northwest to Globe, then northeast through the large Fort Apache Indian Reservation. Both drives have scenic attributes.

If you drive east on Highway 70-666, then branch north on 666 you'll hit the small hamlet of Clifton, seat of skinny, sparsely-populated Greenlee County. Just above is Morenci, home to a huge Phelps Dodge open pit copper mine.

Clifton *is an old-fashioned mining town terraced into a brushy slope above the San Francisco River. It had its brief day of glory when copper was discovered and a town was laid out in 1872. It still retains that yesterday look, with brick and stone buildings lining Chase Creek Street (Highway 666). You can peek into the old* **town jail,** *carved into a rock cliff face. Beside it sits* **Copper Head,** *an 1880 narrow-gauge locomotive that hauled ore to the smelter.*

Morenci is a modern company town, built by the Phelps Dodge Corporation in 1969 when it saw the need to bury the original town with its copper tailing dump.

Morenci Open Pit Mine ● *Call (602) 865-4521 to arrange a free tour.* Phelps Dodge offers two-hour tours of the Morenci open pit mine—the world's second largest. This thing is so huge you could toss Bisbee's Lavender Pit inside and lose it. The guide will dazzle you with statistics as you stare down into the terraced pit at giant ore haulers with tires taller than a man. From your vantage point, they look like Tonka toys. The tour also includes the mine's crushers and concenrators.

Coronado Trail ● Clifton's first visitor was Francisco Coronado, who trekked through here in 1540. The Coronado Trail—Highway 66—follows the conquistador's route north through the mountains of Apache-Sitgreaves National Forest. It winds and twists into some of the Southwest's prettiest alpine scenery. Campgrounds and picnic areas line the winding roadway and trailheads lure hikers deeper into the wilds. For a map and camping-hiking brochures, stop in at the **district ranger office** at the west end of Clifton, or write Apache-Sitgreaves National Forest, P.O. Box 698, Clifton, AZ 85533; (602) 865-2432.

San Carlos Indian Reservation

Taking the other route from Safford, you'll climb from Graham County's farm lands into high desert and enter the 1,853,841-acre San Carlos Indian

Reservation. It was here, in the arid Gila River Valley that Geronimo and his Chiricahua followers were crowded with other Apache tribes. Twice, he bolted to resume his long guerrilla war with the U.S. Army.

A roadside monument between the hamlets of Fort Thomas and Geronimo—now outside the reservation—marks the site of Camp Thomas, the army post built to try and keep the restless Apaches in line. It describes the government's futile attempts to turn the warriors into tillers of the soil. Sadly, the town of Geronimo is completely abandoned. All that survives of the great warrior's namesake are a dead motel and general store.

The San Carlos reservation climbs into the White Mountain foothills, sharing borders with the Fort Apache reservation. San Carlos Indians run cattle in this grassy high desert and low foothills; they're sometimes called the "Cowboy Indians" because of their skills with rope and horse.

Parts of the San Carlos reservation offer hiking, camping and fishing opportunities. Some areas can be reached from the main highway; you should have a four-wheel drive to tackle any of the unpaved roads. Fees are required for camping, recreation, hunting and fishing. These are in lieu of a state fishing or hunting license, which is not needed on Arizona Indian reservations. Stop at the tribal administration office in **San Carlos** to make the necessary arrangements, or contact: San Carlos Recreation and Wildlife Department, P.O. Box 97, San Carlos, AZ 85550; (602) 475-2361.

San Carlos Lake ● *c/o Box 0, San Carlos, AZ 85550; (602) 475-2361.* This large reservoir within the reservation offers camping, picnicking and fishing. Use permits are available at the lake or from the tribal office.

Globe-Miami

Elevation: 3,544 feet   **Population: 6,265**

Set into the arid Cobre Valley just west of the San Carlos reservation, Globe is an old copper town that still retains that old copper town look. It's a quiet place with a turn-of-the-century main street, complete with an old-fashioned J.C. Penney Store.

Globe is very much into tourism; the chamber of commerce even has a toll-free number for visitor information: (800) 448-8983. It's a good base for exploring the surrounding mountains and Indian reservations and it has one of the West's finest Indian archaeological sites. Neighboring Miami has a similar oldstyle downtown, which we find to be a bit more rustic. Some of Globe's structures were "modernized" during the 30s to 50s decades, while Miami still retains an oldstyle look.

Both were early mining camps. Tailing dumps and grim-looking slag heaps tell of those busy days when eager men dug into these rough hills for their fortunes. But at least someone has a sense of humor about this brutalized landscape. They've erected three dummy camels that appear to be trudging up the barren slope of a large tailing dump between the two towns.

Globe, the seat of Gila County, started life in 1886 after prospectors found a silver strike on the Apache reservation. Their activities irritated the Indians, so the government merely carved off that chunk of the reservation and a town was laid out. It was named for a rounded silver nugget with markings resembling the continents. The silver soon ran out, but then rich copper deposits were discovered. The Depression shut down the mines, and Globe has been dozing in the sun since.

Salado Indian pueblo realistically re-created at Besh-Ba-Gowah Archaeological Park in Globe.

Miami was established in 1907 at the site of a copper strike. There are two versions for the naming of this town, which bears not the slightest resemblance to the original Miami. One is that it was named for Miami, Ohio. We prefer the second story: founder Black Jack Newman named it Camp Mima after his fiance Mima Tune. Then it was distorted into "Miami" when the town was incorporated in 1918. The Cyprus-Miami Mining Corporation is still digging copper here, but there were no tours at this writing.

Greater Globe-Miami Chamber of Commerce office is at 1360 N. Broad St. (Highway 60 just north of downtown); it's open weekdays from 8 to 5 and Saturdays from 8 to 2; it's sometimes staffed on Sundays.

THE BEST ATTRACTIONS

Besh-Ba-Gowah Archaeological Park ● *Near Globe Community center, a mile southwest of town, off Jesse Hayes Road; (602) 425-0320. Daily 9 to 5; adults $1, kids 12 and under free.* Archaeologists and craftsmen have re-created Arizona's most realistic ancient Indian dwellings at Besh-Ba-Gowah. They're so believable that you almost expect to be greeted by the ghost of an occupant—hopefully a friendly one.

Climb a rough wooden ladder and peer into a second-floor room where pottery, gourds, ears of corn and a plant fiber whisk broom are arranged as they might have been 600 years ago. A pot hangs over the firepit and a loom with a half-finished blanket stands in a corner. In another area, a cutaway shows precisely how the roof was constructed of poles, yucca fiber, reed matting and mud.

An adjacent museum offers fine graphics and implements of the Salado. An advanced hunting and gathering band, they inhabited the Gila River Valley from 1100 to 1400 A.D. They were accomplished potters and weavers; the results of their handiwork are on display.

Ironically, this rich find was nearly lost before restoration was begun. Since this huge 200-room ruin was on an exposed hilltop, only a few wall fragments remained when excavations began in the 1920s. However, it yielded one of the richest collections of artifacts in the Southwest, including more than 350 burial sites.

A scientist named Irene Vickery spent years sorting through the ruins and cataloging her finds, but after her death, the site was neglected. And— good grief!—a parking lot for the adjacent community center was paved over several of the rooms. Fortunately, Arizona State University's anthropology department became interested in 1981 and has rescued and restored this excellent find.

Gila County Historical Museum • *1330 N. Broad St. (Highway 60, north of town), Globe; (602) 425-7385. Monday-Saturday 10 to 4. Free; donations appreciated.* The museum occupies a 1914 Spanish-style bungalow that served as the Dominion Mine rescue station. Behind its garage doors (now sealed off) is parked a shiny red Seagrave fire engine. Other exhibits include a furnished turn-of-the-century miner's cabin, a tack room with saddles and other cowboy stuff, an early bedroom setting with some attractive floor-length dresses, a wet-plate camera and other relics.

THE REST

Gila County Courthouse • *100 Broad St. (Oak); now housing the Cobre Valley Center for the Arts; (602) 425-0884.* This sturdy brick, vaguely Spanish-style structure is the focal point of the downtown historic district. It contains art galleries and shops.

Historic Globe Downtown Walking Tour • *Brochure available at the Chamber of Commerce.* This hike takes you past—and identifies—the old town's turn-of-the-century buildings.

Antique shops • If you like antiques, you'll find a sizable selection of shops in Globe and next-door Miami. An *Antique Trails* brochure available at the chamber will direct you to about a dozen of them.

Old Dominion Mine • *Opposite the museum on Broad Street.* You can peer at what's left of one of the world's richest copper mines.

Historic downtown Miami • *Town Hall information desk on Keystone Avenue, open 8:30 to 12 and 1 to 5; (602) 473-4403.* You can pick up a walking map of old town Miami at the Town Hall, just off Highway 60.

ANNUAL EVENTS

Gila County Gem and Mineral Show, last weekend of January; **Historic Home and Building Tour,** and antique show, third weekend of February; **Copper Dust Stampede,** third weekend of April; **Old Time Fiddlers' Contest,** last weekend of July; **Apache Day Celebration,** third weekend of October.

WHERE TO DINE & RECLINE

Jerry's Restaurant • △△ $
699 E. Ash St. (Highway 60), Globe; (602) 425-5282. Dinners $5 to $10; no alcohol. Open 24 hours. MC/VISA, AMEX, DC. Family-style restaurant serving steaks, chops, seafood, meatloaf and other typical American fare, plus some Mexican entrees.

Budget Host El Rey Motel • △ $$
1201 Ash St. (Highways 60 and 70), Globe, AZ 85502; (602) 425-4427. Doubles $30 to $35, singles $28 to $32. TV, room phones; playground, picnic area; RV parking with no hookups.

Cloud Nine Motel ● △△ $$$ ∅
*1699 E. Ash (Highways 60 and 70), P.O. Box 1043, Globe, AZ 85502;
(602) 425-5741 or (800) 432-6655 (Arizona only). Doubles $49 to $69,
singles $40 to $69. Major credit cards.* TV, room phones, some refrigerators
and spa tubs; pool, spa.

Two regions north of Globe, tucked into alpine forests, are popular sum-
mer retreats. Payson to the northwest is reached via highways 88 and 188.
It's above Roosevelt Lake and Dam, which we visited back in Chapter 8. The
Show Low-Pinetop-Lakeside area is northeast, beyond the large Fort Apache
Indian Reservation.

Payson

Elevation: 4,930 feet   **Population: 6,500**

Payson first saw life in 1881 when prospectors found a bit of gold. But it
was only a small bit, so the town—named by the first postmaster in honor of
Senator Louis Payson to repay a political favor—grew up as a ranching cen-
ter. Author Zane Grey loved the timbered land below the Mogollan Rim and
built a hunting cabin northeast of town, where he wrote many of his books.

It's now a commercial center and recreation area for folks drawn to the
surrounding Tonto National Forest's lakes, streams, campgrounds and
hiking trails.

Payson Chamber of Commerce, at Beeline Highway (route 87) and
Main Street, is open 8 to 5 weekdays and 10 to 2 weekends; (602) 474-
4515. **Tonto National Forest** district office is half a mile east on Highway
260; open weekdays from 8 to 5. The mailing address is P.O. Box 100,
Payson, AZ 85541; (602) 474-2269.

WHERE TO SHOP

Swiss Village, a mile north on the Beeline Highway, is a themed shop-
ping complex with boutiques offering western regalia, Indian handicrafts,
home baked goodies, jewelry and antiques.

ANNUAL EVENTS

Country Music Festival, second weekend of June; **Loggers Saw-
dust Festival** with tree-felling and ax-throwing competition, last weekend
of July; **Payson Rodeo** (rivaling Prescott's claim as the world's oldest),
second weekend in August; **State Champion Old Time Fiddlers' Con-
test,** third weekend of September.

WHERE TO DINE

Country Kitchen Restaurant ● △ $ ∅
*210 E. Highway 260 (Walmart Shopping Center), Payson; (602) 474-
1332. American, dinners $2 to $10; full bar service. Daily 6 a.m. to 10 p.m.
MC/VISA.* Family restaurant serving homestyle American fare.

Heritage House Garden Tea Room ● △△ $ ∅
*202 W. Main Street, Payson; 474-5501. Lunches only, meals from $3.25 to
$5. Weekdays 11 to 3. MC/VISA.* An attractive tea room in a 1925 tree-
shaded bungalow with an outside patio; sandwiches, soups and salads.

Mario's Restaurant ● △△ $ ∅
*600 E. Highway 260 (just east of Walmart), Payson; (602) 474-5429.
Italian and American, dinners $5 to $11; full bar service. Daily 11 a.m. to 9
p.m. MC/VISA.* Specialties include homemade lasagna, pizzas, plus steaks
and ribs. Adjoining lounge with live music occasionally.

WHERE TO SLEEP

Best Western Paysonolo Lodge ● ΔΔΔ $$$ ∅
1005 S. Beeline Hwy. (downtown), Payson, AZ 85541; (602) 474-2382 or (800) 8-PAYSON in Arizona and (800) 7-PAYSON outside. Doubles and singles $45 to $95. Major credit cards. TV movies, phones, refrigerators, free breakfasts, some fireplaces; pool, spa.

Charleston Motor Inn ● ΔΔ $$ ∅
302 S. Beeline Hwy. (downtown), Payson, AZ 85541; (602) 474-2201. Doubles $42 to $49, singles $24 to $34; lower off-season rates. MC/VISA, AMEX, DC. TV movies, phones, free coffee; refrigerators, some fireplaces.

Lazy D Ranch Motel ● Δ $$
Highway 260 (four miles east), P.O. Box 547, Payson, AZ 85541; (602) 474-2442. Doubles, singles and kitchenettes $28 to $42, suites $55 to $65; lower off-season rates. MC/VISA. TV, some fireplaces.

Payson Pueblo Inn ● ΔΔΔ $$ ∅
809 E. Highway 260 (half mile east of Highway 87), Payson, AZ 85541; (602) 474-5241 or (800) 888-9828. Doubles $35 to $70, singles $33 to $70; lower prices are off-season rates. MC/VISA, AMEX, DC. New rooms with TV movies, phones, free coffee, refrigerators. Picnic areas.

Swiss Village Lodge ● ΔΔΔ $$$ ∅
801 N. Beeline Hwy., P.O. Box 399, Payson, AZ 85541; (602) 474-3241 or (800) 24-SWISS. Doubles, singles and kitchenettes $49 to $59, suites $79 to $109, lower off-season rates. MC/VISA, AMEX. TV, phones, refrigerators, free breakfast and newspapers; attractively landscaped grounds in alpine setting. **Swiss Village Inn** restaurant serves 6 a.m. to 9 p.m. (to 10 on weekends), American menu, Swiss decor, full bar service.

Trail's End Motel ● ΔΔ $$ ∅
811 S. Beeline Hwy. (downtown), Payson, AZ 85541; (602) 474-2283 or (800) 266-2283. Doubles $30 to $40, singles $22 to $30, kitchenettes $45 to $50, suites $50 to $85; lower off-season rates. MC/VISA, AMEX. TV, room phones, free coffee.

NEARBY ATTRACTIONS

Tonto Natural Bridge and Lodge ● *Ten miles north on Highway 87, P.O. Box 1600, Pine, AZ 85544; (602) 476-3440. Daily 9 to 6 April-September and 9 to 5 the rest of the year. Bridge admission $3.50, lodge rooms $55 to $85 per couple including continental breakfast (full breakfast on weekends), campsites with no hookups $9.50. MC/VISA.* Privately owned, this formation is one of the world's largest natural travertine arches, spanning a 150-foot canyon. After studying it from a viewpoint, you can scramble down a steep trail and explore the lower canyon with its travertine grottoes and traces of ancient civilizations.

You can spend the night at the restored 1927 Tonto Natural Bridge Lodge or at a primitive campground. The lodge has rooms with period furnishings, a main lobby with Western decor, a fireplace and a gift shop.

Zane Grey Cabin ● *17 miles northeast on 260, then five miles north, P.O. Box 787, Payson, AZ 85547; (602) 478-4243. Open 9 to 5 April-October and 10 to 4 November-March. Admission $2, kids under 12 free.* The West's most prolific and famous cowboy author loved this country below the Mogollon Rim, know hereabouts as the Tonto. He had a cabin built in the 1920s and returned frequently to pen such novels as *Code of the West*, *Hash Knife Outfit* and—of course—*Beneath the Tonto Rim*.

Now on the National Register of Historic Places, the lodge has been restored as a private museum. Inside, you'll find period furniture and Zane Grey memorabilia, including photos, original manuscripts and first editions of his novels.

Payson Zoo ● *Six miles east at Highway 260 and Lion Springs Road; Star Route Box 75, Payson, AZ 85541; (602) 474-5435. Daily 10 to 5; adults $3, kids $1.* Started as a training facility for movie and TV animals, this small privately-owned animal park exhibits a few big cats, monkeys, and birds. It's a mix of wild and farm animals, including regional critters such as javelinas, cougars and bobcats.

Fort Apache Indian Reservation

North of Globe, the Fort Apache Reservation—also called the White Mountain Reservation—occupies one of the most scenic alpine areas of any Indian land in America. It sprawls over 1,664,872 acres of foothills, valleys and peaks of the White Mountains. More than 30 campgrounds offer 1,000 campsites; 25 lakes and streams are stocked with trout. Three lakes—Hon-Dah, Hawley and Reservation have cabins, groceries, boat rentals and stuff. The reservation is home to **Sunrise,** probably Arizona's best ski resort. The White Mountain Reservation has been called "the largest privately-held recreation area in America."

For information on activities, facilities and the necessary use permits, contact: White Mountain Apache Enterprises, P.O. Box 220, Whiteriver, AZ 85941; (602) 338-4385 or 338-4386. As we mentioned above, a state hunting or fishing license isn't required; tribal permits serve that purpose.

Highways 60-77 heading northeast from Globe traverse the spectacular **Salt River Canyon,** an unexpected bonus on your way to the Fort Apache Indian lands. The highway ribbons dizzily down into this rugged, terraced chasm, crosses the Salt River, then winds dizzily back up the other side. The buttes, fluted ridges and peaks rival Oak Creek Canyon in grandeur. Several picnic spots along the way tempt you to spend more time admiring one of Arizona's most impressive ravine.

A side road on the canyon's northern slope leads to the tiny Apache hamlet of **Cibecue.** There's not much to see here but you can hike, camp and picnic along Cibecue Creek, with a permit available from the Apache Traders store here.

The Cibecue are a tiny band that once figured prominently in Apache history. A medicine man who taught a religion predicting expulsion of the whites was killed in 1880 when army troops tried to arrest him. The army's own Apache scouts mutinied and killed several soldiers. It was the only such revolt in the 75-year history of the Apache scout corps. The Cibecue incident sent a wave of unrest through the already restless Chiricahua Apaches of the San Carlos Reservation. It led eventually to Geronimo's departure to resume his campaign against the army.

Continuing north out of Salt River Canyon, we follow Highway 73, which dips into the heart of the Fort Apache Reservation.

Kinishba Ruins ● *Two miles off Highway 73, just west of Fort Apache.* A crumbling but still intact adobe ruin dating to 1300 can be reached by taking a dirt road two miles north of the highway. It's too fragile to be entered but you can view it from outside. This is all that remains of a huge complex that once contained 700 rooms. University of Arizona researchers excavated a rich find of pottery, jewelry and other artifacts here during the 1930s.

Continuing to the disheveled town of **Fort Apache**, we encounter what's left of a once legendary army post. Now a small Indian community of weathered homes, it bears no resemblance to the Fort Apache made famous by Hollywood. A few shabby structures of the original fort are about a mile off the highway. One houses a small museum, behind the imposing red brick Theodore Roosevelt Indian Boarding School.

Fort Apache Museum • *A mile east of town. Monday-Saturday 8 to 5 in summer, weekdays only the rest of the year.* In an ironic twist of history, a tattered log building that once housed Geronimo-pursuer General George Crook now shelters this small Indian museum. Exhibits are limited because the main museum and its treasures were destroyed by fire in 1985. It does display some nice Apache beadwork, basketry and other crafts. Graphics and photos tell the story of the Apaches of yesterday and today.

Whiteriver, sitting in a forested valley just north of Fort Apache, is the reservation's administrative and commercial center, with a shopping complex and a motel-restaurant. At the tribal office, you can get recreational information and permits.

White Mountain Apache Motel and Restaurant • △△ $$
P.O. Box 1149, Whiteriver, AZ 85941; (602) 338-4927. Doubles and singles from $40. MC/VISA. Modern rooms with two double beds, TV. **Restaurant** serves from 6 a.m. to 9 p.m., American, Mexican and Indian fare, weekday noon and evening buffets, dinners $6 to $12.

Sunrise Resort • △△△ $$$
P.O. Box 217, McNary, AZ 85930; (800) 55-HOTEL in Arizona, (800) 882-7669 in Western U.S. Doubles $50 to $110, suites $150 to $250; lower off-season rates. Ski packages with two nights lodging and two-lift tickets from $170 per couple. Lift tickets $25 all day, $19 half day and $10 for night skiing. Sunrise is a year around resort with plush lodgings, a **restaurant**, fireplace lounge, swimming pool, spa and a lake for swimming, sailing and fishing.

In winter, it becomes one of the Southwest's largest ski areas with 1,800 vertical feet and sixty trails on three mountains. Four quad lifts carry skiers to Sunrise Peak at 10,700 feet, Apache Ridge at 11,000 and Cyclone Circle ridge at 10,700. There's a separate bunny slope for beginners; other runs vary from intermediate to advanced. A cross-country ski area has ten miles of groomed trails.

In addition to the lodge, nearby Pinetop and Lakeside—just above the reservation—offer a variety of motels, cabins, resorts and restaurants.

Show Low, Pinetop & Lakeside

Show Low elevation: 6,300 feet   **Population: 5,410**

We're already in high country as we pass through the White Mountains of Apache land. Then we climb even higher—up the steep incline of the Mogollan Rim—to Pinetop and Lakeside. They're woodsy hamlets comprised mostly of pine-shaded cabins, motels, resorts and RV parks. They extend along a forested ridge between the White Mountain Apache reservation and Apache-Sitgreaves National Forest.

The **district ranger station** in Lakeside (opposite Lakeside Campground) is open weekdays from 8 to 5. Folks there can sell you a $2 map and give you information on hiking, fishing, camping, backpacking and whatever in the surrounding forests. The address is Route 3, Box 5-50, Lakeside, AZ 85929; (602) 368-5111.

Show Low, down the mountain a bit from Pinetop, is the region's commercial center. Initially, it was the hub of a ranching area. The unusual name comes from a low-ball poker expression; if you "show low"—have the lowest cards, you win. It seems that C.E. Cooley and Marion Clark had built up a 100,000-acre cattle spread in the 1870s. After six years, they decided to break up the partnership, and drew cards to see who would buy who out. Cooley drew the deuce of clubs; Clark moved on. Show Low's main drag is called Deuce of Clubs in honor of that draw.

Thousands of Arizonans have been lured to these cool summer heights and many have stayed, or they've built summer cabins. Thus, Show Low, Pinetop and Lakeside are fast-growing resort communities. The highway linking them has become a rather untidy string of lodgings, restaurants, service stations and small businesses.

The **Chamber of Commerce,** west of downtown on Deuce of Clubs (sounds silly, doesn't it?) near Eighth Avenue, has lists of motels, RV parks, restaurants and other facilities. Phone (602) 537-2326.

This region offers no specific attractions that we could find, other than recreational lures in the surrounding forests—which is quite enough for many folks.

Pinetop Adventure Tours ● *P.O. Box 76, Pinetop, AZ 85935; (602) 367-5337.* This company runs four-wheel drive trips into the surrounding Apache-Sitgreaves National Forest. Guides discuss the flora, fauna, geology and history of the area.

ANNUAL EVENTS

National Triple Crown Softball Tournament, third weekend of June; **White Mountain Square Dance Festival,** second weekend of July; **Shoot-Out in Show Low,** gunfights and skits, second weekend of October.

WHERE TO DINE

Branding Iron Steak House ● △△ $$
1261 E. Deuce of Clubs, Show Low; (602) 537-5151. American; dinners $9 to $25; full bar service. Daily, lunch 11 to 2 and dinner 5 to 9 (to 10 Friday-Saturday). MC/VISA. Western-style place with Native American artwork; specializing in prime rib, steak and seafood. Cowboy Bar adjacent.

Charlie's Steakhouse ● △△ $$ ∅
Highway 260 (near First Interstate Bank), Pinetop; (602) 367-4900. American; dinners $9 to $20; full bar service. Daily from 5 p.m. to 10 in summer, closed Mondays in winter; reservations accepted. MC/VISA. Thick Western atmosphere with trophy animals and such. Steaks, seafood, ribs, prime rib, some Cajun dishes. Adjacent sports bar and piano bar.

WHERE TO SLEEP

Best Western Maxwell House ● △△ $$
480 W. Deuce of Clubs (west end of town), P.O. Box 2437, Show Low, AZ 85901; (602) 537-1254 or (800) 528-1234. Doubles $46 to $56, singles $42 to $50; lower off-season rates. Major credit cards. TV movies, phones; pool. **Restaurant** serves 6 a.m. to 9:45 p.m., American and Mexican, dinners $5.50 to $10, non-smoking areas, full bar service.

Best Western Paint Pony Lodge ● ∆∆∆ $$$
581 Deuce of Clubs (west end of town), P.O. Box 2437, Show low, AZ 85901; (602) 537-5773 or (800) 528-1234. Doubles $60 to $70, singles $55 to $69. Major credit cards. TV, room phones, refrigerators. **Paint Pony Steakhouse** serves from 5 p.m. to 9:45 Monday-Saturday, noon to 8:45 Sunday (closed Sunday in winter), American (prime rib specials), dinners $7.50 to $26, non-smoking areas, full bar service. Nightly dancing in adjoining lounge.

Hidden Rest Resort ● ∆∆ $$
Off Highway 260, Route 3, Box 2590, Lakeside, AZ 85929; (602) 368-6336. All cabins with kitchens, $38 to $65. MC/VISA. Rustic housekeeping cabins nestled in a pine forest; porches, picnic tables; TV.

KC Motel ● ∆∆ $$ ∅
60 W. Deuce of Clubs (downtown), P.O. Box 175, Show Low, AZ 85901; (602) 537-4433. Doubles $34 to $56, singles $32 to $38; lower off-season rates. Major credit cards. New motel; large rooms with TV movies and phones.

Lake of the Woods Resort ● ∆∆ $$$
2244 White Mountain Blvd. (Highway 260), P.O. Box 777, Lakeside, AZ 85929. All kitchenettes, $60; lower off-season rates. MC/VISA. Fully-equipped housekeeping cabins on a private trout lake. **Lakewood Inn** serves from 11 a.m. to 10 p.m., mixed menu, dinners $6 to $17, rustic dining room overlooking lake, non-smoking areas, full bar service.

The Pines ● ∆∆∆ $$$$ ∅
2700 S. White Mountain Rd. (Highway 260), Show Low, AZ 85901; (602) 537-1888 or (800) BEDTIME. All condo units, doubles $68 to $108, singles $48 to $78; lower off-season rates. Major credit cards. Resort in woodsy setting; fully equipped condos with kitchens, fireplaces, spas, laundry facilities and barbecues.

Whispering Pines Resort ● ∆∆ $$$
237 White Mountain Blvd. (near Safeway Shopping Center), P.O. Box 307, Pinetop, AZ 85935; (602) 367-4386. Rustic and delux cabins, doubles and singles $52 to $85, two-bedroom units from $80; lower off-season rates. MC/VISA. Woodsy resort with spa, laundry, free athletic club privileges. Cabins have TV, fully-equipped kitchens and fireplaces

WHERE TO CAMP

Camp Town ● *1221 W. McNeil St. (half mile west from Highway 60), Show Low, AZ 85901; (602) 537-2578. RV and tent sites, $15 with or without hookups. No credit cards.* Shaded sites in piney forest, some pull-throughs; flush potties, showers, coin laundry; shuffleboard, horseshoes, golf chipping green.

Ponderos Mobile Home Park ● *Rt. 1, Box 570 (Woodland Road), Lakeside, AZ 85929; (602) 368-6989. RV sites, full hookups $12. No credit cards.* Adult park with clubhouse, pool tables, cards, potlucks and other activities. Flush potties, showers, coin laundry, Propane.

White Mountain KOA ● *Route 60, box 726 (a mile out of town), Springerville, AZ 85938; (602) 333-4632. RV and tent sites, full hookups $18, water and electric $16, no hookups $14. Reservations accepted; MC/VISA.* Pull-throughs; shaded sites. Flush potties, showers, coin laundry, convenience store, Propane, dump station; playground, petting zoo, game room, mini-golf, horseshoes.

Holbrook

Elevation: 5,080 feet   **Population: 5,890**

By the time we reach Holbrook, we've dropped down from the White Mountains into a high desert and grassland. Founded in 1882 as a railroad terminal and ranching center, Holbrook is noted mostly as the gateway to Petrified Forest National Park.

A century ago, it was better known as the shipping center for the Aztec Ranch, one of the largest cattle spreads in America. Running 60,000 head over a million acres of open range, it was nicknamed the Hashknife outfit because of its spade-shaped brand. Bad management and falling beef prices shut down the huge operation at the turn of the century.

Holbrook is an ordinary-looking community alongside the Little Colorado River, with an oldstyle, clean-swept downtown. It offers a few motels and restaurants and a lot of rock shops selling gems, thunder eggs and things petrified. Only part of the prehistoric rock trees of this area are enclosed in Petrified Forest National Park. Many are on private land, feeding a steady flow of souvenirs to gift and rock shops in and outside the park.

Holbrook is the seat of sparsely populated Navajo County. The former yellow brick 1898 courthouse now houses a museum and the **Chamber of Commerce.**

Courthouse Museum and chamber office ● *100 East Arizona St. (Navajo Street); (602) 524-6558. Monday-Saturday 8 to 5 and Sunday 10 to 4 in summer, weekdays 8 to 5 and Saturday 10 to 4 the rest of the year.* A counter in the museum serves as the chamber, where you can get the usual brochures and maps. The museum itself, while interesting, is an unprofessional clutter. Its jumbled exhibits include old photos, pioneer relics, tortoise-shell combs, a turn-of-the-century living room, and a scene recreating the card game leading to the naming of Show Low. An old-fashioned pharmacy displays such wonder drugs as Dr. Beaumont's tonic for snake bites, ticks and fleas, pneumonia, rheumatism, blood disorders, senility and fevers. Something every travel writer needs.

Historic downtown tour ● *Brochure available at the chamber.* Holbrook has a good selection of turn-of-the-century wood frame and stone buildings and this map-guide will lead you past several of them.

ANNUAL EVENTS

Sheriff's Posse Ride is the re-creation of a Pony Express run from Holbrook to Scottsdale, in January or February. You can have a letter carried and endorsed by the Pony Express by sending it to the Holbrook postmaster. It should be stamped, marked "Via Pony Express," and enclosed in another letter addressed to: Postmaster, Holbrook, AZ 86025.

Other events include **Holbrook Old West Days and Bucket of Blood Races** (named for a famous local saloon), third weekend of May; **Quilt Show and Old-Time Fiddlers' Contest,** first Saturday of August; **Navajo County Fair,** third weekend of August; **All Indian Pow Wow,** rock and gem show and art show, late August to early September.

WHERE TO DINE & RECLINE

Butterfield Stage Co. Restaurant ● △△ $$ ∅

609 Hopi Dr. (downtown), Holbrook; (602) 524-3447. American, dinners $7 to $23; full bar service. Daily 4 to 10 p.m. MC/VISA, AMEX. Steak and barbecue specialties; western decor with a stagecoach on display.

Holbrook Super 8 Motel ● ΔΔ $$ ∅
*1989 Navajo Blvd. (I-40 exit 286), Holbrook, AZ 86025; (602) 524-2871
or (800) 843-1991. Doubles $32.88 to $56.88, singles $31.88 to $44.88,
suites $41.88 to $68.88; lower off-season rates. Major credit cards.* TV,
phones, free coffee; pool. Suites have wet bars and hot tubs.
Rainbow Inn ● ΔΔ $$ ∅
*2211 E. Navajo Blvd. (I-40 exit 289), Holbrook, AZ 86025; (602) 524-
2654. Doubles $38 to $56, singles $30 to $36; lower off-season rates. Major
credit cards.* TV movies, phones, room refrigerators.
Whiting Brothers Motor Hotel ● Δ $$
*2402 E. Navajo (downtown), Holbrook, AZ 86025; (602) 524-6298.
Doubles $30, singles $24 to $30, suites $50 to $60; lower off-season rates.
Major credit cards.* TV, room phones; pool.

Petrified Forest & Painted Desert

Petrified Forest National Park ● *P.O. Box 217, Petrified Forest, AZ
86028; (602) 524-6228. Park gates open daily 7 a.m. to 8 p.m. in summer, 8
to 5 the rest of the year; visitor center hour 7 to 8 in suumer; shorter hours the
rest of the year. Fees are $5 per car or $2 per hiker or biker.* **NOTE**: Because
of the vulnerability of these petrified formations to souvenir hunters, anyone
attempting to remove material from the park will face a heavy fine and pos-
sibly a jail term.

Scientists say the odds of a tree being petrified are about a million to
one, yet thousands managed to beat the odds in this high, grassy tableland
east of Holbrook. They are scattered, like broken columns of fallen temples,
over the preserve's 93,533 acres.

The park has two entrance stations—one just off I-40, 25 miles east of
Holbrook and another off U.S. 180 southeast of town. A 27-mile scenic drive
links the two stations, so you can view the park's features without back-
tracking. Visitors actually get two attractions for the price of one. The road
from the north entrance loops through a section of the Painted Desert before
wandering south past the petrifactions. This multi-chrome desert stretches
for 300 miles across Arizona, along the northern edge of the Little Colorado
River.

The **Painted Desert Visitor Center**, just outside the north entrance,
offers a few museum exhibits and a book shop. An orientation film is shown
every half hour. An adjacent Fred Harvey complex has a service station and
large gift shop and cafeteria, open the same hours as the visitor center.
There's also a post office here. The **Rainbow Forest Museum**, inside the
south entrance station, has more extensive exhibits. Another Fred Harvey
gift shop and snack bar are adjacent.

Two more curio shops, **Petrified Forest Trading Post** and **Crystal
Forest Museum and Gift Shop,** stand just outside the south entrance.
They sell every conceivable petrified gimmick from bolo ties and bookends
to polished table tops costing up to $8,500. Both have small museums with
exhibits of petrifactions, Indian relics and fossils.

Despite an excessively gushy narration, the orientation film at the north
visitor center does an effective job of explaining the process of petrification.
It uses photos of crystal growth to demonstrate how microscopic silica crys-
tals gradually replace wood cells in buried timber.

The author, sitting like a hump on a petrified log.

Creation of these stone logs began about 225 million years ago in the late Triassic period when fallen trees were washed onto a flood plain. Mud, silt and volcanic ash covered them, cutting off oxygen and slowing their decay. Eventually, ground water saturated with silica seeped in and replaced the wood cells with crystals. Some of the results are remarkably pretty. They have a luminous gemstone quality, with rich yellow, orange, gold and purple in their crystal patterns. The wood grain is still evident in many of the logs.

From the north visitor center, you enter the park and drive past the **Painted Desert** with its soft, feminine contours of off-white, russet, beige and gray-green. What you're seeing is an erosion of Chinle Formation clay; it was this same erosion that exposed the fallen stone trees nearby.

The park drive then takes you south, with turn-outs at assorted points of interest. Fragmented walls of the **Puerco Indian Ruin** are all that remain of a pueblo occupied 600 to 800 years ago. At **Newspaper Rock**, you can view squiggles, spirals, stick-men and hand prints left by some unidentified ancients. **Agate Bridge** is a remarkable petrified log that not only stayed intact but formed a natural span across a small wash. Supposedly, a cowboy won a $10 bet in 1886 by riding his horse across it. It has since been reinforced with a concrete beam, should anyone else be so tempted.

At **Jasper Forest,** logs are scattered in the desert sand like remnants of a sloppy lumbering operation. The **Rainbow Forest Museum** offers some fine exhibits, with reconstructions of critters that roamed this area during the Triassic, and a display concerning present-day trees that may be distant relatives of the stone ones outside. The **Giant Logs Trail** behind the museum offers the park's best examples of petrified trees, so save some film for this.

Chapter 13

THE HOPI-NAVAJO CORNER

> *The only way we can save the old traditions is to recognize the forces at work in our lives. That way, we can survive and preserve a part of our mind for the old values. If you don't survive, you don't have anything.*
>
> —Albert Yava, Hopi Indian

 THE GREAT HOPI-NAVAJO reservation in northeastern Arizona encompass some of the state's most interesting terrain, from starkly beautiful canyons to netherworld sandstone spires. They also provide an opportunity to witness two proud nations in transition—working to preserve their old ways while embracing many of our new ones.

The combined reservations cover about 29,000 square miles, encompassing all of northeastern Arizona and spilling over into Utah and New Mexico. That's nearly as big as New Hampshire, Vermont, Massachusetts and Connecticut combined.

The Navajo Nation covers 25,000 square miles; it's the largest Indian reservation in America. The Hopi reservation is much smaller—about 4,000 square miles. By an unfortunate whim of the federal government, Hopi turf is entirely surrounded by the Navajo reservation. The Hopi Nation does, however, encompass some of the tribe's ancestral lands. One pueblo, Oraibi, has existed for more than 800 years. It may be oldest continually occupied settlement in America.

When you enter reservation lands, you technically leave Arizona and enter sovereign nations. You don't need a passport, of course, and both tribes welcome visitors. But they are self-governing and some of their laws differ from those outside. Alcohol is prohibited; you cannot buy a drink at any reservation establishment or a can of beer in a market. Safety belt use is required and Navajo police use radar to enforce the 55 mph speed limit—although they don't appear to be fanatics about it. As on other reservations, permits are required for hunting or fishing, and you don't need Arizona licenses. These permits are readily available through tribal offices and at several trading posts and stores; fees are modest.

Here's a point of minor confusion: Arizona does not switch to daylight saving time, and neither does the Hopi Nation, but the Navajo Nation does. Don't spend a lot of time setting your watch; just build an extra hour into your schedule.

Most guidebooks to Navajo and Hopi lands are too preoccupied with what you should or shouldn't do. The prospective traveler becomes a bit intimidated. In our wanderings through this corner of the state, we were greeted with everything from open friendliness to stoic indifference. We never experienced a shred of resentment. Contrary to overkill advise in some guidebooks, the Hopi and Navajo generally observe a live-and-let-live attitude.

So we suggest a simple rule of conduct: Just be nice. You know the difference between showing an interest in someone's way of life and regarding them as a tourist curiosity.

Hopefully, you'll come away as we did—with a warm feeling of respect—not sympathy—for these people whose culture we nearly destroyed, who are still seeking their niche in this sometimes overwhelming society that engulfed them.

THINGS TO KNOW BEFORE YOU GO

Best time to go • Summers are busy in the tourist areas; reservations at the few motels should be made **several months** in advance. Campgrounds fill early. We prefer the spring and fall, when the weather is cool but not cold. Of course, many special events occur in the summers, but Hopi ceremonial dances are held year around. Some small gift shops—particularly in the Hopi pueblos—keep regular hours only in the summer, but larger ones are open all year.

Climate • The reservations occupy a high plateau, offering warm summers and cool to cold winters. July average (from Oraibi Weather Station)—high 90 to 95; low 55 to 60. January average—high 40 to 45, low 15 to 20. Rainfall—8 inches; snowfall—7 inches.

Useful contacts

Navajo Tribe Office of Tourism, P.O. Box 663, Window Rock, AZ 86515; (602) 871-6659 or (602) 871-6436.

Office of Public Relations, The Hopi Tribe, P.O. Box 123, Kykotsmovi, AZ 86039; (602) 734-2331, ext. 360.

Area radio stations

The Navajo-Hopi nations are served by powerful **KTNN** at **AM-660** out of Window Rock. You'll get Indian news (and a chance to hear the fascinating Navajo language), Arizona and network news and plenty of "hit kickin' country music"—which must be said carefully.

As you travel, you'll pick up these stations on the reservation perimeter:

KXAZ-FM, 93.5, Page—Easy listening and new wave.

KMGN-FM, 93.9, Flagstaff—pop, light rock and country.

KAFF-FM, 92.9 Flagstaff—country.

KNAU-FM, 89.7, Flagstaff—National Public Radio.

KTLF-FM, 99.1, Gallup, N.M.—country, light rock.

KIWN-FM 92.9, Farmington, N.M.—light rock, pop, oldies.

The land may surprise you. Much of it is barren grassland, punctuated by startling scenery. Canyon de Chelly is one of the most interesting chasms we've ever seen; Monument Valley looks even more dramatic than it is in photos. After you've driven for hours, seeing nothing but an occasional Navajo farmhouse, a great redwall butte may appear on the horizon.

Don't expect quaint Indian villages. You'll see occasional log and mud Navajo hogans, and some modern ones made of lumber. However, most Navajo towns differ little from ours.

The Hopi pueblos, while intriguing, are not models of neatness. The earthy style of these ancient dwellings does not blend well with non-biodegradable objects such as car parts and tin cans. The gentle Hopi are more into spiritual things than landscaping. Look beyond the litter and realize that you are seeing people and dwellings that were here before Columbus set sail, before the Spanish began their obscene intrusions into this peaceful land.

THE WAY THEY WERE • The Hopi may have occupied this area for as long as man has wandered in the Southwest. Anthropologists say they're likely descendants of the Anasazi. The Hopi themselves feel they have occupied their mesas for a hundred generations or more.

Spanish padres tried to sell them on Christianity in the 1600s. But tensions built over the years, exploding into a violent Hopi revolt in 1680. They wiped out Spanish settlements and ripped mission buildings apart. Men were killed and women and children were captured and distributed among the Hopi villages. That brought an abrupt halt to Spanish influence in the area.

It was one of the few violent acts in the Hopi's recorded history. Wanting only to be peaceful farmers, they grudgingly retreated as Navajo raiders and later American settlers began moving in on their land.

The Navajos, as we've mentioned before, are descendants of Athabascan clans from northwestern Canada. Originally a nomadic and warlike group, they moved into the Southwest from 1300 to 1500 A.D. Navajo and Apaches are distant cousins; through the decades, each settled in opposite ends of the state.

Like the Apaches, they resisted outside intrusion, raiding white settlements and clashing with the army. They were rounded up in the 1860s and forced to make the agonizing "Long Walk" to a bleak area of New Mexico at Fort Sumner. Then, in 1868 they were given most of northeastern Arizona as a reservation—a blow to the Hopi who had occupied these lands for uncounted decades.

In 1882, the government finally granted the Hopi their own reservation—in the middle of the Navajo Nation. Border disputes between the two tribes continue to this day—fought in the courts and before Congress.

THE WAY THEY ARE • The Hopi cling to the old ways much more than the Navajos, still occupying their centuries-old pueblos. Their ritualistic dances, unchanged for centuries, are a major tourist lure in this corner of Arizona (See box.)

Their villages—some hundreds of years old—occupy three high peninsulas, simply called First, Second and Third Mesas. Tribal offices are located at Kykotsmovi on Third Mesa. The modern Hopi Cultural Center at Second

Mesa is the tourist core, with an attractive restaurant, motel, gift shop and museum.

Navajos are America's largest Indian tribe, numbering about 150,000 on the reservation, with several thousand more living elsewhere. Hopi population on the reservation is around 7,000. Navajos tend to live on their ranches and farms, while the Hopi prefer village life—commuting to the their agricultural lands.

Navajo Tribal headquarters is at Window Rock on the eastern edge of the reservation. It's a town not unlike other small communities in Arizona, although museums and crafts shops exhibit the Navajo's pride in their traditions. Other small towns are spotted about the reservation.

The decision that gave the Navajos the lion's share of this land also—by a further twist of fate—gave them most of the area's resources. Extensive coal fields, oil, natural gas and even uranium lie beneath the arid soil, and some of it is being tapped. Forests cover the Defiance Plateau around Window Rock and some of the highlands to the northwest. Navajos cash in on tourist dollars as visitors pause to shop and gas up enroute to Canyon de Chelly National Monument. Perhaps even more famous, Monument Valley in Arizona and Utah is a Navajo Tribal Park.

Shopping • Navajos have long been noted for their artistry with wool hand-woven blankets and turquoise and silver jewelry—particularly the squash-blossom necklace. The Hopi produce fine basketry, pottery, silver and detailed, brightly-colored *kachina* (or *katsina*) dolls, carefully whittled out of cottonwood. Traditional *kachinas* are regarded as spiritual messengers. However Hopi artistry, like all native crafts, has been altered by the tourist market. Don't be surprised to see a Levi-clad *kachina*, or one toting a camera.

Scores of roadside stands offer a bewildering variety of crafts, particularly Navajo silver. Prices generally are better than those in the shops, although there's a small chance that you might get something less than authentic. Poor-quality turquoise can be dyed to increase its brilliance, and silver may be not-quite-sterling. In shopping for a Navajo blanket, you certainly want to know that you're getting Navajo virgin wool, and not cotton or treated synthetic fabric.

Most of the stuff we've seen at the roadside stands seems authentic however, and the tribal councils oversee the handiwork of their craftsmen. If you're in doubt, you may want to shop at established gift centers, although you'll pay a bit more for your treasures.

Night driving • Most of the Navajo and Hopi reservations are open range and livestock exhibit a sometimes fatal disdain for motor vehicles. We prefer to drive during daylight hours.

Touring • Natural wonders and interesting towns are spread widely over this New England-sized land. So we've devised a driving route—with accompanying map—that will take you to most of them. If you have the time and inclination to learn more about this intriguing Arizona corner, a couple of comprehensive guides are available, listed in Chapter 15. An easy-to-follow map, *Visitor's Guide to the Navajo Nation,* is sold at most souvenir and curio shops for $2.50. However, it doesn't list all the Hopi villages, and the villages themselves don't always have signs, so you may have to ask and wander a bit to locate them.

NAVAJO-HOPI NATION DRIVE

THE NAVAJO NATION WEST

Page, just outside the northwestern tip of the reservation, is our starting point. That area originally was Navajo land, but the government offered an exchange for other acreage when the Glen Canyon Dam project was started.

From Page, you head south on Highway 89, entering the Navajo Nation a few miles from town. The route follows the base of the redwall Echo Cliffs, then passes through a tiny settlement called The Gap, with a stone trading post dating back to 1900. Then you hang a left onto Highway 160 and drive through a cleft in this dramatic face, passing gentle contours of a portion of the Painted Desert.

To the west of here, farther south on Highway 89, then west on Highway 64, is **Little Colorado River Gorge Navajo Tribal Park**. We mentioned this chasm in Chapter 5 as a side trip north of Flagstaff. If you haven't seen it, this mini-Grand Canyon with its sheer, fluted cliff edges is worth a look:

Traveling east on 160 toward Tuba City, you'll see signs directing you to **dinosaur tracks.** They're a short distance to the north on a bumpy road. Reptilian critters strolled along a muddy shoreline here 200 million years ago, leaving hundreds of pawprints that have hardened in the sandstone. A few locals from the nearby village of Moenave are usually on hand to help you find them. They'll obligingly pour water into the tracks to accent them for photographs. A small offering for their helpfulness would be nice. Several jewelry stands are nearby.

Business was slow when we arrived late one March afternoon, so young Morris A. Chee, Jr., had plenty of time to spend with us.

"You're only my fifth and sixth people today," he said. "In summer, we go through maybe 80 gallons of water to make the tracks show up. We have to pack it from the village up there." He gestured toward tiny Moenave, across the sparse prairie. "When I'm done here, I'm going to celebrate my twentieth birthday. Sure wish more people had come."

We took the hint and doubled his gratuity, then we gave him a ride back to his village.

Tuba City

Elevation: 4,940 feet   **Population: 5,100**

The largest community on the reservation, Tuba City was established in 1877 when Mormon farmers settled around a nearby spring. The odd name comes from a Hopi chief, T Ivi, which settlers distorted to "Tuba." Apparently not realizing they'd settled on Indian land, the Mormons tried to get title to it. Failing this, they sold out to the government in 1903.

Tuba City offers an interesting architectural mix. Many of the original buildings—including government offices— are of cut sandstone, standing alongside tree-shaded streets. Neighborhoods are a mix of ordinary bungalows, modular and mobile homes and some interesting "modern" pre fab wooden octagonal hogans. Like any typical American city, it has a couple of fast-food places. The main part of town is about a mile north of the highway.

Tuba Trading Post is worth a browse. It's an interesting hexagonal tufa block structure with a raised center floor offering a good array of Indian crafts such as blankets, basketry, pottery and silver. The perimeter is a general store offering everything from groceries to VCR movie rentals to tricycles. It's open daily from 7:30 a.m. to 8:30 p.m.

WHERE TO DINE & RECLINE

Note: no alcohol is served in reservation restaurants

Tuba City Truck Stop Cafe ● △ $

Highway 160-264 junction, Tuba City; (602) 283-4975. American and Navajo; dinners $4 to $7. Open 24 hours. No credit cards. Basic formica cafe popular with locals. It offers chicken, chops, sandwiches and the best Indian taco in Arizona (see box).

Pancho's Family Restaurant ● △△ $

Downtown, between Tuba City Motel and trading post, Tuba City; (602) 283-3302. American, Mexican and Navajo; dinners $6 to $13. Daily 6 a.m. to 9 p.m. Major credit cards. Attractive place with pottery chandeliers, Navajo rugs on the walls; American and Mexican entrees plus Navajo fry bread. **CJ's Old Fashioned Ice Cream Parlor** behind the restaurant is open weekdays from 2 to 9 p.m.

Tuba Motel ● ∆∆ $$
*Downtown, P.O. Box 247, Tuba City, AZ 86045; (602) 283-4545. Singles
and doubles $45. Major credit cards.* Modern rooms with phones, TV; gift
shop.

THE HOPI NATION

Heading south into Hopi country, Highway 264 passes through seamless
high prairie stretching to the horizons. As you begin climbing gradually
toward Third Mesa, look for a dirt road to the left (15 miles from Tuba City)
leading to **Coal Canyon.** It's a small chasm where locals dig coal for their
stoves. There's no sign, so it's easy to miss. Look for a windmill, then turn
across a cattle guard.

The Hopi occupy a dozen small villages with a few hundred residents
each, perched on or below three mesas that jut southward like chubby
fingers from the Black Mesa tableland.

A few miles after you've crossed into the Hopi Nation (whose border isn't
marked), you're greeted by a "Welcome to Hopi-Land" signboard. When you
visit the pueblos, you'll find other signs that seem less friendly. They
prohibit photography or sketching of any village, ceremonial dance or other
activity. Tape-recording is forbidden as well.

This brings us to sensitive point about the Hopi and visitors. They're a
much more private people than the Navajo. While both groups embrace
tourism, the Hopi are more touchy about intrusion into their private lives.
Understandably, they don't appreciate a lot of outsiders clambering over
their ancient villages, pointing and gawking. So please, leave your camera in
the trunk and take home images in your mind.

Bacobi, comprised mostly of pre-fab homes, is the first Hopi village
you'll encounter. **Hotevilla** *(HOAT-vih-la),* to the left off the highway, is
what you might call a "transition pueblo," a mix of adobe and cinderblock
homes, perched on the edge of a mesa. It's a relatively new village, estab-
lished in 1906 by a group that left Oraibi to start their own community after
an internal dispute.

Old Oraibi *(Oh-RYE-bee),* just down the highway at the junction of In-
dian Route 2, is one of the more fascinating of the Hopi pueblos. Many
structures are little changed from those we've seen in reconstructed ruins.
Other, more modern dwellings are being built upon the foundations of the
old. **Monongya Gallery,** run by a *kachina* carver, sells an assortment of
handicrafts. Hours are 9 to 5, but it may be closed in the off-season.

Adjacent to Old Oraibi is **Kykotsmovi** *(Kee-KOTS-mo-vee),* the ad-
ministrative center of the Hopi Nation. Begun in 1890, it's sometimes called
"New Oraibi" because it's a spin-off from the original village. The more
traditional name means "mound of pueblo ruins."

Following Highway 264 to Second Mesa, you'll see **Shungopovi**
(Shung-O-PO-vee) on your right, sitting at cliff's edge with a view of the val-
ley below. It's the largest Second Mesa village with about 750 residents, and
it may be the most ancient of all, even predating Oraibi. **Dawa's Arts and
Crafts**, open mostly in summer, offers a selection of Hopi handicrafts.

Within ten minutes, you encounter the **Hopi Arts and Silvercraft
Center,** run by the Hopi Arts and Silvercrafts Cooperative Guild. It's one of
the best places to find Hopi art, with a good selection of *kachinas,* clay pot-

Hopi ceremonial dance performed for tourists in the 1930s.

THE HOPI CEREMONIAL DANCE:
IN TOUCH WITH SPIRITS

The Hopi are a highly spiritual people and they often conduct elaborate ceremonial dances, garbed in brightly-colored beaded costumes and jewelry. The dances may be to appeal for rain, or to ask for good health and seek harmony with nature.

They're held throughout the year, some in private and others on village plazas, where visitors may observe them. Most dances open to the public are held on weekends, beginning at sunup and continuing all day, with stops for lunch and rest.

Plazas are small and not set up for visitors, so crowds aren't encouraged. Dance schedules aren't posted, but you can check at the Hopi Cultural Center, or call these village community development offices. They're open Monday through Friday, 8 to 5.

Bacavi, 734-2404; First Mesa, 737-2670; Hotevilla, 734-2420; Kykotsmovi, 734-2474; Mishongnovi, 737-2520; Moenkopi, 283-6684; Shungopavi, 734-2262 and Shipaulovi, 734-2570.

Photography, sketching and tape recording Hopi dances are strictly forbidden. You're expected to watch respectfully, aware that this is a sacred religious ritual and not a tourist gimmick. While this may sound ambivalent, the Hopi are very private about these public ceremonies and they don't encourage visitors to ask a lot of questions.

Hopi Ceremony Schedule

Dance schedules are determined by village elders, who must consider the sun and moon positions and suitable spiritual vibrations. This is determined only a few days in advance, so consult local sources.

January—Buffalo dances; February—bean dances; March—*kachina* night dances; April through June—*kachina* day dances; July—social dances; August—snake and flute dances; September—social dances; October—ladies' society dances; November—men's society dances; December—men's Prayer Feather Ceremony.

Bean dances are for crop fertility; "social" dances concern inter-tribal relationships and *kachina* dances are the most colorful, when performers wear masks and costumes representing various spiritual messengers.

tery, beautifully finished woven basketry and silver work such as watch bands, belt buckles and ladies' jewelry.

Hopi Cultural Center and Museum • *On Highway 264, just beyond the arts and crafts center, P.O. Box 7, Second Mesa, AZ 86043; (602) 734-6650. Museum open Monday-Saturday 9 to 4; $3; gift shops generally open daily 9 to 5; MC/VISA.* This attractive sandstone-colored pueblo-style complex features a museum, gift shops and a restaurant and motel (listed below).

The nicely-done museum offers collections of modern and ancient pottery, murals of traditional villages, a hand-woven bridal robe and other things Hopi. A diorama of Keet Seel, a ruin in Navajo National Monument, shows how it might have appeared in 1200 A.D. Another display reveals how Hopi make pottery without a wheel, shaping and smoothing it with a gourd rind scraper and rounded pebble, then painting it with a yucca leaf brush.

Below the cultural center, just short of the Highway 87 junction, you'll see the twin villages of **Shipaulovi** *(Shih-PAW-lo-vee)* and **Mishongnovi** *(Mih-SHONG-no-vee)* above, on your left. These weathered pueblos, perched on a narrow shelf, were founded in 1680 when valley dwellers fled from the Spanish during the Hopi rebellion. To reach them, turn left at an Exxon service station and follow a paved road. Don't attempt to drive through the narrow village streets. Park and walk, enjoying the lofty views. You can see the San Francisco peaks on the far Western horizon—to which the Hopi *kachina* spirits retreat each year.

Back on the highway, you can get provisions at the large **Fecakuku** market at the route 264-87 junction; there's a post office as well.

Continuing east on 264, you'll drop down through some attractive rock formations to **First Mesa.** The only town on the highway is **Polacca.** It's a scatter of a modern settlement at the foot of the mesa, with none of the pueblo mystique. From here, a winding road leads up to three classic Hopi villages—the twin towns of **Hano** and **Sichomovi** *(Si-CHO-MO-vee),* and charming little **Walpi.** Hano is occupied by a small group of Tewa Pueblo Indians from the Rio Grande. They were given refuge here after fleeing from the Spanish in 1696. After all these decades, they still retain their original language and customs.

Perched on the tip of a steep-walled peninsula like a village in the sky, Walpi is the most distinctive of all the pueblos. It could be an Anasazi village come to life. Timeless houses seem part of the narrow stone finger they occupy. The tiny village of 30 people is tied to the mesa by a 15-foot-wide strip of stone. Walpi is undergoing restoration to shore up its structures and preserve its classic look.

Down off the mesas, you pass Keams Canyon, a government administrative center on the eastern edge of the Hopi Nation. **Keams Canyon Shopping Center** and small a motel sit alongside the highway. The main town—not a Hopi village—occupies an attractive wooded canyon north of the highway. It consists mostly of Bureau of Indian Affairs offices and a hospital.

WHERE TO DINE IN THE HOPI NATION
Tunosvongya Restaurant • ∆∆∆ $ ∅

In the Hopi Cultural Center on Second Mesa; (602) 734-2401. American and traditional Hopi food, dinners $5 to $12. Daily 7 a.m. to 8 p.m. MC/VISA. This attractive restaurant earns three points because it's the best place on the Hopi-Navajo reservations to find traditional foods. Try Hopi dishes such as *chil-il ou gya va*, a lively blend of pinto beans, beef and chilies, or *nok qui vi*, stew with lamb, baked green chilies and Indian fry bread. The place serves good Indian tacos as well. It's a non-smoking cafe, with comfortable booths.

Keams Canyon Restaurant • △ $
In Keams Canyon Shopping Center; (602) 738-2296. Indian and American, dinners $4 to $10. Monday-Friday 7 a.m. to 8 p.m., Saturday 8 to 3, closed Sunday. MC/VISA. It's a simple little formica place serving light American fare and Indian tacos.

WHERE TO SLEEP
Hopi Cultural Center Motel • △△ $$
P.O. Box 67, Second Mesa, AZ 86043; (602) 734-2401. Doubles $55, singles $50. MC/VISA. Attractive rooms with Indian decor; TV and phones.

Keams Canyon Motel • △ $
Adjacent to Keams Canyon Shopping Center, P.O. Box 188, Keams Canyon, AZ 86034; (602) 738-2297. Doubles $35, singles $30, kitchenettes $45. MC/VISA. Basic lodging with vaguely Indian decor.

WHERE TO CAMP
There are no organized campgrounds on the reservation, but you can camp at a site 100 yards from the Hopi Cultural Center (ask at the desk for directions), and across the highway from Keams Canyon Shopping Center. Both are fee-free and both have two-day limits.

THE NAVAJO NATION EAST
Leaving the Hopi reservation at Keams Canyon, you pass some interesting sandstone formations including **Steamboat Rock,** near the trading post of the same name. With a bit of imagination, this formation becomes an old sternwheeler; there's even a water line along the side. Eleven miles beyond is the Navajo town of **Ganado** and a historic site that's still functioning.

Hubbell Trading Post National Historic Site • *P.O. Box 150, Ganado, AZ 86505; (602) 755-3475. Daily 8 to 6 in summer and 8 to 5 the rest of the year. Free.* Trading posts occupied a special place on the Western frontier. Traders formed a vital link between the Native Americans and the newcomers—a bridge between the two societies. They provided a market for Indian crafts while offering them essential white man's gadgetry such as tools, sewing machines and canned goods. Traders taught the Indians how to use these new tools; often, they interceded with government officials on their behalf. The trading post also was a social center, where both whites and Indians met to talk and swap lies.

Hubbell is an historic landmark and a still-active trading post. You can buy canned goods, bolts of cloth or harnesses—should you should you need them—or Indian curios, souvenirs and books. A large barn next to the venerable stone store once housed the post's livestock. Several old wagons are on display out back. At the visitor center museum, you'll learn about the vital role of the Western trading post. Navajo craftspeople often come to demonstrate their skills at weaving and jewelry-making.

Guided tours are conducted periodically, or you can buy a $1 brochure that will steer you around the extensive grounds.

Window Rock—sculpted through Kayenta sandstone.

The oldest active post on the reservation, it was established in nearby Ganado by John Lorenzo Hubbell in 1876. It was moved to its present site just west of town two years later.

East of Ganado, Highway 264 climbs a high tableland and passes through pinons and ponderosas of Navajo Nation Forest. It tops out at 7,750 feet, then drops down to the Navajo tribal center.

Window Rock

Elevation: 6,764 feet   **Population: 2,200**

Like Tuba City, Window Rock was established by whites. Indian Affairs Commissioner John Collier took a fancy to a natural sandstone arch and decided to locate the Navajo administration center here in 1934. It's now the Navajo Nation's tribal capital. Most of the administration buildings, many dating back to the 1930s, sit just below the arch near a wooded park.

The downtown area, at the intersection of highway 264 and Indian route 12, has the usual ration of service stations and fast food chains.

ATTRACTIONS

Navajo Tribal Museum ● *In the arts and crafts center, 27002 Highway 264, P.O. Box 308, Window Rock, AZ 86515; (602) 871-6673. Weekdays 9 to 4:45. Free; donations appreciated.* This small, well-planned museum exhibits the skeleton of a 180 million-year-old *dilophosaurus,* plus displays tracing Indian occupation of the region from basketmakers of 50 A.D. to the present. Artifacts include pottery, projectile points, metates and such. One exhibit traces the development of Navajo silvercraft. Contemporary life is shown in a clever display within the outline of the Navajo's most essential tool—the pickup.

Navajo Arts and Crafts Center • *P.O. Drawer A, Window Rock, AZ (602) 871-4090.* Operated by the Navajo Arts and Crafts Enterprise, the center offers the largest selection of native handicrafts on the reservation. Products include silver and turquoise jewelry, un-set turquoise stones, blankets, curios, bolo ties, squash blossom necklaces, dolls, sand paintings, pottery from Navajo, Jemez and Hopi tribes, and books on Indian lore.

Navajo Nation Zoological Park • *Just beyond the arts and crafts center. Open daily 8 to 5; $1.* The most interesting thing about this small zoo is its setting—amidst several sandstone monoliths 70 or more feet high. The critters, some in cages, others in fenced-off areas against a steep sandstone cliff, are mostly from the Southwest. You first pass through an exhibit building with spiders, rattlesnakes, scorpions and other uglies. Outside, you can learn Navajo names of creatures as you pass their enclosures, such as *ma'ii* for coyote (which sounds like their howl) and *shash tazhinii,* a properly ferocious-sounding name for a black bear.

Tse Bonito Tribal Park • *Between the zoo and the highway.* This informal park has a couple of picnic tables and rest rooms. You can park your RV here, although there are no hookups or water.

Window Rock Tribal Park • *Half mile north of the main junction to a traffic signal, then half a mile east, past the tribal administration buildings.* This is a pretty spot, with a landscaped park and picnic area shaded by junipers. Window Rock is a Kayenta sandstone ridge with a circular arch cut through it by wind an erosion. It's fenced off, but you can follow a trail beyond and behind it, where you will discover more weather-sculpted shapes.

WHERE TO DINE & RECLINE

Navajo Nation Inn and Dining Room • ∧∧ $$
Highway 264 (just past the main intersection), P.O. Box 1687, Window Rock, AZ 86515; (602) 871-4108. Doubles $50, singles $45; lower off-season rates. MC/VISA, AMEX. Nicely decorated rooms with TV and phones. **Navajo Nation Restaurant** is open daily from 6:30 a.m. to 9 p.m.; American, Navajo and Mexican fare, dinners $6 to $11. Entrees include Navajo mutton and beef stew, Navajo tacos, American chicken, steaks and chops.

Chinle & Canyon de Chelly

Elevation: 5,058 feet   **Population: approx. 2,000**

To reach your next stop, back-track to Ganado, then drive north on U.S. 191. Most of the route passes through uninteresting prairie country. Chinle is an ordinary-looking community spread over a good part of this prairie, offering the usual service stations, a large supermarket and fast food places.

Canyon de Chelly National Monument • *P.O. Box 588, Chinle, AZ 86503; (602) 674-5436. Visitor center open 8 to 6 from May to September and 8 to 5 the rest of the year; free.* Save a day for Canyon de Chelly, and yes it does rhyme. Canyon de Chelly and its adjoining Canyon del Muerto are unexpectedly beautiful steep-walled ravines, dropping a thousand feet to neat patchwork farms on the valley floor. Lining the banks of a meandering stream, these lands are still being tilled, as they have been since the 1300s.

Knife-edged ridges and pinnacles rise from the canyon floor and serpentine side canyons cut into the sheer walls. Cliff dwellings are tucked into hidden recesses, suddenly appearing as you scan the vertical walls with your

Spider Rock juts skyward in Canyon de Chelly National Monument.

binoculars. There are few places on earth offering such a dramatic mix of natural formations and archaeological ruins.

The **Visitor Center** has a small museum with graphics tracing canyon occupation from basketmakers to Anasazi cliff dwellers of the 12th and 13th centuries. Ranger programs, from late May through early September, include coffee talks at the campground amphitheater, canyon hikes, nature walks, lectures at Thunderbird Lodge and campfire programs.

Canyon hiking: Because the Navajo are even more sensitive than we are about protecting prehistoric ruins, most of canyon cannot be entered without a guide. Free half-day ranger hikes leave the visitor center daily, usually from May through September. Also, you can hire a Navajo guide for $7.50 and hour and explore the canyon's inner secrets. This can can be arranged at the visitors center.

The White House Ruins trail can be followed without a guide. It starts at the White House overlook, about six miles from the visitor center on the South Rim Drive. The broad trail switchbacks down to the canyon floor, where you skirt the edge of a farmer's field, wade an icy stream (Take dry socks!), and cross to the dwelling. White House Ruin, named because the ancients whitewashed one of the structures, occupies a niche about 50 feet above you. Another ruin, fenced off from vandals, sits at its base. The walls here are so sheer and smooth that your voices bounce off them like vocal ping pong balls.

Two **rim drives** take you to turnouts for an assortment of awesome views of the canyons and hidden Anasazi dwellings.

The **SOUTH RIM DRIVE,** about 25 miles long, starts at the visitor's center. **Tsegi Overlook** provides your first startling glimpse down the sheer canyon face to farm fields below. At **Junction Overlook,** you can see a tall, pie-shaped peninsula where Canyon del Muerto joins Canyon de Chelly. **White House Overlook** provides canyon floor access, 500 feet down from the rim. **Sliding House Overlook** offers a look at ruins perched on a ledge so narrow that they seem ready to slip into the canyon. **Wild Cherry** provides more canyon vistas and **Face Rock Overlook** faces some cliff dwellings high in the opposite wall.

Spider Rock overlook at the end of the route is the most impressive, with a half mile rim hiking trail offering several vantage points. Here, the walls drop a thousand feet. Spider Rock is an unbelievably slender freestanding, spiked monolith rising 800 feet from the canyon floor.

NORTH RIM DRIVE along Canyon del Muerto follows Navajo Route 64, leading to Tsaile, home of Navajo Community College. From there, roads travel to the northern part of the reservation. **Ledge Ruin Overlook** is a broad caprock peninsula with views up and down the canyon; two different viewpoints provide glimpses of canyon ruins. **Antelope House** also has two overlooks. Here, another great free-standing wedge is formed where Canyon del Muerto and Black Rock Canyon merge.

Several miles up the highway, a turnoff leads to **Mummy Cave** and **Massacre Cave** viewpoints. At Mummy Cave, you see a remarkably intact pueblo; Massacre Cave was so-named because the Spanish slaughtered more than a hundred men, women and children at a pueblo here. Go to the right, along the edge of the canyon, and you'll see ruins and remnants of a kiva, only 35 feet below.

Hatathli Museum • *On the campus of Navajo Community College in Tsaile, northeast of Canyon de Chelly; (602) 724-6156. Weekdays 8:30 to noon and 1 to 4:30; donations appreciated.* This all-Navajo museum is housed in the octagonal Hatathli Center on the college campus. Exhibits trace Navajo and other Native American cultures. Handicrafts and artworks are available at a sales gallery. There's also a cafeteria, open to visitors.

TOURS

Canyon de Chelly Jeep Tours • *Thunderbird Lodge, P.O. Box 548, Chinle, AZ 86503; (602) 674-5841 or 674-5842. Major credit cards.* Half-day tours depart at least twice daily, at 9 a.m. and 1 p.m.; price is $25.20.

WHERE TO DINE & RECLINE

Thunderbird Lodge • ΔΔ $$$
Near visitor center, P.O. Box 548, Chinle, AZ 86503; (602) 674-5841 or (602) 674-5842. Doubles $60 to $75, singles $54 to $69, suites $125 to $136; lower off-season rates. Major credit cards. TV, phones; gift shop. **Cafeteria** open 6:30 a.m. to 8:30 p.m. (to 7:30 in the off-season), American (steaks, soup, sandwiches), $8 to $12. It's rather attractive for a cafeteria dining room, done in a Southwest-Indian style.

Canyon de Chelly Motel • ΔΔ $$
On Highway 7 enroute to Canyon de Chelly, east of Highway 191, P.O. Box 295, Chinle, AZ 86503; (602) 674-5875. Doubles $68, singles $64. MC/VISA, AMEX. Attractive Southwest-style motel surrounding a large lawn area; TV, room phones.

Canyon de Chelly Restaurant • Δ $
On Route 7, just beyond Canyon de Chelly Motel; (602) 674-5900. American, Native American; dinners $5 to $10. Daily 10 to 8. Basic formica place; all-you-can-eat buffet from 11 to 2.

WHERE TO CAMP

Cottonwood Campground • *Adjacent to Thunderbird Lodge, near visitors center. Tent and RV sites, no hookups; free.* Attractive sites shaded by cottonwoods; flush potties, picnic and barbecue areas, dump station. Water and restrooms shut down during winter; pit toilets available.

THE NAVAJO NATION NORTH

North from Chinle, Highway 191 travels through bunchgrass country accented by occasional redwall mesas. Two of the more impressive ones, visible to the northwest, are **White Top Mesa** and **Carson Mesa Red Rocks.** You pass Many Farms and Round Rock—little more than village trading posts—then turn east at Mexican Water onto Highway 160. Destination: Four Corners, probably the most pointless part of our trek through Hopi-Navajo land.

Four Corners Monument • When we made this trip, we expected very little from Four Corners, and we were not disappointed. This monument marking the merger of Arizona, Utah, Colorado and New Mexico is a concrete slab with a bronze benchmark at the precise spot. The four state lines are seamed through the slab with the their names and seals embedded.

Thus, you can do utterly pointless things like placing one finger in each state, taking a four-state walk in four seconds and whatever else amuses you. An elevated photo stand is nearby, so your companion can record your mindless moments.

A graveled parking lot surrounds the marker, so you drive through four states as you leave. Also surrounding the marker are souvenir stands, should you want an authentic Four-Corner T-shirt. The hawkers sell jewelry and soft drinks, as well. Nearby is a string of porta-potties that you probably won't want to use.

Your route now takes you along the upper edge of Arizona on Highway 160, past sandstone shapes that give promise of more to come at legendary Monument Valley. Along the way, you pass the serrated red limestone **Comb Ridge** on the right, just beyond **Dennehotso,** and a curious little formation called **Baby Rocks** near the trading post of the same name. Here, a mesa breaks into small columns of pinnacles that look like red clay soldiers marching off the end of the butte. A couple of miles farther, just west of the Navajo Route 59 junction, **Church Rock** juts skyward like the spirals of a complicated cathedral.

Kayenta & Monument Valley

Elevation: 5,798 feet   **Population: 3,400**

You've seen thousands of images of Monument Valley, in travelogues and Western movies, and on pretty posters. Ad agencies like to park cars on top of the tall spires.

But you have to be there to get the full Cinemascopic impact of these awesome shapes. They rise from the desert in great tapered spires and broad-shouldered buttes, looking too alien to be earthly. From the distance, there is no more beautiful sight than a panorama of Monument Valley with puffy clouds rising to a high, blue sky.

Kayenta, gateway to Monument Valley Tribal Park, occupies an arid valley about 20 miles south, providing a few motels and restaurants for visitors. **Gouldings,** just opposite the Monument Valley park entrance on the Utah side, also offers lodging, shopping, a restaurant and campground.

Driving north toward the monument, you'll pass **Agathla Peak,** the pointed black core of an ancient volcano that's nearly as impressive as the beige and rose sandstone shapes ahead.

Monument Valley Tribal Park ● *P.O. Box 93, Monument Valley, UT 84536; (801) 727-3287. Daily from 7 a.m. to 8 p.m. mid-March through September and 8 to 5 the rest of the year; last admission 30 minutes before closing. Adults $1, seniors 50 cents, kids under 12 free.* You must first pause at the small visitor center to pay your fees, permitting you to follow a 17-mile drive among the park's formations. The center, perched on a ridge, offers great views of the valley below.

The road through the park is extremely bumpy; you may feel like you're doing the Baja 500 in slow motion. Low clearance vehicles might have a problem, particularly on the steep climb back out. It occurred to us that the Navajos should raise the entry fee and improve the road. Perhaps they have by now. If you prefer, you can save your car and book a van or jeep tour (see below). They offer the advantage of taking you into areas where private vehicles aren't allowed.

We were dazzled by the scenery but slightly put off by the excess of signs telling you where you can't go and what you can't do. As in Canyon de Chelly, the Navajos are very conservative about their natural areas. Hiking, rock-climbing and wandering off the designated route are prohibited.

An iceberg tip of Monument Valley is in Utah, but the bulk of it is in Arizona. The scenic drive covers only a small part of it, but it does take you past many of the valley's most striking formations.

Artist's Point, a slight rise offering views of the natural wonders around you, is a nice place to pause for a picnic. It's about midway through the drive. The formations are remnants of an early Rocky Mountain range, eroded about 160 million years ago and fused into sandstone. The gradual uplifting of the Colorado Plateau created cracks and seams that eroded into canyons and gullies. As more of the land eroded, softer portions weathered away, leaving buttes and gravity-defying pinnacles.

If you have time, spend a full day here—from sunup to sundown. Changing light and shadows cast their magic on these free-standing formations. Although park gates are open only during daylight, the valley shapes are visible from many areas. Nearby Gouldings and a campground just below the visitor center are good places to spend the night.

TOURS
Monument Valley Tours • *c/o Monument Valley Tribal Park, P.O. Box 93, Monument Valley, UT 84536; (801) 727-3287.* Make arrangements at the visitor's center; two and a half hours, $15. Departures on demand.

Gouldings Tours • *P.O. Box 1, Monument Valley, AZ 84536; (801) 727-3231.* Booked out of Gouldings Lodge at Monument Valley or Wetherill Inn Motel in Kayenta. Full day with lunch, $41 for adults and $21 for kids under 12; half day, $21 adults and $11 kids. Departures at 9 a.m. and 1:30 p.m.

WHERE TO RECLINE & DINE
Gouldings Lodge • △△△ $$$
Six miles from the park entrance, P.O. Box 1, Monument Valley, UT 84536; (801) 727-3231. Doubles or singles $78; lower off-season rates. Major credit cards. Rooms have balconies or patios with views of Monument Valley. Attractively furnished with TV, phones; pool, gift shop. Monument Valley tours (see above). **Stagecoach Restaurant** serves breakfast, lunch and dinner, American, dinners $9 to $15. The Western-style dining room is decorated with props from the film *She Wore a Yellow Ribbon,* for which it was built.

The Goulding complex also includes a service station and store. The original stone trading post has a small museum, with relics from the days when it was established by Harry and Lenore (Mike) Goulding in 1924.

Holiday Inn • △△ $$$
On Highway 160, P.O. Box 307, Kayenta, AZ 86033; (602) 697-3221 or (800) 465-4329. Doubles $74, singles $69; lower off-season rates. Major credit cards. Phones, TV; pool, gift shop, coin laundry. **Monument Valley Restaurant** serves from 6 a.m. to 10 p.m., American (chicken, chops, steaks, fish, plus a Navajo "pocket sandwich"), dinners $7 to $14. Southwest-style dining room.

Tsegi Canyon Inn Motel and Cafe • △ $
Ten miles west of Kayenta on Route 160, P.O. Box 1543, Kayenta, AZ 86033; (602) 697-3793. Doubles $26, singles $20. Major credit cards. Small motel in an attractive forest setting between Kayenta and Navajo National Monument; TV movies, room phones. **Cafe** serves from 6 a.m. to 10 p.m., American and Navajo, dinners $5 to $10.

Wetherill Inn • △△ $$$ ∅
Uptown Kayenta, on road to Monument Valley (Highway 163), P.O. Box 175, Kayenta, AZ 86033; (602) 697-3231. Doubles $68, singles $62; lower

off-season rates. Major credit cards. TV, phones, free room coffee; Monument Valley tours (see above).

Golden Sands Cafe ● △△ $
Uptown, on Highway 163, Kayenta; (602) 697-3684. American; dinners $5 to $10. Daily 6 a.m. to 9 p.m. MC/VISA. Charmingly rustic place with

---

INDIAN TACO: A CULINARY CURIOSITY

If Arizona's Indians had developed this weapon a century ago, they might not have lost their war with the white intruders. The U.S. Army would have been too bogged down to attack the Apaches, pursue the Papagos or nab the Navajos.

The Indian taco is a delicacy of dubious pedigree. It is neither Indian nor taco, but a sort of Italian-Mexican tostada. The base is Indian fry bread, a puffy and pleasantly chewy dough akin to soft pizza crust. Upon this is layered pinto beans—sometimes with chili—and ground beef, plus grated cheese, chopped onions and shredded lettuce. Diced tomatoes and other salad veggies are optional.

Once devoured, the beans and gruel unite in your stomach and begin expanding. Perhaps it is some mystical amalgam unknown to nutritional science. An hour after consuming an Indian taco, you feel like you've been force-fed a Thanksgiving dinner after winning a watermelon-eating contest.

You won't need another meal for hours—perhaps days. Averaging under $5, the Indian Taco is a dining bargain. In our ongoing pursuit of culinary enrichment, we sampled many of them—perhaps too many—and compiled this list of the best in Arizona.

1. Truck Stop Cafe ● *Highway 160 and 264, Tuba City; open 24 hours.* Immodestly called the "World Famous Navajo Taco," this monstrous thing arrives on a platter, not a plate. The underlying fry bread is thick and poofy with a nice fried-fat flavor that you just *know* is cholesterol city. It's topped with about a pound of chili beans and ground beef, with a generous sprinkling of finely shredded lettuce and cheese. A spicy slice of cold, cooked green chili is draped across this tasty consortium. Although the taco is quite spicy, there's Tabasco sauce on the table to give it added authority. **Price: $4.75.**

2. Navajo Nation Inn ● *Highway 264 at Navajo Route 12, Window Rock; open 6:30 a.m. to 9 p.m.* The Inn's Navajo Taco was barely edged out by the Truck Stop's number. This hefty version arrived with the cheese melted and the plate warmed; nice touches! A choice of red or green salsa is served on the side. However, the pinto beans, ground beef and chopped lettuce and tomatoes weren't quite as spicy as the Truck Stop's chili topping. **Price: $4.85.**

3. Hopi Cultural Center Cafe ● *Highway 87 and 264, Second Mesa; open 7 a.m. to 8 p.m.* Called the Hopi Taco, this lively version had chili with pinto beans, lettuce, tomato and onions, served on a tasty, puffy base. Spicy salsa comes on the side. **Price: $3.85.**

4. Golden Sands Cafe ● *Highway 163 in uptown Kayenta; open 6 a.m. to 10 p.m.* The Golden Sands' Navajo Taco rivals the Truck Stop's entry in size, and it's topped with excellent chili beans, chopped lettuce, tomatoes, onions, shredded cheese and chopped green chilies. It's tasty, but a rather greasy fry bread keeps it from scoring higher. **Price: $4.75 or $3.75 for a mini-version.**

5. Havasupai Tribal Cafe ● *Supai (Havasu Canyon); open 7:30 to 5.* A standard but tasty version of the Indian Taco, it's served with red beans and the traditional chopped lettuce, onions and grated cheese. We liked the chewiness of the fry bread, but the beans needed chili or salsa to give them a lift. **Price: $4.50.**

checkered oilcloth, Western decor, wood stove; American steaks, chicken and chops, Navajo tacos.

As the sun sinks into our adjectives and we near the end of our Arizona trail, we offer one final jewel. Drive 21 miles west of Kayenta on Highway 160, then turn north on Route 564.

Navajo National Monument ● *HC 71, Box 3, Tonalea, AZ 86044; (602) 672-2366 or 672-2367. Visitor center open 8 a.m. to 4:30 p.m. Lookout trail open during daylight hours. Campground open from mid-April through mid-October; RV and tent sites, no hookups; free.* Navajo National Monument contains three of the most complete Anasazi ruins and one of the finest small museums in the state. It takes advance planning to see the ruins; the museum can be enjoyed any day. The visitor center occupies a piney ridge at 7,286 feet, so dress warmly for the off-season.

The three ruins sheltered by this small national monument are Betatakin, Inscription House and Keet Seel. **Betatakin** can be seen from an overlook not far from the visitor center, or visited by ranger-guided tours. **Inscription House**, 30 miles from the monument, is so fragile that it's closed to visitors. **Keet Seel**, the "star" of Southwest's Indian ruins, is eight miles away and can be visited only with an advance permit.

Two-and-a-half hour hikes to Betatakin leave the visitor center daily at 11 a.m. in the off-season and 9 a.m. and 1 p.m. in summer. It takes five to six hours, involving a difficult 700-foot descent into a canyon. You must sign up on the day of the hike; group sizes are limited, so arrive early. Hikes are conducted from early spring through October.

The hike to Keet Seel, a large, amazingly intact ruin with many roofs and timbers still in place, must be reserved early. Write or call two months prior to your trip; reservations aren't accepted before then. Visits are permitted only from Memorial Day through Labor Day weekend. Once at the site, you can't enter the ruin without a ranger, who will be on duty during visiting periods. When we last checked, the park service was considering limiting Keet Seel hikes to weekends because of personnel shortages, so permits may be *very* hard get. The permit also allows overnight stays at a primitive campground near the ruin.

Because these ruins were hidden from pot-hunters in a ruggedly beautiful canyon, they yielded a rich treasure of relics. Many have been used to create an excellent small museum. Stone tools, implements and pottery are focal points of simple, uncluttered displays that teach us much about the Anasazi, perhaps the most dominant prehistoric tribe of the Southwest. You can crawl inside a reconstructed living unit that's so complete it seems the occupants just stepped out for a bit.

A film about these people who prevailed in the Southwest for 13 centuries is shown periodically. You can ask the ranger on duty to push a button for a five-minute slide show about the monument. An adjacent gift shop open from mid-April to mid-November offers Hopi, Navajo and some Zuni handicrafts, along with books and guides.

Nearest overnight lodging to Navajo National Monument—other than the campground—is Tsegi Canyon Inn, listed above.

From the monument, you can follow Highway 160 southwest toward Tuba City, passing a pair of sandstone buttes near Red Lake; they've earned the appropriate name of **Elephants Feet.** Or, swing northwest on Highway 98 and complete your loop back to Page.

NAVAJO NATION ANNUAL EVENTS

Woozhchid Indian Pro Rodeo, Window Rock, fourth weekend in March; **Dave Gorman Memorial Rodeo,** Chinle, first weekend in May; **Eastern Navajo Fair,** Crownpoint, N.M., fourth weekend of June; **West World Rodeo,** Chinle, fourth weekend of August; **Central Navajo Fair,** Chinle, late August to early September; **Navajo Nation Fair,** the largest annual celebration with a rodeo, pow wow, arts and crafts, horse races, Miss Navajo pageant, in Window Rock, first weekend of September; **Coyote Calling Contest,** Window Rock, third weekend of October.

Chapter 14

SNOWBIRD DIRECTORY

 EVERY YEAR, MILLIONS of Americans and Canadians, mostly retirees, pull up winter roots and head for warmer climes. If you're one of these, you know that you've been nicknamed Snowbird. Arizona ranks second to Florida and ahead of California and Texas as a leading Snowbird retreat.

Exact figures are hard to find for this migratory flock, but Arizona may draw upwards of a million each winter. A recent Arizona State University survey indicated that most long-term winter visitors to the Valley of the Sun visitors arrive in November (32 percent) and depart in April (55 percent). Sunbelt chambers of commerce report similar trends.

The ASU survey—taken at several Mesa-Apache Junction RV and mobile home parks—revealed some interesting statistics. About half of Arizona's long-term winter visitors occupy RVs or mobile homes; the others check into apartments or condos or own winter homes in Arizona. A surprising 70 percent of mobile home park dwellers leave their unit there year-around; only 30 percent tow a trailer or drive a motor home to the state.

And these are indeed migrants. Only five percent of those responding to the survey said they planned to stay permanently. The average length of winter stay is between four and five months. Two thirds have been doing the Snowbird bit for five or more years.

Where do you folks come from? A surprising 20 percent are from Canada. Most of the Americans surveyed came from Minnesota (13 percent), with Iowa and Washington tied for second at 11 percent. Number four was North Dakota with seven percent—an amazing figure, since it has a population of less than 700,000. Others were Colorado, six percent; Illinois, four percent; California, Oregon and Wisconsin, all three percent.

Not surprisingly, 88 percent of those surveyed are between 60 and 79 years old.

Winter visitors don't come just for suntans and golf. A different survey revealed that three-fourths of Arizona's Cactus Baseball League ticket-buyers are from out of state. Two-thirds of the fans say they head south *specifically* for spring hardball.

Since about half of the long-term winter visitors lease apartments and condos, Tucson, Phoenix and some other cities list short-term lodgings in their accommodations guides. Tucson even has an apartment locator service for individuals.

Most Arizona RV parks offer special rates for long-term visitors. Many are elaborate resorts, with swimming pools, golf courses, marinas, recreational programs and other amenities.

Incidentally, whether you plan to winter in Arizona for two weeks or six months, remember to bring your sweater—perhaps even a down jacket. Compared with Bismark, North Dakota, and Edmonton, Ontario, much of Arizona is a winter paradise. But nighttime tempertures sometimes dip down to freezing in the Phoenix and Tucson areas. Days generally are in the balmy 60s, climbing often into the 70s. Tucson is more than a thousand feet higher than Phoenix and therefore slightly cooler.

If you require balmier winter nights, the Colorado River corridor is warmer than the desert interior. Yuma, for instance, is less than 200 feet above sea level. Parker and Bullhead City often report the nation's highest temperatures, in both winter and summer.

Arizona offers a rich panorama of enticements for Snowbirds. If you're thinking about joining this flock, or if you'd like to find a new roost next winter, this directory of communities catering to Snowbirds should help. The list ranges from cosmopolitan Phoenix to dusty Quartzsite, and it includes some sun-country places you may not be aware of. Chambers of commerce can provide more specific information. Most have lists of RV parks and mobile home resorts that cater to long-term visitors.

We don't list planned retirement communities such as Sun City and Arizona City, since they're set up more for permanent resident-retirees.

All of the communities listed below are discussed in more detail elsewhere in this book. Chapter locations are shown at the bottom of each listing.

Important note • Many RV parks with long term rates—particularly those near metropolitan areas—book up early, so make your plans as soon as possible.

APACHE JUNCTION

Elevation: 1,175 feet   **Population: 17,266**

Location • South central Arizona, 40 miles east of Phoenix, in the foothills of the Superstition Mountains.

Winter Climate • Warm and dry with chilly evenings; less than 8 inches annual rainfall. Average January high 65, low 35.

Characteristics • A fast-growing community on the outer fringe of the Valley of the Sun's metropolitan core. It's a major Snowbird and retirement area, drawing about 40,000 winter visitors.

Attractions • Phoenix and Scottsdale; Salt River Canyon reservoirs and Superstition Mountains with boating, fishing and other outdoor activities.

Long-term visitor accommodations • About a hundred RV parks and resorts are in the area.

Advantages • It offers a nice balance between cosmopolitan lures of Phoenix and a rural desert atmosphere. It's beyond the congestion, yet close enough for a quick commute.

Disadvantages • Area recreational facilities become very crowded with Valley of the Sun residents on weekends. There's no direct freeway link to Phoenix, but one is under construction.

Contact • Apache Junction Chamber of Commerce, P.O. Box 1747, Apache Junction, AZ 85217; (602) 982-3141.

See Chapter 8.

BULLHEAD CITY

Elevation: 540 feet   **Population: 13,600**

Location • Northwestern Arizona on the Colorado River, near the California-Nevada border.

Winter climate • Warm and very dry with cool evenings; less than 4 inches of rain. Average January high 80, low 38.

Characteristics • Fast-growing community scattered alongside Lake Mohave reservoir. The rising new casino town of Laughlin, Nevada, is just across the water. The area's economy is based almost entirely on tourism and water recreation.

Attractions • Fishing, boating and swimming on Lake Mohave; casino shows and gaming in Laughlin. Lake Mead National Recreation Area is immediately north.

Long-term visitor accommodations • Dozens of RV parks stand alongside the river, mostly on the Arizona side, with a few on the Nevada shore.

Advantages • The area offers some of the most temperate winter climate in the Southwest; frost is rare. There's plenty of Nevada-style amusement across the river.

Disadvantages • Bullhead is not a well-planned city; the business area is rather scattered. There are few cultural opportunities here.

Contact • Bullhead City Chamber of Commerce, P.O. Box 66, Bullhead City, AZ 86403; (602) 754-4121.

See Chapter 4.

CAVE CREEK & CAREFREE

Elevation: 2,350 feet   **Population: Approx. 3,500**

Location • About 15 miles north of Phoenix in central Arizona.

Winter climate • Warm days, cool evenings; moderate rainfall (12 inches a year). Average January high 60, low 40.

Characteristics • Cave Creek is a deliberately rustic Western-style town; adjacent Carefree—a planned community—is more contemporary. They sit side-by-side, just beyond reach of the Valley of the Sun's congestion, in a scenic rocky desert area.

Attractions • Phoenix and its sundry lures, plus the golf courses, restaurants and elegant resorts of next-door Scottsdale.

Long-term visitor accommodations • A few—but not many—RV parks are in the area.

Advantages • The cultural and night life offerings of Phoenix are nearby, yet the area is desert rural.

Disadvantages • Limited RV facilities; the few available are rather expensive. Trips to Phoenix must pass through sprawling suburbs, although a freeway is being built in that direction.

Contact • Carefree-Cave Creek Chamber of Commerce, P.O. Box 734, Carefree, AZ 85377; (602) 488-3381.

See Chapter 7.

CASA GRANDE

Elevation: 1,398 feet   **Population: 16,000**

Location • In south central Arizona, midway between Phoenix and Tucson, just off Interstate 10.

Winter climate • Warm with chilly evenings, annual rainfall, 8 inches. Average January high 66, low 35.

Characteristics • An agricultural community; starting to catch a little of the Phoenix-Tucson growth fever, but still rural.

Attractions • Phoenix is less than an hour by freeway; Tucson's lures are 70 miles south.

Long-term visitor accommodations • A few RV parks are in the area, and more are being built.

Advantages • It's ideally located between two metropolitan centers, linked by freeway.

Disadvantages • Set in a farming area, it lacks the appeal of desert gardens, and it's a bit on the cool side in winter; it can get windy here.

Contact • Greater Casa Grande Chamber of Commerce, 575 N. Marshall, Casa Grande, AZ 85222; (602) 836-2125.

See Chapter 8.

LAKE HAVASU CITY

Elevation: 482 feet   **Population: 20,000**

Location • In west central Arizona, across the Colorado River from California.

Winter climate • Very warm with cool evenings; less than 4 inches of annual rainfall. Average January high 79, low 37.

Characteristics • It was started several years ago as a planned community by the McCulluch Corporation, with the transplanted London Bridge as its centerpiece. It has since become the largest city on the Colorado River corridor between Arizona and California.

Attractions • Adjacent Lake Havasu offers all sorts of water sports and of course, there's that bridge.

Long-term visitor accommodations • There are many RV parks in the area, including a new full-service resort on Lake Havasu Peninsula.

Advantages • Lake Havasu City is better planned than most river corridor communities and it's large enough to offer essential services and good shopping. The winter climate is warm enough for all those water sports.

Disadvantages • It's a long way from anywhere; the nearest freeway is 19 miles and that only gets you to Needles, California. Phoenix is 200 miles away.

Contact • Lake Havasu City Area Chamber of Commerce, 1930 Mesquite Ave., Suite 3, Lake Havasu City, AZ 86403; (602) 855-4115.

See Chapter 4.

LAKE MEAD NATIONAL RECREATION AREA

Elevation (Boulder City, Nev.): 1,232 feet   Population: 11,100

Location • Northwestern Arizona, encompassing Lake Mead and Lake Mohave.

Winter climate • Similar to Bullhead City; warm and dry with cool evenings; less than 4 inches of rain. Average January high 80, low 38.

Characteristics • A shoreline longer than the California coast provide water sports for more than eight million year-around visitors on Lake Mead above Hoover Dam and Lake Mohave below.

Attractions • Colorado River corridor water sports; the glitter of Las Vegas is a short drive northwest.

Long-term visitor accommodations • Nine marinas occupy Lake Mohave and Lake Mead shorelines and most offer long-term rental spaces. Others are in nearby Boulder City, Nevada.

Advantages • Proximity to water sports; lower monthly rental fees that urban areas.

Disadvantages • There are no city services there. However, Boulder City is just seven miles from the dam and Bullhead City is a short drive south.

Contacts • For a list of marinas, contact: Lake Mead National Recreation Area, 601 Nevada Hwy., Boulder City, NV 89005-2426; (702) 293-8907. For area information: Boulder City Chamber of Commerce, 1497 Nevada Hwy., Boulder City, NV 89005; (702) 293-2034.

See Chapter 4.

MESA-TEMPE

Elevation: 1,200 feet   Mesa: 250,000; Tempe: 150,000

Location • Just east of Phoenix in central Arizona.

Winter climate • Balmy, with chilly evenings. Rainfall less than 8 inches. Average January high 65, low 35.

Characteristics • These two cities account for most of the Valley of the Sun's eastward suburban sprawl. They're primarily bedroom communities, among the fastest growing in the state.

Attractions • Phoenix-Scottsdale, of course, plus Arizona State University in Tempe; both communities have their own fine museums.

Long-term visitor accommodations • Several RV resorts and parks in the area, plus some winter apartment rentals (but scarce in Tempe because of ASU).

Advantages • These large communities offer all essential services and plenty of shopping, plus their own cultural activities in addition to those in Phoenix.

Disadvantages • This is suburbia with sunshine and traffic.

Contacts • Mesa Convention & Visitors Bureau, 120 N. Center, Mesa, AZ 85201; (602) 969-1307; Tempe Chamber of Commerce, 60 E. Fifth St., Suite 3, Tempe, AZ 85281; (602) 894-8158.

See Chapter 7.

PARKER

Elevation: 450 feet **Population: 3,035**

Location • West central Arizona, across the Colorado River from California.

Winter climate • Warm with cool evenings. Rainfall less than 4 inches. Average January high 67, low 37.

Characteristics • Parker, on the Colorado River Indian Reservation, is one of the smaller river corridor winter resort communities. It has more of a quiet, small-town America atmosphere.

Attractions • Water sports are pretty much the main focus; Parker Dam is 20 miles north.

Long-term visitor accommodations • The 20-mile "Parker Strip" between here and Parker Dam is practically a solid row of RV parks and resorts, lining both the Arizona and California shores.

Advantages • Parker is a quiet community offering an abundance of rather inexpensive RV parks.

Disadvantages • It's almost as far from nowhere as Lake Havasu City, with few cultural opportunities

Contact • Parker Area Chamber of Commerce, P.O. Box 627, Parker, AZ 85344; (602) 669-2174.

See Chapter 4.

PHOENIX-SCOTTSDALE

Elevation: 1,083 feet **Phoenix: 1,036,000; Scottsdale: 121,000**

Location • Central Arizona, in the heart of the Valley of the Sun.

Winter Climate • Balmy, with some chilly evenings. Rainfall, 7 inches. Average January high 65, low 35.

Characteristics • Phoenix and Scottsdale need no further introduction. Phoenix is the big, booming heart of the Arizona sunbelt.

Attractions • Museums, major league sports, live theater, good restaurants, adjacent mountains, beautiful desert gardens—you name it. The Valley of the Sun is host to five of the eight Cactus League baseball clubs.

Long-term visitor accommodations • There are many RV parks and resorts, particularly on the outskirts, plus winter apartment and condo rentals.

Advantages • Phoenix offers a great mix of culture, night life, recreation and sunshine.

Disadvantages • You may not care for the busy metropolitan bustle; RV park prices are on the high side.

Contacts • Phoenix and Valley of the Sun Convention and Visitors Bureau, 505 N. Second St., Suite 300, Phoenix, AZ 85004-3998; (602) 254-6500; Scottsdale Chamber of Commerce, 7333 Scottsdale Mall, Scottsdale, AZ 85251-4498; (602) 945-8481.

See Chapter 7.

QUARTZSITE

Elevation: 875 feet **Population: 1,200**

Location • Southwestern Arizona, 20 miles from the California border on Interstate 10.

Winter climate ● Warm and dry; cool evenings. Rainfall less than 4 inches. Average January high 65, low 35.

Characteristics ● Quartzsite is a scraped-away patch of desert that has become one huge RV park. Its population zooms to 200,000 in winter; it's probably the world's largest concentration of rec vehicle facilities.

Attractions ● Colorado River recreation areas are 20 miles west. Huge gem shows and flea markets from mid-January to early February draw up to half a million visitors to this dusty desert hamlet.

Long-term visitor accommodations ● There are wall-to-all RV parks; too many to count.

Advantages ● Quartzsite offers the cheapest RV rates in the state, and there's free parking out in the boonies.

Disadvantages ● It's a cultural desert in the desert, sitting in the middle of nowhere, next-door to nothing. And it's just hound-dog homely.

Contact ● Quartzsite Chamber of Commerce, P.O. Box 85, Quartzsite, AZ 85346; (602) 927-5600.

See Chapter 4.

SIERRA VISTA

Elevation: 4,623 feet   **Population: 34,000**

Location ● Southeastern Arizona, 70 miles southeast of Tucson.

Winter Climate ● Warm to cool days, chilly nights. Rainfall, 15 inches, snowfall 10 inches. Average January high 58, low 34.

Characteristics ● This is an Arizona surprise—a growing community the otherwise thinly-populated southeast. This open, well-planned city is rimmed by mountains.

Attractions ● Historic Tombstone, Chiricahua National Monument and mountain wilderness areas; short drives to Tucson and the Mexican border.

Long-term visitor accommodations ● Several RV parks in the area; mostly toward Huachuca City; relatively inexpensive.

Advantages ● It's away from the hustle, yet close to Tucson. And it's large enough to offer most services and conveniences.

Disadvantages ● Sierra Vista is a bit on the cool side for a winter retreat, but you may never want to leave. It offers one of the most temperate year-around climates in America.

Contact ● Sierra Vista Chamber of Commerce, 77 Calle Portal, #140-A, Sierra Vista, AZ 85635; (602) 458-6940.

See Chapter 11.

TUBAC

Elevation: Approx. 3,700 feet   **Population: 600**

Location ● South central Arizona, 40 miles south of Tucson and 20 miles north of Nogales, Mexico.

Winter Climate ● Warm days, chilly nights. About 11 inches of rain; occasional traces of snow. Average January high 66, low 31.

Characteristics ● If you like history mixed with artistic funk, you'll like tiny Tubac. It's Arizona's oldest settlement and a popular artists' colony.

Attractions ● It's less than an hour from Tucson and half an hour from the border. Historic sites such as Tubac Presidio State Park and Tumacacori National Monument are nearby; so are several mountain recreation areas.

Long-term visitor facilities ● There are a few RV parks in the area.

Advantages ● Tubac is quiet, funky and remote, yet close to the Tucson action.

Disadvantages ● You may not like quiet and funky places. It's a bit cool for a winter resort, although it's warmer and closer to Tucson's attractions than nearby Sierra Vista.

Contact ● Tubac Chamber of Commerce, P.O. Box 1866, Tubac, AZ 85646; (602) 398-9201.

See Chapter 9.

TUCSON

Elevation: 2,584 feet   Population: 664,000

Location ● South central Arizona, 100 miles southeast of Phoenix and 65 miles north of Mexico (at Nogales).

Winter climate ● Balmy days, some cool to chilly evenings. Noted for its cloud-free days; rainfall about 11 inches. Average January high 66, low 37.

Characteristics ● It offers the metropolitan lures of Phoenix, with more small city charm; the pace is a bit slower here.

Attractions ● Fine cultural offerings, good restaurants, skiing at nearby Mount Lemmon, surrounding desert gardens, excellent museums and galleries; good Mexican handicraft shopping in nearby Nogales.

Long-term visitor accommodations ● Tucson has a good selection of RV parks, winter apartments and condos. The visitor's bureau has an apartment-locator service.

Advantages ● Think of it as a flat San Francisco with warm sunshine. (It's our favorite city in the Southwest.)

Disadvantages ● We can't think of any, unless you prefer a more rural setting. Also, RV parks are on the expensive side.

Contact ● Metropolitan Tucson Convention & Visitors Bureau, 130 S. Scott Ave., Tucson, AZ 85701; (602) 624-1817.

See Chapter 9.

YUMA

Elevation: 138 feet   Population: 50,000

Location ● On interstate 8 in Arizona's southwestern corner, 20 miles from Mexico (at San Luis).

Winter climate ● Warm days, cool evenings, occasionally chilly. It's the driest corner of the state; rainfall less than 3 inches. Average January high 68, low 37.

Characteristics ● Yuma is another Arizona surprise—a burgeoning mini-metropolis far from the rest of civilization. Snowbirds nearly double this fast-growing sunshine resort's population each winter.

Attractions ● Occupying the site of Yuma Crossing (the old Colorado River gateway to California), it has several historic sites, plus water recreation; Mexico shopping is 20 miles south.

Long-term visitor accommodations ● Several RV parks and resorts are on both shores of the Colorado River, and many more are inland along Interstate 8.

Advantages ● A small-town atmosphere, with adequate facilities and services. Relatively inexpensive RV parks; water recreation. If you like your climate dry, Yuma's the place.

Disadvantages ● It's remote from any metropolitan center and offers limited cultural resources.

Contact ● Yuma County Chamber of Commerce, P.O. Box 6468, Yuma, AZ 85366; (602) 344-3800.

See Chapter 10.

Chapter 15

AFTERTHOUGHTS

OTHER USEFUL ARIZONA BOOKS

As far as we know, all of these books are still in print. If you can't find them at a bookstore, they should be available directly from the publishers. Prices are subject to change, of course.

GENERAL TRAVEL INFORMATION

Arizona Travel Planner published by the Arizona Office of Tourism, 1100 W. Washington Ave., Phoenix, AZ 85007. A "quick study" guide of the state, section by section, listing attractions, mileages, campgrounds, chambers of commerce, tour operators and other essentials. 120 pages, **free.**

Grand Canyon National Park by John F. Hoffman, a National Parkways publication, World-Wide Research and Publishing Co., P.O. Box 3073, Casper, WY 82602. Attractive guide with background, visitor information, maps and lots of pretty color photos; available at most Grand Canyon National Park museums and gift shops. 120 pages, **$5.95.**

Grand Canyon Perspectives by W. Kenneth Hamblin and Joseph R. Murphy, (c) 1969. H & M Distributors, P.O. Box 7085, University Station, Provo, UT 84602. The Grand Canyon as seen from various viewpoints, with detailed sketches of geographic features by illustrator William L. Chesser. 48 pages, Available at park museums and gift shops. **$4.25.**

The Grand Canyon: Temple of the World, an Arizona Highways Book, 2039 W. Lewis Ave., Phoenix, AZ 85009. Quotes from various authors who have been moved to pen poetic prose about the canyon, along with the usual Arizona Highways-style beautiful photos; available at park museums and gift shops. 48 pages, **$3.95.**

Scenic Sedona by Lawrence W. Cheek, (c) 1989. An Arizona Highways Book, 2039 W. Lewis Ave., Phoenix, AZ 85009. Prettily-illustrated guide to

Sedona, Oak Creek Canyon, Jerome, Mingus Mountain and the Verde Valley. 64 pages, **$4.95.**

The Sonoran Desert by Christopher S. Helms, (c) 1980. KC Publications, Inc., Box 14883-A, Las Vegas, NV 89114. Attractive color photos, maps and background on the Sonoran Desert. 48 pages, **$4.50.**

Travel Arizona by Joseph Stocker, (c) 1987. An Arizona Highways Book, 2039 W. Lewis Ave., Phoenix, AZ 85009. Sixteen suggested tours of the state, with illustrations and maps; nice color photography. 128 pages. **$8.95.**

Tucson Official Visitors Guide, produced annually by the Metropolitan Tucson Convention and Visitors Bureau, 130 S. Scott Ave., Tucson, AZ 85701. Assorted listings of attractions, museums, tour operators, restaurants and hotels. Bear in mind that most are paid-for listings. **Free.**

Visitors Guide to Phoenix-Scottsdale and the Valley of the Sun, produced annually by the Phoenix-Valley of the Sun Convention and Visitors Bureau, 502 N. Second St., Suite 300, Phoenix, AZ 85004. Helpful lists of attractions, museums, tour operators, restaurants and hotel. As with the Tucson guide, most listings are paid by the listees. **Free.**

What Is Arizona Really Like: A Guide to Arizona's Marvels by Reg Manning, (c) 1989. Published by Reganson Cartoon Books, P.O. Box 5242, Phoenix, AZ 85010. Humorously written insider's look at Arizona with cartoon illustrations, by Pulitzer Prize-winning cartoonist for the *Arizona Republic.* 120 pages, **$5.95.**

GHOST TOWNS AND BACK ROADS

Travel Arizona: The Back Roads. An Arizona Highways Book, 2039 W. Lewis Ave., Phoenix, AZ 85009. Lots of pretty color photos and route maps. 136 pages, **$9.95.**

Arizona's Best Ghost Towns by Byrd Howell Granger, (c) 1980. Published by Northland Press, P.O. Box N, Flagstaff, AZ 86002. A helpful guide with maps and nice sketches. 142 pages; **$12.95.**

DINING

100 Best Restaurants in Arizona by John and Joan Bogert, issued annually. Published by Arizona Desert Minerals Company, Inc., P.O. Box 10462, Phoenix, AZ 85064-0462. Reviews of restaurants throughout the state, but focused mostly in Phoenix and Tucson. 208 pages, **$3.95.**

HIKING & CAMPING

A Hiker's Guide to Arizona by Steward Aitchison and Bruce Grubbs, (c) 1987. Falcon Press, P.O. Box 279, Billings, MT 59103. A well-written guide with maps and black and white photos. 160 pages, **$9.95.**

Outdoors in Arizona: A Guide to Camping by Bob Hirsch, (c) 1986. An Arizona Highways Book, 2039 W. Lewis Ave., Phoenix, AZ 85009. A good mix of campsite listings, color photos and history and vignettes about the state's out-of-doors. 128 pages, **$12.95.**

Outdoors in Arizona: A Guide to Hiking and Backpacking by John Annerino, (c) 1987. An Arizona Highways Book, 2039 W. Lewis Ave., Phoenix, AZ 85009. Suggested hikes from desert to mountain to prairie, with maps and photos. 136 pages, **$12.95.**

HISTORY & REFERENCE

Arizona Place Names, re-print of a 1935 edition by Will C. Barnes, (c) 1988. University of Arizona Press, Tucson. Thorough, comprehensive and scholarly guide to the origin of Arizona's geographic names. 504 pages, **$15.95.**

Desert Wildflowers, (c) 1988. An Arizona Highways Book, 2039 W. Lewis Ave., Phoenix, AZ 85009. Gorgeous photos of desert blossoms, with descriptions, zones and times to catch peak blooming periods. 112 pages, **$9.95.**

History of Arizona by Robert Woznicki, PH.D. (c) 1987. Messenger Graphics, 110 S. 41st Ave., Phoenix, AZ 85009. A highly-readable treatment of the state's history; not comprehensive, but filled with interesting vignettes and personality sketches. 172 pages, **$4.95.**

The Story of Superstition Mountain and the Lost Dutchman Mine by Robert Joseph Allen, (c) 1971. Pocket Books, 1230 Avenue of the Americas, New York, NY 10020. A readable narrative of the Dutchman mine mystery but with some very questionable suppositions. 212 pages, **$3.95.**

INDIANS: TODAY AND YESTERDAY

A Clash of Cultures: Fort Bowie and the Chiricahua Apaches by Robert M. Utley, (c) 1977. For sale by the Superintendent of Documents, U.S. Government Printing Office, Washington, DC 20402. Also available at national monuments and historic sites, particularly in southeastern Arizona. 88 pages, **$2.95.**

American Indians of the Southwest by Bertha P. Dutton, (c) 1984. University of New Mexico Press. A good general guide to present and past Southwestern Indians. 286 pages, **$7.95.**

The Complete Family Guide to Navajo-Hopi Land by Bonnie Brown and Carol D. Bracken, (c) 1986. Published by Bonnie Brown and Carol Bracken, P.O. Box 2914, Page, AZ 86040. It's a bit unprofessionally done, but helpful, with lists of attractions, places to dine and sleep; several children's pages to amuse the youngsters. 112 pages, **$7.95.**

Geronimo: A Man, His Time, His Place by Angie Debo, (c) 1976. University of Oklahoma Press, Norman, OK 73019. An award-winning biography of the famous Apache warrior; probably the most comprehensive Geronimo study ever written. 480 pages, **$10.95.**

Hohokam Indians of the Tucson Basin by Linda M. Gregonis and Karl J. Reinhard, (c) 1979. University of Arizona Press, Tucson. Scholarly, readable account of Tucson's prehistoric peoples. 48 pages, **$1.95**

Southwestern Indian Tribes by Tom Bahti, (c) 1989. KC Publications, Inc., Box 14883-A, Las Vegas, NV 89114. Attractive easy-reference guide to Arizona and New Mexico tribes with maps and color and black and white illustrations; nice detail photos of artifacts. 72 pages, **$4.50.**

Visitor's Guide to Arizona's Indian Reservations by Boye De Mente, (c) 1988. Phoenix Books/Publishers, P.O. Box 32008, Phoenix, AZ 85064. A thorough, well-written guide with lots of detail and maps. 160 pages; **$6.**

HOW TO SPEAK LIKE AN ARIZONAN

Well, of course Arizonans speak English, but there's a sprinkling of Spanish and Indian words in there. And many Arizona place names have Spanish and Indian roots. This pronunciation guide—prepared with the aid of Brian C. Catts of the University of Arizona's Office of Public Service—will help you talk like a native.

Ajo *(AH-hoe)* — Town in southern Arizona; means "garlic" in Spanish.

Anasazi *(Ana-SAH-zee)* — Early Arizona Indian tribe; the name means "the ancient ones."

Apache *(Ah-PAH-chee)* — Central and southeastern Arizona tribe.

Arcosanti *(Ar-ko-SAN-tee)* — Futuristic habitat north of Phoenix, built by Italian visionary-architect Paolo Soleri.

Athabaskan *(A-tha-BAS-kan — "a's" pronounced as in apple)* — Canadian Indian tribe; ancestors of the Navajo and Apache.

Bowie *(BOO-ee)* — Fort in southeastern Arizona, now a national historic site; also a tiny town on Interstate 10.

Canyon de Chelly *(du SHAY)* — Arizona national monument.

Canyon del Muerto *(MWAIR-toh)* — "Canyon of Death," a ravine adjacent to Canyon de Chelly.

Carne *(CAR-nay)* — Meat.

"Cerveza fria, por favor" *(Sehr-VE-sa FREE-ah, por fah-VOR)* — "Bring me a cold one, please."

Chemehuevi *(Tchem-e-H'WAY-vee)* — Southern Colorado River tribe of Yuman origin; located mostly in southeastern California. Meaning is unknown.

Chinle *(Chin-LEE)* — Navajo town, the gateway to Canyon de Chelly National Monument.

Chiricahua *(Cheer-i-COW-wa)* — Southeastern Arizona Apache tribe made famous by Cochise and Geronimo's rebellions; also the name of a mountain range and national monument.

Cholla *(CHOY-ya)* — Large family of Arizona cactus.

Coconino *(Co-co-NEE-no)* — Arizona place name, given to a national forest, county and plateau south of the Grand Canyon.

Colorado *(Coh-lo-RAH-doh)* — Red; obviously, a very common Arizona geographic name.

El Tovar *(El To-VAR)* — Historic hotel at South Rim of Grand Canyon National Park.

Gila *(HEE-la)* — A river in southern Arizona.

Guadalupe Hidalgo *(Wa-da-LU-pay Hee-DAL-go)* — The treaty ending the Mexican War, signed in 1848.

Havasupai *(Hah-vah-SOO-pie)* — "Blue-green water people" who occupy beautiful Havasu Canyon, tributary of the Grand Canyon; also called Supai.

Hohokam *(Hoe-hoe-KAHM)* — Prehistoric Indian tribe occupying deserts of Southern Arizona about AD 200 to 500; means "those who have gone."

Huachuca *(Hwa-CHOO-ka)* — Army fort in southern Arizona with an historic museum; also the name of a mountain range.

Hopi *(HOE-pee)* — Indian tribe, probably descended from the Anasazi.

Hotevilla *(HOAT-vih-la)* — Hopi village on Third Mesa. The name means "skinned back" or cleared off.

Hualapai *(HWAL-a-pie or WAH-lah-pie)* — Western Arizona Indian tribe; the name means "pine tree people."

Huevos Rancheros *(WHEY-vose ran-CHER-ohs)* — Popular Spanish-style breakfast with eggs and picante sauce.

Javalina *(Ha-va-LEE-na)* — Wild boar.

Kykotsmovi *(Kee-KOTS-mo-vee)* — Hopi tribal administrative center, on Third Mesa below Oraibi, also called New Oraibi. It means "the place of the mound of ruins."

Maricopa *(Ma-ri-KOH-pah)* — A name given to the Pipa tribe, which shares a reservation with the Pima.

Mescalero *(Mess-kah-LAIR-O)* — Eastern Arizona and Western New Mexico Apache tribe. The name is Spanish, referring to mescal cactus, a traditional food source.

Moenkopi *(Mu-en-KO-pee)* — Hopi village on Third Mesa; means "place of running water."

Mogollan *(MUGGY-yon)* — Ancient Indian tribe occupying eastern Arizona about AD 200 to 500; also Mogollan Rim, the abrupt southern edge of the Colorado Plateau.

Mohave *(Mo-HA-vay)* — Arizona place name, referring to Indian tribe and a county along the western border.

Mojave — Same pronunciation as above, with Spanish spelling, commonly used in California.

Navajo *(NAH-VAH-hoe)* — America's largest Indian tribe, descended from Athabascan band of Canada.

Nogales *(No-GAH-less)* — Twin Arizona-Mexico border towns; the word is Spanish for "walnuts."

Ocotillo *(O co-TEE-yo)* — Spiny-limbed desert bush with red spear-like blossoms.

Oraibi *(Oh-RYE-bee)* — Hopi settlement on Third Mesa; means "place of the Orai stone."

Paloverde *(PAW-lo-VAIR-day)* — Desert tree distinctive for the green bark of its limbs.

Papago *(PAH-pu-go)* — Spanish word for "bean eaters," referring to a Southern Arizona Indian tribe, which has since re-adopted its traditional name of "Tohono O'odham."

Pima *(PEE-mah)* — Central and southern Arizona tribe. The name was a Spanish mistake. When questioned by early explorers, they responded *"Pi-nyi-match,"* which means "I don't understand." The Spanish thought they were identifying themselves.

Prescott *(PRESS-kit)* — Town in central Arizona.

Quechan *(KEE-chan or KAY-chan)* — Indian tribe near Yuma area; also known as Yuma Indians.

Saguaro *(Sa-WHA-ro)* — Large cactus; its blossom is Arizona's state flower.

San Xavier *(Sahn Ha-vee-YAY)* — Spanish mission south of Tucson; some locals pronounce it *Ha-VEER.*

Sichomovi *(si-CHO-MO-vee* — Hopi settlement on First Mesa; means "a hill where the wild currants grow."

Sinagua *(Si-NAU-wa)* — Ancient north central Arizona tribe; lived in the area about 900-1000 A.D. It comes from the Spanish words *sin agua*—"without water."

Shungopovi *(Shung-O-PO-vee)* — Hopi settlement on Second Mesa; means "a place by the spring where tall reeds grow."

Tempe *(Tem-PEE)* — City east of Phoenix.

Tohono O'odham *(To-HO-no ah-toon)* — Traditional tribal name of the Papago Indians. It means "people of the desert who have emerged from the earth."

Tubac *(TU-bahk)* — Arizona's first settlement; below Tucson.

Tumacacori *(Too-mawk-ka-COR-ee)* — Spanish mission below Tucson; now a national monument.

Tusayan *(TU-sigh-yan or TUSSY-yan)* — Sinagua Indian ruin near Desert View in Grand Canyon National Park; also a community just outside the park's south entrance station.

Ute *(Yoot)* — Large Great Basin Indian tribe; few members are in Arizona. The name simply means "the tribe" in the Shoshoni and Comanche language.

Verde *(VAIR-day)* — Spanish for "green."

Wahweap *(WAH-weep)* — Ute Indian for "bitter water"; the name of a large marina at Glen Canyon National Recreation Area.

Wupatki *(Wu-PAT-key)* — National monument northeast of Flagstaff. The word is Hopi for "tall house."

Yaqui *(Ya-KEE)* — Small Indian tribe southwest of Tucson, near Tohono O'odham Reservation. Origin of name unknown; it might simply mean "the people," a self-reference commonly used by many early tribes. Yaqui are more numerous in northern Mexico and may be an off-shoot of early Apache tribes.

Yavapai *(YA-va-pie)* — Central Arizona tribe. Origin of the name is not sure; might mean "crooked mouth people" or "people of the sun."

Yuma *(YOO-mah)* — Large tribal group near the city of Yuma; the name is derived from *lum,* which means tribe. Original name is Quechan.

INDEX